MW00567573

# the CANADIAN WRITER'S WORKPLACE

## SIXTH EDITION

*Gary Lipschutz*
*Centennial College*

*John Roberts*
*Mohawk College*

*John Scarry*
*Hostos Community College,*
*City University of New York*

*Sandra Scarry*
*Formerly with the Office of Academic Affairs,*
*City University of New York*

THOMSON
NELSON

Australia Canada Mexico Singapore Spain United Kingdom United States

THOMSON
NELSON

*The Canadian Writer's Workplace,*
**Sixth Edition**

by Gary Lipschutz, John Roberts,
John Scarry, and Sandra Scarry

**Associate Vice President, Editorial Director:**
Evelyn Veitch

**Editor-in-Chief, Higher Education:**
Anne Williams

**Executive Editor:**
Laura Macleod

**Marketing Manager:**
Shelley Collacutt Miller

**Developmental Editor:**
Theresa Fitzgerald

**Photo Researcher and Permissions Coordinator:**
Sandra Mark

**Senior Content Production Manager:**
Natalia Denesiuk Harris

**Copy Editor:**
Lisa Berland

**Proofreader:**
Wayne Herrington

**Indexer:**
Edwin Durbin

**Production Coordinator:**
Ferial Suleman

**Design Director:**
Ken Phipps

**Interior Design Modifications:**
Katherine Strain

**Cover Design:**
Wil Bache

**Cover Image:**
VisionsofAmerica/Joe Sohm/
Getty Images

**Compositor:**
Nelson Gonzalez

**Printer:**
Webcom



Printed and bound in Canada
1 2 3 4 10 09 08 07

For more information contact Nelson, 1120 Birchmount Road, Toronto, Ontario, M1K 5G4. Or you can visit our Internet site at http://www.nelson.com



**Library and Archives Canada Cataloguing in Publication Data**

The Canadian writer's workplace / Gary Lipschutz ... [et al.]. — 6th ed.

Fourth ed. written by: John Roberts, John Scarry and Sandra Scarry.

Includes index.
ISBN 978-0-17-610466-5

1. English language—Rhetoric—Textbooks. 2. English language—Rhetoric—Problems, exercises, etc. 3. English language—Grammar—Problems, exercises, etc.
I. Lipschutz, Gary, 1964–
II. Roberts, John A., 1944–
Canadian writer's workplace.

PE1413.C355 2008 808'.042
C2007-905235-5

ISBN-13: 978-0-17-610466-5
ISBN-10: 0-17-610466-6

# Brief Contents


| | | |
|---|---|---|
| PREFACE | | xvii |
| **UNIT I** | **Grammar** | **1** |
| CHAPTER 1 | Parts of Speech: Overview | 3 |
| CHAPTER 2 | Recognizing Subjects and Verbs | 13 |
| CHAPTER 3 | More Work with Verbs | 30 |
| CHAPTER 4 | Subject-Verb Agreement | 47 |
| CHAPTER 5 | Coordination and Subordination | 56 |
| CHAPTER 6 | Correcting Fragments | 78 |
| CHAPTER 7 | Correcting Run-ons | 92 |
| CHAPTER 8 | Parallel Structure | 102 |
| CHAPTER 9 | Pronouns | 109 |
| CHAPTER 10 | Modifiers: Misplaced and Dangling | 120 |
| CHAPTER 11 | Punctuation | 126 |
| CHAPTER 12 | Capitalization | 147 |
| CHAPTER 13 | Unit I Review: Using All You Have Learned | 152 |
| **UNIT II** | **The Writing Process** | **161** |
| CHAPTER 14 | The Four Stages of Writing for a Paragraph or an Essay | 163 |
| CHAPTER 15 | The Paragraph I: Structure and Topic Sentence | 175 |
| CHAPTER 16 | The Paragraph II: Supporting Details | 183 |
| CHAPTER 17 | The Essay | 194 |
| CHAPTER 18 | Revising and Editing | 213 |
| CHAPTER 19 | Summarizing and Paraphrasing | 221 |
| CHAPTER 20 | Research and Documentation | 229 |

## UNIT III Writing Strategies for the Paragraph and Essay 255

CHAPTER 21 Narration 257

CHAPTER 22 Description 267

CHAPTER 23 Process 279

CHAPTER 24 Comparison and/or Contrast 290

CHAPTER 25 Definition 302

CHAPTER 26 Classification 311

CHAPTER 27 Cause and Effect 322

CHAPTER 28 Argumentation 334

## UNIT IV Readings 351

ROSEMARY SULLIVAN Don Juan/Doña Juana 352

DAVID SUZUKI Hidden Lessons 355

MARYA FIAMENGO In Praise of Old Women 359

JEAN VANIER Heart of Loneliness 362

GRANT ROBERTSON The $2-Million Comma 367

TOMSON HIGHWAY Canada, My Canada 370

NAHEED MUSTAFA My Body Is My Own Business 373

JOHN ARTIBELLO Leaving the Cave 376

RITA JOE I Lost My Talk 383

W. FRANK EPLING Rats 385

HIMANI BANNERJI The Other Family 389

COLIN CAMPBELL How R Tngz, Dude? 394

NEIL BISSOONDATH Selling Illusions 397

GARY LIPSCHUTZ Lessons of Love from Stories of Old 402

SHARI GRAYDON Bad Girls 409

CAMERON AINSWORTH-VINCZE Till Fraud Do Us Part 414

LEONARD COHEN In My Secret Life 416

UNIT V Appendices 419

APPENDIX A Distinguishing between Words Often Confused 420

APPENDIX B Solving Spelling Problems 435

APPENDIX C Irregular Verbs 451

APPENDIX D Answer Key to Practices 455

CREDITS 468

INDEX 470

# Contents


PREFACE xvii

UNIT I Grammar 1

CHAPTER 1 Parts of Speech: Overview 3

Quick Quiz 3
1. What Are Nouns? 4
2. What Are Pronouns? 5
3. What Are Adjectives? 6
4. What Are Verbs? 6
5. What Are Adverbs? 8
6. What Are Prepositions? 9
7. What Are Conjunctions? 9
8. What Are Interjections? 11
9. What Are Articles? 11
Working Together: *Puzzle Pieces and Sentence Parts* 12

CHAPTER 2 Recognizing Subjects and Verbs 13

Quick Quiz 13
Why Should We Use Complete Sentences When We Write? 13
What Is a Complete Sentence? 14
How Do You Find the Subject of a Sentence? 14
Finding the Subject in Sentences with Prepositional Phrases 17
What Are the Other Problems in Finding Subjects? 21
How Do You Find the Verb of a Sentence? 23
Chapter Review Exercises 27
Working Together: *Singling Out Subjects* 29

CHAPTER 3 More Work with Verbs 30

Quick Quiz 30
What Are the Principal Parts of the Irregular Verbs? 30
Avoiding Unnecessary Shifts in Verb Tense 35
What Is the Sequence of Tenses? 37
How Do You Use the Present Perfect and the Past Perfect Tenses? 39
What Is the Difference between Active and Passive Voice? 41

What Is the Subjunctive? 44
Other Problems with Verbs 45
Chapter Review Exercises 45
Working Together: *Verbs, Not Verbiage* 46

CHAPTER 4 **Subject-Verb Agreement** **47**
Quick Quiz 47
Subject-Verb Agreement within the Sentence 47
Chapter Review Exercises 53
Working Together: *Magazine Mayhem* 55

CHAPTER 5 **Coordination and Subordination** **56**
Quick Quiz 1 56
Quick Quiz 2 56
What Is Coordination? 57
Combining Sentences Using Coordination 57
What Is Subordination? 65
Combining Sentences Using Subordination 65
How Do You Punctuate a Clause with a Relative Pronoun? 72
Chapter Review Exercises 74
Working Together: *Practising Coordination and Subordination* 77

CHAPTER 6 **Correcting Fragments** **78**
Quick Quiz 78
Recognizing and Correcting Sentence Fragments 78
What Is a Fragment? 79
How Do You Correct a Fragment? 81
Don't Confuse Phrases with Sentences 83
Making a Complete Sentence from a Fragment That Contains a Verbal 85
Chapter Review Exercises 89
Working Together: *Editing Ad Copy* 91

CHAPTER 7 **Correcting Run-ons** **92**
Quick Quiz 92
Run-ons Are Not "Long Sentences" 92
What Kinds of Run-ons Are There? 93
How Do You Make a Complete Sentence from a Run-on? 93
Chapter Review Exercises 99
Working Together: *Operation "Plot without Run-ons"* 101

CHAPTER 8 **Parallel Structure** **102**
Quick Quiz 102
What Is Parallel Structure? 102

| | | |
|---|---|---|
| | Chapter Review Exercises | 106 |
| | Working Together: *Practise Making Sentences Parallel* | 108 |
| **CHAPTER 9** | **Pronouns** | **109** |
| | Quick Quiz | 109 |
| | Pronouns and Case | 110 |
| | Pronoun-Antecedent Agreement | 112 |
| | Missing, Ambiguous, or Repetitious Pronouns | 115 |
| | Chapter Review Exercises | 117 |
| | Working Together: *Practise with Pronouns* | 119 |
| **CHAPTER 10** | **Modifiers: Misplaced and Dangling** | **120** |
| | Quick Quiz | 120 |
| | What Are Modifiers? | 120 |
| | What Are Misplaced Modifiers? | 121 |
| | What Are Dangling Modifiers? | 122 |
| | Chapter Review Exercises | 123 |
| | Working Together: *Modifiers Making the Difference* | 125 |
| **CHAPTER 11** | **Punctuation** | **126** |
| | Quick Quiz | 126 |
| | Correct Punctuation: A Strong Indicator of a Writer's Competence | 126 |
| | The Eight Basic Rules of the Comma | 126 |
| | Other Marks of Punctuation | 134 |
| | Chapter Review Exercises | 144 |
| | Working Together: *Designing Punctuation Tests* | 146 |
| **CHAPTER 12** | **Capitalization** | **147** |
| | Quick Quiz | 147 |
| | Ten Basic Rules for Capitalization | 147 |
| | Working Together: *Designing Capitalization Tests* | 151 |
| **CHAPTER 13** | **Unit I Review: Using All You Have Learned** | **152** |
| | Editing Sentences for Errors | 152 |
| | Editing Paragraphs for Errors | 158 |
| | Working Together: *Remembering 9/11* | 159 |
| **UNIT II** | **The Writing Process** | **161** |
| **CHAPTER 14** | **The Four Stages of Writing for a Paragraph or an Essay** | **163** |
| | Stage One: Prewriting | 163 |
| | Stage Two: Outlining (or Organizing) | 169 |

| | | |
|---|---|---|
| | Stage Three: The Rough Draft | 170 |
| | Stage Four: Postwriting (Revising, Editing, and Proofreading) | 171 |
| | Working Together: *Prewriting Activities* | 173 |
| **CHAPTER 15** | **The Paragraph I: Structure and Topic Sentence** | **175** |
| | What Is a Paragraph? | 175 |
| | What Does a Paragraph Look Like? | 175 |
| | What Is a Topic Sentence? | 176 |
| | How Do You Find the Topic in a Topic Sentence? | 178 |
| | What Is a Controlling Idea? | 179 |
| | Choosing Your Own Controlling Idea | 180 |
| | Chapter Review Exercises | 181 |
| | Working Together: *Controlling Ideas* | 182 |
| **CHAPTER 16** | **The Paragraph II: Supporting Details** | **183** |
| | What Is a Supporting Detail? | 183 |
| | Using Examples as Supporting Details | 185 |
| | Avoid Restating the Topic Sentence | 187 |
| | How Do You Make Supporting Details Specific? | 189 |
| | The Concluding Sentence | 191 |
| | Outline Format | 192 |
| | Working Together: *Supporting Details* | 193 |
| **CHAPTER 17** | **The Essay** | **194** |
| | Writing Is a Skill | 194 |
| | The Components of an Essay | 195 |
| | What Is a Thesis Statement? | 197 |
| | The Introductory Paragraph | 203 |
| | Using Transitions to Move from One Idea to the Next | 206 |
| | The Concluding Paragraph | 207 |
| | Titles | 209 |
| | Model Outline | 209 |
| | Working Together: *Education Endangered?* | 211 |
| **CHAPTER 18** | **Revising and Editing** | **213** |
| | The Final Stage | 213 |
| | Proofreading | 213 |
| | The Right Conditions for the Tasks | 214 |
| | A Sample Student Essay in Its Fourth Stage | 217 |
| | Preparing the Final Copy | 218 |
| READ | *"Sonata in C Major, Opus 35" by Allison Hickman* | *218* |
| | Working Together: *Revising and Editing Activity* | 220 |

CHAPTER 19 **Summarizing and Paraphrasing** **221**

Summarizing 221
Paraphrasing 225
Avoid Unintentional Plagiarism 227
Analyzing and Critiquing 228
Working Together: *Summarizing Opposing Points of View* 228

CHAPTER 20 **Research and Documentation** **229**

The Research Paper 229
The Literary Research Paper 230
The General Topic Research Paper 230
Internet vs. Library Research 230
Analyzing the Legitimacy of Online Sources 232
Using Quotations 233
Documentation 235
Two Mandatory Parts of Documentation: Internal and End 236
American Psychological Association (APA) 237
Modern Language Association (MLA) 240
*Sample Research Paper: "The Cell Phone: Tomorrow's Medical Menace?" by Leila Sayeed* 244
Working Together: *Finding Appropriate Sources* 253

## UNIT III Writing Strategies for the Paragraph and Essay 255

CHAPTER 21 **Narration** **257**

What Is Narration? 257
Developing Paragraphs: Narration 257
Working with Narration: Using Narration to Make a Point 258
Coherence in Narration: Placing Details in Order of Time Sequence 259
Writing the Narrative Paragraph Step by Step 260
On Your Own: Writing Narrative Paragraphs from Model Paragraphs 263
Writing the Narrative Essay 263
*Model Essay: "Transparent Silhouette" by Akis Stylianou* 264
Working Together: *Spontaneous Creativity or Combustion?* 266

CHAPTER 22 **Description** **267**

What Is Description? 267
Developing Paragraphs: Description 268

Working with Description: Selecting the Dominant Impression 268
Working with Description: Sensory Images 271
Coherence in Description: Putting Details in Spatial Order 272
Writing the Descriptive Paragraph Step by Step 273
On Your Own: Writing Descriptive Paragraphs from Model Paragraphs 274
Writing the Descriptive Essay 275
READ *Model Essay: "A Profile of Daphne" by Alexandra Savage-Ferr* *276*
Working Together: *The Hunt for a Roommate* 278

**CHAPTER 23 Process** **279**

What Is Process? 279
Developing Paragraphs: Process 279
Coherence in Process: Order in Logical Sequence 281
Writing the Process Paragraph Step by Step 282
On Your Own: Writing Process Paragraphs from Model Paragraphs 283
Writing the Process Essay 284
READ *Model Essay: "Replacing a Tire" by Cara Watters* *286*
Working Together: *Campus Woes* 288

**CHAPTER 24 Comparison and/or Contrast** **290**

What Are Comparison and Contrast? 290
Developing Paragraphs: Comparison and/or Contrast 290
Two Methods: Point-by-Point and Block 292
Tips on Transitions: *Like* vs. *As* 296
Writing the Comparison and/or Contrast Paragraph Step by Step 296
The Comparison and/or Contrast Essay 297
READ *Model Essay: "City Life Beats the Small Town Blues" by Zack Goodman* *298*
Working Together: *Reaching Consensus* 301

**CHAPTER 25 Definition** **302**

What Is Definition? 302
Developing Paragraphs: Definition 303
Writing the Definition Paragraph Step by Step 305
Developing an Essay of Definition 307
READ *Model Essay: "Love Hurts" by Jenny Yuen* *307*
Working Together: *What Does the Cover Mean to You?* 310

**CHAPTER 26 Classification** **311**

What Is Classification? 311
Developing Paragraphs: Classification 311
Making Distinct Categories 313
Writing the Classification Paragraph Step by Step 314
Developing an Essay of Classification 316
*Model Essay I: "Booting Out Boredom" by Hussain Mohamdally* *316*
*Model Essay II: "The Evolution of Spirituality" by Margo Fine* *318*
Working Together: *Brainstorming for Classification* 321

**CHAPTER 27 Cause and Effect** **322**

What Is Cause and Effect? 322
Two Types of Cause and Effect Paragraph or Essay 322
Developing Paragraphs: Cause and Effect 323
Writing the Cause or Effect Paragraph Step by Step 327
On Your Own: Writing Cause and Effect Paragraphs from Model Paragraphs 328
Developing the Cause and Effect Essay 329
*Model Essay I: "Whose Choice Is It, Anyway?" by Donald Pianissimo* *330*
Working Together: *Identifying Causes* 332
*Model Essay II: "Anything but Peaceful" by Zack Goodman* *332*

**CHAPTER 28 Argumentation** **334**

What Is Argumentation? 334
Argumentation vs. Persuasion 334
Persuasive Appeals That Are Not Logical 334
Other Argumentative Strategies 335
What Is Critical Thinking? 335
More Tools and Components of Argumentation 336
Underlying Assumptions 337
Analyzing the Intention of Argument: The Importance of Virtue 338
We Become What We Communicate 338
Argumentative Techniques 338
Common Fallacies 340
Writing the Argumentative Paragraph 342
Developing Essays: Argumentation 343
*Model Essay: "Individuals Must Spur Change" by Leanne C. Southall* *343*

*Annotated Model Essay: "It's Time We Helped Patients Die" by Dr. Howard Caplan* 345
Working Together: *Identifying Good and Bad Arguments* 350

**UNIT IV Readings** 351

**DON JUAN/DOÑA JUANA** 352
References to the literary character of the infamous lover seem appropriate in Rosemary Sullivan's examination of both men and women who apparently need many lovers to be happy.

**HIDDEN LESSONS** 355
Scientist David Suzuki looks at bad influences on our attitudes and behaviour toward the environment as much of the reason for its demise. He says the worst influences are the ones of which we are entirely unaware.

**IN PRAISE OF OLD WOMEN** 359
One of three poems in this section, this one by Marya Fiamengo contrasts women of Eastern Europe and Asia with women of America.

**HEART OF LONELINESS** 362
In this excerpt from his book *Becoming Human*, Jean Vanier examines the universal human condition of loneliness and how it can be viewed as a vehicle to a higher place.

**THE $2-MILLION COMMA** 367
Rogers is a leader in the communications industry. So it seems ironic that this company would make a mistake with a punctuation mark that would end up costing a fortune. Grant Robertson tells this uncommon story of the common comma.

**CANADA, MY CANADA** 370
Born and raised on the Brochet Reserve in Northern Manitoba, Tomson Highway paints a proud and vibrant picture of the country he calls home.

**My Body Is My Own Business** 373
Naheed Mustafa explains why she wears the traditional Muslim headscarf, the hijab.

**Leaving the Cave** 376
Philosophy professor John Artibello paints a picture of Plato's cave and shows how this ancient Greek story bears just as much relevance today as it did 2400 years ago.

**I Lost My Talk** 383
Micmac poet Rita Joe writes from the perspective of someone whose school experience was not a good one.

**Rats** 385
Are animal rights activists hypocrites? University of Alberta Professor W. Frank Epling takes a humorous approach to this question as he examines people's motivations for fighting for the rights of animals.

**The Other Family** 389
In this short story by Himani Bannerji, a young Indo-Canadian girl finds herself being torn between two worlds, that of her schoolmates and that of her family and culture.

**How R Tngz, Dude?** 394
Research shows we are getting much more than convenience from the current cell phone boom. Colin Campbell of *Maclean's* tells us that the wireless craze may be causing an entire generation to undergo undesirable social changes.

**Selling Illusions** 397
Neil Bissoondath, in this excerpt from his book by the same name, relates how his experience at York University first acquainted him with the unease he felt over Canada's approach to multiculturalism.

**Lessons of Love from Stories of Old** 402
*The Canadian Writer's Workplace* author Gary Lipschutz discusses the popular misinterpretation of the story "Sleeping Beauty" and its damaging influence on our ideas about love.

BAD GIRLS 409
Writer and educator Shari Graydon examines the case of Reena Virk, the fourteen-year-old British Columbian girl who was brutally murdered in November 1997, and explores the topic of female teen violence. In this essay, Graydon interviews one of Reena's convicted murderers, a sixteen-year-old girl.

TILL FRAUD DO US PART 414
If threats of terrorism weren't enough, fraudulent marriage is now another fear many Canadians face. Cameron Ainsworth-Vincze explains how more people are getting married just to get into Canada and to start a more prosperous life. And they do this in spite of the harm to the people they are marrying.

IN MY SECRET LIFE 416
Montreal-born poet Leonard Cohen reflects on a conflict from which he cannot seem to escape.

UNIT V **Appendices** 419

APPENDIX A **Distinguishing between Words Often Confused** 420

APPENDIX B **Solving Spelling Problems** 435

APPENDIX C **Irregular Verbs** 451

APPENDIX D **Answer Key to Practices** 455

CREDITS 468

INDEX 470

# Preface

It's been said that the first casualty of war is truth. Well, the first casualty of writing is often clarity. Writing without clarity is bad writing. *The Canadian Writer's Workplace,* Sixth Edition, is an easy-to-use textbook that aims to inspire and guide students on the road to achieving clarity in their writing. With this book, students are expected to develop solid **paragraph and essay writing skills** needed not only in English courses, but also in many other courses taken in college and/or university and, subsequently, wherever written communication is required. *The Canadian Writer's Workplace* can help students get the most out of any endeavour that calls for the ability to write clearly and effectively.

## Everything You Need between Two Covers

*The Canadian Writer's Workplace* is a **three-in-one textbook of grammar, rhetoric (writing steps and strategies), and readings.** When you use this book, there is no need to look for a supplemental book containing work on grammar or a book to teach writing skills or a reader providing material that inspires the students to generate thoughtful and well-written composition. Everything you need is already between two covers.

## Reinforcement and Flexibility

With examples and figures, *The Canadian Writer's Workplace* offers constant reinforcement of every definition stated and every writing technique taught at every step of the way. Numerous practice exercises and writing assignments throughout the entire book offer further reinforcement of what is being learned. The format of *The Canadian Writer's Workplace* features flexibility in that the book enables an instructor to work on different exercises with an entire class, gives individual students opportunity to work by themselves or with a tutor in a lab, and encourages students to work in groups. Certain sections can be skipped if the material is not needed for a particular class—or a class might begin with a later section, with the earlier chapters being used as a review. Students or faculty can also use the **Quick Quiz** at the beginning of each chapter in Unit I to determine whether students' skills are strong enough in a particular area to move on right away or not.

## Stimulating Content

The reading content in this edition has been expanded to include more cutting-edge essays with particular appeal to postsecondary students. Overall, the readings throughout the text are extremely varied: they include model paragraphs and essays (including a new model research essay about cell phones and their potential harm to our health) in Unit III and new major readings in Unit IV. Some of the works in Unit III are by student writers; others are taken from a wide range of novels, essays, short stories, and books of nonfiction by world-famous authors. Unit IV is made up of mostly nonfiction and some short fiction and poetry—all carefully chosen to evoke thoughtful and well-structured written responses from students. The writers of the readings in Unit IV are exclusively Canadian, and they are all seasoned writers and/or academics. The strong Canadian flavour of the text offers the postsecondary student in Canada an insight into various aspects of Canadian culture. The assignments in the book feature material that deals with events or subjects that are of contemporary interest. And many of the exercises are based on material from such fields as history or science.

## Features of the Sixth Edition

Many features of the first five Canadian editions of the book have been retained. As mentioned earlier, they include the comprehensive package of grammar, rhetoric, and readings. This sixth edition, however, offers some exciting and innovative changes:

- A brand new chapter (Chapter 20) entitled "Research and Documentation" is a major feature of this new edition of *Canadian Writer's Workplace*. This chapter showcases tips on research, especially in the electronic world in which we now live; APA and MLA documentation; and a model research paper on the timely and controversial topic of cell phones and their potential long-term effects on our health.
- The chapter entitled "Argumentation" (Chapter 28) has been expanded to include a new section on **critical thinking and analysis**. This new section includes discussion on persuasive appeals that are not logical, common fallacies (with examples), and clear definitions that are designed to help the student identify the necessary components of a solid argument.
- Other new readings, in addition to the new model research essay in the brand new chapter on research and documentation, have been added to both Unit III and Unit IV. These include several student model essays (in Unit III) and three magazine articles by Canadian journalists (in Unit IV).
- The chapter on the essay (Chapter 17) has been expanded, particularly in the area of thesis statements.

- Additional practices and exercises have been incorporated into various chapters in Unit I (Grammar), especially chapters on subject-verb agreement, fragments, and run-ons.

An **Instructor's Manual** and a **Test Bank** that accompany this text have been updated. Although available online, these documents, if requested by the instructor, can also be made available on hard copy. The Instructor's Manual contains transparency masters that support much of the material in the text and that offer students a visual perspective of grammar and writing strategies; answers to the "Exercises" (answers to "Practices" are already in the Answer Key of the text); suggested answers to all questions following every reading in the text (Units III and IV); hints for teaching students writing skills, including techniques for group work in the classroom; and specific suggestions for activities that can be used with the material in the textbook.

The Test Bank for *The Canadian Writer's Workplace,* Sixth Edition, contains an extensive selection of exercises corresponding to every point of grammar discussed in Unit I and the first three appendices in the back of the book.

## Features Retained from the Fifth Edition

Many of the features that proved successful for students and faculty who worked with the fifth edition of the book have been retained in this sixth edition.

- Most of the readings in Unit IV of the fifth edition have been retained due to an overwhelmingly positive response.
- Each chapter in Unit I begins with a Quick Quiz, designed to assess students' skills in the material in that chapter. Based on the results of this quiz, the instructor can choose either to skip over the material in the chapter, or to spend extra time on the material in question if the students' skills in this area are shown to be weak.
- The nature of the "Practices" and "Exercises" in the fifth edition has been maintained in that the answers for the "Practices" are provided in the Answer Key at the back of the textbook, and the answers to the "Exercises" are not. The main reason for the deliberate absence of answers to the exercises in the book is so that instructors can assign these exercises for in-class testing or homework. Answers to the "Exercises" are provided, however, in the Instructor's Manual that accompanies the sixth edition of *Canadian Writer's Workplace.*
- A valuable and popular feature, "Working Together," can still be found at the end of every chapter in the book. "Working Together" gives the student an additional opportunity to confirm the work that has just been finished. Each "Working Together" section enables the class to break into groups, an approach that provides opportunities for the peer editing and peer review that many instructors use to enhance their classes today.

## Acknowledgments

For their advice and/or personal support, the author is indebted to John Artibello, Ben Labovitch, Denvil Buchanan, Leah Robinson, Rose Lipschutz, Sofia Phillips, Andrea Jacobs, and George Thomas.

Kudos and thanks go to the winning team at Nelson—Laura Macleod, Theresa Fitzgerald, and Natalia Denesiuk Harris. Their hard work and dedication have helped make this edition what it is.

The comments and advice from the following reviewers of the fifth edition and the first draft of the sixth edition were invaluable:

Veronica Baig, Athabasca University
Neil Carter, Sault College
Jo Ann Foote, Lambton College
Karen Hebb, Southern Alberta Institute of Technology
Chandra Hodgson, Humber College
Christina Horgan, Southern Alberta Institute of Technology
Linda Maloney, Humber College
Sandi Mills, Centennial College
Nina Pyne, Sault College

To the student essayists who have generously given permission to publish their work in this edition of *The Canadian Writer's Workplace,* the author and editors wish to thank them most sincerely. They are Margo Fine, Zack Goodman, Allison Hickman, Hussain Mohamdally, Donald Pianissimo, Alexandra Savage-Ferr, Leila Sayeed, Leanne C. Southall, Akis Stylianou, Cara Watters, and Jenny Yuen.

# UNIT ONE I

# Grammar


| | |
|---|---|
| CHAPTER 1 | PARTS OF SPEECH: OVERVIEW |
| CHAPTER 2 | RECOGNIZING SUBJECTS AND VERBS |
| CHAPTER 3 | MORE WORK WITH VERBS |
| CHAPTER 4 | SUBJECT-VERB AGREEMENT |
| CHAPTER 5 | COORDINATION AND SUBORDINATION |
| CHAPTER 6 | CORRECTING FRAGMENTS |
| CHAPTER 7 | CORRECTING RUN-ONS |
| CHAPTER 8 | PARALLEL STRUCTURE |
| CHAPTER 9 | PRONOUNS |
| CHAPTER 10 | MODIFIERS: MISPLACED AND DANGLING |
| CHAPTER 11 | PUNCTUATION |
| CHAPTER 12 | CAPITALIZATION |
| CHAPTER 13 | UNIT I REVIEW: USING ALL YOU HAVE LEARNED |

CHAPTER ONE

1

# Parts of Speech: Overview

*The Canadian Writer's Workplace* begins with an overview of grammar to ensure that you have an understanding of basic terms. Such an understanding will help you succeed with the rest of this text. Words can be divided into nine categories called **parts of speech.** Understanding these categories will help you work with language, especially when it comes to revising your own writing.

## QUICK QUIZ

Test your knowledge of the various parts of speech. Determine the correct part of speech for the underlined words in the following sentences. There is no need to actually write the answers in the blanks. The Quick Quiz is primarily for self-assessment only. The answers to the questions are upside down beside the quiz.

1. By installing the service, you agree to the following conditions.

   ______ ______ ___

2. Follow the instructions on the screen to uninstall the older version of the

   ______ ___ ______ ___

   program.

   ______

3. Running the program is easily handled if you pay attention to the next part of the

   ______ ______ ___ ______

   video.

4. Everything you need to do is explained in ten easy steps.

   ______ ______ ___ ___

5. If you have any questions, call our toll-free number.

   ___ ______ ___ ______

**Answers:**
1. noun, verb, article
2. verb, preposition, adjective, preposition, noun
3. gerund (-*ing* word acting as a noun), adverb, pronoun, adjective
4. pronoun, infinitive (*to* + a verb), preposition, adjective
5. conjunction, noun, verb, adjective

**Most Common Parts of Speech**

1. Nouns
2. Pronouns
3. Adjectives
4. Verbs
5. Adverbs
6. Prepositions
7. Conjunctions
8. Interjections
9. Articles

## 1. What Are Nouns?

**DEFINITION ➤** A **noun** is a word that refers to a person, place, or thing.

***Example:*** The student is doing her homework.

Both *student* and *homework* are nouns.

### Types of Nouns

There are two types of nouns: common nouns and proper nouns.

**Types of Nouns**

| **Common Nouns** | **Proper Nouns** |
|---|---|
| officer | Michael Johnson |
| station | Union Station |
| magazine | *Canadian Geographic** |
| university | Centennial College |

* When a title is that of a major publication such as a book or a magazine, the title should be italicized or underlined (the equivalent of italicizing when handwriting).

Common nouns are nouns that are not names or titles. For this reason, common nouns do not begin with a capital letter (unless, of course, the word begins a sentence):

I plan to attend university next fall.

The word *university* is a common noun in this sentence because it is not part of a specific name or title. The *u* must not be capitalized.

Proper nouns are names or titles. Every significant word of these titles starts with a letter that must be capitalized.

Carleton University is in Ottawa, our nation's capital. The University College of Cape Breton, on the other hand, is in Sydney, Nova Scotia.

In the above two sentences, the *U* in University (the word immediately following *Carleton* and the second word in the second sentence) must be capitalized because the word *University* in both cases is now a proper noun; it is part of the title of a specific university. (See Chapter 12: "Capitalization.") The University College of Cape Breton includes the word *of,* whose first letter is not capitalized because *of* is a *preposition* (see p. 9), and a preposition is not considered a significant word in a title.

### Concrete vs. Abstract Nouns

Nouns are said to be **concrete** if they represent things you can see or touch.

| | |
|---|---|
| window | river |
| paper | finger |

Nouns are said to be **abstract** if they represent things you cannot see or touch. These words can be concepts, ideas, or qualities.

| | |
|---|---|
| meditation | carelessness |
| honesty | fearlessness |

To test for a noun, it may help to ask these questions:

- Can I put the article *the* in front of the word?
- Is the word used as the subject or object of the sentence?

A noun may be the subject of a sentence, but it may not be. All subjects are nouns. But not all nouns are subjects. For example, a noun might be an object, instead.

Marissa gave me the book.

*Marissa* is the first noun in the sentence. *Marissa* is also the subject of the sentence. The word *me* is the second noun (more specifically, a pronoun); it is also an indirect object (the indirect receiver of the action). Finally, *book* is the third noun of the sentence. It is a direct object. It is the direct receiver of the action.

### Countable Nouns vs. Non-countable Nouns

Countable nouns, quite simply, can be counted.

There are three *marbles* on the floor.

Non-countable nouns, just as simply, cannot be counted.

The *water* spilled onto the floor.

Do not put an indefinite article (*a* or *an*) in front of a non-countable noun. For example, the following is not correct: *A* water spilled onto the floor.

## 2. What Are Pronouns?

**DEFINITION ➤** A **pronoun** is a word that takes the place of a noun. Just like a noun, it is used as the subject or object of a sentence. Pronouns can be divided into several cases (*see next page*).

***Example:*** *He* is dating the girl next door.

(The pronoun *he* can replace a noun such as *Johnny* or *The boy.*)

### Pronoun Cases

A personal pronoun will be in one of three cases depending on how it is used in a sentence: subjective, objective, or possessive. Possessive adjectives (last column) are not pronouns because they do not replace nouns; they modify them instead.

| | Personal Pronouns | | | Possessive |
|---|---|---|---|---|
| | **Subjective** | **Objective** | **Possessive** | **Adjectives** |
| **Singular** | | | | |
| 1st person | I | me | mine | my |
| 2nd person | you | you | yours | your |
| 3rd person | he | him | his | his |
| | she | her | hers | her |
| | it | it | its | its |
| **Plural** | | | | |
| 1st person | we | us | ours | our |
| 2nd person | you | you | yours | your |
| 3rd person | they | them | theirs | their |

| **Relative Pronouns** | **Demonstrative Pronouns** | **Indefinite Pronouns** |
|---|---|---|
| who, whom, whose | this | all, both, each, one |
| which | that | nothing, nobody, no one |
| that | these | anything, anybody, anyone |
| what | those | something, somebody, someone |
| whoever, whichever | | everything, everybody, everyone |

## 3. What Are Adjectives?

**DEFINITION ➤** An **adjective** is a word that modifies a noun or pronoun.

***Example:*** The *red* car is hers.

Adjectives usually come before the nouns they modify, but they can also come after the verb.

The *unusual* letter was delivered to my house.
It felt *heavy*.

## 4. What Are Verbs?

**DEFINITION ➤** A **verb** is a word that is used to indicate an action, state, or occurrence as well as the time at which the action, etc., takes place.

***Example:*** The Edmonton Oilers *advanced* to the Stanley Cup Finals in 2006.

Verbs can be divided into three classes: action verbs, linking verbs, and helping verbs.

## Action Verbs

An action verb tells us what the subject is doing. Most verbs are action verbs.

The athlete *cycles* 20 km every morning.
(The action takes place in the present.)

The crowd *applauded* the sax player.
(The action takes place in the past.)

## Linking Verbs

A linking verb joins the subject of a sentence to one or more words that describe or identify the subject.

She *is* a jazz musician in her twenties.
He *seemed* excited about getting married.

| Common Linking Verbs | | |
|---|---|---|
| be (am, is, are, was, were, have been) | become | look |
| act | feel | seem |
| appear | grow | taste |

## Helping Verbs (also called Auxiliary Verbs)

A helping verb, or an "auxiliary," is any verb used before the main verb.
It could show the tense of the verb:

It *will* rain tomorrow.
(Shows future tense.)

It could show the passive voice (see pp. 41–44 for more on active and passive voice):

The new concert hall *has been* finished.

It could give a special meaning to the verb:

Avril Lavigne *may be* singing at that concert.

The most common auxiliary verbs are forms of the irregular verbs *do, have,* and *be.*

A *modal* auxiliary is a helping verb that comes before the main verb and expresses probability, obligation, ability, or necessity.

| Common Modal Auxiliary Verbs |
|---|
| can, could<br>may, might, must<br>shall, should<br>will, would |

See Appendix C at the back of the text for more on irregular verbs.

## 5. What Are Adverbs?

**DEFINITION ➤** An **adverb** is a word that modifies a verb, an adjective, or another adverb. It often ends in *-ly*, but a better test is to ask yourself if the word answers the question how, when, or where.

***Example:*** The children ran *quickly.*

She is sure to succeed *eventually.*

- The adverb *eventually* answers the question "When?"
- It ends in *-ly*, and it modifies the verb *succeed.*

It will be *very* cold tomorrow.

- The adverb *very* answers the question "How?"
- It modifies the adjective *cold.*

Winter has come *too* early.

- The adverb *too* answers the question "How?"
- It modifies the adverb *early.*

Here are some adverbs to look out for:

**Adverbs**

| Adverbs of Frequency | Adverbs of Degree | |
|---|---|---|
| always | even | quite |
| ever | extremely | surely |
| never | just | too |
| often | more | very |
| seldom | much | |
| sometimes | only | |

## 6. What Are Prepositions?

**DEFINITION ➤** A **preposition** is a relatively short word that indicates time, place, or means. It is used to relate a noun or pronoun to some other word in the sentence. The preposition with its noun or pronoun (object of the preposition) is called a prepositional phrase.

***Examples:*** The gift is *from* my mother.
The card is addressed *to* my aunt.

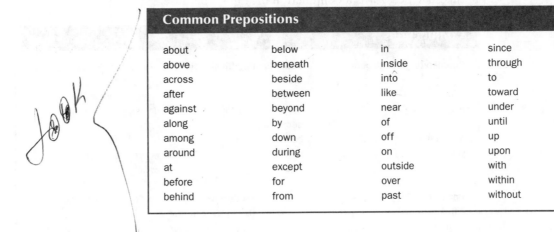

**Common Prepositions**

| | | | |
|---|---|---|---|
| about | below | in | since |
| above | beneath | inside | through |
| across | beside | into | to |
| after | between | like | toward |
| against | beyond | near | under |
| along | by | of | until |
| among | down | off | up |
| around | during | on | upon |
| at | except | outside | with |
| before | for | over | within |
| behind | from | past | without |

## 7. What Are Conjunctions?

**DEFINITION ➤** A **conjunction** is a word that joins or connects other words, phrases, or clauses.

***Examples:*** I was sick, *but* I still came to work.
She had eggs *and* pancakes for breakfast.

Connecting two words

Sooner *or* later, you will have to pay.

Connecting two phrases

The story was on the radio *and* in the newspaper.

Connecting two clauses

Dinner was late *because* I had to work overtime at the office.

**Since one word can function differently or have different forms or meanings, you must often study the context in which the word is found to be sure of its part of speech.**

The parent makes sacrifices *for* the good of the children.

In this sentence, *for* is a preposition.

The parent made sacrifices, *for* the child needed a good education.

In this sentence, *for* is a conjunction meaning "because."

## Conjunctions

**Coordinating Conjunctions**
and
but
nor
or
for (meaning "because")
yet
so

**Subordinating Conjunctions**
after
although
as, as if, as though
because
before
how
if, even if
provided that
since (meaning "because")
unless
until
when, whenever
where, wherever, whereas
while

**Correlative Conjunctions**
either ... or
neither ... nor
both ... and
not only ... but also

**Adverbial Conjunctions** (also known as "conjunctive adverbs")

| | |
|---|---|
| To add an idea: | furthermore |
| | moreover |
| | likewise |
| To contrast: | however |
| | nevertheless |
| To show results: | consequently |
| | therefore |
| To show an alternative: | otherwise |

**TIP**

**Where coordinating conjunctions are concerned, you can use the word *FANBOYS* (an acronym) as a way to remember them: *F* for *for*, *A* for *and*, *N* for *nor*, *B* for *but*, *O* for *or*, *Y* for *yet*, and *S* for *so*.**

For
And
Nor
But
Or
Yet
So

## 8. What Are Interjections?

**DEFINITION ➤** An **interjection** is a word that expresses a strong feeling and is not connected grammatically to any other part of the sentence.

***Examples:*** *Oh,* I lost my wallet. *Well,* that means I'll have to borrow cash from a friend.

## 9. What Are Articles?

**DEFINITION ➤** An **article** is a word that identifies a noun in a general sense.

***Examples:*** *The* dogs were mistreated for years by *a* previous owner.

Articles are considered to be adjectives. There are two types of articles: definite (*the*) and indefinite (*a, an*).

She read *the* magazine (a particular magazine).
She read *a* magazine (some magazine not identified).

Do not use *a* or *an* with non-countable nouns (things that can't be counted separately, such as *water*).

Water leaked under my roof during the rainstorm.

Use the indefinite article *a* or *an* before nouns that can be counted when you don't specify the thing counted.

*An* open window allowed the fresh air in (any one of a number of windows).

Use *a* before nouns beginning with a consonant or *u* pronounced as *y*. Use *an* before words beginning with a vowel or a silent *h*.

*a* vacation
*a* unit, *a* eulogy (*u* and *eu* in these words are pronounced "*yu*")
*an* automobile
*an* hour

## Working Together: Puzzle Pieces and Sentence Parts

Review the names for sentence parts by doing this crossword puzzle. Feel free to look back in the chapter for the answers.

### Crossword Puzzle: Reviewing the Terms for Sentence Parts

**Across**

1. Verbs like *hop, sing,* and *play* are called _________ verbs.
4. A helping verb
6. Every sentence has a _________ and a verb.
8. A helping verb
9. Which of the following is a preposition?
   *must, upon, they*
12. A preposition
14. *Word, witch, wall,* and *willow* are examples of the part of speech called a _________.
15. Most nouns are _________ nouns. They are not capitalized.
18. In the following sentence, which word is an adjective? *His pet theory was disproved.*
21. A preposition
22. In the following sentence, which word is an abstract noun?
    *The era was not economically successful.*
23. A preposition
24. A word that can take the place of a noun

**Down**

1. *Joy, confidence, peace* are examples of this kind of noun; the opposite of a concrete noun.
2. Which word is the subject in the following sentence?
   *Here is the tube of glue for Toby.*
3. An indefinite pronoun
4. A plural pronoun
5. *Look, appear, feel,* and *seem* are examples of _________ verbs.
7. Which word is the object of the preposition?
   *He made sure to call her before ten.*
10. The opposite of a common noun
11. A pronoun
13. A preposition
16. A helping verb
17. Which of the following is a proper noun?
    *king, Nero, hero, teen*
19. Which of the following is an adjective?
    *net, tan, Nan, man*
20. Which word is the verb in the following sentence?
    *Run down to the car for our bag.*
21. A common linking verb

CHAPTER TWO

2

# Recognizing Subjects and Verbs

**QUICK QUIZ** Test yourself on your knowledge of subjects and verbs. In each of the following sentences, find the subject and verb. Write your answers in the spaces provided. The answers to the questions are upside down beside the quiz.

| Subject | Verb | |
|---|---|---|
| ____________ | ____________ | 1. The definition of marriage has become a major issue in Canada. |
| ____________ | ____________ | 2. Studies show that many people are getting married later than their parents did. |
| ____________ | ____________ | 3. In Quebec, a large proportion of people have chosen to live in common-law relationships. |
| ____________ | ____________ | 4. Researchers have given more attention to divorces than to successful marriages. |
| ____________ | ____________ | 5. A positive attitude toward the partner appears to be the most important quality in a successful marriage. |

**Answers:**
1. Subject: definition
Verb: has become
2. Subject: studies
Verb: show
3. Subject: proportion
Verb: have chosen
4. Subject: researchers
Verb: have given
5. Subject: attitude
Verb: appears

## Why Should We Use Complete Sentences When We Write?

If you walk up to a friend at noon and say "Lunch?" you are expressing an idea by using a short form of a complete thought: you are asking your friend to join you for lunch. Even though we do not always use complete sentences in daily conversation, we usually have complete thoughts in mind. We say and hear words and phrases such as "Lunch?" every day, and these words and phrases seem to be complete thoughts because both the speaker and the listener supply the missing words in their own minds. When your friend hears you say "Lunch?" he or she is able to quickly understand the meaning: "Would you like to join me for lunch?"

You are free to use language in this way when you speak, but you must use a different approach in more formal speaking and writing situations. In writing down your thoughts, you cannot assume that another person will finish your thoughts for you. Each of your written thoughts must be a complete expression of what is in your mind.

The purpose of writing is to communicate something of value to a reader. Once you understand how the parts of a complete sentence work, you will be able to focus as much attention on *what* you are saying as on *how* you are saying it. Once you understand how the parts of a complete sentence work, you can take control of the sentence. You will have the power to make words work for you.

## What Is a Complete Sentence?

**DEFINITION ➤** A **complete sentence** must contain a subject and a verb, as well as express a *complete thought.*

***Example:*** The cat drank.

(*Cat* is the subject; *drank* is the verb. You need not know what the cat drank in order for the sentence to be complete.)

A *complete thought* is difficult to describe. It may be best understood by means of an example:

1. If you want an "A" in this course.
2. If you want an "A" in this course, you should do all your assignments and homework, attend all your classes, and communicate to your professor any difficulties you're having.
3. You want an "A" in this course.

The first thought is incomplete. The second thought is complete. The third thought is complete. Obviously, length does not determine completeness.

## How Do You Find the Subject of a Sentence?

The subject of a sentence is the person or thing about which the rest of the sentence makes an assertion. Any sentence must be about someone or something; therefore, every sentence must have a subject. To find the subject of any sentence, ask yourself this question: Who or what is the sentence about? When you have answered this question, you have found the subject of the sentence. Try to zero in on one word that is the subject. Although it may not always be possible, it is possible most of the time. The subject in sentence #3 above is *you*. The words "*A*" and *course* are also nouns, but neither is the subject of the sentence.

**EXERCISE**

## Recognizing Subjects

Examine each of the following sentences and ask yourself who or what each sentence is about. Draw a line under the subject in each sentence. (Underline only one word where possible.) The answers and explanations immediately follow the sentences.

1. The student graduated in the spring.
2. The unemployed Rick Daniels spent the summer looking for work.
3. He took a job as a security guard.
4. The building was near the waterfront.
5. The warehouse grew bitterly cold.
6. Cowardice was not the issue.
7. Tina and Margot listened to his complaints whenever they got together.

Since the subject of a sentence is made up of either one or more nouns (or a word, phrase, or clause that functions as a noun), learning some of the different terms used in traditional grammar to describe these different nouns is helpful.

1. The student graduated in the spring.

The sentence is about the *student*. In this case, the subject is a common noun.

**DEFINITION ➤** **Nouns** refer to persons, places, and things. Most nouns are common nouns.

**Common nouns** are the general terms for all the persons, places, and objects around us. They are not specific names; therefore, they are not capitalized.

***Examples:*** woman, city, cola

2. The unemployed Rick Daniels spent the summer looking for work.

The sentence is about *Rick Daniels*. In this case, the subject *Rick Daniels* is made up of two proper nouns.

**DEFINITION ➤** **Proper nouns** name particular persons, places, or things. Proper nouns are always capitalized.

***Examples:*** Juanita, Calgary, Pepsi

Notice that words such as *unemployed* can be put in front of nouns to describe them further. These words are called **adjectives.** *The, a,* and *an* are called **articles.** An article is also a form of adjective because it modifies a noun (***Example:*** *the* cat).

3. He took a job as a security guard.

The sentence is about *he*.

**DEFINITION ➤** Words that can be used in place of nouns are called **pronouns.**

***Examples:*** *she, he, it, we, I, you,* and *they*

4. The building was near the waterfront.

The sentence is about the *building*, a common noun. Can you replace this noun first with a proper noun and then with a pronoun?

_______________ was near the waterfront.

_______________ was near the waterfront.

5. The warehouse grew bitterly cold.

The sentence is about the *warehouse.* Here the common noun is not about a person or place but a thing. What pronoun could take the place of *warehouse*?

_______________ grew bitterly cold.

6. Cowardice was not the issue.

The sentence is about *cowardice.*

7. Tina and Margot listened to his complaints whenever they got together.

The sentence is about *Tina* and *Margot.* The subject is made up of two proper nouns joined by *and.*

**DEFINITION ➤** A **compound subject** is made up of two or more nouns joined together by *and, or, either/or,* or *neither/nor.*

***Example:*** Neither the *teacher* nor the *students* know the answer.

Not *every* noun or pronoun functions as a subject. Nouns and pronouns can also function as **objects.** Can you find a noun in the following sentence that is not the subject of the sentence?

Marc bought a ticket.

The word *ticket* is an object; it receives the action of the verb. It does not do it. The subject *Marc* does the action.

## Guide to Finding the Subject of a Sentence

*Definition:* The subject of a sentence is who or what the sentence is about.
How to find the subject: Ask yourself, "Who or what is this sentence about?" or ask the question, "Who or what is doing the main action?"

- Subjects usually come early in the sentence.
- Subjects can be modified by adjectives.
- Subjects can be compound.

Look for these two kinds of words as your subjects:

1. **Nouns**: the names of persons, places, or things

| **Common** | or | **Proper** | **Concrete** | or | **Abstract** |
|---|---|---|---|---|---|
| aunt | | Aunt Giselle | face | | loneliness |
| country | | Ghana | people | | patriotism |
| watch | | Timex | jewellery | | time |

2. **Pronouns:** take the place of nouns

| **Personal** | **Indefinite** | **Relative** | **Demonstrative** |
|---|---|---|---|
| I | one | who | this |
| you | each | that | that |
| he, she, it | some, someone, somebody, something | what | these |
| we | any, anyone, anybody, anything | which | those |
| they | nobody, nothing | | |
| | everyone, everybody, everything | | |
| | all | | |
| | many | | |
| | several | | |

**PRACTICE**

### Finding the Subject of a Sentence

Underline the subject in each of the following sentences. An example is done for you. Check your answers against those in the Answer Key on p. 455.

The seat belt sign switched on.

1. The plane landed.
2. Michelle Bates gathered her bags.
3. She was so excited.
4. Strange sounds filled her ears.
5. A mother and her three children shared a lunch.
6. The battered red taxi idled outside.
7. A light rain had fallen recently.

## Finding the Subject in Sentences with Prepositional Phrases

The sentences you worked with in the Practice above were short and basic. If we wrote only such sentences, our writing would sound choppy. Complex ideas would be difficult to express. One way to expand the simple sentence is to add prepositional phrases.

He put his suitcase on the seat.

*On* is a preposition. *Seat* is a noun used as the object of the preposition. *On the seat* is the prepositional phrase.

**DEFINITION ➤** A **prepositional phrase** is a group of words containing a preposition and an object of the preposition with its modifiers. Prepositional phrases contain nouns, but these nouns are never the subject of the sentence.

***Example:*** The dog buried the bone *under the porch.*

In sentences with prepositional phrases, the subject may be difficult to spot. Consider the following sentence:

In the young woman's apartment, paintings covered the walls.

In the sentence above, what is the prepositional phrase? Who or what is the sentence about?

To avoid making the mistake of thinking that a noun in the prepositional phrase could be the subject, it is a good practice to cross out the prepositional phrase.

~~In the young woman's apartment,~~ paintings covered the walls.

With the prepositional phrase crossed out, it now becomes clear that the subject of the sentence is the noun *paintings*.

**TIP** **When you are looking for the subject of a sentence, do not look for it within the prepositional phrase.**

You can easily recognize a prepositional phrase because it always begins with a preposition. Study the following list so that you will be able to quickly recognize all of the common prepositions.

**Common Prepositions**

| | | | |
|---|---|---|---|
| about | below | in | since |
| above | beneath | inside | through |
| across | beside | into | to |
| after | between | like | toward |
| against | beyond | near | under |
| along | by | of | until |
| among | down | off | up |
| around | during | on | upon |
| at | except | outside | with |
| before | for | over | within |
| behind | from | past | without |

In addition to these common prepositions, English has a number of prepositional combinations that also function as prepositions.

**Common Prepositional Combinations**

| | | |
|---|---|---|
| ahead of | in addition to | in reference to |
| at the time of | in between | in regard to |
| because of | in care of | in search of |
| by means of | in case of | in spite of |
| except for | in common with | instead of |
| for fear of | in contrast to | on account of |
| for the purpose of | in the course of | similar to |
| for the sake of | in exchange for | |

**TIP**

**Notice that when a prepositional phrase begins a sentence, a comma usually follows the phrase. (Sometimes, if the prepositional phrase is short, the comma is omitted.)**

**EXERCISE 1**

## Creating Sentences with Prepositional Phrases

Use each of the prepositions in the list below to write a prepositional phrase. Then write a sentence containing that prepositional phrase. Two examples are done for you.

| **Preposition** | **Prepositional Phrase** | **Sentence** |
|---|---|---|
| before | before breakfast | My cousin called before breakfast. |

| **Preposition** | **Prepositional Phrase** | **Sentence** |
|---|---|---|
| between | between the two barns | Between the two barns, the old Buick lay rusting. |

| Preposition | Prepositional Phrase | Sentence |
|---|---|---|
| 1. in | ______________________ | ______________________<br>______________________ |
| 2. with | ______________________ | ______________________<br>______________________ |
| 3. of | ______________________ | ______________________<br>______________________ |
| 4. from | ______________________ | ______________________<br>______________________ |
| 5. during | ______________________ | ______________________<br>______________________ |
| 6. by | ______________________ | ______________________<br>______________________ |
| 7. for | ______________________ | ______________________<br>______________________ |

## EXERCISE 2 Finding Subjects in Sentences with Prepositional Phrases

Remember that you will never find the subject of a sentence within a prepositional phrase. In each of the following sentences, cross out any prepositional phrases. Then underline the subject of each sentence. An example is done for you.

> ~~On the circus grounds,~~ <u>Lisa</u> wandered ~~among the elephants, horses, and camels~~.

1. Young people in the circus search for travel, adventure, danger, and romance.
2. However, after a few weeks of pulling cages and sleeping on hay, most of these people get tired of the circus and go back home.
3. The art of clowning, for instance, is very serious work.
4. Today, a circus clown must graduate from Clown College in Venice, Florida.
5. The staff of Clown College looks across the country for applicants.
6. Admission to the college is not easy.
7. Only 60 people out of 3000 applicants are admitted.

## What Are the Other Problems in Finding Subjects?

### Sentences That Are Questions

Some sentences begin with words that indicate that a question is being asked. Such words as *why, where, how,* and *when* give the reader the signal that a question will follow. Such opening words are not the subject. The subject will be found later on in the sentence. The following sentences begin with question words:

Why is *he* going away?
How did *he* find his sister in the city?

Notice that in each sentence the subject is not found in the opening part of the sentence. By answering questions or changing the question into a statement, you can make the subject easier to spot.

*He* is going away ...
*He* found his sister ...

### Using *here* and *there*

The words *here* and *there* can never be the subject of a sentence.

There is a new teacher in the department.

Who or what is this sentence about? This sentence is about a teacher. *Teacher* is the subject of the sentence.

Here is the book. (The subject is *book*.)

### Commands

Sometimes a sentence contains a verb that gives an order:

Go to Halifax.
Help your sister.

In these sentences, the subject *you* is not written, but it is understood. This is the only case where the subject of a sentence may be left out when you write a sentence.

### Sentences That Contain Appositive Phrases

**DEFINITION ➤** An **appositive phrase** is a group of words in a sentence that gives us extra information about a noun in the sentence.

***Example:*** Don Koyama, *the retired chemist,* sat at his desk.

In the example above, the words *the retired chemist* make up the appositive phrase because they give you extra information about Don Koyama. Notice that commas separate the appositive phrase from the rest of the sentence. If you leave out the appositive phrase when you read the sentence, the thought will still be complete.

Don Koyama sat at his desk.

Now the subject is clear: *Don Koyama.*

**TIP**

**When you are looking for the subject of a sentence, you will not find it within an appositive phrase.**

The word *chemist* in the example in the box at the bottom of p. 21 cannot be the subject because it is in an appositive phrase.

## Subjects That Look like Verbs

Words that end in *-ing* but have no helping verb in front are called *gerunds*. They act as nouns, not verbs. A gerund, therefore, can be the subject of a sentence.

Jogging is good for your health.

**PRACTICE**

### Finding Hidden Subjects

Each of the following sentences contains an example of a special problem in finding the subject of a sentence. First, cross out any prepositional phrases or appositive phrases. Then underline the subject of each sentence. An example is done for you. Check your answers against those in the Answer Key on p. 455.

What can <u>we</u> learn ~~from the study of an ancient civilization~~?

1. Look at a map of South America.
2. Where is the ancient city of Chan Chan?
3. Here on the coastal desert of northern Peru stand the remains of this city of the kings.
4. Chan Chan, once the fabulously wealthy centre of the Chimor, is situated in one of the driest, bleakest regions in the world.
5. It was the largest pre-Columbian city in South America.
6. In the ruins of this city, scientists have found fragments to piece together the mystery of the past.
7. How could this civilization have survived this hostile environment and become so advanced?

## How Do You Find the Verb of a Sentence?

Every sentence must have a verb. Verbs can be divided into three classes:

1. Action: An **action verb** tells what the subject is doing.

   Canada's Cassie Campbell *played* hockey in the Olympics.

2. Linking: A **linking verb** indicates a state of being or condition.

   The crowd *seemed* exhausted during the triathlon.

3. Helping: A **helping verb** combines with a main verb to form a verb phrase and gives the main verb a special time or meaning.

   Canadians *can* expect strong performances from their Olympic athletes in the future.

*Verbs tell time.* Use this fact to test for a verb. If you can put the verb into different tenses in the sentence, that word is a verb.

***Present:*** (Today) he *runs*.
***Past:*** (Yesterday) he *ran*.
***Future:*** (Tomorrow) he *will run*.

### Action Verbs

**DEFINITION ➤** **Action verbs** tell us what the subject is doing and when the subject does the action.

***Example:*** The woman *studied* ballet.

Look at the example in the box above.

| | |
|---|---|
| What was the woman doing? | studying |
| What is the time of the action? | past (*-ed* is the past tense ending) |

**Action Verbs**

Most verbs are action verbs. Here are a few examples:

| | | | |
|---|---|---|---|
| arrive | learn | open | watch |
| leave | forget | write | fly |
| enjoy | help | speak | catch |
| despise | make | teach | wait |

**PRACTICE**

## Finding Action Verbs

Each of the following sentences contains an action verb. Find the action verb by first crossing out any prepositional or appositive phrases and underlining the subject of the sentence. Then circle the verb (the word that tells what the subject is doing). Note also the time of the action: past, present, or future. An example is done for you. Check your answers against those in the Answer Key on p. 455.

Many people (begin) hobbies ~~in childhood~~ (present).

1. Some people collect very strange objects.
2. One man saved the fortunes from fortune cookies.
3. A group of people in Alberta often met to discuss their spark plug collections.
4. People in Brandon will gather many types of barbed wire.
5. Collectors take pride in the possession of unusual items.
6. A collection, like odd rocks or unique automobiles, will let a person express his or her individuality.
7. Collections keep us entertained from childhood to old age.

**EXERCISE**

## Finding Action Verbs

Each of the following sentences contains an action verb. Find the action verb by first crossing out any prepositional or appositive phrases and underlining the subject of the sentence. Then circle the verb (the word that tells what the subject is doing). Note also the time of the action: past, present, or future. An example is done for you.

Attitudes ~~toward medical practices~~ (will change) (future).

1. Traditional Chinese medicine harnessed ancient healing techniques in the practice of "qigong" (pronounced *chee gong*).
2. Masters of this Chinese practice claimed the ability to cure many diseases.
3. The master will project a mysterious force into his students.
4. The hands of the Chinese qigong practitioner will pound at the air above a patient.
5. Many patients respond to this invisible force.
6. Some patients sway their bodies with the power of the force.
7. Some doctors conducted research in China in hopes of finding the secrets of this ancient art.

## Linking Verbs

**DEFINITION ➤** A **linking verb** is a verb that joins the subject of a sentence to one or more words that describe or identify the subject.

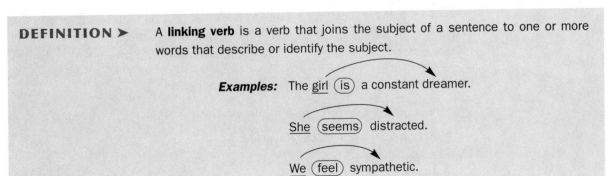

***Examples:*** The girl (is) a constant dreamer.

She (seems) distracted.

We (feel) sympathetic.

In each of the examples above, the verb links the subject to a word that identifies or describes the subject. In the first example, the verb *is* links *girl* with *dreamer*. In the second example, the verb *seems* links the pronoun *she* with *distracted*. Finally, in the third example, the verb *feel* links the pronoun *we* with *sympathetic*.

| Common Linking Verbs | |
|---|---|
| act | feel |
| appear | grow |
| be (am, is, are, was, were, have been) | look |
| become | seem |
| | taste |

**EXERCISE 1**

### Finding Linking Verbs

Each of the following sentences contains a linking verb. Find the linking verb by first underlining the subject of the sentence. Then draw an arrow to the word or words that identify or describe the subject. Finally, circle the linking verb. An example is done for you.

Dreams (are) very important to the Aboriginal peoples of Canada.

1. My dream last night was wonderful.
2. I had become middle-aged.
3. In a sunlit kitchen with a book in my hand, I appeared relaxed and happy.
4. The house was empty and quiet.
5. In the morning light, the kitchen felt cozy.
6. I seemed to have grown calmer.
7. I felt satisfied with life.

**EXERCISE 2**

## Finding Linking Verbs

Each of the following sentences contains a linking verb. Find the linking verb by first underlining the subject of the sentence. Then draw an arrow to the word or words that identify or describe the subject. Finally, circle the linking verb. An example is done for you.

Colds (can be) miserable.

1. Monica was afraid of catching a cold.
2. She felt healthy.
3. Everyone in her family became sick.
4. Her brother looked horrible.
5. She seemed immune to the cold.
6. Soon Monica's head grew stuffy.
7. The chicken soup from the deli down the street tasted delicious.

## Helping Verbs (also called Auxiliary Verbs)

Some verbs that come before the main verbs can be used to help the main verbs express a special time or meaning.

| Sentence Using Helping Verb | Time or Meaning Expressed |
|---|---|
| He *is* sleeping. | right now |
| He *might* sleep. | maybe now or in the future |
| He *should* sleep. | ought to, now or in the future |
| He *could have been* sleeping. | maybe in the past |

A **modal auxiliary verb** is a helping verb or auxiliary verb that comes before the main verb and expresses probability, obligation, ability, or necessity.

| Modal Auxiliary Verbs |
|---|
| can, could |
| may, might, must |
| shall, should |
| will, would |

*Be*, *do* and *have* are the most common auxiliary verbs. REMEMBER that *be*, *do*, and *have* are also used as main verbs of sentences. In such cases, *be* is a linking verb while *do* and *have* are action verbs. All other helping verbs are usually used only as helping verbs.

WATCH OUT for adverbs that may come in between the helping verb and the main verb.

**DEFINITION ➤** **Adverbs** are words that can modify verbs, adjectives, or other adverbs.

***Example:*** Dreams can *often* frighten young children.

The word *often* is an adverb coming between the verb phrase *can frighten*. For a list of adverbs, see p. 8.

**EXERCISE**

### Finding Helping Verbs

Each of the following sentences contains a helping verb in addition to the main verb. In each sentence, first underline the subject. Then circle the entire verb phrase. An example is done for you.

In some writing classes, students (must keep) a diary of their work.

1. Keeping a diary could have several advantages.
2. In a journal, a person can safely express true feelings without fear of criticism by family or friends.
3. You will be able to capture your memories before they fade.
4. Important, too, would be the development of a writing style and the improvement of language skills.
5. A journal might awaken your imagination.
6. It may unexpectedly bring pleasure and satisfaction.
7. You should seriously consider the purchase of one of those lovely fabric-bound notebooks.

## Chapter Review Exercises

**PRACTICE**

### Finding Subjects and Verbs in Simple Sentences

In each of the following sentences, cross out any prepositional phrases or appositive phrases. Then underline the subject and circle the complete verb. An example is done for you. Check your answers against those in the Answer Key on p. 455.

The modern family (has been disrupted) ~~by many negative outside influences~~.

1. Mother and Dad always blame me for any trouble with my sister.
2. My sister, the most popular girl in her class, is two years older than I.
3. Yesterday, for instance, she was trying on her new graduation dress.
4. Helpfully, I took out her new shoes and purse for her.
5. Margaret instantly became furious with me.
6. I was only sharing Margaret's excitement about her new clothes.

## EXERCISE 1 Finding Subjects and Verbs in Simple Sentences

In each of the sentences in the following paragraph, cross out any prepositional or appositive phrases. Then underline the subject and circle the complete verb.

Go West! Western Australia, one of the remaining great boom areas of the world, constitutes one-third of the Australian continent. Why did people by the tens of thousands go to western Australia in the late 1800s? In 1894, Leslie Robert Menzies jumped off his camel and landed in a pile of gold nuggets. In less than two hours, this man gathered over a million dollars in gold. He eventually took 5 tonnes of gold to the bank by wheelbarrow! Kalgoorlie and Boulder, the two boom towns that grew up there, boast the richest golden mile in the world. With all the gold seekers, this surface gold did not last very long. Now the only bands of rich ore lie more than 1200 metres down under the ground. There are many ghost towns with their empty iron houses and rundown chicken coops.

## EXERCISE 2 Composing Complete Sentences

Below are two lists, one of subjects and one of verbs. Using any subject from one list and any verb from the other list, compose complete sentences. Use each subject and each verb only once. Try to vary the position of the subject in the sentence. An example is done for you. (Do not use it as one of your own sentences.)

The dentist looks very tired today.

| | |
|---|---|
| 1. dogs | is |
| 2. nose | chased |
| 3. she | are |
| 4. dentist | was |
| 5. Saskatchewan | singing |
| 6. fishing | has |
| 7. problems | screams |
| 8. obeying | see |
| 9. mailbox | approaches |
| 10. storm | looks |

1. ______________________________

2. ______________________________

3. ______________________________

4. ______________________________

5. ______________________________

6. ______________________________

7. ____________________

8. ____________________

9. ____________________

10. ____________________

## Working Together: Singling Out Subjects

Student Profile: On a separate piece of paper, answer the following five questions about yourself. Write on every other line to make your writing more readable. Write freely for twenty minutes. Then exchange papers with another student. Using a pencil, circle the one-word (in most cases) subject in every sentence in your classmate's writing. Are you confusing subjects with objects (nouns that receive the action instead of do it)? Be prepared to share examples with the class.

1. Tell about the first book you remember looking at or reading.
2. Who was your most memorable teacher in elementary school? What is it about this teacher that you remember?
3. Who was the person outside of school who taught you the most?
4. What are the magazines you subscribe to or would like to subscribe to and why?
5. When you have a day or half day to yourself, how do you spend that time?

CHAPTER THREE

3

# More Work with Verbs

**QUICK QUIZ**

Test yourself on your knowledge of verb forms. In each of the following sentences, choose the correct verb tense for the verb in the dependent clause. Answers to the questions are upside down beside the quiz.

1. The soccer game will continue only after the lightning and rain __________. (to stop)
2. Since he was poor and unappreciated by the music world when he died in 1791, Mozart did not realize the importance that his music __________ (to have) in the twenty-first century.
3. My aunt told me yesterday that she __________ (to buy) a new condo the day before that.
4. Hemingway wrote only about subjects that he __________. (to like)
5. I __________ (to see) the woman buy the purple hat yesterday.

**Answers:**
1. have stopped, stop
2. would have
3. had bought
4. liked
5. saw

Since every sentence contains at least one verb, and this verb can take one of many forms, it is worth a good deal of your time and effort to understand these many forms and their uses. In Chapter 2, you have learned to *recognize* verbs. In this chapter, you will study several other areas with respect to verbs that often cause difficulty for writers:

Irregular verbs
Verb tense consistency
Sequence of verb tenses
Present perfect and past perfect tenses
Active and passive voice
The subjunctive

## What Are the Principal Parts of the Irregular Verbs?

The English language has more than 100 verbs that do not form the past tense or past participle with the usual *-ed* ending. Their forms are irregular. When you listen to young children, you often hear them utter expressions such as "Yesterday I *cutted* myself." Later on, they will learn that the verb *cut* is unusual, and they will change to the irregular form: "Yesterday I *cut* myself." The best way to learn these verbs is to listen to how they sound. Pronounce them out loud over and over until you have learned them. If you find that you don't know a particular verb's meaning, or you cannot pronounce a verb and its forms, ask your instructor for help. Most irregular verbs are very common words that you will be using often in your writing and speaking. You will want to know them well.

**DEFINITION ➤** An **irregular verb** takes a past tense form or past participle that is not with the usual *-ed* ending that regular verbs take.

***Example:*** Yesterday, he *cut* himself. (The word *cut* is the past tense form of the irregular verb *to cut.*)

See more on "Irregular Verbs" in Appendix C in the back of the text.

## Practising 50 Irregular Verbs

These are the three principal parts of irregular verbs:

| **Simple Form** (also called **Bare Infinitive Form**) | **Past Form** | **Past Participle** (used with perfect tenses after *has, have,* or *will have,* or with passive voice after the verb *to be*) |
|---|---|---|

I. The following verbs do not change their forms:
(Notice they all end in *-t* or *-d.*)

| **Simple Form** | **Past Form** | **Past Participle** |
|---|---|---|
| bet | bet | bet |
| cost | cost | cost |
| cut | cut | cut |
| fit | fit | fit |
| hit | hit | hit |
| hurt | hurt | hurt |
| quit | quit | quit |
| spread | spread | spread |

II. The following verbs have the same simple present form and past participle:

| **Simple Form** | **Past Form** | **Past Participle** |
|---|---|---|
| come | came | come |
| become | became | become |

**EXERCISE 1** **Knowing the Irregular Verb Forms**

Fill in the correct form of the verb in the following sentences.

(cost) 1. Last year the tuition for my education ___________ 7 percent more than the year before.

(quit) 2. I have ___________ trying to guess my expenses for next year.

(spread) 3. The message has ___________ that college costs continue to spiral.

(hit) 4. Most parents have been ___________ with large tax increases.

(become) 5. Financing a child's higher education has ___________ a difficult task.

III. The following verbs have the same simple past form and past participle:

| Simple Form | Past Form | Past Participle |
|---|---|---|
| bend | bent | bent |
| lend | lent | lent |
| send | sent | sent |
| spend | spent | spent |
| creep | crept | crept |
| keep | kept | kept |
| sleep | slept | slept |
| sweep | swept | swept |
| weep | wept | wept |
| teach | taught | taught |
| catch | caught | caught |
| bleed | bled | bled |
| feed | fed | fed |
| lead | led | led |
| speed | sped | sped |
| bring | brought | brought |
| buy | bought | bought |
| fight | fought | fought |
| think | thought | thought |
| seek | sought | sought |

**EXERCISE 2**

## Knowing the Irregular Verb Forms

Fill in the correct form of the verb in the following sentences.

(buy) 1. Last year the school district __________ new chemistry texts.

(spend) 2. Some parents felt they had __________ too much money on these new books.

(bleed) 3. They claimed the taxpayers were being __________ dry.

(keep) 4. These parents argued that the school should have __________ the old books.

(think) 5. The teachers __________ the old books were worn out.

IV. The following verbs have all different forms:

| Simple Form | Past Form | Past Participle |
|---|---|---|
| blow | blew | blown |
| fly | flew | flown |
| grow | grew | grown |
| know | knew | known |
| throw | threw | thrown |
| begin | began | begun |
| drink | drank | drunk |
| ring | rang | rung |
| shrink | shrank | shrunk |
| sink | sank | sunk |
| sing | sang | sung |
| spring | sprang | sprung |
| swim | swam | swum |
| bite | bit | bitten (or bit) |
| hide | hid | hidden (or hid) |
| drive | drove | driven |
| ride | rode | ridden |
| stride | strode | stridden |
| rise | rose | risen |
| write | wrote | written |

## EXERCISE 3 Knowing the Irregular Verb Forms

Fill in the correct form of the verb in the following sentences.

(grow) 1. Adventure holidays ___________ in popularity during the last decade.

(fly) 2. Years ago, travellers ___________ to Spain to see bullfights.

(throw) 3. Today, some clients dream of being ___________ by the bull.

(ride, swim) 4. As part of adventure trips, people have ___________ horseback, have ___________ across rivers, and have walked for days to get to their destinations.

(shrink) 5. Clients of a new trend called "reality tours" do not even ___________ from visiting jails.

## EXERCISE 4 Knowing the Irregular Verb Forms

Supply the past form or the past participle for each verb in parentheses.

Ever since people ___________ (begin) to write, they have ___________ (write) about the great mysteries in nature. For instance, no one ___________ (know) why the dinosaurs disappeared. Scientists now have ___________ (bet) on one strong possibility. That possibility is that 65 million years ago, a 10-km-wide chunk of rock ___________ (hit) the earth and ___________ (throw) up a thick cloud of dust. The dust ___________ (keep) the sunlight from the earth; therefore, certain life forms disappeared. Some scientists have ___________ (think) that this could also have ___________ (shrink) the earth's animal population by as much as 70 percent. Other scientists are not so sure that this is the answer. They believe time has ___________ (hide) the real reason for the disappearance of the dinosaurs.

**EXERCISE 5**

## Knowing the Irregular Verb Forms

Supply the past form or the past participle for each verb in parentheses.

Medical researchers have ____________ (seek) a cure for the common cold, but so far they have ____________ (fight) without success. The cold virus has ____________ (spread) throughout the world, and the number of cold victims has ____________ (rise) every year. Past experience has ____________ (teach) us that people who drink plenty of liquids and take aspirin get over colds more quickly than those who do not, but this is not a good enough remedy. People have also believed that you ____________ (feed) a fever and starved a cold, but recent research has ____________ (lead) to a refutation of this belief. It has ____________ (cost) a lot of time and effort to search for a vaccine, but so far the new knowledge has not ____________ (bring) a cure.

# Avoiding Unnecessary Shifts in Verb Tense

Do not shift verb tenses (move from past to present, for example) as you write unless you intend to change the time of the action.

***Shifted tense:*** The customer *asked* (past tense) for the prescription, but the pharmacist *says* (present tense) that the ingredients *are being ordered* (present tense).

***Revised:*** The customer *asked* (past tense) for the prescription, but the pharmacist *said* (past tense) that the ingredients *were being ordered* (past tense).

**PRACTICE 1**

## Correcting Unnecessary Shifts in Verb Tense

Each of the following sentences has an unnecessary shift in verb tense. Revise each sentence so that the tense remains consistent. There may be more than one correct answer for each sentence. Check your answers against those in the Answer Key on p. 455.

1. After I complete that writing course, I took the required history course.

______________________________________________

______________________________________________

2. In the beginning of the movie, the action was slow; by the end, I am sitting on the edge of my seat.

3. The textbook gives the rules for writing a works cited page, but it didn't explain how to do parenthetical references.

4. I was walking in the park when all of a sudden I see her running toward me.

5. The encyclopedia gave several pages of information about astronomy, but it doesn't give anything about black holes.

6. The invitation requested that Juan be at the ceremony and that he will attend the banquet as well.

7. That website gives you excellent information, but it was too cluttered.

**PRACTICE 2**

## Correcting Unnecessary Shifts in Verb Tense

The following paragraph contains unnecessary shifts in verb tense. Change each incorrect verb to past tense. Check your answers against those in the Answer Key on p. 456.

Doctor Norman Bethune grows up in Gravenhurst, Ontario. He was educated in Toronto and serves as a stretcher bearer in World War I. He contracted tuberculosis and thereafter devotes himself to helping other victims of the disease when he practises surgery in Montreal. He also invents or redesigned twelve medical and surgical instruments. Bethune travelled to Russia in 1935, joined the Communist party, and goes to Spain in 1936, where he organized the first mobile blood transfusion service during the Spanish Civil War. After returning to Canada, he shortly left for overseas again, this time to China, where he helped the Chinese Communists in their fight against Japan. "Spain and China," he writes, "are part of the same battle." While there, he contracted an infection and died. Mao's essay "In Memory of Norman Bethune," prescribed reading during China's Cultural Revolution, urges all Communists to follow Bethune's example of selfless dedication to others. Bethune is the best-known Canadian to the Chinese, and many Chinese visit his Canadian birthplace.

## What Is the Sequence of Tenses?

Sentences often contain two or more verbs that carry different tenses according to the times at which the actions are taking place. The type of sentence in which this happens is *complex*. A complex sentence is one that contains an independent clause and a dependent clause (although the dependent clause might come before the independent clause).

Before introducing the term **sequence of tenses,** which refers to the proper order of verb tense when a sentence contains more than one action, it is first necessary to introduce the terms **independent** and **dependent clauses.**

**DEFINITION ➤** The **independent clause (IC)** is a group of words that can be a simple sentence. *Independent* means that the words can stand alone as a sentence, and *clause* means there is a subject and a verb. The *independent clause* is a **complete thought.**

***Example:*** The students worked on their papers all night long.

**DEFINITION ➤** The **dependent clause (DC)** cannot stand alone as a simple sentence. It is an **incomplete thought.** Even though it has a subject and a verb, it depends on the rest of the sentence for completeness.

***Example:*** Because their assignments were due in the morning

The word *assignments* is the subject of the verb *were,* but this group of words is not a complete sentence. It is a ***dependent clause*** (DC).

**DEFINITION ➤** The term **sequence of tenses** refers to the proper use of verb tenses in complex sentences (sentences that have an independent clause and a dependent clause).

***Example:*** The students had worked on their papers all night long because their assignments were due the following morning.

The verb *had worked* in the independent clause is in the past perfect tense, and the verb *were* in the dependent clause is in the past tense. The first action takes place before the second one.

The verb tense in the independent clause determines the tense of the verb in the dependent clause. The guide that follows shows the relationship between the verb in the independent clause (IC) and the verb in the dependent clause (DC).

**Sequence of Tenses**

| Independent Clause | Dependent Clause | Time of the DC in Relation to the IC |
|---|---|---|
| If the tense of the independent clause is in the **present** (he *knows*), here are the possibilities for the dependent clause: | | |
| He knows | that she *is* right. | same time |
| | that she *was* right. | earlier |
| | that she *will be* right. | later |
| If the tense of the independent clause is in the past (he *knew*), here are the possibilities for the dependent clause: | | |
| He knew | that she *was* right. | same time |
| | that she *had been* right. | earlier |
| | that she *would be* right. | later |
| If the independent clause is in the future (he *will tell*), here are the possibilities for the dependent clause: | | |
| He will tell us | if she *goes.* | same time |
| | if she *has gone.* | earlier |
| | if she *will go.* | later |

**PRACTICE**

## Using the Correct Tense

In each of the following sentences, choose the correct tense for the verb in the dependent clause. Use the guide above if you need help. Check your answers against those in the Answer Key on p. 456.

1. The golf tournament will continue only after the thunder and lightning __________ (to stop).
2. Since he thought that he was buying a well-maintained car, Enzo did not realize the problems that this car __________ (to have) in the months to come.
3. I will know when I get my next paycheque whether or not I __________ (to buy) a stereo next week.
4. Albert Einstein failed the entrance exam at the Swiss Federal Institute of Technology because he __________ ((to be) + never) a very disciplined student.
5. Jacob ate only those foods that he __________ (to like).
6. Sasha believes that with a lot of hard work and a little luck, she __________ ((to be) + soon) successful.
7. I know that my best course of action __________ (to be) to tell the truth.

# How Do You Use the Present Perfect and the Past Perfect Tenses?

## Forming the Perfect Tenses

*Present perfect tense:* *has* or *have* + past participle of the main verb
has worked
have worked

*Past perfect tense:* *had* + past participle of the main verb
had worked

## What Do These Tenses Mean?

**DEFINITION ➤** The **present perfect tense** describes an action that started in the past and continues to the present time.

***Example:*** Elena *has worked* at the hospital for ten years.

The example in the box above indicates that Elena began to work at the hospital ten years ago and is still working there now.

Examine the following time line. What does it tell you about the present perfect tense?

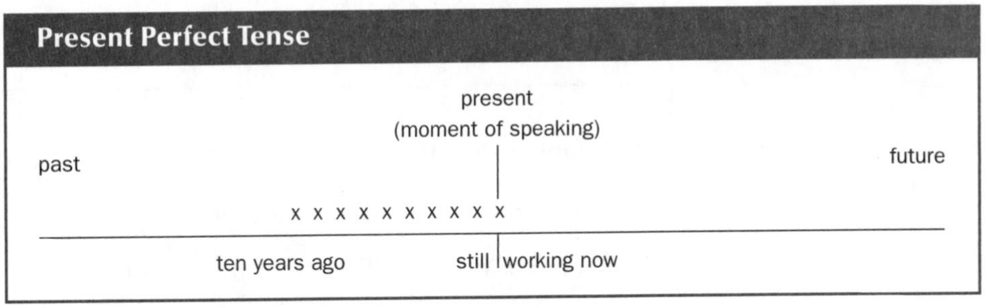


Other example sentences of the present perfect tense:

She *has studied* French since 2004.
I *have* always *despised* that television show.

**DEFINITION ➤** The **present perfect tense** can also describe an action that has just taken place, or an action whose exact time in the past is indefinite.

***Examples:*** *Has* Elena *found* a job yet?
Elena *has* (just) *found* a new job in Moncton.
*Have* you ever *been* to Kapuskasing?
Yes, I *have been* there three times.

If the time were definite, you would use the simple past:

> Elena *found* a new job yesterday.
> Yes, I *was* there last week.

**DEFINITION ➤** The **past perfect tense** describes an action that occurred before another activity or before another point in the past.

***Example:*** Elena *had worked* at the hospital for ten years *before* she *moved* away.

In the example in the definition above, there are two past actions: Elena *worked,* and Elena *moved.* The action that took place first is in the past perfect (*had worked*). The action that took place later, and was also completed in the past, is in the simple past (*moved*).

**Past Perfect Tense**

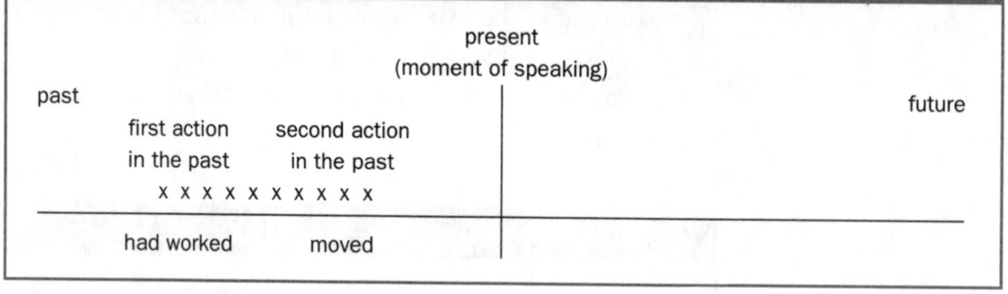


Other examples using the **past perfect tense:**

> I *had* just *arrived* when the alarm *rang*.
>
> She *said* that Marty *had told* the class about the essay deadline.
>
> He *had provided* the report *long before* last week's meeting.

**EXERCISE**

## Using the Correct Verb Tense

Complete the following sentence by filling in each blank with either the present perfect tense or the past perfect tense of the verb given.

1. Yolanda told us that she ________________ (live) in Fort Smith before she moved to Mexico City.

2. Mexico City ________________ (fascinate) visitors for many years.

3. This city ____________ (become) the largest city in the world, and people ____________ (watch) it grow larger every year.

4. The suburbs of the city ________ (overwhelm) old villages that ________ (exist) peacefully since the days of the Aztecs.

5. Today, Mexico City ________ (build) a computer-controlled subway system to deal with its huge transportation problem.

## What Is the Difference between Active and Passive Voice?

In the active voice, the subject does the acting. In the passive voice, the subject is acted upon. (See examples in the box below.) But which one is usually better to use? And does this mean the other should never get used at all?

**Active Voice Is Generally Best**

Stylistically speaking, a sentence employing the active voice is most often considered the stronger sentence when compared to its passive voice counterpart:

***Active:*** The dog buried its bone.

***Passive:*** The bone was buried by the dog.

Not only is the first sentence stronger because it is shorter than the second, but it is in the first sentence that the subject does the action. In the second sentence, *the bone* is the subject. But the bone does not do the burying. *The dog* has still done the burying, but *the dog* is not the subject. In fact, it is part of a prepositional phrase, so it cannot be the subject. (See the definition of a prepositional phrase on p. 18.)

### The Place for Passive Voice

Although active voice is generally better than passive voice, there are situations in which passive voice is the more appropriate voice to use:

1. You might find yourself to be in a position of authority and, in an official capacity, you are required to give bad news to someone. Sometimes it is advisable to speak deliberately vaguely about what the cause of your bad news is. You can do this, in part, by using the passive rather than the active voice.

   Unfortunately, it was decided that the job go to an internal candidate.

   The above sentence is in the passive voice. The person who made the decision is not mentioned. This wording might have been chosen to protect whoever did the deciding because it was such a controversial move. This way, there's less chance the recipient of the bad news will ask specific questions that might be embarrassing if not legally troubling to the employer.

2. It is also better to use the passive rather than active voice when the subject that has been acted upon is more important than the doer of the action.

   The Conservatives have been given more seats than the Liberals in the House of Commons.

   Who is the doer of the action here? Who actually gave more seats to the Conservatives? The answer is the *people of Canada who voted in the election.* So why aren't these people mentioned at all? Well, it's obvious. That's how elections work. What isn't obvious is who won. And that's why the word *Conservatives* becomes the subject of the sentence even though they are not the doer of the action. The sentence, therefore, is better in the passive voice.

3. Yet another reason for putting a sentence in the passive voice is that the action itself is more important than the doer of the action. People in the sciences and in legal affairs often report events this way.

   Ice was found on Mars today.
   Michael Jackson was acquitted today.

   In the first sentence above, there is no need to report that scientists found the ice. Nor is there need to mention, in the second sentence, that Jackson was acquitted by a jury of his peers.

### Active and Passive Voice

In the **active voice**, the subject does the acting:

**The committee made the decision.**

**Choose the active voice generally in order to achieve direct, economical, and forceful writing. Most writing, therefore, should be in the active voice.**

In the **passive voice**, the subject is acted upon:

**The decision was made by the committee**
or
**The decision was made.**

Notice in these passive sentences that the actor is not only de-emphasized by being moved out of the subject place but may be omitted entirely from the sentence.

**Choose the passive voice to de-emphasize the actor or to avoid naming the actor altogether.**

Study the two sentences below. The first is in the active voice and the second is in the passive. Which one is more appropriate and why? What are the disadvantages of each?

Chris Hadfield orbited the earth in 2001.
The earth was orbited by Chris Hadfield in 2001.

## How Do You Form the Passive Voice?

The passive voice of a verb consists of a form of *be* (*am, is, are, was, were, being, be,* or *been*) plus the past participle of the main verb.

Cars and trucks *are built* in Oshawa.

1. Use the past participle, not the base form or past tense of a verb, to form the passive voice.
2. Identify the subject and make sure the form of the auxiliary verb *be* agrees with it.
3. Use only transitive verbs (verbs that take a direct object) in the passive voice.

| Subject Acted Upon | + Verb *to be* | + Past Participle | + *by* Phrase (Optional) |
|---|---|---|---|
| The race | was | won | (by the runner) |
| The fish | was | cooked | (by the chef) |
| The books | are | illustrated | (by the artists) |

**PRACTICE**

### Choosing the Right Voice

Rewrite the following sentences, changing the active voice to passive, and the passive voice to active. Then decide which one is best and why. Check your answers against those in the Answer Key on p. 456.

1. No policy or funding announcements were made by the Canadian health minister at the International AIDS Conference in Toronto.
2. Six hundred and fifty million dollars (U.S.) was given by Microsoft founder Bill Gates to the war against HIV/AIDS.
3. Canadian authorities allowed Zimbabwe's foreign minister into Canada for the international conference despite a ban on visits by senior officials from that country.
4. The audience was told by former U.S. President Bill Clinton that a lot of mistakes were made during his presidency, but underfunding AIDS research was not one of them.
5. The International AIDS Conference in 2006 was attended by 22 000 delegates and 8000 journalists, exhibitors, volunteers, and staff.
6. The impact that poverty has on HIV and AIDS in developing countries was discussed in great detail at the conference.
7. Actor and activist Richard Gere stressed the importance of the role of media in spreading the word about HIV/AIDS.

**EXERCISE**

### Choosing the Right Voice

Fill in the following chart by making all sentences on the left active voice and all sentences on the right passive voice. Then discuss with your classmates and instructor why you might choose the active voice or the passive voice in each case.

| **Active Voice** | **Passive Voice** |
| --- | --- |
| 1. the child dialled the wrong number by mistake. | 1. The wrong number was dialled by the child by mistake. |
| 2. many shoes were available to be purchased ~~when we~~ at the store we went. | 2. We went to the store where many shoes were available to be purchased. |
| 3. The tornado struck Cherry Creek last spring. | 3. Cherry Creek was struked by a tornado last spring. |
| 4. The wind blew the leaves across the yard. | 4. the leaves were blown by the wind across the yard. |
| 5. Many fashionable young men and women wore platform shoes in the 1970's. | 5. In the 1970s, platform shoes were worn by many fashionable young men and women. |

## What Is the Subjunctive?

**DEFINITION ➤** The **subjunctive** is a verb form found in a sentence that expresses desire or demand.

***Examples:*** If I *were* a millionaire, I would travel around the world.
She demanded that he *arrive* on time.

Verbs in italics are in the subjunctive form. They are found in dependent clauses.

Recognize these three situations that call for the subjunctive:

1. Unreal conditions using *if*, *wish*, *as if*, *as though*

   *If he were* my teacher, I would be pleased.
   He *wishes he were* in France.
   Try to act *as though you were* proud.

   Note that *as if* and *as though* don't always call for the subjunctive. It is correct to say: "It looks as if it is snowing." In this case, the speaker is simply describing what is very likely true. The difference is in the degree of doubt.

   The subjunctive verb form *were* shows that what is being wished for, or considered, is not (or not yet) a fact. **Use *were* whether the subject is plural or singular.** For example:

   If *I were* you ... (I can't be you.)
   I wish *I were* rich. (I'm not.)
   He acts as if *he were* the boss. (He's not.)

2. Clauses starting with *that* expressing demands, resolutions, or requests (after verbs such as *ask*, *command, demand, insist, move, order, recommend, suggest*, or *urge*)

   I *demand* that *she work* harder.
   Sullivan *insisted* that *Jones report* on Tuesday.

   Use the simple form of the verb (see p. 33) whether the subject is singular or plural.

3. Clauses starting with *that* after adjectives expressing urgency, as in *it is necessary, it is imperative, it is urgent, it is important,* and *it is essential*

   *It is necessary* that *she wear* a net covering her hair.
   *It is essential* that Robert *understand* the concept.

   Again, use the simple form of the verb.

## Other Problems with Verbs

Do not use more than one **modal auxiliary** (*can, may, might, must, should, ought*) with the main verb.

*Incorrect:* Ethan *shouldn't ought* to drop that course.
*Correct:* Ethan *ought not* to drop that course.
or
Ethan *shouldn't* drop that course.

Do not use *should of, would of,* or *could of* to mean *should have, would have,* or *could have.*

*Incorrect:* Alana *would of* helped you if she *could of.*
*Correct:* Alana *would have* helped you if she *could have.*

See more on helping verbs in Chapter 1, pp. 7–8.

## Chapter Review Exercises

**PRACTICE**

### Solving Problems with Verbs

Revise each of the following sentences to avoid problems with verbs. Check your answers against those in the Answer Key on p. 457.

1. He hadn't ought to drive so fast.

   ______________________________

2. It is essential that Lynn takes her dog to the vet.

   ______________________________

3. I wish I was a chef.

_______________________________________________

4. She sung for a huge crowd Saturday night.

_______________________________________________

5. I was shook up by the accident.

_______________________________________________

6. The hill was climbed by the skiers.

_______________________________________________

7. My father ask me last night to help him build a deck.

_______________________________________________

**EXERCISE**

### Solving Problems with Verbs

Some of the verbs in the following paragraph are incorrect. Find the errors and correct them.

I knowed I was in big trouble in chemistry when I took a look at the midterm exam. My semester should of been a lot better. The first day I had my new textbook, I put it on the back shelf of a taxi and forgot it when I got out. Then I catched a cold and miss the next two classes. When I finally start off for class, I missed the bus and walked into the classroom half an hour late. The teacher scowls at me and ask to speak to me after class. I use to always sit in the front row so I could see the board and hear the lectures, but now that I am late I have to take a seat in the last row. I wish I was able to start this class over again the right way. No one had ought to have such an unlucky start in any class.

## Working Together: Verbs, Not Verbiage

Student Profile: On a separate piece of paper, answer the following five questions about yourself. Double space or write on every other line to make your writing more readable. Write freely for twenty minutes. Then exchange papers with another student. Using a pencil, circle each verb in your classmate's writing. Are any of the verbs incorrect in their form or in their tense? Be prepared to share examples with the class.

1. Tell about the first car you remember owning or driving.
2. Who was the first person you were ever attracted to? What is one thing about this person that you remember?
3. Who was the person in school who taught you the most?
4. What is one television program you enjoy and why?
5. When you go away for the weekend, where is one place you like to go?

CHAPTER FOUR

4

# Subject-Verb Agreement

**QUICK QUIZ**

Test yourself on your knowledge of subject-verb agreement. On the line before each sentence below, write the correct form of the verb. Answers to the questions are upside down beside the quiz.

_______________ 1. The history of humankind's attempts to fly (goes, go) back hundreds of years.

_______________ 2. An ancient myth that describes men trying to fly with wings made of feathers and wax (has, have) been passed on.

_______________ 3. The famous inventor Leonardo da Vinci made designs for a helicopter that (was, were) very detailed.

_______________ 4. Every aviator who set a new flying record in the early years of flight (was, were) treated as a hero.

_______________ 5. Not only helicopters but also the jet engine (was, were) among the advances that occurred during the Second World War.

**Answers:**
1. goes
2. has
3. were
4. was
5. was

For your sentences to be logical, all parts of each sentence must agree. Agreement is the correspondence between words in number, gender, or person. Subjects and verbs agree in number (singular or plural) and person (first, second, or third).

Since many students have problems with agreement in their writing, you should work through this chapter carefully so that you will be able to identify and deal effectively with these trouble spots in your own writing.

## Subject-Verb Agreement within the Sentence

**DEFINITION ➤** There is subject-verb agreement in a sentence when a verb agrees with its subject in **number** and in **person.**

***Examples:*** The girl plays.
The girls play.
I am here on Thursdays.

The verb *plays* in the first sentence is singular. It agrees with the singular subject *girl.*

The verb *play* in the second sentence is plural. It agrees with the plural subject *girls.*

The verb *am* in the third sentence is first person. It agrees with the first-person subject *I.*

If the subject is singular, the verb must also be singular. Notice how singular and plural subjects are handled in the following chart:

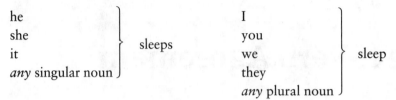

| Subject | Verb | Subject | Verb |
|---|---|---|---|
| he<br>she<br>it<br>*any* singular noun | sleeps | I<br>you<br>we<br>they<br>*any* plural noun | sleep |

***Example:*** The baby *sleeps*. ***Example:*** The babies *sleep*.

**TIP** **Remember that a singular verb that goes with a singular noun or pronoun (except *I* or *you*) needs a final *s*.**

**PRACTICE 1**

## Making the Subject and Verb Agree

Underline the correct verb in the following sentences. Check your answers against those in the Answer Key on p. 457.

1. My uncle (cycle, cycles) 30 km a day.
2. He (amaze, amazes) the family.
3. His routes (varies, vary) with his mood.
4. Friends (cheers, cheer) him on.
5. I (hopes, hope) I'm that energetic at his age.

## Special Problems in Making Verbs Agree with Their Subjects

**RULE 1 ➤** **The subject is not always the noun closest to the verb.** Remember, you will not find the subject of the sentence within a prepositional phrase.

In the example that follows, the subject is underlined, the prepositional phrase is crossed out, and the verb is circled.

> The hairline cracks ~~in the engine~~ (present) a serious threat to passengers' safety.

**PRACTICE 2**

## Making the Subject and Verb Agree

Underline the correct verb in the following sentences. Check your answers against those in the Answer Key on p. 457.

1. The rules of the game of chess (is, are) very complicated.
2. The pawns on the board (moves, move) only one square at a time except on the first move when they can move up to two squares.
3. The rooks on the four corners of the board (moves, move) straight and not diagonally.

4. Several versions of the musical about the game and by the same name—"Chess"—(is, are) being performed throughout the world.
5. If, for example, all the pawns on the white side (is, are) gone from the board, no white pieces can any longer be retrieved.

**RULE 2 ➤** **Many indefinite pronouns take a singular verb.**

### Indefinite Pronouns

**Indefinite Pronouns Taking a Singular Verb:**

| | | | | |
|---|---|---|---|---|
| -one | everyone | someone | anyone | no one |
| -body | everybody | somebody | anybody | nobody |
| -thing | everything | something | anything | nothing |
| | each | another | either | neither |

**Everyone *is* expecting a miracle.**

**Indefinite Pronouns Taking a Plural Verb:**

| | | | |
|---|---|---|---|
| both | few | many | several |

**The talks between the two countries failed.**
**Both *were* to blame.**

**Indefinite Pronouns Taking a Singular or Plural Verb Depending on the Meaning in the Sentence:**

| | | |
|---|---|---|
| any | all | more |
| none* | some | most |

**The books are gone.** **All were very popular.**
**The sugar is gone.** **All of it was spilled.**

*in informal usage

The English language is constantly evolving. The word *none,* for example, is one of those words that is still in transition. The letters *one* inside the word *none* suggest that this indefinite pronoun should be singular. In formal usage, this is so. An example, therefore, of the correct formal usage of the word *none* would be the following:

None of my pens *is* working.

(*None,* being singular [in formal usage], would take a singular verb, in accordance with the subject-verb agreement rule.)

In general (less formal) usage, *none* (like the other indefinite pronouns listed with it above) is either singular or plural depending on the noun that the indefinite pronoun refers to (the noun that usually follows the preposition *of* which immediately follows the word *none*).

None of the sugar is wasted.
None of the people are here yet.

This may be a case where you, the individual, have to make a decision. Do you go with formal or general usage? Your decision might depend on your audience and purpose (see pp. 168–69 in Chapter 14: "The Four Stages of Writing"). You might also want to ask your instructor about what he or she prefers.

**PRACTICE 3**

## Making the Subject and Verb Agree

Underline the correct verb in the following sentences. Check your answers against those in the Answer Key on p. 457.

1. Everyone in the four classes (is, are) studying for exams.
2. Neither book (has, have) the answer to her question.
3. Everybody in all programs (is, are) expected to bring a student card to the exam.
4. Each question on all exams (specifies, specify) how many marks the question is worth.
5. No one, except for emergency purposes, (is, are) allowed to leave the exam until it is over.
6. Both the English exam and the math exam (is, are) on Tuesday.
7. None of these pencils (is, are) sharp enough for the SCANTRON portion of the math exam.

**RULE 3 ➤** **When a pair of conjunctions is used, the verb agrees with the subject closer to the verb.**

Neither the textbook nor my lecture notes (explain) the meaning of the term "tidal wave."

*Textbook* and *notes* together make up the compound subject. Since *notes* is closer to the verb, the verb agrees with *notes*.

| Pairs of Conjunctions | | |
|---|---|---|
| neither ... nor | either ... or | not only ... but also |

**PRACTICE 4**

## Making the Subject and Verb Agree

Underline the correct verb in the following sentences. Check your answers against those in the Answer Key on p. 457.

1. Neither the students nor the teacher (is, are) smoking on the patio.
2. It was obvious that not only the automotive students but also their dean (was, were) noticeably outraged by the college president's decision to shut the campus down.
3. Neither the police officer nor the firefighters (seems, seem) afraid in spite of people's continuous screams.
4. Not only the children but also their mother (takes, take) the bus every day.
5. Either the buses or the subway (has, have) resumed service, but not both.

| | |
|---|---|
| **RULE 4 ➤** | **In some sentences, the subject can come after the verb. In these cases, be sure that the verb agrees with the subject.** |

Here (is) the <u>surprise</u> I promised you.

Who (were) the <u>people</u> with you last night?

**PRACTICE 5**

## Making the Subject and Verb Agree

Underline the correct verb in the following sentences. Check your answers against those in the Answer Key on p. 457.

1. In the room, there (is, are) two windows.
2. If they are ever late, there (is, are) always a good reason.
3. Who (is, are) her real friends as opposed to those who just want things from her?
4. There (is, are) plenty of marbles on the floor.
5. Here (is, are) some salt for your fries.

| | |
|---|---|
| **RULE 5 ➤** | **A group noun in Canadian English usually takes a singular verb if the group acts as a unit.** (The test is to substitute the word *it* in place of the group noun.) |

The town <u>council</u> (is planning) a Canada Day celebration.

In this sentence, the council is acting as a unit. *It* is planning a celebration. Therefore, the verb is singular.

| | |
|---|---|
| **RULE 6 ➤** | **A group noun takes a plural verb if the members of the group act as individuals.** (The test is to substitute the word *they* for the group noun and see if it sounds right.) |

The town <u>council</u> (are preparing) their speeches for this event.

In this sentence, the council members are individually preparing speeches. *They* substitutes for the group noun in this sentence. Since the individuals are acting separately, the verb is plural.

| Common Group Nouns | | | | |
|---|---|---|---|---|
| audience | class | committee | council | crowd |
| family | group | jury | number | team |

**PRACTICE 6**

## Making the Subject and Verb Agree

Underline the correct verb in the following sentences. Check your answers against those in the Answer Key on p. 457.

1. The class (is, are) performing their presentations this week.
2. The family (is, are) all eating at separate times throughout the week.
3. The committee (has, have) decided to go ahead with the construction of the public swimming pool.
4. The group (has, have) voted 5–4 in favour of joining forces with their opponents.
5. The crowd (claps, clap) whenever the "applause" sign lights up.

**RULE 7 ➤**

**The verbs *do* and *be* are often troublesome. Remember that standard English uses *s* for the third person singular in the present tense (and for the verb *to be* [*was*] in the past tense).**

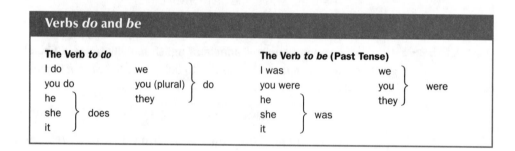

### Verbs *do* and *be*

**The Verb *to do***

| | |
|---|---|
| I do | we, you (plural), they } do |
| you do | |
| he, she, it } does | |

**The Verb *to be* (Past Tense)**

| | |
|---|---|
| I was | we, you, they } were |
| you were | |
| he, she, it } was | |

She *does* the signage for the Christmas pageant every year.
They *do* everything they can to help others.
You *were* at the scene of the crime.
He *was* elected to the position.

**PRACTICE 7**

## Making the Subject and Verb Agree

Underline the correct verb in the following sentences. Check your answers against those in the Answer Key on p. 457.

1. The boy and his date (does, do) the samba every time they go to a Latin dance club.
2. She and he (was, were) the first ones to arrive.
3. It (does, do) feel like 40 degrees outside today.
4. Jake and Amelia (does, do) their homework together every weekend.
5. Cameron and she (was, were) here for three hours before they talked to each other.

## Chapter Review Exercises

**PRACTICE 1**

### Making the Subject and Verb Agree

Underline the verb that agrees with the subject. Check your answers against those in the Answer Key on p. 457.

1. He (doesn't, don't) study in the library anymore.
2. We (was, were) hoping to find him there.
3. The library (doesn't, don't) close until eleven o'clock.
4. (Was, Were) you late tonight?
5. Ann (doesn't, don't) care if you stay until closing time.

**PRACTICE 2**

### Making the Subject and Verb Agree

In the blanks next to each sentence, write the subject of the sentence and the correct form of the verb. An example is done for you. Check your answers against those in the Answer Key on p. 457.

| | **Subject** | **Verb** |
|---|---|---|
| The eleven proposals for the development of a new building at Laurier Circle (has, have) been submitted to the city. | proposals | have |
| 1. The price of airline tickets to England (has, have) remained fairly reasonable. | ______ | ______ |
| 2. His decision (requires, require) a lot of thought. | ______ | ______ |
| 3. She (doesn't, don't) know the answer to any of the test questions. | ______ | ______ |
| 4. Either the guide or the security guard (see, sees) every visitor. | ______ | ______ |
| 5. The committee (agree, agrees) to the fundraising projects for this year. | ______ | ______ |
| 6. Potato chips and cola (is, are) most of her diet. | ______ | ______ |
| 7. One of the people in the audience (is, are) my brother. | ______ | ______ |

## EXERCISE 1 Making the Subject and Verb Agree

In the blanks next to each sentence, write the subject of the sentence and the correct form of the verb.

| | Subject | Verb |
|---|---|---|
| 1. Included in the price of the trip (was, were) five nights in a lovely hotel and all meals. | ________ | ________ |
| 2. None of the members (wants, want) to go. | ________ | ________ |
| 3. Jerry and Aldo (works, work) well together. | ________ | ________ |
| 4. The number of essay questions on the apprenticeship exam (seems, seem) to be increasing. | ________ | ________ |
| 5. When (does, do) your parents return from their holiday? | ________ | ________ |
| 6. In the whole town there (is, are) only two good restaurants. | ________ | ________ |
| 7. Neither a piano nor Jim's guitar (was, were) available. | ________ | ________ |

## EXERCISE 2 Making the Subject and Verb Agree

Take your answers from the blanks in Exercise 1, and use them as the main subjects and verbs in your own sentences. For example, if the subject in the first column is *cars,* and the verb in the second is *perform,* your own sentence might look something like this:

> Cars from Japan generally perform better than cars from the U.S.

The sentence *I prefer cars from Japan because they perform better than cars from the U.S.* does not work in this exercise because in this sentence, the subject is not *cars* but *I.*

## EXERCISE 3 Making the Subject and Verb Agree

The following paragraph may have several occurrences of subject-verb disagreement. Rewrite the paragraph, making sure all verbs agree with their subjects.

> Going to the movies are a favourite thing for me to do on the weekends. If I don't have someone "special" in my life, I still go to the movies either with friends or even by myself. I like all kinds of movies: horror flicks, comedies, drama, adventure film, etc. And not all the movies I watch comes from Hollywood. I also like independent film, foreign films with subtitles, and Bollywood movies as well. When I go with my friends, they often want to see

something I've already seen. They can't believe I see so many on a regular basis. But because I like movies so much, I sometimes sees them twice, especially since sometimes it's more fun to see the same movie with friends than a brand new one by myself. Except for the astronomically high prices the cinema charge for popcorn, pop, and candy, there's not many more exciting things to do than go to a great movie on a weekend night. For two hours or so, the problems of the world disappears, and I'm very content to be lost in a world outside of myself.

## Working Together: Magazine Mayhem

**To the Instructor:** Bring a magazine (that you don't mind destroying) to class. If your class is made up of students from one particular program, you might want to bring a magazine in which there is related subject matter. Circulate the magazine among your students along with a pair of scissors. Announce to the students how much time they have for the following activity. Students may use their text if they think it can help.

**To the Students:** Cut out any one paragraph (of at least five sentences) that looks interesting to you, and then pass the magazine and scissors onto the next person.

Then underline every subject of every sentence in the paragraph, and circle every verb that goes with that subject. Then rewrite the paragraph on a separate sheet of paper, but deliberately make every verb that you have circled **disagree** with its subject. Write as legibly as possible, and double space your work so that someone else can easily read it.

Now trade your rewritten paragraph with that of someone else who is sitting close to you, but keep the original paragraph with the underlined subjects and the circled verbs. On the separate sheet of paper you now have from someone else, underline all the subjects of all the sentences, and circle all the verbs that go with them, correct or incorrect. Make the corrections above the incorrect verbs, making sure all verbs agree with their subjects. Hand the separate sheet of paper back when you're finished.

Now compare the answers on the separate sheet of paper to the answers on the original paragraph. Discuss any discrepancies with the person with whom you traded paragraphs.

CHAPTER FIVE

5

# Coordination and Subordination

**QUICK QUIZ 1** Test yourself on your knowledge of combining sentences using **coordination.** The following pair of sentences could be combined into a single sentence using coordination. Among the four choices given, place a check mark in front of the example that is correct. The answer to the question is upside down beside the quiz.

Chocolate became a popular drink throughout Europe. It was thought to be good for your health.

______ 1. Chocolate became a popular drink throughout Europe, it was thought to be good for your health.

______ 2. Chocolate became a popular drink throughout Europe because it was thought to be good for your health.

______ 3. Chocolate became a popular drink throughout Europe, for it was thought to be good for your health.

______ 4. Chocolate became a popular drink throughout Europe and good for your health.

**Answers:**
Sentence 3 is correct. Sentence 1 is a run-on and sentence 4 is not parallel. Sentence 2 is grammatically correct, but it shows subordination rather than coordination.

**QUICK QUIZ 2** Test yourself on your knowledge of combining sentences using **subordination.** Combine each of the following pairs of sentences using either a subordinating conjunction or a relative pronoun. More than one correct answer is possible. Sample answers are upside down beside the quiz.

1. I live alone with two cats.
   They sleep on the braided rug in my bedroom.

   ______________________________________________

2. The police stood by the door.
   They blocked our entrance.

   ______________________________________________

3. She wore high heels.
   They made marks in the wooden floor.

   ______________________________________________

**Answers:**
1. I live alone with two cats, who sleep on the braided rug in my bedroom.
2. The police stood by the door so that they could block our entrance.
3. She wore high heels that made marks in the wooden floor.

4. My aunt is my favourite relative.
   Her name is Bharati.

   ______________________________________________

5. He wore expensive designer clothes.
   He claimed to be struggling financially.

   ______________________________________________

**Answers:**
4. My aunt, whose name is Bharati, is my favourite relative.
5. He wore expensive designer clothes although he claimed to be struggling financially.

Reading the above sentences, you will see that writing only simple sentences would result in a choppy style. Also, you would have trouble trying to express more complicated ideas.

You will therefore want to learn how to combine sentences. You can do this by using particular marks of punctuation and special connecting words called **conjunctions.** The two major ways of joining sentences together are called **coordination** and **subordination.**

## What Is Coordination?

**DEFINITION ➤** The pairing of similar elements—words, phrases, or clauses—to give equal weight to each pair is called **coordination.** Coordination can link two independent clauses to form a compound sentence.

***Example:*** I was sick. I went to work anyway.
I was sick, but I went to work anyway.

## Combining Sentences Using Coordination

You can use coordination whenever you have two sentences that are related and that contain ideas of equal importance. There are three ways to combine such sentences. All three ways result in a new kind of sentence called a **compound sentence.** Before you study these three methods, however, it is important to understand the term *independent clause.* The **independent clause** is a group of words that can be a simple sentence. In a compound sentence we can say we are combining simple sentences, or we can say we are combining *independent clauses.* Don't let the term confuse you. *Independent* means that the words could stand alone as a sentence, and *clause* means a group of words that includes a subject and predicate (what is said about the subject). *IC* will mean *independent clause* in the work that follows.

### Use a Comma Plus a Coordinating Conjunction

**TIP** **The first way to combine independent clauses (or complete thoughts) is to use a comma plus a coordinating conjunction. A conjunction is a connecting or joining word.**

| IC | , and | IC |
|---|---|---|
| He spoke forcefully | , and | I felt compelled to listen. |

## Connectors: Coordinating Conjunctions

| For easier remembering, spell *FANBOYS:* | Logical use: |
|---|---|
| **F**or | to introduce a reason |
| **A**nd | to add an idea |
| **N**or (negative of "or") | to add an idea when the first clause is in the negative |
| **B**ut | to contrast two opposing ideas |
| **O**r | to show a choice |
| **Y**et | to contrast two opposing ideas (like *but*) |
| **S**o | to introduce a result |

**Used in Pairs (correlative conjunctions)**
either ... or
neither ... nor
not only ... but also

**TIP** **If any of the above coordinating conjunctions ("FANBOYS") is used to separate two independent clauses, always place a comma before it.**

When the sentence is short, the comma before the coordinating conjunction becomes less necessary, but to be safe, it is wise to leave the comma in every time.

I arrived late**, and** most people had already finished the exam.

**PRACTICE**

### Recognizing the Comma and Coordinating Conjunction

In each of the following compound sentences, draw a single line under the subject and draw two lines under the verb for each independent clause. Then circle both the coordinating conjunction and the comma. An example is done for you. Check your answers against those in the Answer Key on p. 457.

The speaker rose to his feet (, and) the room became quiet.

1. The audience was packed into the room, for this was a man with an international reputation.
2. He could have told about all his successes, but instead he spoke about his disappointments.
3. His words were electric, so the crowd was attentive.
4. I should have brought a tape recorder, or at least I should have taken notes.

Did you find a subject and verb for both independent clauses in each sentence?

Now that you understand the structure of a compound sentence, you need to think about the meanings of the different coordinating conjunctions and how they can be used to show the relationship between two ideas, with each idea given equal importance.

**EXERCISE**

## Combining Sentences Using Coordinating Conjunctions

Each of the following examples contains two simple sentences. In each case, join the sentences to form a new compound sentence. Use a comma and one of the seven coordinating conjunctions. There can be more than one correct answer for each example. Be sure the conjunction you choose makes sense in the sentence. An example is done for you.

***Two simple sentences:*** Many farmers are desperate. They are going bankrupt.

***Compound sentence:*** Many farmers are desperate, for they are going bankrupt.

1. The farmers in Canada want to work.
   Some are experiencing severe financial difficulty.

   the farmers in Canada want to work, (~~but~~) yet
   some are experiencing severe financial difficulty.

2. Some people are losing their farms.
   The banks are refusing to make further loans.

   Some people are losing their farm, (~~and~~) for.
   the banks are refusing to make further loans

3. Many government programs have not been effective.
   The public cannot do anything.
   (Use *nor.* You will have to change the word order in the second sentence.)

   Many government programs have not been effective ~~nor~~
   the public ~~cannot~~ (~~nor can~~) do anything.

   nor can

4. The farmers feel neglected.
   They are protesting against the government.

   the farmer feel neglected so they are
   protesting against the government.

5. There is an increased need for farm products, but
   The government pays farmers not to grow food.

6. Everyone needs what the farmers produce, therefore
   We should be concerned about their problems.

7. In the future, fewer people will become farmers.
   The problem is likely to become increasingly serious.

## Coordinating Conjunctions That Do Not Combine Two Independent Clauses

Remember that a coordinating conjunction such as *and* is not always used to combine two independent clauses. Often, it is used simply to combine two items. In this case, do not place a comma before the coordinating conjunction.

> I had bacon *and* eggs for breakfast.

The word *and* does not separate two independent clauses, so there is no comma before it.

> I had bacon and eggs for breakfast, *and* then I had a salad for lunch.

In this sentence, the second *and* does combine two independent clauses. Therefore, the comma is required.

The coordinating conjunction *but* is the exception here. It is always a good idea to put a comma before *but* regardless of whether it combines two independent clauses or not. This is because *but* is a strong indication of an opposite point of view. The comma gives the reader a chance to focus on this abrupt shift in thinking.

> He is short, *but* powerful.
> He is short, *but* he exudes a powerful aura.

Use a comma for both situations involving the word *but*.

## Use a Semicolon, an Adverbial Conjunction, and a Comma

**TIP**

**A second way to combine independent clauses (or complete thoughts) is to use a semicolon, an adverbial conjunction, and a comma.**

| IC | ; adverbial conjunction, | IC |
|---|---|---|
| I had worked hard | ; therefore, | I expected results. |

Another set of conjunctions, which have meanings similar to the common coordinating conjunctions, are called **adverbial conjunctions** (or conjunctive adverbs). These connecting words will give the compound sentence you write more emphasis. They may also sound slightly more formal to you than the shorter conjunctions *and* and *but*. If an adverbial conjunction separates two independent clauses, place a semicolon before it. If it does not, use a comma before it instead.

**TIP**

**Unlike the combination of a comma and a coordinating conjunction, the combination of a comma and an adverbial conjunction *cannot* separate two independent clauses.**

*Incorrect:* I had worked hard, therefore, I expected results.

The above is a run-on sentence. See Chapter 7 on run-ons.

*Correct:* I had worked hard, so I expected results.
*Correct:* I had worked hard; therefore, I expected results.

Look

**Connectors: Frequently Used Adverbial Conjunctions**

| **Addition (and)** | **Alternative (or)** | **Result (so)** |
|---|---|---|
| in addition | instead | accordingly |
| also | otherwise | consequently |
| besides | | hence |
| furthermore | | therefore |
| likewise | | thus |
| moreover | | |
| **Contrast (but)** | **Emphasis** | **To Show Time** |
| however | indeed | meanwhile |
| nevertheless | in fact | |
| nonetheless | | |

**PRACTICE 1**

## Recognizing the Semicolon, Adverbial Conjunction, and Comma

In each of the following compound sentences, draw a single line under the subject and draw two lines under the verb for both independent clauses. Then circle the semicolon, adverbial conjunction, and comma. An example is done for you. Check your answers against those in the Answer Key on p. 457.

The jet was the fastest way to get there ; moreover, it was the most comfortable.

1. The restaurant is always too crowded on Saturdays; nevertheless, it serves the best food in town.
2. The land was not for sale; however, the house could be rented.
3. The lawsuit cost the company several million dollars; consequently, the company went out of business a short time later.
4. The doctor told him to lose weight; furthermore, she insisted he also stop smoking.

**PRACTICE 2**

## Combining Sentences Using Adverbial Conjunctions

Combine each pair of sentences below to make a compound sentence. Use a semicolon, an adverbial conjunction, and a comma. Be sure the conjunction you choose makes sense in the sentence. There can be more than one correct answer. An example is done for you. Check your answers against those in the Answer Key on p. 457.

***Two simple sentences:*** Our family would like to purchase a computer. We must decide on which computer best serves our needs.

***Compound sentence:*** Our family would like to purchase a computer; however, we must decide on which computer best serves our needs.

1. People once preferred to write with a pen or pencil, however
   The computer has now become a favourite writing tool. (Show contrast.)

   ______________________________________________

   ______________________________________________

2. Computers provide a powerful way to create and store pieces of writing.
   They make the editing process fast and efficient. (Add an idea.)

   ______________________________________________

   ______________________________________________

3. Computers have revolutionized today's offices.
   No modern business is without them. (Show result.)

   ______________________________________________

   ______________________________________________

4. Computers have become relatively inexpensive.
   Most people own a computer. (Show result.)

   ______________________________________________

   ______________________________________________

5. Many children know more about computers than many adults.
   Many children are teaching adults how to operate computers. (Add an idea.)

   ______________________________________________

   ______________________________________________

6. Professional writers have become enthusiastic about the use of computers.
   There are still some writers who will use only a ballpoint pen. (Show contrast.)

   ______________________________________________

   ______________________________________________

7. We have many technological aids for writing.
   Let us not forget that the source of all our ideas is the human brain. (Show contrast.)

**EXERCISE**

## Combining Sentences Using Adverbial Conjunctions

For each example, add the suggested adverbial conjunction and another independent clause that will make sense. There can be more than one correct answer for each example. Remember to punctuate correctly.

1. (however) I'll be at the library for a few hours
2. (therefore) James asked to borrow my notes
3. (otherwise) I'm thinking about taking a part-time job
4. (instead) Marcus is not going home for reading week
5. (in fact) They haven't won a game this year
6. (furthermore) Suzie has given up coffee and cigarettes
7. (consequently) My computer keeps crashing

## Use a Semicolon

**TIP** **The third way to combine two independent clauses is to use a semicolon by itself (that is, without an adverbial conjunction).**

Remember, do not capitalize the letter of the first word after the semicolon unless the word already begins with a capital letter because of its spelling.

| IC | ; | IC |
|---|---|---|
| He arrived at ten | ; | he left at midnight. |
| He arrived at ten | ; | I left at midnight. |

This third method of combining sentences is used less often. No connecting word is used. The semicolon takes the place of the conjunction.

*Two independent clauses:* I used to watch the Toronto Blue Jays play baseball at Exhibition Stadium. Tonight, I'm going to see them play at Rogers Centre.

*Compound sentence:* I used to watch the Toronto Blue Jays play baseball at Exhibition Stadium; tonight, I'm going to see them play at Rogers Centre.

The semicolon was used in this example to show that the content of the two clauses is closely related and, therefore, belongs together in one sentence.

When sentences are combined by using a semicolon, the grammatical structure of each independent clause is often similar:

Gasoline prices increased; ***vacations*** became less frequent.

Both independent clauses above begin with a subject. (See Chapter 8: "Parallel Structure.")

**EXERCISE**

### Combining Sentences Using the Semicolon

For each of the independent clauses below, add your own independent clause that is a related idea with a similar grammatical structure. Join the two clauses with a semicolon. There can be more than one correct answer for each example. An example is done for you.

***Independent clause:*** He wrote the speech.

***Compound sentence:*** He wrote the speech; she gave it.

1. The apartment was light and airy.

_______________________________________________

_______________________________________________

2. Many students decorate their rooms wonderfully.

______________________________________________

______________________________________________

3. I plan to learn two foreign languages.

______________________________________________

______________________________________________

4. I tried to explain.

______________________________________________

______________________________________________

5. This rain will never stop.

______________________________________________

______________________________________________

## What Is Subordination?

When you use coordination to combine sentences, the ideas in both of the resulting clauses are given equal weight. However, ideas are not always equally important. Subordination allows you to show which idea is the main idea.

**DEFINITION ➤** **Subordination** is the method used to combine sentences whose ideas are not equally important. It is a combination of an independent clause and a dependent clause.

***Example:*** I stayed home today (Independent clause) because I was sick. (Dependent clause)

## Combining Sentences Using Subordination

When you combine sentences using subordination, you make the most important idea an independent clause and the less important idea a dependent (subordinate) clause. The sentence that results is called a **complex sentence.** We identify the two or more ideas that are contained within this complex sentence by calling them **clauses.** The relationship between the main and secondary parts of a complex sentence is shown by the method of subordination you use. The various methods of subordination will be discussed below.

In a complex sentence, the main idea is called the **independent clause** because it could stand alone as a simple sentence. The less important idea is called the

**dependent clause** because even though it has a subject and a verb, it is dependent on the rest of the sentence for its meaning. Consider the following clauses:

***Independent clause:*** That girl leaves.
***Dependent clause:*** If that girl leaves

Notice that both clauses in the example above have a subject and a verb. (The subject is *girl*, and the verb is *leaves*.) The difference is that the dependent clause has an additional word. *If* is a special kind of connecting word that makes the clause "dependent" on an additional idea. A dependent clause contains a thought that is not complete; it cannot stand on its own. Below is the same dependent clause with an independent clause added to it.

If that girl leaves, then I can finish my homework.

Now the thought is complete.

In your work with sentences, you will want to be comfortable writing sentences with dependent clauses. For this, you will need to practise using two kinds of "connecting" words: subordinating conjunctions and relative pronouns. First, practise using subordinating conjunctions.

## Use a Subordinating Conjunction to Create a Complex Sentence

Following is a list of subordinating conjunctions. These connecting words signal the beginning of a dependent clause. Be sure to learn them. It is a good idea to memorize them, especially for the purpose of preventing fragments. (See more on fragments in Chapter 6.)

Look

**Connectors: Common Subordinating Conjunctions**

| | | |
|---|---|---|
| after | if, even if | unless |
| although | in order that | until |
| as, as if | provided that | when, whenever |
| as long as, as though | rather than | where, wherever, whereas |
| because | since | whether |
| before | so that | while |
| even though | though | |

You might recall teachers in elementary school telling you never to begin a sentence with *because*. They might have told you this because they were afraid you wouldn't finish the sentence.

***Incomplete:*** Because the child was sick
***Complete:*** Because the child was sick, she stayed home yesterday.

With the addition of an independent clause to the dependent clause, the sentence is now complete.

### Function of Subordinating Conjunctions

To introduce a *condition*: if, even if, as long as, provided that, unless

**I will go *as long as* you go with me.**
**I won't go *unless* you go with me.**

To introduce a *contrast*: although, even though, though

**I will go *even though* you won't go with me.**

To introduce a *cause*: because, since

**I will go *because* the meeting is very important.**

To show *time*: after, before, when, whenever, while, until

**I will go *whenever* you say.**
**I won't go *until* you say it is time.**

To show *place*: where, wherever

**I will go *wherever* you send me.**

To show *purpose*: in order that, so that

**I will go *so that* I can hear the candidate for myself.**

You can choose between two ways of writing the complex sentence. You can begin with either the dependent clause or the independent clause.

| | | | |
|---|---|---|---|
| *First way:* | **DC** | **,** | **IC** |
| *Example:* | If Barbara leaves | , | we can finish our homework. |

| | | |
|---|---|---|
| *Second way:* | **IC** | **DC** |
| *Example:* | We can finish our homework | if Barbara leaves. |

**TIP**

**Use a comma when you begin a sentence with a dependent clause. Do not use a comma when the independent clause comes first.**

From the above examples you can see that when a sentence begins with an independent clause, a comma may not always be needed. For example, the comma is omitted if the dependent clause is essential to the main idea of the speaker. This point of grammar is further discussed in Chapter 11, page 129, on punctuation.

**PRACTICE 1**

## Recognizing Dependent and Independent Clauses

In the blank to the side of each group of words, write the letters *IC* if the group is an independent clause (a complete thought) or *DC* if the group is a dependent clause (not a complete thought even though it contains a subject and a verb). Check your answers against those in the Answer Key on p. 458.

DC ______ 1. while the photographer was getting ready

DC ______ 2. before the guests arrived

ID ______ 3. I've been a bridesmaid for two of my friends

DC ______ 4. even though we're all in our teens

~~DC~~ ID ______ 5. this one was more fun than most

DC ______ 6. whenever I see you

DC. ______ 7. since I did not take the subway

**PRACTICE 2**

## Combining Sentences Using Subordination

Combine each pair of sentences using subordination. Look back at the list of subordinating conjunctions if you need to. There may be more than one correct answer for each of these exercises. Check your answers against those in the Answer Key on p. 458.

1. He was eating breakfast.
   The results of the election came over the radio.
   The results of the election came over the radio when he was eating breakfast.

2. Simon gave up his plan to launch a dot-com company. because – no comma.
   He felt it was too risky.
   Simon gave ... company because he felt it was too risky.

3. I will see my teacher tonight. as (no punctuation).
   She is speaking at the university this evening.
   ______________________________
   ______________________________ (even though)

4. The designer hoped for a promotion. ~~but~~ (since) (no comma).
   Not one person in the department was promoted last year.
   ______________________________
   ______________________________

5. The designer hoped for a promotion. ~~[illegible]~~
   She made sure all her work was done accurately and on time. because the designer hoped for a promotion.

## EXERCISE 1

## Combining Sentences Using Subordination

Below are three pairs of sentences. Combine each pair by using a subordinating conjunction. Write the sentence two different ways. First, begin the sentence with the dependent clause, and use a comma. Second, begin the sentence with the independent clause, and use a comma only if necessary.

1. (Use *since*.) Wildlife habitats are being destroyed.
   Many species are in danger.
   a. wildlife habitats are being destroyed, since many species are in danger.
   b. Many species are in danger since wildlife habitats are being destroyed.
2. (Use *after*.) He won the wrestling match.
   He went out to celebrate.
   a. He went out to celebrate after He won the wrestling match.
   b. He won the wrestling match, afer he went OUT to celebrate.
3. (Use *when*.) Halyna returned from Europe this spring.
   The family was excited.
   a. ______
   b. ______

## EXERCISE 2

## Combining Sentences Using Subordination

Rewrite the following paragraph using subordination to combine some of the sentences wherever you feel it would be effective. Be prepared to discuss the reasons for your choices. You might also want to discuss places where coordination might be a good choice. More than one correct answer is possible.

Many Canadian communities collect refuse from its source. Waste is delivered to a waste disposal site. Very little waste is recycled. Very little waste is burned. Many smaller towns and villages cannot afford a waste collection service or a proper waste disposal site. Smaller communities are prevalent in Canada. Improperly operated dumps outnumber the better-operated facilities used by larger communities. Over the next few years, many of our landfills will close. They are getting full. Some places in Ontario already truck their trash to the United States. The garbage continues to pile up. The newspapers print stories about it every week. Trash is not a very glamorous subject. People in every town talk about the problem.

Here is a summary so far of how clauses (dependent and independent) can be combined to form complete sentences.

***Remember:*** IC stands for independent clause (complete thought)
DC stands for dependent clause (incomplete thought)

| | | |
|---|---|---|
| **IC** | **, coordinating conjunction** | **IC** |
| **IC** | **; adverbial conjunction,** | **IC** |
| **IC** | **;** | **IC** |
| **DC** | **,** | **IC** |
| **IC** | | **DC** |

Note the absence of any comma between IC and DC in the last row above.

## Use a Relative Pronoun to Create a Complex Sentence

Often sentences can be combined with a relative pronoun.

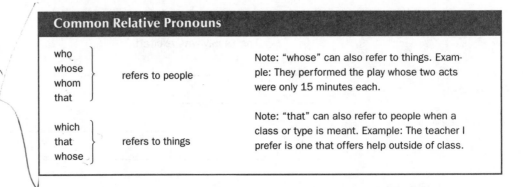

**Common Relative Pronouns**

| | | |
|---|---|---|
| who<br>whose<br>whom<br>that | refers to people | Note: "whose" can also refer to things. Example: They performed the play whose two acts were only 15 minutes each. |
| which<br>that<br>whose | refers to things | Note: "that" can also refer to people when a class or type is meant. Example: The teacher I prefer is one that offers help outside of class. |

*Two simple sentences:* The researcher had a breakthrough.
He was studying diabetes.

These sentences are short and choppy. To avoid this choppiness, a writer could join these two related ideas with a relative pronoun.

*Combining sentences with a relative pronoun:* The researcher who was studying diabetes had a breakthrough.

Now join a third idea to the sentence (use *which*).

*Third idea:* He reported the breakthrough to the press.

**TIP** **Remember to put the relative pronoun directly after the word it relates to.**

*Incorrect:* The researcher, which he reported to the press, had a breakthrough who was studying diabetes.

*Correct:* The researcher who was studying diabetes had a breakthrough, which he reported to the press.

The relative pronoun *who* and its clause *who was studying diabetes* refers to *the researcher*, not to *a breakthrough*. See more on the relative pronoun *who* (vs. *whom*) on p. 111. The relative pronoun *which* and its clause *which he reported to the press* does refer to *breakthrough*. This clause will follow the noun *breakthrough*. (See Chapter 10 on modifiers.)

**PRACTICE**

## Combining Sentences Using a Relative Pronoun

Combine each of the three pairs of sentences below into one complex sentence by using a relative pronoun. Do not use commas. More than one correct answer is possible for each example. An example is done for you. Check your answers against those in the Answer Key on p. 458.

***First sentence:*** That woman created the flower arrangement.

***Second sentence:*** She visited us last weekend.

***Combined sentence:*** That woman who visited us last weekend created the flower arrangement.

1. The chemistry lab is two hours long.
   I attend that chemistry lab.

   Combined: ____________________________________________

   ____________________________________________

2. The student assistant is very knowledgeable.
   The student assistant is standing by the door.

   Combined: ____________________________________________

   ____________________________________________

3. The equipment was purchased last year.
   The equipment will make possible some important new research.

   Combined: ____________________________________________

   ____________________________________________

## How Do You Punctuate a Clause with a Relative Pronoun?

Punctuating relative clauses can be tricky because there are two types of relative clauses.

1. One type of relative clause is basic to the meaning of the sentence:

   Never eat fruit *that hasn't been washed* first.

   The basic meaning of the sentence is not "never eat fruit." The relative clause is necessary to restrict the meaning. This clause is called a **restrictive clause** and does not use commas to set it off. *Note:* Clauses beginning with the pronoun *that* are usually in this category.

2. The other type of relative clause is **not** basic to the meaning of the sentence:

   Kim's famous salad, *which included spinach and almonds,* was delicious.

   In this sentence, the relative clause is not basic to the main idea. In fact, if the clause were omitted, the main idea would not be changed. This clause is called a **nonrestrictive clause.** Commas are required to indicate that the information is nonessential. *Note:* Clauses beginning with the pronoun *which* are usually in this category. Remember, the relative pronoun *which* always refers to things.

   *Note:* While *which* refers to things in a nonrestrictive clause and *that* refers to things in a restrictive clause, the relative pronouns that refer to people (*who, whom,* and *whose*) are used either for nonrestrictive or restrictive clauses. Remember, restrictive clauses do not take commas to separate them from the rest of the sentence while nonrestrictive clauses do. (See Chapter 11: "Punctuation" for more on commas.)

**PRACTICE**

### Recognizing Restrictive and Nonrestrictive Clauses

Choose whether or not to insert commas in the sentences below. Two examples have been done for you. Check your answers against those in the Answer Key on p. 458.

The man *who is wearing the Hawaiian shirt* is the bridegroom.

(The relative clause is essential. There are no commas.)

Al, *who was wearing a flannel shirt,* arrived late to the wedding.

(The relative clause is nonessential. Commas, therefore, are necessary.)

1. Canada's first census, which was taken in 1667 showed 3215 non-Native inhabitants in 668 families.
2. Most of the families who lived near the St. Lawrence River were French Canadians.
3. By the time of Confederation, the population of the country had risen to 3 463 000 which was an increase of 1077 percent over 200 years.
4. If the population which is about 30 000 000 persons in Canada now increases by a similar percentage, we'll have a population of 280 200 000 by the year 2167.
5. Where do you think will we put everyone who will live in Canada then?

**EXERCISE 1**

## Combining Sentences Using Relative Pronouns

Add a clause that begins with a relative pronoun to each of the sentences below. Use each of these possibilities at least once: *who, whose, whom, which, that.* Be sure to punctuate correctly. There may be more than one correct answer for each sentence. An example is done for you.

***Simple sentence:*** The leader was barely 1.5 metres tall.

***Complex sentence:*** The leader, who was always self-conscious about her height, was barely 1.5 metres tall.

1. The figure skaters, who finished 1st place in the competition, began their program.
2. The music, that was playing, had a Latin beat.
3. Their first figure ~~wich was~~ that assigned, was a triple toe loop.
4. The crowd, that assisted the ~~play~~ game, cheered wildly.
5. Even the judges, who were very observative, seemed impressed.
6. Her triple axel, which she did last, was a little ragged.
7. Their coach, whose excitement was overexcited, was thrilled by the final score.

**EXERCISE 2**

## Combining Sentences Using Relative Pronouns

Combine the following pairs of sentences using a relative pronoun. There may be more than one correct answer for each example.

1. Stress can do a great deal of harm.
   We experience stress every day.

~~We experience stress every day~~

We experience stress, wich can do a great deal of harm, every day.

non restrictive → Stress, wich we experience every day, can do a great deal of harm.

Restrictive: Stress that we experience ---- (no commas)

2. People often use food to help them cope.
   Some people work long hours at demanding jobs.

   Some people, who work long hours at demanding jobs, often use food to help them cope.

3. The practice of eating to cope with stress is often automatic.
   The practice of eating to cope often goes back to childhood.

   The practice of eating to cope stress, that is often automatic, often goes back to childhood.

4. Foods can actually increase tension.
   People turn to foods in times of stress.

   People that turn to foods in times of stress, ~~can~~ can actually increase tension.

5. One of the biggest mistakes people make is to use alcohol as an aid to becoming calm.
   Alcohol is really a depressant.

6. People should eat three light meals a day and two small snacks.
   People want to feel a sense of calm.

   People, who want to feel a sense of calm should eat three light meals a day an two small snacks.

7. Eat a good meal at regular intervals to help reduce stress.
   Binge eating puts on pounds, drains you of energy, and increases your stress level.

## Chapter Review Exercises

**PRACTICE**

### Combining Sentences Using Coordination and Subordination

Look over the following simple sentences, and rewrite the paragraph, combining sentences where you think it would improve the meaning and style. The Answer Key will give you one possible answer, but there are many ways of revising. Be creative, and don't be afraid to alter the wording to accommodate the changes you want to make. Check your answers against those in the Answer Key on p. 458.

The wind is strong. The waves are choppy. They are growing larger. I paddle my kayak harder. My arms are getting tired. The energy is draining from them. They grow limp and heavy. The other side of the harbour seems distant. The glow of the setting sun is behind me. It spreads orange and purple fingers across the sky. A wall of rocks lies offshore. It picks up the last light of the setting sun. It is a silver beacon. I focus on that wall and paddle harder. The sea smashes against my bow. It seems to push me away from shore. Flecks of spray hit my face. I taste the salt on my lips. With that taste of the sea, the beauty of the sea and shore strikes me. I am distracted from my labour and absorbed by the world around me. My kayak finally glides past the rocks to the sheltered beach beyond. I am exhilarated and exhausted.

## EXERCISE 1 Combining Sentences Using Coordinating and Adverbial Conjunctions

Combine each pair of sentences below to make a compound sentence. Use a coordinating, subordinating, or adverbial conjunction, but be sure that the conjunction clearly shows the relationship between the ideas. There can be more than one correct answer for each example.

1. For many people, mathematics is a necessary evil.
   To a few, mathematics provides a lifetime of challenge and fun.

   ______________________________

   ______________________________

2. Most Canadians have studied math only to Grade 12.
   This limits their ability to understand new scientific developments.

   ______________________________

   ______________________________

3. Their knowledge extends to little more than basic arithmetic.
   People in the seventeenth century knew as much about math as most Canadians today.

   ______________________________

   ______________________________

4. Few Canadians study math at the university level.
   Many promising mathematics graduates are offered employment in the United States.

   ______________________________

   ______________________________

5. Many schools form math teams to compete in area contests.
   Other schools encourage interest in math with math clubs.

   ______________________________________________

   ______________________________________________

6. Some schools suffer from a lack of science and math teachers.
   Mathematicians can find well-paid employment in industry.

   ______________________________________________

   ______________________________________________

7. It is important to increase the number of mathematics graduates.
   Canadian students may continue to trail behind those of many other countries in math and science ability.

   ______________________________________________

   ______________________________________________

## EXERCISE 2 Combining Sentences with a Subordinating Conjunction or a Relative Pronoun

Combine each of the following pairs of sentences using either a subordinating conjunction or a relative pronoun. Be sure that the word you use makes sense in the sentence. There may be more than one correct answer for each example.

1. People have been fascinated for centuries by the problem of stuttering.
   Modern science is only beginning to understand some of the underlying causes of the problem.

   ______________________________________________

   ______________________________________________

2. For some people, stuttering disappears by itself.
   For others, stuttering continues into adulthood.

   ______________________________________________

   ______________________________________________

3. Stutterers usually keep their condition.
   They seek professional help.

   ______________________________________________

   ______________________________________________

4. It is true that there is some psychological basis for stuttering.
   It is true that psychologists have not been able to solve the problem.

   ______________________________________________

   ______________________________________________

5. All kinds of scientists have looked at the problem from all different angles.
   There is no single answer to stuttering.

   ______________________________________________

   ______________________________________________

6. Stuttering runs in families.
   Children of such families have greater chances of becoming stutterers.

   ______________________________________________

   ______________________________________________

7. You often hear someone say he or she knows the causes of stuttering.
   You know that person cannot be speaking scientifically.

   ______________________________________________

   ______________________________________________

## Working Together: Practising Coordination and Subordination

A controversial issue today concerns the wide gap between the wages earned by people in some professions and the wages earned by people in other professions. For instance, some sports figures and entertainers earn millions every year. How are wages determined in our society? How do you think wages should be determined? Should there be a minimum wage in Canada? Should everybody earn the same salary? Divide into groups and discuss the subject for fifteen minutes.

Following the general discussion, practise combining sentences using coordination by writing ten sentences on the subject of wage differences. If you like, you may try to summarize the ideas of your group. The goal is to use each of the following coordinating conjunctions to combine two independent clauses:

**F**or, **A**nd, **N**or, **B**ut, **O**r, **Y**et, **S**o (FANBOYS)
either/or, neither/nor, not only/but also (correlative conjunctions)

Now, in each sentence you've written, combine two independent clauses with subordinating conjunctions instead. Consult the list of subordinating conjunctions on page 66.

After working on these sentences for fifteen minutes, exchange papers and answer the following questions about the sentences on the paper you have:

1. In each case, has the writer combined two independent clauses?
2. In each sentence, does the coordinating or subordinating conjunction carry the correct meaning for the sentence?
3. Is the punctuation correct?

CHAPTER SIX

6

# Correcting Fragments

**QUICK QUIZ** Test yourself on your knowledge of fragments. Some of the examples below are complete sentences; some are fragments (only parts of sentences). Write *C* if the example is a complete sentence. Write *F* if the example is a fragment. The answers to the questions are upside down beside the quiz.

____________ 1. Whale watching is a popular tourist activity in British Columbia.

____________ 2. Although its effects are being studied.

____________ 3. Whales coping with heavy boat traffic.

____________ 4. The noise from engines can disturb the whales' communication.

____________ 5. Which may be changing their habitat.

Answers:
1. C
2. F
3. F
4. C
5. F

## Recognizing and Correcting Sentence Fragments

Once you have learned that a sentence must have a subject and a verb, and that a sentence must also express a complete thought, you are on your way to correcting one of the most frequent errors in student writing—the fragment. A fragment is an incomplete sentence. Although many of our daily conversations are informal and sometimes contain fragments, standard writing is always more formal and requires complete sentences.

Although you will occasionally spot incomplete sentences in professional writing, such as newspaper writing, advertising, novels, and so on, it is hoped that the writer is using these fragments intentionally. In such cases, the fragment may capture the way a person thinks or speaks, or it may create a special effect. A student developing his or her writing skills should be sure to use only **standard sentence form** so that thoughts will be communicated effectively. Most of the writing you will do in your life—business correspondence, papers in school, or reports in your job—will demand standard sentence form. Fragments will be looked upon as a sign of poor writing skills rather than creative style!

The fragment is a major problem for many student writers. In the writer's mind, a thought may be clear; however, on paper the idea may turn out to be incomplete, missing a subject or a verb. In this chapter, you will improve your ability to spot incomplete sentences or fragments, and you will learn how to correct them. This practice will prepare you to avoid such fragments in your own writing.

Remember the definition of a sentence:

**DEFINITION ➤** A **complete sentence** has a subject and a verb and expresses a complete thought.

***Example:*** The cat drank.

Notice that it is not necessary to know what the cat drank in order for the sentence to be grammatically complete.

### A Typical Casual Conversation

The following conversation is one that a couple of students might have at the start of their English class.

JOHN: Early again.
LESIA: Want to get a front-row seat.
JOHN: Your homework done?
LESIA: Nearly.
JOHN: Think he'll give a quiz today?
LESIA: Hope not.
JOHN: Looks like rain today.
LESIA: Better not; haven't got a bag for these new books.
JOHN: Going to the game Saturday?
LESIA: Probably.

Remember, when you write in complete sentences, this writing is likely going to be quite different from the way you would express the same idea in everyday conversation with a friend. Every single idea in the conversation above is incomplete. Not one sentence is complete. There is at least one fragment on every line. (The eighth line has two fragments, with a semicolon incorrectly separating them.) If this dialogue, with the proper quotation marks, were to appear in a novel, it would be perfectly acceptable. But for standard English form, fragments are, quite simply, an example of poor writing skills.

## What Is a Fragment?

**DEFINITION ➤** A **fragment** is a piece of a sentence.

***Examples:*** Which is not what the teacher wanted to hear.
Because the bus was late.
Whereas she was better at math.

Fragments often begin with the relative pronoun *which* or the subordinating conjunctions *because* and *whereas.*

A fragment is not a sentence for one of the following reasons:

a. The subject is missing.

delivered the plans to my office

b. The verb is missing.

the architect to my office

c. Both the subject and verb are missing.

to my office

d. The group of words might be a dependent clause. In other words, a subject and a verb are present, but the words do not express a complete thought.

when the architect delivered the plans
which the architect identified as her favourite design
because the bus was late

Sometimes the group of words might look like a complete sentence because it is fairly long, and it starts with a capital letter and ends with a period. Obviously, these criteria are not sufficient in determining a complete sentence.

**PRACTICE 1**

## Understanding Fragments

Each of the groups of words below is a fragment. In the blank to the right of each fragment, identify what sentence part could be added to make the fragment into a sentence. An example is done for you. Check your answers against those in the Answer Key on p. 458.

a. Add a subject.
b. Add a verb.
c. Add a subject and a verb.
d. It is a dependent clause. A subject and a verb are present, but you need to add or delete words to express a complete thought.

| | **Fragment** | **Add** |
|---|---|---|
| | the red fox | b. verb |
| 1. | returned to the river | ______________ |
| 2. | a bird on the oak branch | ______________ |
| 3. | between the island and the mainland | ______________ |
| 4. | the hawk in a soaring motion | ______________ |
| 5. | the fishing boats on the lake | ______________ |
| 6. | dropped like a stone into the water | ______________ |
| 7. | because the fisherman put the net away | ______________ |

## How Do You Correct a Fragment?

You can eliminate fragments in one of two ways:

1. Add the missing part or parts to develop the fragment into a complete sentence:

   *Fragment:* along the coastal road
   *Add:* subject and verb
   *Sentence:* He drove along the coastal road.

2. Join the fragment to another sentence. In order to do this, you will need to make use of the comma, the colon, or the dash, or you may not need to use punctuation. For example,

   a. Using the comma

   *Fragment:* including a stop at the shoe store
   *Other sentence:* He has to make a number of purchases.
   *Fragment eliminated:* He has to make a number of purchases, including a stop at the shoe store.

   b. Using the colon

   *Fragment:* action, science fiction, and comedy
   *Other sentence:* I like three types of movies.
   *Fragment eliminated:* I like three types of movies: action, science fiction, and comedy.

   c. Using the dash

   *Fragment:* more often than she should
   *Other sentence:* She goes to the casino every day.
   *Fragment eliminated:* She goes to the casino every day—more often than she should.

   d. Using no punctuation

   *Fragment:* on top of the mountain
   *Other sentence:* We planned to plant the flag.
   *Fragment eliminated:* We planned to plant the flag on top of the mountain.

**PRACTICE 2**

### Turning Fragments into Sentences

Change the fragments of Practice 1 into complete sentences by adding the missing part or parts that you have already identified. There can be more than one correct answer. Check your answers against those in the Answer Key on p. 459.

1. returned to the river

   ______________________________

2. a bird on the oak branch

3. between the island and the mainland

4. the hawk in a soaring motion

5. the fishing boats on the lake

6. dropped like a stone into the water

7. because the fisherman put the net away

**PRACTICE 3**

## Turning Fragments into Sentences

The following groups of words may or may not be fragments. If the group of words is complete, write "complete." Otherwise, rewrite the group of words adding whatever is necessary to correct the fragment. There can be more than one correct answer. Check your answers against those in the Answer Key on p. 459.

1. As long as it's a windy day.

2. Into the forest, armed with a machine gun.

3. It's great.

4. Along a deserted and dusty road.

5. Where the deer and the antelope play.

6. The groundhog run over by three different cars.

7. A jeep has parked.

**EXERCISE**

### Turning Fragments into Sentences

Each of the following passages contains one or more fragments. First read each passage. Then locate the fragments in it. Correct the fragments by joining them to other sentences, using either a comma, a colon, a dash, or no punctuation.

1. Fishing is one of the oldest sports in the world. And can be one of the most relaxing. Someone with a simple wooden pole and line can have as much fun as a professional angler. With expensive equipment. For busy executives, overworked teachers, and even presidents of nations. Fishing can be a good way to escape from the stress of demanding jobs.
2. The first electric car was built in 1887. Six years later, it was sold commercially. At the turn of the century, people had great faith in new technology. In fact, 300 electric taxicabs were operating in New York City by 1900. However, electric cars soon lost their popularity. The new gasoline engine became more widely used. With our concern about pollution. Perhaps electric cars will become desirable once again.
3. Most sports evolve over many years. But not basketball. A Canadian-born teacher invented basketball in December 1891. Working at a YMCA training school in Massachusetts. The coach needed an indoor game to keep his students fit over the winter. Dr. James Naismith created goals. By nailing two peach baskets to the gym balcony.

## Don't Confuse Phrases with Sentences

Fragments are usually made up of phrases. These phrases are often mistaken for sentences because they are groups of words. However, they do not fit the definition of a sentence.

### What Is a Phrase?

**DEFINITION ➤** A **phrase** is a group of words that go together but that lack one or more of the elements necessary to be classified as a sentence.

***Example:*** In the barn at the back of the house

In the example above, two prepositional phrases have been put together. See number 2 below. It is another example of a fragment.

### How Many Kinds of Phrases Are There?

In English, there are a number of types of phrases that you should learn to recognize. Some of them you have already studied in the previous chapter. Remember, a phrase is not a complete sentence; it is a sentence fragment, and as such must be either joined to another sentence or made into a complete sentence.

1. **Noun phrase:** a group of words that functions as a noun.

   *Noun phrase*: large square bricks
   *Complete sentence*: The garage is built out of large square bricks.

   **Gerund phrase:** a type of noun phrase; a group of words beginning with a gerund (an *-ing* word that looks like a verb, but functions as a noun).

   *Gerund phrase:* jogging every morning at 6:00
   *Complete sentence:* Jogging every morning at 6:00 is something I cannot miss.

2. **Prepositional phrase:** a group of words beginning with a preposition. (See the list of common prepositions on page 9.)

   *Prepositional phrase:* on the porch
   *Complete sentence:* Many of our neighbours are sitting on the porch.

3. **Verb phrase:** a group of words that functions as a verb.

   *Verb phrase*: is walking
   *Complete sentence:* My best friend is walking to my house.

4. **Infinitive phrase:** a group of words beginning with an infinitive.

   *Infinitive phrase:* to have a good job
   *Complete sentence:* I think it's important to have a good job.

**PRACTICE 1**

### Identifying Phrases

Identify each of the underlined phrases in the following sentences. Check your answers against those in the Answer Key on p. 459.

1. <u>To visit Montreal</u> is a thrill for most Canadians.
2. Many people love <u>to see the French culture</u>.
3. Museums, restaurants, shopping, and the varied night life offer endless possibilities <u>for the tourist</u>.
4. <u>On the subways</u>, tourists experience one of the cleanest underground transit systems in North America.
5. <u>My brother Don</u> rode the subway under the St. Lawrence River.
6. <u>A landowner from the country</u>, he enjoyed the continental atmosphere of Quebec's largest city.
7. Montreal's continual fascination is its rich mix <u>of cultures and lifestyles</u> from all over the world.

**PRACTICE 2**

### Identifying Phrases

Identify each of the underlined phrases in the following sentences. Check your answers against those in the Answer Key on p. 459.

| | |
|---|---|
| 1. In Canada,① crime seems to be increasing② at an alarming rate.③ | 1. ______ |
| | 2. ______ |
| 2. Stories about many major crimes④ can be seen⑤ almost daily in the newspapers.⑥ | 3. ______ |
| | 4. ______ |
| | 5. ______ |
| 3. To avoid⑦ the issue will not solve the problem. | 6. ______ |
| | 7. ______ |
| 4. Citizens should be concerned⑧ and try to make their views known⑨ to their elected officials.⑩ | 8. ______ |
| | 9. ______ |
| | 10. ______ |

## Making a Complete Sentence from a Fragment That Contains a Verbal

**DEFINITION ➤** **Verbals** are words that look like verbs, but that function as nouns, adjectives, or adverbs. There are three types of verbals: **infinitives, participles,** and **gerunds.** All three of these types of verbals appear in phrases. Such phrases by themselves are not complete sentences. They are fragments.

*Infinitive phrases:* to kill a mockingbird
to tour the West
*Complete sentence:* He began to tour the West.

Participial phrases function as adjectives.

*Participial phrases:* beaten to a pulp
running like the wind
*Complete sentence:* Running like the wind, he's never looked more afraid in his life.

*Gerund phrases:* working on the car
sitting on the bench
*Complete sentence:* Working on the car can wait until she's finished her supper.

Gerund phrases can look like (present) participial phrases (both end in *-ing*), but when they appear in complete sentences, they function as nouns rather than adjectives.

**TIP**

**Watch out for *-ing* words. No word ending in *-ing* can be the complete verb of a sentence.**

You can form a sentence from a fragment that contains a participle in any of the following ways.

*Fragment:* he talking in his sleep

1. Add a helping verb to the participle:

   He *is talking* in his sleep.

2. Change the participle to a different form of the verb:

   He *talks* in his sleep.

3. Use the participle as an adjective, being sure to provide a subject and verb for the sentence:

   *Talking in his sleep*, he muttered something about his boss.

4. Use the participle as a subject (gerund phrase):

   *Talking in his sleep* got him into trouble.

**PRACTICE 1**

## Correcting the Fragment That Contains a Participle

Make four complete sentences from each of the following fragments. Use this example as your model. There can be more than one correct answer for each example. Check your answers against those in the Answer Key on p. 459.

***Fragment:*** using the back stairway

a. He *is using* the back stairway.
b. He *uses* the back stairway.
c. *Using the back stairway,* he got away without being seen.
d. *Using the back stairway* is not a good idea.

1. climbing in the Rockies

   a. ______________________________

   b. ______________________________

   c. ______________________________

   d. ______________________________

2. playing video games

   a. ______________________________

   b. ______________________________

   c. ______________________________

   d. ______________________________

3. going clubbing on Tuesdays

   a. ______________________________

   b. ______________________________

   c. ______________________________

   d. ______________________________

**PRACTICE 2**

## Recognizing the Fragment

The paragraph below contains fragments. Read the paragraph. Then write *complete* after each example that is a complete sentence. Write *fragment* after each example that is a phrase or piece of a sentence. Keep in mind that a sentence must have a subject and verb as well as express a complete thought. Check your answers against those in the Answer Key on p. 459.

That summer, she cycled through the backcountry of southern France. Discovering early that her bike was ideal. The perfect mode of transportation. Because they are cycling fanatics. The French almost always treated her with respect and kindness. In spite of her halting attempts at the language. They would shout encouragement. As she puffed up a hill. The waitress in a café where she stopped to rest. Urged her to eat more, slipping an extra portion onto her plate.

1. That summer, she cycled through the backcountry of southern France. ______________
2. Discovering early that her bike was ideal. ______________
3. The perfect mode of transportation. ______________
4. Because they are cycling fanatics. ______________
5. The French almost always treated her with respect and kindness. ______________
6. In spite of her halting attempts at the language. ______________
7. They would shout encouragement. ______________
8. As she puffed up a hill. ______________

9. The waitress in a café where she stopped to rest. ______________________
10. Urged her to eat more, slipping an extra portion onto her plate. ______________________

**PRACTICE 3**

## Editing for Fragments

The paragraph below may contain fragments. Rewrite the paragraph, correcting any fragments that appear. Correct the fragments using any method you have learned, but make as few changes to the content as possible. Circle any changes you have made. Check your answers against those in the Answer Key on p. 459.

Soccer's World Cup in 2006 was won by Italy for the first time in 24 years, but it is public disgrace for which the game will be remembered by the world. By half time, the final game between Italy and France was tied 1–1. After 120 minutes, the game was still tied. The final victory depended on the penalty shootout. Which took the game to 5–3 for Italy. But 10 minutes before the end of extra time. France's illustrious captain, Zinedine Zidane, was expelled. For head-butting Marco Materazzi. Apparently, Marco had called him a terrorist. And had insulted both his mother and his sister. Was this a deliberate, desperate, and cheap attempt to achieve final victory in what had become a gruelling final game? Celebrations by Italians around the world were unstoppable. Partying with abandon. But soccer scandal continues to loom over the Italian team. And Zinedine Zidane exited from his last World Cup under an umbrella of shame. Because he didn't take the moral high road. While millions of fans watched his every move.

**EXERCISE**

## Correcting the Fragment That Contains a Participle

The following passage contains four fragments containing participles. Circle the fragments and correct them in one of the four ways shown in Practice 1. There can be more than one correct answer.

At last taking the driving test. I felt very nervous. My mother was sitting in the back seat. All my papers sitting on the front seat. The inspector got into the car and sat on my insurance form. He looked rather sour and barely spoke to me. Trying not to hit the curb. I parallel parked surprisingly well. I managed to get through all the manoeuvres. Now tensely waiting for the results.

## Chapter Review Exercises

**EXERCISE 1**

### Correcting the Fragment

Rewrite each fragment so that it is a complete sentence. There can be more than one correct answer.

1. early morning a time of peace in my neighbourhood

   ______________________________

2. the grey mist covering up all but the faint outlines of nearby houses

   ______________________________

3. the shapes of cars in the streets and driveways

   ______________________________

4. to sit and look out the window

   ______________________________

5. holding a steaming cup of coffee

   ______________________________

6. the only sound the rumbling of a truck

   ______________________________

7. passing on the highway a kilometre away

   ______________________________

**EXERCISE 2**

### Correcting the Fragment

Rewrite the paragraph in the exercise "Correcting the Fragment That Contains a Participle" on page 88. Correct the fragments in one of the following three ways. There can be more than one correct answer.

a. Join the phrase to the sentence preceding it.
b. Join the phrase to the sentence that follows it.
c. Add a subject, a verb, or both so that the sentence is complete.

## EXERCISE 3 Correcting the Fragment

Each of the following passages contains a fragment. Underline the fragment, and on the lines beneath each passage, rewrite the passage so that it is composed of complete sentences. There can be more than one way to correct each fragment.

1. The moon rose high in the sky. All of us worked quickly to pitch the tent. Then making a fire.

   Revised passage: ______________________________

   ______________________________

   ______________________________

2. Raising the drinking age to 21 saves the lives of all drivers. The drinkers and nondrinkers. Every province should raise the drinking age to 21.

   Revised passage: ______________________________

   ______________________________

   ______________________________

3. Companies do a lot of research before they name a new product. Based on the results of a market research team. The company makes its final selection.

   Revised passage: ______________________________

   ______________________________

   ______________________________

4. The day of my eighteenth birthday, the reservations made at a fine restaurant. My father came home early from work.

   Revised passage: ______________________________

   ______________________________

   ______________________________

5. In 1930, Clint Benedict of the Montreal Maroons donned professional hockey's first facemask. It was a crude leather device intended to protect his broken nose. During the game, an opponent jammed the mask into Benedict's face. Causing further injury. Benedict tore off the mask and quit the game forever.

   Revised passage: ______________________________

   ______________________________

   ______________________________

## Working Together: Editing Ad Copy

Read the Audi advertisement illustrated below. Notice that this advertisement contains many fragments. The writing we must produce for academic or professional purposes is often very different from the kind of writing we find in advertisements and other kinds of popular writing. This kind of writing is short and snappy. Why do you think the advertiser would choose to write in this way? Rewrite the entire advertisement using only complete sentences. There can be more than one way to rewrite this advertisement.

Audi

Traction. Like a lot of things in life you take it for granted, then boom. It's taken away. And oh how you want it back. It doesn't take much. Gravel on the offramp. A soft shoulder on a rainy night.

That's why we developed quattro™ all-wheel drive for our luxury cars. Very serious grip. High performance traction. Quattro continuously distributes power between the front and back wheels, whichever has the best hold of the road. It happens instantly. And the extra traction quattro provides could be the difference between being in a collision, or avoiding a collision. So which is better, protection or traction? Get both. In an Audi quattro all-wheel drive. For more information call 1-800-668-AUDI.

Audi 90 quattro

Audi Quattro. Reprinted with kind permission of Volkswagen Canada.

CHAPTER SEVEN 7

# Correcting Run-ons

**QUICK QUIZ** Test yourself on your knowledge of run-ons. Some of the examples below are complete sentences; some are run-ons (two or more independent clauses inadequately separated). Write *C* if the example is correct. Write *R* if the example is a run-on. Answers to the questions are upside down beside the quiz.

__________ 1. Strong competition exists among computer companies, each carefully guards its new software designs.

__________ 2. Last year, newspapers carried the story of the great video game design robbery, in fact, it sounded like a spy movie.

__________ 3. A young worker for a California company wanted money to buy a sports car, so he tried to sell the secret company designs to an Asian competitor.

__________ 4. The worker thought the designs were safely hidden on a disk in an airport locker, however, the police caught him and recovered the disk.

__________ 5. The company pressed charges, the worker was given a suspended sentence.

**Answers:**
1. R
2. R
3. C
4. R
5. R

## Run-ons Are Not "Long Sentences"

Too many people think that a run-on is simply a sentence that "runs on and on and on." This is not the definition of a run-on. The question of whether a sentence is a run-on or not does not depend on length. The following is a run-on sentence despite its length: *I did, he didn't.* Quite simply, a run-on is two or more independent clauses without adequate separation. While there are many ways to provide this separation, what's most important is that runs-ons in your writing be recognized and that proper separation be used to solve the problem.

**DEFINITION ➤** A **run-on** is two or more complete thoughts without adequate separation. (A comma alone is NEVER adequate separation.)

***Examples:*** Everyone watched silently as the bus pulled into the school parking lot, then each person stepped onto the bus in a very orderly fashion.

I came to school, however, I was late.

Both examples in the definition box on the previous page are run-on sentences. In the first sentence, the word *then* is used incorrectly as if it were a coordinating conjunction. It is not. It is not one of the "FANBOYS" (see Chapter 5, p. 58). In the second sentence, the adverbial conjunction *however* separates two complete thoughts. It, therefore, requires a semicolon before it, not just a comma.

## What Kinds of Run-ons Are There?

**The Different Kinds of Run-on Sentences**

1. *The fused run-on:* two or more independent clauses that run together without any punctuation

   **I met Diana again we were happy to see each other.**

2. *The comma splice:* two or more independent clauses that run together with only a comma

   **I met Diana again, we were happy to see each other.**

   (The comma splice is the most common type of run-on sentence.)

3. *The "and" run-on:* two or more independent clauses that run together with a coordinating conjunction but no punctuation

   **I met Diana again and we were happy to see each other and we talked for hours.**

*Note:* A long sentence is not, in itself, a run-on sentence. The following sentence may be considered long, but it is **not** a run-on:

> I met Diana again, and despite the fact that we hadn't seen each other in years, we both felt as if we hadn't parted at all, as strange as that may seem to everyone.

## How Do You Make a Complete Sentence from a Run-on?

**Guide for Correcting Run-ons**

1. Make two simple sentences with end punctuation:

   **I met Diana again. We were happy to see each other.**

2. Make a compound sentence using one of the three methods of coordination:

   **I met Diana again, and we were happy to see each other.**
   **I met Diana again; furthermore, we were happy to see each other.**
   **I met Diana again; we were happy to see each other.**

   (For more on using the semicolon correctly—either with adverbial conjunctions or alone—see Chapter 5, pp. 60–64.)

3. Make a complex sentence using subordination:

   **When I met Diana again, we were happy to see each other.**
   **We were happy to see each other when I met Diana again.**

**EXERCISE**

## Recognizing and Correcting Run-ons

The following story is written as one sentence. Rewrite the story, making sure to correct the run-on sentences. Put a period at the end of each complete thought. You may have to omit some of the words that loosely connect different ideas, or you may want to use coordination and subordination (see Chapter 5). Remember to start each new sentence with a capital letter. More than one correct answer is possible.

My best friend is accident-prone if you knew her you'd know that she's always limping, having to write with her left hand, or wearing a bandage on her head or ankle, last week for example, she was walking down the street minding her own business when a shingle from someone's roof hit her on the head and she had to go to the emergency ward for stitches, then this week one of her fingers is purple because someone slammed the car door on her hand, in fact, sometimes I think it might be better if I didn't spend too much time with her, you know her bad luck might be catching!

**PRACTICE 1**

## Correcting Run-ons

Each of the following examples is a run-on. Supply four possible ways to correct each run-on. There may be more than one correct answer for each example. Check your answers against those in the Answer Key on p. 460. Use the guide on page 93 if you need help.

1. Five-year-old Davie asked Grandpa for an iPod for his birthday, he started crying because Grandpa didn't know what that was.

   Two simple sentences (sentences with a single subject, verb, and one complete thought):

   ________________________________________

   ________________________________________

   Two kinds of compound sentence (two simple sentences connected with either a comma and a coordinating conjunction, a semicolon and an adverbial conjunction, or just a semicolon):

   a. ________________________________________

   ________________________________________

   b. ________________________________________

   ________________________________________

   Complex sentence (use subordination):

   ________________________________________

   ________________________________________

2. Many people are opposed to gambling in all its forms, therefore, they will not even buy a lottery ticket.

   Two simple sentences:

   ______________________________

   ______________________________

   Two kinds of compound sentence:

   a. ______________________________

   ______________________________

   b. ______________________________

   ______________________________

   Complex sentence:

   ______________________________

   ______________________________

3. Hockey may be Canada's national sport, the game can be quite brutal.

   Two simple sentences:

   ______________________________

   ______________________________

   Two kinds of compound sentence:

   a. ______________________________

   ______________________________

   b. ______________________________

   ______________________________

   Complex sentence:

   ______________________________

   ______________________________

4. Many young people manage to travel, they find ways to do it cheaply.

   Two simple sentences:

   ______________________________

   ______________________________

Two kinds of compound sentence:

a. ______________________________

______________________________

b. ______________________________

______________________________

Complex sentence:

______________________________

______________________________

5. The need for a proper diet is important in any health program, however, all the junk food on the grocery shelves makes it hard to be consistent.

Two simple sentences:

______________________________

______________________________

Two kinds of compound sentence:

a. ______________________________

______________________________

b. ______________________________

______________________________

Complex sentence:

______________________________

______________________________

**PRACTICE 2**

## Correcting Run-ons

Each of the following examples is a run-on. Supply four possible ways to revise each run-on. There may be more than one correct answer for each example. Check your answers against those in the Answer Key on p. 460. Use the guide on page 93 if you need help.

1. The airline has begun its new route to the islands everyone is looking forward to flying there.

Two simple sentences:

______________________________

______________________________

Two kinds of compound sentence:

a. ______________________________

______________________________

b. ______________________________

______________________________

Complex sentence:

______________________________

______________________________

2. The movie begins at nine o'clock, therefore, let's have dinner before the show.

Two simple sentences:

______________________________

______________________________

Two kinds of compound sentence:

a. ______________________________

______________________________

b. ______________________________

______________________________

Complex sentence:

______________________________

______________________________

3. The studio audience screamed at the contestant, after all, they wanted her to try for the big prize.

Two simple sentences:

______________________________

______________________________

Two kinds of compound sentence:

a. ______________________________

______________________________

b. ______________________________

______________________________

Complex sentence:

4. Maya needs new shoes, she is running in the marathon.

Two simple sentences:

Two kinds of compound sentence:

a.

b.

Complex sentence:

5. My actor friend grabbed my arm, she wanted to tell me about her new part in the movie.

Two simple sentences:

Two kinds of compound sentence:

a.

b.

Complex sentence:

PRACTICE 3

## Editing for Run-ons

Rewrite the following paragraph, and correct the run-on sentences using any of the methods you have learned. Check your answers against those in the Answer Key on p. 461.

Mythology is the study of myths and myths are known as the oldest form of literature and the oldest myths are creation myths. Cultures from around the world have their own creation myths all of them are amazingly similar despite the vast geographical distances between these cultures and the fact that there are no known ways in which communication could have taken place between certain ones. Details of these myths change from one culture to the next, however, various themes of the myths remain the same. For example, although characters (most of the time, but not all of the time) take on new names from one culture to another, every culture refers to the existence of a creator, also the number of gods often differs from one mythology to another, nevertheless, every mythology has at least one god or one heroic figure in it. All in all, myths are incredible stories that, in many cases, have lasted thousands of years no matter where they come from and what they are about, they bear striking similarities from one culture to another, and they all share a wisdom about something that never changes: our human nature.

PRACTICE 4

## Editing for Run-ons

Rewrite the following paragraph, and correct the run-on sentences using any of the methods you have learned. Check your answers against those in the Answer Key on p. 461.

Sigmund Freud and Carl G. Jung were both psychiatrists, they have had a great deal of influence on the study of psychology to this day, for example, each was famous for his own model of the human psyche. In Freud's model, there are three main parts, they are the ego, the id, and the superego. In Jung's model, there are also three main parts, they are the conscious, the personal unconscious, and the collective unconscious. Freud (Jung's teacher and subsequent collaborator until they parted due to a major disagreement in 1912) and Jung both believed that dreams come from the unconscious part of our psyche (for Freud, this meant the id and superego), nevertheless, they disagreed a great deal in the area of dream interpretation.

# Chapter Review Exercises

EXERCISE 1

## Editing for Run-ons

Rewrite the following paragraph, correcting all run-on sentences. More than one correct answer is possible.

Commercial farming in Atlantic Canada is concentrated in the dairy, poultry, and horticultural sectors, the most important crop in the region, particularly in New Brunswick and Prince Edward Island, is potatoes. In Ontario and Quebec, farming is highly diversified and includes specialty crops such as soybeans, tobacco, fruit, and vegetables. In the Prairie region, most of the country's wheat, oats, barley, rye, flaxseed, canola, mustard, and sunflowers are grown livestock raising is also very important in Canada with the majority of ranches being located in the three prairie provinces.

## EXERCISE 2 Editing for Run-ons

Rewrite the following paragraph, correcting all run-on sentences. More than one correct answer is possible.

Although the metric system was legalized in Canada in 1871, the British Imperial system of units, based on yards, pounds, gallons, etc., continued to be used until the 1960s, with rapidly expanding technology and worldwide trade, the need for an international measurement system became apparent. Britain decided to convert to the system the United States was studying a similar move. A number of Canadian businesses favoured the metric system in January 1970 the government passed legislation stating that a single, coherent measurement system based on metric units should be used for measurement purposes in this country.

## EXERCISE 3 Editing for Run-ons

Correct the following run-on sentences by using the different methods you have learned. Correct the sentences in at least two different ways.

1. I had to buy a new DVD, I gave my only copy to my brother.
2. I'm taking guitar lessons, four of us want to start a band.
3. It was hot outside, I wanted to get some exercise.
4. The storm came on suddenly, we were lost.
5. There were no right answers to the questions, we tried to answer them.
6. He is a politician, he serves his community well.
7. Where is Kanata, I think it's near Ottawa.
8. When did Canada last win the World Junior Hockey Championships, I think it was a long time ago.
9. Our tour was interesting, four of us became lost in Edmonton.
10. We tried our hardest, the exam was too difficult.

## EXERCISE 4 Editing for Run-ons

Correct any run-on sentences by using the different methods you have learned. Correct the run-ons in at least two different ways. If the sentence is already correct, write *C* beside the number.

1. The right answer was not at the end of the chapter, it was at the beginning of the next one.
2. I was late for school, however, the teacher wasn't in class today.
3. The pizza was cold, then again, it was still good.
4. At the edge of the table, the marble slowed down and began to roll the other way.
5. The time was right, it was now or never.
6. Listening to the radio at dawn, I found myself singing the words to every song.
7. My teacher is dedicated to her profession, furthermore, she's the best teacher I've ever had.

## Working Together: Operation "Plot without Run-ons"

Choose a movie or book you have seen or read recently, and retell the plot. In about twenty minutes, write as much of the story as you can remember, being careful to write only on every other line, separating each word, and writing clearly so your classmates can read what you have written. Exchange papers and read the paper you receive in order to check for run-ons. When you have found what you believe to be a run-on, put a mark beside that sentence, and be ready to read the sentence or put it on the board for class discussion.

CHAPTER EIGHT

8

# Parallel Structure

**QUICK QUIZ**

Test yourself on your knowledge of parallel structure. The underlined portion of each sentence is not parallel with the rest of the sentence. Replace the underlined portion with the correct words, making the entire sentence parallel. Answers are upside down in the margin.

1. While the men go out in their boats, the women and children stay in camp, cook meals, and to take care of the dog teams.
2. The weather on the East Coast is often wet, windy, and the temperatures are low.
3. His office is without windows, on the fourth floor, and you have to go down a dark hallway to get there.
4. Carmelita does her work quickly, accurately, and with cheerfulness.
5. The mayor promised lower taxes, less crime, and the number of jobs would be higher.

**Answers:**
1. take care of the dog teams
2. cold
3. down a dark hallway
4. cheerfully
5. more jobs

## What Is Parallel Structure?

**DEFINITION ➤** **Parallel structure** is balance in a sentence containing a list. The list might consist of words, phrases, or clauses. Balance occurs when all the items in the list are of the same grammatical form, such as nouns, adjectives, and so on.

***Example:*** ***Parallel:*** She went out with him because of the twinkle in his eye, the swagger in his step, and his love for movies.

***Unparallel:*** She went out with him because of the twinkle in his eye, swaggering, and he loves movies.

In the first sentence above, at the heart of all three items in the list is a noun: twinkle, swagger, and love. They are all nouns (with modifiers), so the sentence is parallel.

In the second sentence, the first item starts with a noun: the *twinkle* in his eye; the second item is a verbal (a gerund): *swaggering*; and the third item starts with the pronoun *he* (not to mention that the word refers back to the man being talked about rather than the qualities he possesses). These grammatical forms are all different. This sentence is unparallel.

Which of the following sentences is better balanced?

> Her favourite pastimes are reading novels, listening to jazz, and to go to films.
> Her favourite pastimes are reading novels, listening to jazz, and going to films.

If you selected the second sentence, you made the right choice. The second sentence uses parallel structure (all three items in the list begin with *–ing* words: reading, listening, and going). By giving each first word of the items in the list the same *-ing* structure, the sentence becomes easier to understand and more pleasant to read. You can make words, phrases, and even sentences in a list parallel:

| RULE 1 ➤ | **Words in a list should be the same parts of speech.** |
|---|---|

*Incorrect:* The town was small, quiet, and the atmosphere was peaceful.

(The list is composed of two adjectives and one clause.)

*Correct:* The town was small, quiet, and peaceful. (*Small, quiet*, and *peaceful* are adjectives.)

| RULE 2 ➤ | **Phrases in a list should be the same kind of phrase (infinitive phrases, prepositional phrases, verb phrases, noun phrases, participial phrases).** |
|---|---|

*Incorrect:* Her lost assignment is in her closet, on the floor, and the clothes are hiding it.

(Two prepositional phrases and one clause.)

*Correct:* Her lost assignment is in her closet, on the floor, and under a pile of clothes.

(Three prepositional phrases beginning with *in, on*, and *under*.)

| RULE 3 ➤ | **Clauses in a list should be parallel.** |
|---|---|

*Incorrect:* One clerk polished the antique spoons; they were placed into the display case by the other clerk.

*Correct:* One clerk polished the antique spoons; the other clerk placed them in the display case.

**PRACTICE 1**

## Making Sentences Parallel

Each of the following sentences has an underlined word, phrase, or clause that is not parallel. Make the underlined section parallel. Check your answers against those in the Answer Key on p. 461.

1. My favourite armchair is lumpy, worn out, and has dirt spots everywhere.

______________________________________________

______________________________________________

2. She enjoys reading novels, studying the flute, and also sews her own clothes.

______________________________________________

______________________________________________

3. He admires teachers who make the classroom an exciting place and willingly explaining material more than once.

______________________________________________

______________________________________________

**PRACTICE 2**

## Making Sentences Parallel

Each of the following sentences needs parallel structure. Underline the word, phrase, or clause that is not parallel and revise it so that its structure balances with the other items in the pair or series. There may be more than one correct answer for each sentence. An example is done for you. Check your answers against those in the Answer Key on p. 461.

***Incorrect:*** The best leather comes from Italy, from Spain, and is imported from Brazil.

***Correct:*** The best leather comes from Italy, from Spain, and from Brazil.

1. Winter in Edmonton is very windy and has many bitterly cold days.

______________________________________________

______________________________________________

2. I would prefer to fix an old car than watching television.

______________________________________________

______________________________________________

3. Alex is a talented athlete, a top student, and even generous to her friends.

______________________________________________

______________________________________________

4. The apartment is crowded and without light.

______________________________________________

______________________________________________

5. The dancer is slender and moves gracefully.

______________________________________________

______________________________________________

6. The trees were tall and had a lot of leaves.

______________________________________________

______________________________________________

7. My friend loves to play chess, to read science fiction, and working out at the gym.

______________________________________________

______________________________________________

**PRACTICE 3**

### Making Sentences Parallel

Each of the following sentences lacks parallel structure. Underline the word, phrase, or clause that is not parallel, and revise it so that its structure balances with the other items in the pair or series. There may be more than one correct answer for each sentence. Check your answers against those in the Answer Key on p. 461.

1. The dog had to choose between jumping over the fence, or he could have dug a hole underneath it.

______________________________________________

______________________________________________

2. She was great at swimming, canoeing, and as a rock climber.

______________________________________________

______________________________________________

3. As I looked down the city street, I could see the soft lights from restaurant windows, I could hear the mellow sounds of a nightclub band, and carefree moods of people walking by.

______________________________________________

______________________________________________

4. The singers have been on several road tours, have recorded for two record companies, and they would also like to make a movie someday.

_______________________________________________

_______________________________________________

5. They would rather order a pizza than eating homemade cooking.

_______________________________________________

_______________________________________________

6. I explained to the teacher that my car had broken down, my books had been stolen, and I left my assignment pad at home.

_______________________________________________

_______________________________________________

7. That night the prisoner was sick, discouraged, and filled with loneliness.

_______________________________________________

_______________________________________________

Before trying the chapter review exercises, here is a reminder of all the rules for parallel structure. (For further explanation of these rules, check back to page 103.)

**RULE 1:** Words in a list should be the same parts of speech.
**RULE 2:** Phrases in a list should be the same kind of phrase (infinitive phrases, prepositional phrases, verb phrases, noun phrases, participial phrases).
**RULE 3:** Clauses in a list should be parallel.

## Chapter Review Exercises

**EXERCISE 1**

### Making Sentences Parallel

Each of the following sentences has a part that does not work with the rest of the sentence; therefore, the sentences lack parallel structure. Find the error and correct it. There may be more than one correct answer for each sentence.

1. Now that he was retired, he started tending to his garden, drank his latte at his favourite café every day, and a new book project was something he was eager to launch.

_______________________________________________

_______________________________________________

2. The dancer was used to eating her banana, stretching for an hour, and then rehearsal for the next performance kept her busy for the rest of the day.

3. The car wasn't in the garage, nobody could find it on the street, and we found out the police hadn't towed it.

4. After volunteering at a senior's residence, doing his chores for his parents, and once his homework was finished, he had no time left for his girlfriend.

5. He had to put salt on the ice, food in the dog's dish, and he had to make sure that the driveway was shovelled.

**EXERCISE 2**

### Making Sentences Parallel

Revise each sentence to make it parallel. There may be more than one correct answer for each sentence.

1. Most of the neighbours are friendly, considerate, and they give help.

2. She is charming and has beauty.

3. I enjoy reading, writing, and to conduct laboratory experiments.

4. Either going for a ride or to lie in the sun is my idea of a good time.

5. She got a new job with a higher salary, increased benefits, and she also works fewer hours than before.

_______________________________________________

_______________________________________________

## Working Together: Practise Making Sentences Parallel

Read the following paragraph. Look for lack of parallel structure, and then rewrite your corrected version. When you're finished, check your answers with another student in the group or class, preferably someone with whom you would not normally sit.

I've had a lot of great summer jobs. They include desk clerk for a student residence, cashier for a busy convenience store, and I even worked as an assistant janitor in an elementary school where my boss and I had some of the best conversations I've ever had. The best summer job, however, was organizing the Miss Glace Bay Pageant. The titillation factor associated with a beauty competition was certainly one reason. Other reasons for enjoying the job included auditioning talent for the entertainment component, I wrote the script for the emcee, and meeting a young woman among the contestants whom I'd already met six months earlier. First, because I love music, having a say as to who performed on the big evening was exciting beyond description. Second, I've always enjoyed writing. And writing what the emcee would say that evening gave me experience with a kind of writing I'd never tried before. But most important, when I saw Sherry with her long golden hair among the contestants on the first day of rehearsals, I knew this second meeting was no coincidence. And about a week later when she sat down next to me, laid her head on my shoulder, and "Hello, there," was whispered into my ear, I knew we'd be dating before too long. She didn't win the pageant, but she definitely won my heart. I'd had some great summer jobs, but organizing the pageant was the one that etched that summer onto the wall of my memory storehouse forever.

CHAPTER NINE

9

# Pronouns

**QUICK QUIZ**

Test yourself on your knowledge of pronouns. In each of the following sentences, choose the correct pronouns. Answers are upside down beside the quiz.

1. Between you and (me, I), the reason I can't go is I lost my ticket.
2. The girl I'm dating is taller than (I, me).
3. (We, Us) students are going to Cancun for the spring break.
4. Would you spare some change for my son and (I, me)?
5. (Him, He) and (me, I) spent lots of money on the weekend.

**Answers:**
1. me
2. I
3. We
4. me
5. He, I

A discussion of pronouns never fails to be interesting because of the potential controversy surrounding usage. Even well-educated people disagree sometimes on what is acceptable. Those who tend to support a particular usage even if it's not grammatically correct will argue that it's acceptable because that's what they hear everyone else saying. But what everyone seems to be saying is not always correct, and what is not correct is still most often unacceptable. In the final analysis, the more correct grammar you know, the safer you'll be.

Most people acquainted with a basic knowledge of English grammar know, for example, that it is improper to say, "Me and him are going downtown." But not everyone knows that it is also improper to say, "Between you and I ..." (the correct usage is, "Between you and me ..."). Some English instructors accept "Everyone has their way of doing things," while fewer instructors accept "To who should I give this book?" In any event, this text is still partial to the correct way, and if there is widespread movement toward acceptance of certain pronoun usage that was once and might still be considered incorrect, you might simply have to make a personal decision.

**DEFINITION ➤** A **pronoun** is a word that replaces a noun (person, place, or thing).

***Examples:*** The boy came across his lucky charm quite unexpectedly.

*He* came across *it* quite unexpectedly.

*Note: He* replaces the boy, and *it* replaces his lucky charm.

**DEFINITION ➤** A **personal pronoun** is a pronoun that refers to the person speaking (*I, me, we, us*), the person spoken to (*you*), or the person(s) spoken about (*he, she, it, they, him, her, them*).

## Pronouns and Case

**RULE ➤** **The case of a personal pronoun is determined by the function it serves in a sentence. Pronouns can function as subjects, as objects, or as indicators of ownership (possessive case).**

**Guide to Pronoun Case**

| Pronouns Used as Subjects (Subjective Case) | Pronouns Used as Objects (Objective Case) | Pronouns Used as Possessives (Possessive Case) | Possessive Adjectives |
|---|---|---|---|
| I | me | mine | my |
| you (sing.) | you (sing.) | yours | your |
| he | him | his | his |
| she | her | hers | her |
| it | it | its | its |
| who | whom | whose | whose |
| whoever | whomever | whosever | |
| we | us | ours | our |
| you (pl.) | you (pl.) | yours | your |
| they | them | theirs | their |

Use the guide to choose the correct answers in the following examples:

1. (She, Her) is singing at the concert tonight.
2. He bought those tickets for Jan and (I, me).

**TIP** **When you have a compound subject or object, it is easier to pick the correct pronoun if you read the sentence leaving out one of the subjects.**

**_Example:_ He bought those tickets for (I, me).**

**(The correct answer is more obvious now: _me._)**

3. He sold (us, we) the best seats in the house.
4. To (who, whom) should I address the letter?
5. Her voice is much stronger than (he, him, his).

TIP

**In a comparison, it is easier to pick the correct pronoun if you complete the comparison.**

***Example:*** **Her voice is much stronger than (he, him, his) voice is.**

6. (Who, Whom, Whose) music was left on the piano?
7. She is dating a man who is shorter than (she, her) is.

**DEFINITION ➤** **Possessive adjectives**, technically speaking, are not pronouns; they do not replace nouns. They are adjectives because they modify nouns. But both the possessive adjective and the noun it modifies can be replaced by a possessive pronoun.

***Example:*** He returned *my* book. He returned *mine.*

The word *my* is a possessive adjective. The word *mine* in the second sentence is a possessive pronoun (see p. 110).

## *Who* vs. *Whom*

*Who* is the subjective form; *whom* is the objective form. Use *who* whenever *he, she, they, I,* or *we* could replace *who.* And likewise, use *whom* when *him, her, them, me,* or *us* could replace *whom.* (If this doesn't work, mentally rearrange the clause the way it's done in parentheses after the following examples):

1. To whom were you talking? (Were you talking to him?)

TIP

**Keep in mind the rule that you cannot find a subject in a prepositional phrase.**

In sentence 1 above, *to* is a preposition (see p. 9). So the objective form of *who,* which is *whom,* must come after the preposition.

However, the following two examples show the exception to the rule.

2. The next person to who I get engaged will be the one I marry. (He or she will be the next person I marry.)
3. The matter of who should pay was not decided. (He or she should pay.)

The rule that a subject never follows a preposition is broken in sentences 2 and 3 because the word *who* is, on the one hand, an object of a preposition, but is also the doer of an action. **Choose the *subjective* form of the relative pronoun (who) when it is both an object and a subject in a sentence.**

**EXERCISE 1**

### Choosing Correct Pronoun Forms

Circle the correct pronoun in each of the sentences below.

1. Matthew and (she, her) presented the project today.
2. Between you and (I, me), I think it was outstanding.

3. Their visual materials will help (whoever, whomever) will study the project later.
4. He is usually a better speaker than (she, her).
5. (Whoever, Whomever) heard them agreed that it was an impressive presentation.
6. (Who, Whom) do you think made the best points?
7. I am not as deeply involved in my project as (they, them).
8. Their research was much more detailed than (us, our, ours).
9. The professor gave both Carolyn and (he, him) A's.
10. My partner and (I, me) will have to work harder to reach this standard.

**EXERCISE 2** **Choosing Correct Pronoun Forms**

Circle the correct pronouns in the following paragraph.

When my mother and (I, me) decided to care for my very ill father at home, some of our friends objected. My sister and (they, them) said we would be exhausted and unable to handle the stress. To (who, whom) could we go for help in the middle of the night? My father, (who, whom) we believed would be happier at home, had been our first consideration. Of course, we would have benefited if my mother or (I, me) had been a nurse. However, we did have a visiting nurse available at times. We were more confident than (they, them) that we could handle the situation.

## Pronoun-Antecedent Agreement

**RULE 1 ➤** **A pronoun must agree in number (singular or plural) and gender (masculine, feminine, or neutral) with any other word to which it refers.**

**DEFINITION ➤** That word to which the pronoun refers is known as the **antecedent** of the pronoun. Most errors in pronoun number agreement occur when a plural pronoun is used to refer to a singular noun, and vice versa.

***Example:*** The *school* has its own way of doing things.

The *antecedent* in the sentence above is *school*. Because *school* is singular and neutral (neither masculine nor feminine), use *its* as the pronoun that refers back to it.

The following sentences contain pronoun-antecedent disagreement in **number:**

The *company* changed *their* name last month.
*Everyone* worked on *their* final draft.

In the first sentence, the antecedent *company* is singular in number and neutral in gender. Therefore, the pronoun (or possessive adjective) referring back to it must be singular and neutral as well. The corrected version is *The company changed its name last month*. (The possessive adjective *its* is both singular and neutral. Notice there is no apostrophe in a possessive adjective.)

The problem in the second sentence is that *everyone* is a singular word (see discussion on **indefinite pronouns** below), but *their* is a plural pronoun. You may often have heard people use the plural pronoun *their* to refer to a singular subject. In fact, the second sentence above may sound correct, especially when it is heard during casual conversation, but it is still a mistake in formal writing. Here are two approaches a writer might take to correct this sentence:

Everyone worked on *his* final draft.

Although you may encounter this approach in current writing, it is unpopular because it is widely considered a sexist construction.

Everyone worked on *his or her* final draft.

This form is technically correct, but if it is used several times, it sounds awkward and repetitious.

The best solution is to revise such a construction so that the antecedent is plural:

All the students worked on *their* final drafts.

*Everyone* is an **indefinite** pronoun. It may look plural, but actually, it is singular. For more on indefinite pronouns, see pp. 49–50 in Chapter 4: "Subject-Verb Agreement."

Many indefinite pronouns are singular (any pronoun with *-one*, *-body,* or *-thing* in it).

**Indefinite Pronouns That Are Singular**

| | | | | |
|---|---|---|---|---|
| -one | everyone | someone | anyone | no one |
| -body | everybody | somebody | anybody | nobody |
| -thing | everything | something | anything | nothing |
| | each | another | either | neither |

Another problem with pronoun-antecedent agreement in number occurs when a **demonstrative** pronoun (*this, that, these, those*) is used with a noun. That pronoun must agree with the noun it modifies:

Singular: this kind, that type

***Incorrect:*** *These kind* of shoes hurt my feet.
***Correct:*** *This kind* of shoe hurts my feet.

Plural: these kinds, those types

***Incorrect:*** *Those type* of cars always need oil.
***Correct:*** *Those types* of cars always need oil.

**EXERCISE 1**

## Pronoun-Antecedent Agreement in Number

Rewrite each of the following sentences so that the pronoun agrees with its antecedent in number.

1. Everybody should believe they have choices.

 ______________________________

 ______________________________

2. Each of the children brought their own toys.

 ______________________________

 ______________________________

3. There was no one who invited us to their homes.

 ______________________________

 ______________________________

4. If the bird-watchers hope to see anything, one must get up early.

 ______________________________

 ______________________________

5. The members of the association voted on its constitution.

 ______________________________

 ______________________________

| RULE 2 ➤ | **Pronouns must also agree with their antecedents in person.** |
|---|---|

"Person" refers to the doer of the action—first person (*I*); second person (*you*); third person (*he, she, it* in the singular; *we, you, they* in the plural, among others). First-person pronouns highlight the writer and are suitable for personal writing. Second-person pronouns focus on the reader and are useful for giving instructions. Third-person pronouns emphasize the subject and are useful in informative and academic writing.

The following **incorrect** sentence contains a pronoun-antecedent disagreement in **person:**

> When mountain climbing, *one* must maintain *your* concentration at all times.

The sentence could be correctly rewritten as follows:

> When mountain climbing, *one* must maintain *one's* concentration at all times.

When mountain climbing, *you* must maintain *your* concentration at all times.
When mountain climbing, *I* must maintain *my* concentration at all times.
When mountain climbing, *we* must maintain *our* concentration at all times.

**EXERCISE 2** **Pronoun-Antecedent Agreement in Person**

Rewrite each of the following sentences so that the pronoun agrees with its antecedent in person.

1. I enjoy math exams because you can show what you know.

______________________________________________

______________________________________________

2. When I took geometry, we discovered that frequent review of past assignments helped make the course seem easy.

______________________________________________

______________________________________________

3. People always need to practise your skills in order not to forget them.

______________________________________________

______________________________________________

4. When you study for exams, one should not watch television at the same time.

______________________________________________

______________________________________________

5. Math is a subject we often neglect in school, but later you use it all the time.

______________________________________________

______________________________________________

## Missing, Ambiguous, or Repetitious Pronouns

| | |
|---|---|
| **RULE ➤** | **The antecedent of a pronoun should not be missing, ambiguous, or repetitious.** |

The following is a sentence with a missing antecedent:

*Missing antecedent:* In British Columbia, they have many challenging hiking trails.
*Possible revision:* British Columbia has many challenging hiking trails.

In the first sentence, who is meant by *they*? If the context has not told us that *they* refers to the government or to tourist companies, for instance, then the antecedent is missing. The sentence should be rewritten in order to avoid *they*.

In the next sentence, the antecedent is ambiguous.

*Ambiguous antecedent:* Margaret told Lin that *she* needed to earn $1000 during the summer.

*Possible revision:* Margaret said that Lin needed to earn $1000 during the summer.

In the first example, *she* could refer to either Margaret or Lin. The sentence should be revised in a way that avoids this confusion.

The next example illustrates a repetitious antecedent.

*Repetitious pronoun and antecedent:* The newspaper article, *it* said that Earth Day, 1993, re-established humankind's commitment to the earth.

*Possible revision:* The newspaper article said that Earth Day, 1993, re-established humankind's commitment to the earth.

The subject should be either *article* or, if there is already an antecedent, *it*. Using both the noun and the pronoun results in needless repetition.

EXERCISE

## Sentences with Proper Antecedents

Rewrite each of the following sentences so that the antecedents are not missing, ambiguous, or repetitious. More than one correct answer is possible.

1. The biologist asked the director to bring back his microscope.

______________________________

______________________________

2. In the report, it says that the number of science and engineering students seeking doctoral degrees has fallen considerably since the mid-sixties.

______________________________

______________________________

3. At the laboratory, they said the research had run into serious difficulties.

______________________________

______________________________

4. The testing equipment was accidentally dropped into the aquarium, and it was badly damaged.

______________________________

______________________________

5. You can't believe anything they say in that newspaper.

## Chapter Review Exercises

**PRACTICE**

### Making Pronouns and Antecedents Agree

Each of the following sentences contains errors with pronouns. Revise each sentence so that pronouns agree with their antecedents and there are no missing or ambiguous antecedents. There may be more than one correct answer for each sentence. Check your answers against those in the Answer Key on p. 462.

1. His father mailed him his high school yearbook.

2. No one wants their income reduced.

3. When a company fails to update its equipment, they often pay a price in the long run.

4. The graduate today has many more options open to them than ever before.

5. Everybody knows their own strengths best.

6. Each of the soccer players put effort into their game.

7. If the campers want to eat quickly, each one should help themselves.

**EXERCISE**

## Making Pronouns and Antecedents Agree

Each of the following sentences may contain an error with pronouns. Revise each sentence so that pronouns agree with their antecedents and there are no missing or ambiguous antecedents. There may be more than one correct answer for each sentence. If a sentence is correct, mark a *C* on the lines provided.

1. The manager told Karen she was responsible for the mix-up in orders.

2. The county submitted their proposal for the bridge repairs.

3. We all rushed away from all the trees to our cars because you had to wait for the thunderstorm to stop.

4. A young person does not receive enough advice on how they should choose their career.

5. These type of watches are very popular.

6. People were taken forcibly from our homes.

7. No one ate their lunch in the cafeteria.

## Working Together: Practise with Pronouns

Pair up with someone else in the class, preferably someone with whom you do not normally sit. Together, come up with ten sentences, each with at least three pronouns in it. Each of the three pronouns should be of different cases: subjective, objective, and possessive. Come up with at least one sentence that requires pronoun-antecedent agreement, and one other that contains potential pronoun ambiguity. Between the two of you, make sure all pronouns are correct. If you disagree on any, give the other student an explanation as to why you think yours is correct. Here is an example of a sentence that complies:

> Jacquie and **I** are faster than **they**, so **they** have to not only pay **our** way to the festival, but also give **us** spending money once **we**'re there.
>
> *I, they, they, we*: subjective case
> *our*: possessive adjective
> *us*: objective case

CHAPTER TEN 10

# Modifiers: Misplaced and Dangling

**QUICK QUIZ**

Test your knowledge of dangling and misplaced modifiers by selecting the correct sentence in each pair below. Answers are upside down in the margin.

1. a. Sweeping the dust in the attic, the dead bugs numbered in the thousands.
   b. Sweeping the dust in the attic, I noticed the dead bugs numbered in the thousands.
2. a. Reduce speed when wet.
   b. Reduce speed when roads are wet.
3. a. While shaving in the bathroom, Grant accidentally cut his ear with his razor.
   b. While shaving in the bathroom, the razor cut Grant's ear.
4. a. To make a good impression on your employer, ensure you have a neat and clean appearance.
   b. To make a good impression on your employer, a neat and clean appearance is advisable.
5. a. Though old and shoddy, Uncle Jake made the room in the back of the house look new again.
   b. Though the room in the back of the house was old and shoddy, Uncle Jake made it look new again.

Answers:
1. b
2. b
3. a
4. a
5. b

## What Are Modifiers?

**DEFINITION ➤** **Modifiers** are words or groups of words that function as adjectives or adverbs.

***Example:*** *Coming back from his vacation,* Tanya's father was eager to give his daughter the gift.

The modifier *coming back from his vacation* describes Tanya's father.

Modifiers describe or modify other words in the sentence. If a modifier is put in the wrong place or in an ambiguous or awkward place in the sentence, the meaning will be unclear. If the modifier has no word at all to modify, the result might be confusing or even unintentionally humorous. (See #2a above.)

**RULE ➤** **A modifier must be placed close to the word, phrase, or clause it modifies so that the reader can understand the intended meaning.**

The following shows how two types of modifier problems can be solved to make the meanings clear. Study the examples carefully. After you are able to recognize them in the exercises that follow, you will begin to recognize them in your own writing as well.

## What Are Misplaced Modifiers?

**DEFINITION ➤** **Misplaced modifiers** are modifiers that have been placed in wrong, ambiguous, or awkward positions.

***Examples:*** While eating his cat food, Johnny stepped on his kitten's tail.

Scurrying around with long and hairy legs, Sylvia tried to kill the spiders.

There are three types of misplaced modifiers.

1. **The modifier in the wrong place**

*Wrong:* The salesperson sold the used car to the customer that needed extensive bodywork.

Who or what needs bodywork—the car or the customer?

*Revised:* The salesperson sold the customer the used car that needed extensive bodywork.

The following was found in a personals ad:

> If you are tired of meeting the wrong people like me, please leave me a message.

Does this make sense? Why would anyone leave a message if they were tired of meeting people like the person who made up the ad? Perhaps what the person meant was this:

> If you, like me, are tired of meeting the wrong people, please leave me a message.

Be especially careful to put each of the following words closest to the word, phrase, or clause it modifies.

| Common Modifiers | | | | |
|---|---|---|---|---|
| almost | exactly | just | nearly | scarcely |
| even | hardly | merely | only | simply |

Notice how the meaning of each of the following sentences changes with the placement of the modifier *only.*

Only Charlene telephoned my brother yesterday.
Charlene only telephoned my brother yesterday.
Charlene telephoned only my brother yesterday.
Charlene telephoned my only brother yesterday.
Charlene telephoned my brother only yesterday.

2. **The awkward modifier that interrupts the flow of the sentence**

    ***Awkward:*** Cheryl planned to only call my sister.

    The adverb *only* could be better placed so that it would not split the infinitive *to call.*

    ***Revised:*** Cheryl planned to call only my sister.

3. **The "squinting modifier"—an ambiguous modifier that could describe a word or words on either side of it**

    ***Squinting:*** Cheryl having telephoned secretly appeared at the scene of the crime.

    Did Cheryl telephone secretly or appear secretly?

    ***Revised:*** Having secretly telephoned, Cheryl appeared at the scene of the crime.

## What Are Dangling Modifiers?

**DEFINITION ➤** A **dangling modifier** is a modifier in a sentence that has no word, phrase, or clause that the modifier can describe.

***Example:*** Riding the bicycle, the countryside seemed different.

In the above example, it sounds like the countryside is riding the bicycle. *Riding the bicycle* is the dangling modifier. It has nothing in the sentence to modify.

***Dangling:*** Working on the engine of the car, the dog barked all afternoon.

Who worked on the engine? Was it the dog?

***Revised:*** Working on the engine of the car, I heard the dog barking all afternoon.
or
The dog barked all afternoon while I was working on the engine of the car.

## Chapter Review Exercises

**PRACTICE**

### Revising Misplaced or Dangling Modifiers

Revise each sentence so there is no misplaced or dangling modifier. There may be more than one correct answer for each sentence. Check your answers against those in the Answer Key on p. 462.

1. Victor fed the dog wearing his tuxedo.

_______________________________________________

_______________________________________________

2. Visiting the Vancouver Aquarium, the otters entertained us.

_______________________________________________

_______________________________________________

3. Wanting to make a good impression, my suit was conservative and well cut.

_______________________________________________

_______________________________________________

4. A band was playing in the park that we had heard earlier.

_______________________________________________

_______________________________________________

5. After running over the hill, the farm was visible in the valley below.

_______________________________________________

_______________________________________________

6. The truck caused a traffic jam, which was broken down on the highway, for kilometres.

_______________________________________________

_______________________________________________

7. Hanging from the ceiling in my bedroom, I saw three spiders.

______________________________

______________________________

**EXERCISE**

## Revising Misplaced or Dangling Modifiers

Revise each sentence so there is no misplaced or dangling modifier. There may be more than one correct answer for each sentence.

1. Leaping upstream, we fished most of the day for salmon.

______________________________

______________________________

2. At the age of ten, my family took a trip to Fredericton.

______________________________

______________________________

3. Skimming every chapter, my biology textbook suddenly made more sense.

______________________________

______________________________

4. Waiting at the airport, every minute seemed endless.

______________________________

______________________________

5. Working extra hours last week, my salary increased dramatically.

______________________________

______________________________

6. We watched a movie in the theatre for which we had paid five dollars.

______________________________

______________________________

7. Dressed as Tinkerbell, he thought she looked charming.

______________________________

______________________________

## Working Together: Modifiers Making the Difference

Get into groups of four or five. See the box of common modifiers on page 122. Pick one and include it in a sentence. Then move the modifier around as many times as possible as long as the sentence still makes sense. (See the example of five sentences using the modifier *only* below the box.) Then, figure out exactly what each sentence means with the modifier in a different location each time. What does this difference in meaning suggest about the importance of word placement?

CHAPTER ELEVEN

11

# Punctuation

**QUICK QUIZ** Test yourself on your knowledge of commas. In each of the following sentences, place commas wherever they should go. Answers to the questions are upside down beside the quiz.

1. White-collar criminals dishonest company executives are being exposed in growing numbers.
2. White-collar criminals are found in industrial plants government offices and banks.
3. For example manufacturers have been caught cheating the government and well-known banks have been caught laundering money.
4. In the past white-collar criminals have not been prosecuted very vigorously by the law.
5. However some executives are now being given jail sentences for their white-collar crimes.

**Answers:**
1. criminals, executives,
2. plants, offices,
3. example, government,
4. past,
5. However,

## Correct Punctuation: A Strong Indicator of a Writer's Competence

Many people put commas in where "it feels right." Sometimes, their feelings are absolutely correct, but sometimes, they're not. Others use the dash when they are not quite sure what other punctuation mark to use instead. Like most aspects of writing, correct punctuation is a strong indicator of a writer's competence. Periods, commas, colons, semicolons, dashes, hyphens, quotation marks—all these tiny marks among words have incredible power over their meaning and ultimate effectiveness.

## The Eight Basic Rules of the Comma

Many students feel very uncertain about when to use the comma. The starting point is to concentrate on a few basic rules. These rules will cover most of your needs.

The tendency now in English is to use fewer commas than in the past. There is no one perfect set of rules on which everyone agrees. However, if you learn the eight basic rules explained in this chapter, your common sense will help you figure out what to do in other cases. Remember that a comma usually signifies a pause in a sentence. As you read a sentence out loud, listen to where you pause. This is often your clue that a comma is needed. Notice that in each of the examples for the following eight rules, you can pause where the comma is placed.

**RULE 1 ➤** **Use a comma to separate parallel words, phrases, and clauses in a list.**

The sky was cloudy, grey, and ominous.
I was dreaming of running in the race, finishing among the top ten, and collapsing happily on the ground.

With respect to Rule 1, note the following points:

- A list means more than two items.
- Some writers omit the comma before the *and* that introduces the last item.

  The sky was cloudy, grey and ominous.

- When an address or date occurs in a sentence, each part is treated as a separate item in a list. A comma follows each item even if there are only two items (as in the second example below):

  I lived at 14 Tartan Avenue, Halifax, Nova Scotia, for many years.
  He was born on August 17, 1980, on the same street where his father was born.

- A comma does not follow the last item in a list unless that last item is part of an address or a date.
- A group of adjectives may not be regarded as a list if some of the words "go together." You can test this by putting *and* between each item. If it doesn't work, then don't use commas.

  I carried my *old, dark green* coat.
  In the yard was a *battered old maple* tree.
  I rode in his *new red sports* car.

**PRACTICE 1** **Insert Necessary Commas**

In each of the following sentences, insert commas wherever they are needed. Check your answers against those in the Answer Key on p. 462.

1. Problems with the water supply of Canada the United States Europe and other parts of the world are growing.
2. Water is colourless tasteless odourless and free of calories.
3. You will use on an average day 90 L of water for flushing 120 L for bathing and washing clothes and 95 L for other uses.

4. It took 450 L of water to create the eggs you ate for breakfast 13 250 L for the steak you might eat for dinner and over 200 000 L to produce the steel used to make your car.
5. The English-Wabigoon river system runs through Grand Narrows Ontario and had become polluted with mercury.

**RULE 2 ➤** **Use a comma before a coordinating conjunction that joins two complete thoughts or independent clauses.** (See Chapter 5: "Coordination and Subordination.")

The house was on fire, but I was determined not to leave my place of safety.
The bees are dying, and one theory is that microwaves from cell phones are killing them.

With respect to Rule 2, note the following points:

- Be careful to use the comma before the conjunction only when you are combining independent clauses. If you are combining only words or phrases, no comma is used.

  The weather was hot and dry.
  He grabbed the ball and sent it flying.
  Larry was neither at third base nor at home plate.

- When clauses joined by a coordinating conjunction are short and closely connected, the comma is often omitted.

  Let's sit down and I'll dish out the food.

**PRACTICE 2**

## Insert Necessary Commas

In each of the following sentences, insert commas wherever they are needed. Check your answers against those in the Answer Key on p. 462.

1. The most overused bodies of water are our rivers but they continue to serve us daily.
2. Canadian cities often developed next to rivers and industries followed soon after in the same locations.
3. The people of the industrial age can try to clean the water they use or they can watch pollution take over.
4. The Great Lakes are showing signs of renewal yet the struggle against pollution there must continue.
5. Most people have not been educated about the dangerous state of our water supply nor are all our members of Parliament fully aware of the problem.

**RULE 3 ➤** **Use a comma to follow introductory material—words, expressions, phrases, or clauses that come before complete thoughts or independent clauses.**

The following are examples of introductory material:

A. Introductory words (such as *yes, no, oh, well*)

> Oh, I never thought he would do it.

B. Introductory expressions (transitions such as *as a matter of fact, finally, secondly, furthermore, consequently*). See the transitions chart on the inside back cover.

> Therefore, I will give you a second chance.

C. Introductory phrases. The comma signals the end of the introductory group of words and the beginning of the sentence proper.

> *Long prepositional phrase:* In the beginning of the course, I thought I would never be able to do the work.

Short prepositional phrases don't generally need to be followed by a comma. However, a comma is often used if the phrase ends with a date.

> At night I like to watch the stars.
> In 2001, a moderate earthquake hit the West Coast.

> *Participial phrase:* Walking on tiptoe, the young mother quietly peeked into the nursery.
>
> *Verbal phrase:* By walking daily, I lost weight. (Gerund)
> Confident of her skills, she entered the contest. (Participle)
> To be honest, I don't like it. (Infinitive)

D. Introductory dependent clauses beginning with a subordinating conjunction (see Chapter 5)

> When the food arrived, we all grabbed for it.

**PRACTICE 3**

## Insert Necessary Commas

In each of the following sentences, insert commas wherever they are needed. Check your answers against those in the Answer Key on p. 462.

1. A total solar eclipse when the moon's shadow blots out the sun completely is an outstanding cosmic event.
2. Once you see your first solar eclipse you start looking forward to the next one.
3. However witnessing this spectacle takes planning and the ability to travel to the best viewing spots.

4. In eastern Turkey on August 11 1999 a crowd of astronomers and "eclipse chasers" watched the last total eclipse of the millennium.
5. At the moment of totality people cheer clap and often cry.

**RULE 4 ➤** **Use commas surrounding a word, phrase, or clause when the word or group of words interrupts the main idea.**

Note the following examples of Rule 4:

A. Interrupting word

We will, however, take an X-ray.

B. Interrupting phrase

*Prepositional phrase:* I wanted, of course, to stay.
*Appositive phrase:* Ann, the girl with the red hair, has a wonderful sense of humour.

C. Interrupting clause

He won't, I think, try that again.

Words, phrases, or clauses that interrupt the main idea of a sentence can be *restrictive* or *nonrestrictive.*

A **restrictive** word, phrase, or clause is essential to the meaning of the sentence and is not set off by commas from the rest of the sentence.

The man with the red hat is my father.

Unless you specifically identify the man with the red hat, any number of unidentified men could be the father.

Author Timothy Findley said it takes failure to become a great writer.

Likewise, if the name *Timothy Findley* is not mentioned, the sentence above would make no sense.

A **nonrestrictive** word, phrase, or clause is not essential to the meaning of the sentence, and *is* set off by commas from the rest of the sentence. (See more on nonrestrictive and restrictive clauses on pp. 72–74 in Chapter 5: "Coordination and Subordination.")

Ann, who has red hair, has a wonderful sense of humour.

**TIP** **Some words can have more than one grammatical function.**

She came to the dance; however, she didn't stay long.

In this sentence, *however* is used to combine independent clauses and therefore requires a semicolon before it.

She did, however, have a good time.

In this sentence, *however* interrupts the main idea and therefore requires a comma before it and a comma after it (comma rule #4).

**TIP** **Some clauses can be used in different ways.**

Ann, who has red hair, has a wonderful sense of humour.

In this sentence, *who has red hair* interrupts the main idea of the sentence, and so commas are used.

The girl who has red hair is my sister Ann.

The clause *who has red hair* is part of the identity of "the girl." This clause does not interrupt the main idea but is necessary to and part of the main idea. Therefore, no commas are used.

**PRACTICE 4**

### Insert Necessary Commas

In each of the following sentences, insert commas wherever they are needed. Check your answers against those in the Answer Key on p. 463.

1. Natural disasters I believe have not been historically significant.
2. They have however significantly affected the lives of many Canadians.
3. Canada's worst coal-mine disaster at Hillcrest, Alberta occurred on June 19 1914.
4. In Springhill, Nova Scotia furthermore 424 persons were killed in the mines between 1881 and 1969.
5. Avalanches, storms, and floods which are natural disasters have also made their marks on the face of our country.

**RULE 5 ➤** **Use a comma to set apart or commas to surround a noun being directly addressed.**

Ali, can you help me with this problem?
I wonder, Michaela, if you really know what you're doing.

**PRACTICE 5**

### Insert Necessary Commas

In each of the following sentences, insert commas wherever they are needed. Check your answers against those in the Answer Key on p. 463.

1. Honey I hope you're not planning to wear that hat.
2. I wonder Samir if the game has been cancelled.
3. Dad could I borrow five dollars?

4. Can you help me Doctor?
5. Ayesha is that you?

**RULE 6 ➤** **Use a comma in numbers of 1,000 or larger for non-metric numbers.**

1,999
1,999,999,999

Note that in the metric system of measurement, spaces—not commas—are used in numbers of 1000 or larger. (However, numbers of four digits need not be separated.) This practice is becoming more widespread in Canada.

4000 or 4 000
38 622

**RULE 7 ➤** **Use a comma to set off exact words spoken in dialogue.**

"The pen," she said, "is mightier than the sword."

The comma, as well as the period, is always placed **inside** the closing quotation marks, as shown in the sentence above.

**PRACTICE 6**

## Insert Necessary Commas

In each of the following sentences, insert commas wherever they are necessary. Check your answers against those in the Answer Key on p. 463.

1. "I'm innocent" he cried "of all charges against me."
2. He mumbled "I won't incriminate myself."
3. "I was told" the defendant explained "to answer every question."
4. "This court" the judge announced "will be adjourned."
5. "The jury" said Al Tarvin of *The Star* "was handpicked."

**RULE 8 ➤** **Use a comma where it is necessary to prevent a misunderstanding.**

Before eating, the cat prowled through the barn.

**PRACTICE 7**

## Insert Necessary Commas

In each of the following sentences, insert commas wherever they are needed. Check your answers against those in the Answer Key on p. 463.

1. Kicking the child was carried off to bed.
2. To Maria Suzuki was the boss from hell.
3. When you can come and visit us.
4. Whoever that is is going to be surprised.
5. Skin cancer seldom kills doctors say.

Before trying the following exercises, here is a summary of rules for comma usage:

**The Eight Basic Rules of the Comma**

RULE 1: Use a comma to separate parallel words, phrases, and clauses in a list.
RULE 2: Use a comma before a coordinating conjunction that joins two complete thoughts or independent clauses. (See Chapter 5 on coordination and subordination.)
RULE 3: Use a comma to follow introductory words, expressions, phrases, or clauses that come before independent clauses or complete thoughts.
RULE 4: Use commas surrounding a word, phrase, or clause when the word or group of words interrupts the complete thought.
RULE 5: Use a comma around nouns in direct address.
RULE 6: Use a comma in numbers of 1,000 or larger for non-metric numbers (although this practice is decreasing in Canada).
RULE 7: Use a comma to set off exact words spoken in dialogue.
RULE 8: Use a comma where it is necessary to prevent a misunderstanding.

**EXERCISE 1**

## Insert Necessary Commas

In each of the following sentences, insert commas wherever they are needed.

1. Fog-water collection is a relatively simple way to supply water to certain areas where water is scarce or polluted.
2. The collectors with screens made of a fine polypropylene mesh look like big volleyball nets.
3. The tiny water droplets which are blown sideways by the wind hit the screen and run down into a trough.
4. In El Tofo Chile 88 fog collectors supply clean water to the fishing village of Chungungo.
5. The El Tofo system on a high coastal ridge is the largest project so far.
6. Amazingly these collectors channel 13 000 litres of water per day to the village.
7. Once almost a ghost town Chungungo now boasts homes with running water and lush gardens.

**EXERCISE 2**

## Insert Necessary Commas

In each of the following sentences, insert commas wherever they are needed.

1. The first games known as the British Empire Games attracted 400 competitors from eleven countries.
2. The Commonwealth Games were first held in Hamilton Ontario in 1930.
3. By 1978 during the Commonwealth Games in Edmonton nearly 1500 athletes from 41 countries competed.
4. Canada has been a leading supporter of these games which are held every four years.
5. Memorable performances feats by both Canadian and non-Canadian athletes have become a hallmark of the games.

6. In Edmonton Canadian athletes won 45 gold 31 silver and 33 bronze medals in 1978.
7. Next to the Olympics the Commonwealth Games are one of the world's best international competitions.

## Other Marks of Punctuation

### The Apostrophe

The apostrophe has three uses:

1. Possession
2. Contraction
3. Avoiding confusion

| | |
|---|---|
| **RULE 1 ➤** | **To form the possessive, add *'s* or just an apostrophe.** |

With respect to Rule 1, note the following points and examples.

A. Add *'s* to singular nouns:

the pen of the teacher = the teacher*'s* pen
the strategy of the boss = the boss*'s* strategy

Be careful to choose the right noun to make possessive. Always ask yourself *who* or *what* possesses something. In the phrases above, the teacher possesses the pen and the boss possesses the strategy.

**TIP** **As a rule, nouns that are inanimate things should not be in the possessive. Use a phrase with *of* instead.**

*Examples:* the leg of the table (NOT the table's leg)
the smell of the sewer (NOT the sewer's smell)
the noise of the cars (NOT the cars' noise)

In common expressions that refer to time and measurements and in phrases suggesting personification, possessives are more and more acceptable:

a stone's throw
two weeks' vacation
New Year's resolution

Note these unusual possessives:

*Hyphenated words:* mother-in-law's advice
*Joint possession:* Rita and Ashley's television special
*Individual possession:* John's and Steve's ideas

B. Add *'s* to irregular plural nouns that do not end in *-s*.

the hats of the children = the children*'s* hats
the harness for the oxen = the oxen*'s* harness

C. Add *'s* to indefinite pronouns:

everyone*'s* responsibility
somebody*'s* wallet

**Indefinite Pronouns**

| | | | |
|---|---|---|---|
| anyone | everyone | no one | someone |
| anybody | everybody | nobody | somebody |
| anything | everything | nothing | something |

**TIP**

**Possessive pronouns in English (*his, hers, its, ours, yours, theirs, whose*) do *not* use an apostrophe.**

*Whose* phone is this?
The phone is *his*.
The car is *theirs*.

D. Add only an apostrophe to regular plural nouns ending in *-s*.

the nests of the hornets = the hornet*s'* nests
the store of the brothers = the brother*s'* store

**TIP**

**A few singular nouns ending in the *s* or *z* sound are awkward-sounding if another *s* sound is added. You may, in these cases, drop the final *s*. Let your ear help you make the decision, and be consistent with your choice.**

Jones' car or Jones's car

**RULE 2 ➤** **To show where letters have been omitted in contractions, use an apostrophe.**

cannot = can't
should not = shouldn't
will not = won't (the only contraction that changes its spelling)
I am = I'm
she will = she'll
it is/it has = it's

*Note:* The word *its* (without the apostrophe) is a possessive adjective.

The dog buried its bone.

**RULE 3 ➤** **To form certain plurals in order to prevent confusion, use *'s*.**

*Numbers:* 100's
*Letters:* a's and b's
*Years:* 1800's or 1800s
*Abbreviations:* Ph.D.'s
*Words referred to in text:* He uses too many *and*'s in his writing.

Be sure *not* to use the apostrophe to form a plural in any case other than these types.

Here is a reminder of the uses and rules of the apostrophe:

**The Three Rules of the Apostrophe**

RULE 1: To form the possessive, add *'s* or just an apostrophe.
RULE 2: To show where letters have been omitted in contractions, use an apostrophe.
RULE 3: To form certain plurals in order to prevent confusion, use *'s*.

**PRACTICE 1**

## Using the Apostrophe

Fill in each of the blanks below using the rules you have just studied for uses of the apostrophe. Check your answers against those in the Answer Key on p. 463.

1. shirts for boys ______________ shirts
2. the house of them ______________ house
3. the bakery of Grandpa Moses ______________ bakery
4. the house of Antony and Maria (joint possession) ______________ house
5. the idea of nobody ______________ idea
6. The book belongs to him. The book is ______________.
7. in the century of 1700 in the ______________
8. It is their choice. ______________ their choice.
9. the nightlife of Vancouver ______________ nightlife
10. the dress of Wendy ______________ dress

**PRACTICE 2**

## Using the Apostrophe

Fill in each of the blanks below using the rules you have just studied for uses of the apostrophe. Check your answers against those in the Answer Key on p. 463.

1. the voice of Don Cherry ______________ voice
2. the flight of the geese the ______________ flight
3. the jackets of Carol and Tess (individual possession) ______________ jackets
4. the CD of somebody ______________ CD
5. The drums belong to her. The drums are ______________.
6. the terrible year of two the terrible ______________
7. We cannot leave yet. We ______________ leave yet.

**EXERCISE 1**

## Using the Apostrophe

Fill in each of the blanks below using the rules you have just studied for uses of the apostrophe.

1. the ice cream of Ben and Jerry ______________ ice cream
2. the spirit of the class the ______________ spirit
3. the centre for women the ______________ centre
4. the wish of everybody ______________ wish
5. The ideas belong to them. The ideas are ______________.
6. The student mixes up *b* and *d*. The student mixes up his ______________.
7. I will not leave this house. I ______________ leave this house.
8. the revenue of the company the ______________ revenue
9. the paw of the doggie the ______________ paw
10. the policies of Ridge School and Orchard School (individual possession) ______________ policies

**EXERCISE 2**

## Using the Apostrophe

Add apostrophes where necessary in the following passage:

> Isnt it true that more people in Canada are concerned about the environment? When Canadians were asked to identify the worst problems facing their country today, 13 percent cited the environment as the top issue. The issue of health

> care still tops environmental concerns with 16 percent polled. Its clear that the environment is growing in importance in the eyes of Canadas people, as the percentage of people citing it as the main concern has increased four points since the federal election in early 2006. The percentage was even lower (closer to 3 percent) in the late 1990s.

**EXERCISE 3**

### Using the Apostrophe

Add apostrophes where necessary in the following passage:

> Many college and university students dont accept the fact that theyll be faced with a huge debt when they graduate. Many have part-time jobs, even if they cant see making careers out of these positions, and wont accept anything less than an opportunity to gain experience for future employment situations. While students attitudes are changing, however, students education is still more important than their eventual debt load.

## Quotation Marks

Use quotation marks as follows:

**RULE 1 ➤** **Use quotation marks for a direct quotation (a speaker's exact words).**

> "Please," he begged, "don't go away."

Do not use quotation marks for an indirect quotation (one person's idea put into someone else's words):

> He begged her to stay.

**RULE 2 ➤** **Use quotation marks for material copied word for word from a source.**

> According to Statistics Canada, "Families or individuals spending 58.5 percent or more of their pre-tax income on food, clothing, and shelter are in financial difficulty."

**RULE 3 ➤** **Use quotation marks for titles of shorter works such as short stories, one-act plays, poems, articles in magazines and newspapers, songs, essays, and chapters of books.**

> "A Modest Proposal," an essay by Jonathan Swift, is a masterpiece of satire.
> Mavis Gallant wrote the short story "In Youth Is Pleasure" in 1975.

**TIP**

**Titles of longer works such as novels, full-length plays, and names of magazines or newspapers are underlined when handwritten. When word-processed or published, these titles appear in italics: *Maclean's* magazine, *Country Living*.**

**RULE 4 ➤** **Use quotation marks for words used in a special way.**

"Duckie" is a term of affection used by the British, the way Canadians would use the word "honey."

Here is a summary of rules for quotation mark usage:

| The Four Basic Rules of Quotation Marks |
|---|
| RULE 1: Use quotation marks for a direct quotation. |
| RULE 2: Use quotation marks for material copied word for word from a source. |
| RULE 3: Use quotation marks for titles of shorter works such as short stories, one-act plays, poems, articles in magazines and newspapers, songs, essays, and chapters of books. |
| RULE 4: Use quotation marks for words used in a special way. |

**PRACTICE 1**

### Insert Necessary Quotation Marks

In each of the following sentences, insert quotation marks wherever they are needed. Check your answers against those in the Answer Key on p. 463.

1. The Hot House is one of the stories contained in Rosemary Sullivan's *More Stories by Canadian Women.*
2. Nellie McClung said I'll never believe I'm dead until I see it in the papers.
3. The prime minister told his caucus that they would have to settle the problem in the next few days.
4. To diss is a slang term meaning to show disrespect.
5. She read the article Whiz Kids in *The Review.*

If these five sentences were handwritten or typed, which words would have to be underlined?

## The Semicolon

Use the semicolon as follows:

**RULE 1 ➤** **Use a semicolon to join two independent clauses (or complete thoughts) whose ideas and sentence structure are related.**

He decided to consult the map; she decided to ask the next pedestrian she saw.

**RULE 2 ➤** **Use a semicolon to combine two sentences using an adverbial conjunction.**

He decided to consult the map; however, she decided to ask the next pedestrian she saw.

**RULE 3 ➤** **Use a semicolon to separate items in a list when the items themselves contain commas.**

I had lunch with Linda, my best friend; Mrs. Zhangi, my English teacher; and Jan, my sister-in-law.

Notice in the last example that if only commas had been used, the reader might think six people had gone to lunch.

**PRACTICE 2**

### Using Semicolons

In each of the following sentences, insert a semicolon wherever one is needed. Check your answers against those in the Answer Key on p. 463.

1. One of the best ways to remember a vacation is to take numerous photos one of the best ways to recall the contents of a book is to take notes.
2. The problem of street crime must be solved, otherwise, the number of vigilantes will increase.
3. The meal was composed of bruschetta, an appetizer, roast duck, the house specialty, and lemon mousse, a tart dessert.
4. The bank president was very cordial, however, he would not approve the loan.
5. New methods of production are being used in the factories of Japan eventually they will be common in this country as well.

## The Colon

Use the colon as follows:

**RULE 1 ➤** **Use a colon after a complete thought (or independent clause) when the material that follows is a list, an illustration, or an explanation.**

A. A list

Please order the following items: five dozen pencils, 20 rulers, and five rolls of tape.

Notice that no colon is used when there is not a complete sentence before the colon:

> The courses I am taking this semester are English Composition, Introduction to Psychology, Art Appreciation, and Survey of Canadian Literature.

B. An illustration or explanation

> She was an exceptional child: at seven she was performing on the concert stage.

| RULE 2 ➤ | **Use a colon following the salutation of a business letter.** |
|---|---|

> To whom it may concern:
> Dear Madam President:

| RULE 3 ➤ | **Use a colon in telling time.** |
|---|---|

> We will eat at 5:15.

| RULE 4 ➤ | **Use a colon between the title and subtitle of a book, article, essay, etc.** |
|---|---|

> *Plain English Please: A Rhetoric*
> "Hemingway: His Foreshadowed Suicide"

**PRACTICE 3**

## Using Colons

In each of the following sentences, insert colons wherever they are needed. Check your answers against those in the Answer Key on p. 463.

1. Two Canadian-born comedians have achieved great success in the United States Jim Carrey and Mike Myers.
2. The official has one major flaw in his personality greed.
3. The restaurant has lovely homemade desserts such as German chocolate layer cake and baked Alaska.
4. The college offers four courses in English literature Romantic Poetry, Shakespeare's Plays, The British Short Story, and The Modern Novel.
5. Arriving at 615 in the morning, Marlene brought me a sausage-and-cheese pizza, ginger ale, and a litre of ice cream.

## The Hyphen

Use the hyphen as follows:

**RULE 1 ➤** **Use a hyphen with two or more words that go together before the noun to act as one adjective.**

I am a second-year student.
She is a well-known actor.

**TIP** **If the group of words that describes the noun comes after the noun, do not use a hyphen.**

The actor is well known.

**TIP** **If the group of words contains an *-ly* adverb, do not hyphenate.**

The dimly lit diner closed every night at eleven.

**RULE 2 ➤** **Use a hyphen at the end of a line to divide a word between syllables.**

Make sure you divide the word at the right place. Check a dictionary if you're not sure. Otherwise, avoid splitting words altogether. Never split a one-syllable word.

When Farah saw her boyfriend kissing another woman, she walked away from him for good.

**RULE 3 ➤** **Hyphens are used in some compound words.**

Other compound words are not hyphenated. There is no rule to determine which is which. Use a dictionary to make the right decision. Where there is disagreement between dictionaries, pick one spelling and be consistent in your own writing.

The following are word spellings upon which all dictionaries agree:

| | |
|---|---|
| father-in-law | hairbrush |
| trade-in | stepmother |

**RULE 4 ➤** **Use hyphens with two-word numbers from twenty-one to ninety-nine.**

thirty-seven
seventy-three

| **RULE 5 ➤** | **Use hyphens in words that contain the prefixes *self, ex,* and *all*; prefixes that are followed by proper nouns; and the suffix *elect.*** |
|---|---|

self-respect, self-confidence
ex-husband, ex-police officer
all-Canadian cast
anti-Catholic
Premier-elect Dalton McGuinty

**EXERCISE**

### Inserting Hyphens Where Necessary

In each of the following sentences, insert a hyphen wherever it is necessary.

1. The students in third year weren't in class today, but all the second year students were.
2. Kelly caught the ball in her baseball glove despite its war torn appearance.
3. The all American company of actors was scared to come to Canada because of SARS.
4. Her low self esteem caused her to stay with her husband despite the repeated beatings he inflicted on her.
5. The widely acclaimed impressionist painter received a standing ovation before he accepted his 32 thousand dollar cheque.
6. Julia's forty four year old ex boyfriend returned all thirty three compact discs she had borrowed when she was enrolled in her postgraduate university program.
7. Faisal bought the all purpose cleaner that his mother in law recommended when he and his wife were still a happily married couple.

## The Dash and Parentheses

Like the comma, both the dash and parentheses can be used to show an interruption of the main idea. The particular form you choose depends on the degree of interruption.

| **RULE 1 ➤** | **Use the dash for a less formal and more emphatic interruption of the main idea.** |
|---|---|

He came—I thought—by car.
She arrived—and I know this for a fact—in a pink Cadillac.
I could see you this weekend—for example, Saturday.

**RULE 2 ➤** **Use a dash before such words as *all, these,* and *they* when these words summarize a preceding list of details.**

Periods, commas, colons, semicolons, dashes, hyphens, and quotation marks—all these tiny marks among words have incredible power over their meaning and ultimate effectiveness.

**RULE 3 ➤** **Use parentheses to insert extra information that some of your readers might want to know, but that is not essential to the main idea. Such information is not emphasized.**

Timothy Findley (1930–2002) wrote *The Wars.*
Plea-bargaining (see page 28) was developed to expedite court verdicts.

**PRACTICE**

### Using Dashes or Parentheses

In each of the following sentences, insert dashes or parentheses wherever they are needed. Check your answers against those in the Answer Key on p. 464.

1. Herbert Simon is and I don't think this is an exaggeration a genius.
2. George Eliot her real name was Mary Ann Evans wrote *Silas Marner.*
3. You should in fact I insist see a doctor.
4. Health Canada's website has suggestions to help smokers quit visit www.infotobacco.com.
5. Mass media television, radio, movies, magazines, and newspapers are able to transmit information over a wide range and to a large number of people.

## Chapter Review Exercises

**PRACTICE 1**

### Punctuation Overview

In each of the following sentences, insert marks of punctuation wherever they are needed. Check your answers against those in the Answer Key on p. 464.

1. To measure crime, sociologists have used three different techniques official statistics, victimization surveys, and self-report studies.
2. David is one of the best-loved poems of Earle Birney.
3. That show uses one thing I hate a laugh track.
4. Farley Mowat has written numerous books for adults however, he also writes very popular books for children.
5. Tuberculosis also known as consumption has been nearly eliminated by medical science.
6. The Victorian Period 1837–1901 saw a rapid expansion in industry.
7. He told me I remember the day that he would never give up.

PRACTICE 2

## Punctuation Overview

In each of the following sentences, insert marks of punctuation wherever they are needed. Check your answers against those in the Answer Key on p. 464.

1. Many young people have two feelings about science and technology awe and fear.
2. Mr. Doyle the realtor Mrs. Tong the bank officer and Ivan Petroff the lawyer are the three people to help work out the real-estate transaction.
3. The book was entitled English Literature The Victorian Age.
4. My computer, she said, has been crashing all day.
5. She brought a bathing suit, towel, sunglasses, and several books to the beach.
6. The meeting to discuss a pay increase I'll believe it when I see it has been rescheduled for Friday.
7. The complex lab experiment has these two major problems too many difficult calculations and too many variables.

EXERCISE 1

## Editing for Correct Punctuation

Read the paragraph below, and insert the following marks of punctuation wherever they are needed:

a. commas to separate items in a series
b. comma with coordinating conjunction to combine sentences
c. comma after introductory words, phrases, or clauses
d. commas around words that interrupt main idea
e. comma to set off spoken words
f. parentheses
g. quotation marks
h. lines under titles of full-length works of art
i. semicolon
j. apostrophe

Tom Thomson 1877–1917 is often remembered as the artist of Canada's North. He was born on August 4 1877 near Leith Ontario. During the twenties Thomson apprenticed as a machinist enrolled in business college and then spent a few years in Seattle working as an engraver. In 1906 he took art lessons and first used oil paint. His first important painting done in 1917 and titled A Northern Lake was sold for $250 a great deal of money in those days. Thomson led the vanguard of a new movement in Canadian art. One reviewer said Thomson paints a world of phenomena of colour and of form which will not be touched by another artist. Thomson drowned at Canoe Lake Algonquin Park July 8 1917. Among his many works are Ottawa by Moonlight Autumn's Garland and Jackpine.

## EXERCISE 2 Editing for Correct Punctuation

Read the following paragraph, and insert the following marks of punctuation wherever they are needed:

a. commas to separate items in a series
b. comma with coordinating conjunction to combine sentences
c. comma after introductory words, phrases, or clauses
d. commas around words that interrupt main idea
e. comma in numbers of 1000 or larger
f. parentheses
g. quotation marks
h. lines under titles of full-length works of art
i. semicolon
j. colon
k. apostrophe

Albert Schweitzer was a brilliant German philosopher physician musician clergyman missionary and writer on theology. Early in his career he based his philosophy on what he called reverence for life. He felt a deep sense of obligation to serve humanity. His accomplishments as a humanitarian were great consequently he was awarded the Nobel Peace Prize in 1952. Before Schweitzer was 30 he had won an international reputation as a writer on theology as an organist and authority on organ building as an interpreter of the works of Johann Sebastian Bach and as an authority on Bachs life. When he became inspired to become a medical missionary he studied medicine at the university in Strasbourg Germany. He began his work in French Equatorial Africa now called Gabon in 1913 where his first consulting room was a chicken coop. Over the years he built a large hospital where thousands of Africans were treated yearly. He used his $33 000 Nobel Prize money to expand the hospital and set up a leper colony in fact he even designed all the buildings. One of Schweitzers many famous books which you might like to find in the library is entitled Out of My Life and Thought. His accomplishments were so many music medicine scholarship theology and service to humanity.

## Working Together: Designing Punctuation Tests

Work with a group of your classmates. Each group in the class will make up an exam to test the other students' knowledge of punctuation. From any book, choose a paragraph that uses a variety of punctuation. Have one person from the group carefully write out or type the paragraph without its punctuation. Then make enough copies so a group or the entire class can take the test. Is your test a fair one? Is it too easy or too hard? Does it cover the material studied in this chapter?

CHAPTER TWELVE

12

# Capitalization

**QUICK QUIZ**

Test yourself on your knowledge of capitalization. Correct any errors of capitalization in the following sentences. Answers are upside down in the margin.

1. I am hoping to go to the University in British Columbia in the fall, but if I can't, I'll have more money to spend at christmas.
2. My Doctor's appointment this afternoon is with doctor Shari Mohammed.
3. The pacific ocean is beautiful at Sunset.
4. I told the umpire, "you don't know the rules of baseball any more than grandma does!"
5. Sam and i have travelled through the rockies by Train three times now, for they are absolutely breathtaking.

**Answers:**
1. university, Christmas
2. doctor's, Doctor (or Dr.)
3. Pacific Ocean, sunset
4. You, Grandma
5. I, Rockies, train

Many students are often confused or careless about the use of capital letters. Sometimes they capitalize words without thinking, or they capitalize "important" words without really understanding what makes them important enough to deserve a capital letter. The question of when to capitalize words becomes easier to answer when you study the following rules and carefully apply them to your own writing.

## Ten Basic Rules for Capitalization

| | |
|---|---|
| **RULE 1 ➤** | **Capitalize the first word of every sentence.** |

| | |
|---|---|
| **RULE 2 ➤** | **Capitalize the names of specific things and places.** |

Specific buildings

I went to the Jamestown Post Office.

*but*

I went to the post office.

Specific streets, cities, provinces, states, countries

She lives on Elam Avenue.

*but*

She lives on the same street as my mom and dad.

Specific organizations

He collected money for the Canadian Cancer Society.

*but*

Janice joined more than one club at the school.

Specific institutions

The loan is from the Royal Bank of Canada.

*but*

The loan is from one of the banks in town.

Specific bodies of water

My uncle fishes every summer on Lake Winnipeg.

*but*

My uncle spends every summer at the lake.

**RULE 3 ➤** **Capitalize days of the week, months of the year, and holidays. Do *not* capitalize the names of seasons.**

The second Monday in October is Thanksgiving Day.

*but*

I cannot wait until spring.

**RULE 4 ➤** **Capitalize the names of all languages, nationalities, races, religions, deities, and sacred terms.**

My friend who is Ethiopian speaks very little English.
The *Koran* is the sacred book of Islam.

**RULE 5 ➤** **In a title, capitalize the first word, the last word, and every other word *except* articles, prepositions, and coordinating conjunctions (*for, and, nor, but, or, yet,* and *so*—FANBOYS).**

"Recognizing Subjects and Verbs" and "Revising and Editing" are chapters in the textbook *The Canadian Writer's Workplace.*

**RULE 6 ➤** **Capitalize the first word of a direct quotation.**

The teacher said, "You have been chosen for the part."

*but*

"You have been chosen," she said, "for the part."

*Note: for* is not capitalized because it is not the beginning of the sentence in quotation marks.

**RULE 7 ➤** **Capitalize historical events, periods, and documents.**

the Rebellion of 1837
the Great Depression
the *Canadian Charter of Rights and Freedoms*

**RULE 8 ➤** **Capitalize the words *north, south, east,* and *west* when they are used as places rather than as directions.**

He comes from the East.

*but*

The farm is about 40 kilometres west of Weyburn.

**RULE 9 ➤** **Capitalize people's names.**

Proper names

George Hendrickson

Professional titles when they immediately precede the person's proper name

| | | |
|---|---|---|
| Judge Samuelson | *but* | the judge |
| Professor Shapiro | *but* | the professor |

- Do not capitalize a title if it follows the name:

  George Shapiro, professor of English

Term for a relative (like *mother, sister, nephew, uncle*) when it is used in the place of the proper name

I told Grandfather I would meet him later.

- Notice that terms for relatives are not capitalized if a pronoun, article, or adjective is used with the name.

  I told my grandfather I would meet him later.

**RULE 10 ➤** **Capitalize brand names.**

Band-Aid
Kleenex

*Band-Aid* and *Kleenex* are product names and therefore are proper nouns.

Here is a summary of the rules for capitalization:

| The Ten Rules for Capitalization |
|---|
| RULE 1: Capitalize the first word of every sentence. |
| RULE 2: Capitalize the names of specific things and places. |
| RULE 3: Capitalize days of the week, months of the year, and holidays. Do *not* capitalize the names of seasons. |
| RULE 4: Capitalize the names of all languages, nationalities, races, religions, deities, and sacred terms. |
| RULE 5: In a title, capitalize the first word, the last word, and every other word except articles, prepositions, and coordinating conjunctions (FANBOYS). |
| RULE 6: Capitalize the first word of a direct quotation. |
| RULE 7: Capitalize historical events, periods, and documents. |
| RULE 8: Capitalize the words *north, south, east,* and *west* when they are used as places rather than as directions. |
| RULE 9: Capitalize people's names. |
| RULE 10: Capitalize brand names. |

**PRACTICE**

## Capitalization

Capitalize wherever it is necessary. Check your answers against those in the Answer Key on p. 464.

1. The italian student got a job in the school cafeteria.
2. Our train ride through the canadian rockies was fabulous.
3. The author often made references in his writing to names from the bible.
4. A student at the university of alberta was chosen for the national award.
5. My uncle's children always have a party on hallowe'en.
6. I met the president of bell canada last friday at a convention in winnipeg, manitoba.
7. The cobalt-60 cancer therapy unit was invented by a canadian, dr. donald green.
8. My niece said, "why don't you consider moving farther south if you hate the winter so much?"
9. The canadian auto workers voted not to go on strike over the new contract.
10. The book *women of the klondike* tells the story of the late-1890s gold rush in the north.

**EXERCISE**

## Capitalization

Capitalize wherever it is necessary. Put in lower case any capital letters that are incorrect.

1. Some people think the Cabot trail on Cape Breton island is the most spectacular drive on the North American Continent.
2. I'm taking five courses right now, but math 101 is my favourite.
3. I love the Text called *Canadian Writer's workplace*; I've already read 20 of 28 Chapters.
4. Morris C. Shumiatcher is a Lawyer and Civil Rights Spokesperson who graduated from the University Of Calgary.
5. George Orwell wrote the novel *nineteen eighty-four* about a Government that punishes its people for thinking certain thoughts.
6. Born in Bombay, India, Writer Rohinton Mistry was raised in that City's Parsi Community.
7. The black honda accord and the white ford escape have collided at the Intersection of Chapel street and Bakersville avenue.
8. "I feel your pain," wrote rabbi Wittstein of Temple Israel of london to the muslim community, "And offer you whatever understanding, sympathy and anger I possess ..."
9. Roman Polanski won an oscar for best director in 2002, but was unable to receive the award in person because if he enters the United States, he would be arrested for statutory rape.
10. Socrates was a greek teacher who is considered one of the founders of western philosophy.

## Working Together: Designing Capitalization Tests

Work with a group of your classmates. Each group in the class will make up an exam to test the other students' knowledge of capitalization. From any book, choose a paragraph that uses a variety of capitalization. Have one person from the group carefully write out or type the paragraph without its capitalization. Then make enough copies so a group or the entire class can take the test. Is your test a fair one? Is it too easy or too hard? Does it cover the material studied in this chapter?

CHAPTER THIRTEEN

13

# Unit I Review: Using All You Have Learned

In this chapter of review practices and exercises, you have the opportunity to test yourself on the material in Unit I. Revisit any point of grammar that you know you need to work on a little more. If, for example, you find that you haven't quite understood how to use a semicolon correctly, then it would be a good idea to revisit Chapter 5 ("Coordination and Subordination"), Chapter 7 ("Correcting Run-ons"), and Chapter 11 ("Punctuation"). The index at the back of the book provides a quick reference if you can't find what you're looking for right away.

Often we think that if we can already speak the language to the extent that most people seem to understand what we're saying, we wonder why, then, it is necessary to learn to write so perfectly. When we speak, especially on informal occasions (which is most of the time), we get away with making mistakes every day. We neither check the grammar of those to whom we speak, nor do they check ours. When someone says, "Lunch?" we know what he or she means, and we don't stop to think, "That wasn't a complete sentence." But when we write, especially in formal situations such as those we encounter in our professional lives, we will not so easily get away with making the same types of errors. The extent to which we communicate properly will in part determine how far we go in meeting our professional goals.

Mastering any language is an ongoing process. And this textbook certainly doesn't cover everything there is to know about the English language. Nevertheless, it covers a great deal. So you might want to keep it on your shelf as a reference tool even after your course is finished. That way, if ever you forget why you're supposed to use *whom* instead of *who*, this textbook will always be there for the reminding.

## Editing Sentences for Errors

In the following exercises, you will find all the types of grammatical and mechanical problems that you have studied so far:

| | |
|---|---|
| Fragments | Incorrect pronouns |
| Run-ons | Unparallel structure |

| | |
|---|---|
| Incorrect punctuation | Incorrect capitalization |
| Subject-verb disagreement | Misplaced and dangling modifiers |

**PRACTICE 1**

## Identifying Parts of Speech

Read the following paragraphs taken from Rosemary Ellen Guiley's book *Dreamwork for the Soul.* Identify the part of speech (as specifically as you can) for each underlined word. Feel free to refer back to Chapter 1 ("Parts of Speech: Overview") for help with this exercise. The index at the back of the textbook can help for easy reference. Check your answers against those in the Answer Key on p. 464.

The first one is done for you.

> (Carl G.) Jung's dreams① were a constant② source of③ creativity and④ inspiration to him⑤. Dreams inspired⑥ his study of archaeology and mythology, and later alchemy. Throughout⑦ his life, as he developed his⑧ ideas, Jung was⑨ aided and guided by dreams. When⑩ he searched for answers to questions, dreams often⑪ led him in the⑫ right⑬ direction....
>
> Three days before he died, Jung had⑭ the last of his visionary dreams and a portent of his own impending⑮ death. In the dream, he had become⑯ whole. A⑰ significant symbol was tree roots interlaced with gold, the alchemical symbol⑱ of completion....
>
> The story of Jung's life can be properly⑲ understood only⑳ from his inner experiences. The experiences of the outer㉑ world were pale and thin by comparison for㉒ him. He㉓ said he could㉔ understand himself only in the light of his inner happenings.㉕

Answer: *dreams*: common noun

**PRACTICE 2**

## Editing Sentences for Errors

The following examples contain several types of errors studied in Unit I. If you think the example is a complete and correct sentence, mark it with a *C*. If the example has an error, correct it. More than one correct answer is possible for each example. Check your answers against those in the Answer Key on p. 465. An example is done for you.

***Incorrect:*** A group of Roma people who now live in Ireland.

***Correct:*** A group of Roma people now live in Ireland.

*or*

A group of Roma people, who now live in Ireland, make their living by repairing pots and pans.

1. Roma (also known as Gypsies or Romany Gypsies) now living in many countries of the world.

2. The international community of scientists agree that these Roma originally came from India thousands of years ago.

3. After the original Roma people left India they went to Persia there they divided into groups.

4. One branch of Roma went West to Europe the other group decided to go East.

5. In the middle ages (476–1453), some Roma people lived in a fertile area of Greece called little egypt.

6. Roma often found it hard to gain acceptance in many countries because of their wandering lifestyle.

7. Today Roma families may be found from Canada to Chile living much as his ancestors did thousands of years ago.

**PRACTICE 3**

## Editing Sentences for Errors

The following examples contain sentence errors studied in Unit I. If you think an example is a complete and correct sentence, mark it with a *C.* If the example has an error, correct it. More than one correct answer is possible for each example. An example is done for you. Check your answers against those in the Answer Key on p. 465.

***Incorrect:*** Science fiction writers have imagined magic rays that can destroy entire cities, but in recent years a magic ray in the form of laser beams have become scientific fact.

***Correct:*** Science fiction writers have imagined magic rays that can destroy entire cities, but in recent years a magic ray in the form of laser beams has become scientific fact.

1. The laser beam a miracle of modern science already has many practical uses in today's world.

_______________

_______________

2. Laser beams are narrow, highly concentrated beams of light that burns brighter than the light of the sun.

_______________

_______________

3. Scientists have found many possible military uses for the laser, but they are hoping it can be converted into constructive uses.

_______________

_______________

4. John Polanyi, Canadian winner of the 1986 Nobel Prize for chemistry, conducted early experiments on the use of lasers.

_______________

_______________

5. The possibility of making a laser was first described in 1958 and two years later in California the first laser beam was created.

_______________

_______________

6. Since they are so precise, laser beams are used in medicine to help make a specific diagnosis and to perform operations such as repairing delicate retinas and the removal of cancerous tumours.

_______________

7. The future uses of the laser seems endless, and it is up to us to decide whether we want to use this invention for war or for peaceful purposes.

_______________

_______________

**EXERCISE 1**

## Editing Sentences for Errors

The following examples contain sentence errors studied in Unit I. If you think an example is a complete and correct sentence, mark it with a *C*. If the example has an error, correct it. More than one correct answer is possible for each example. An example is done for you.

***Incorrect:*** Frostbite an injury to the skin and underlying tissues is a serious danger in very cold weather.

***Correct:*** Frostbite, an injury to the skin and underlying tissues, is a serious danger in very cold weather.

1. A common threat to outdoor adventurers frostbite can strike anyone who is not adequately protected against the cold.

2. Risk factors are of three types exposure, faulty judgment, and underlying medical conditions.

3. Ice crystals in the skin possibly starting to form at –6°C.

4. Symptoms of frostbite includes: cold numbness and a feeling of clumsiness or heaviness in the affected part of the body.

5. The first thing to do is find a warm shelter and remove any wet clothing.

6. Prevention measures includes wearing proper clothing, educating yourself about weather conditions, and awareness of risk factors.

7. Frostbite injury which gets worse with time should be treated immediately.

**EXERCISE 2**

## Making Sentence Parts Work Together

Each of the following sentences has a part that does not work with the rest of the sentence. Find the error and correct it. There may be more than one correct answer for each sentence.

1. Two Statistics Canada studies, which have been reported recently on the CBC television network, links stress and obesity now and health problems later in life.

______________________________

______________________________

2. Suffering from stress and obesity, the researchers found that Canadians will probably suffer major health problems as soon as six years later.

______________________________

______________________________

3. People who suffer from stress and obesity become a perfect candidate for health problems such as arthritis and rheumatism, chronic bronchitis or emphysema, and stomach or intestinal ulcers.

______________________________

______________________________

4. One study shows that for men, diseases also include heart disease, and for a woman, asthma and migraine.

______________________________

______________________________

5. According to one of the studies, stress in men appeared to be worse where economic issues are concerned: job loss, demotions and taking pay cuts, for example.

______________________________

______________________________

6. An obese adult's chance of suffering from arthritis is 60 percent higher than an adult who is not obese.

______________________________

______________________________

7. They say stress goes down with age and up in low-income people.

______________________________

______________________________

## Editing Paragraphs for Errors

### EXERCISE 1 Making Sentence Parts Work Together

Read the following paragraph. Look for errors in agreement, for lack of parallel structure, and for misplaced or dangling modifiers, and then rewrite your corrected version. More than one correct answer is possible.

Cowboys became important in the United States after the American Civil War who lived on large ranches in Texas, Montana, and other western states. Canada, too, had its cowboys working on ranches on the prairies. One of the traditional names for cowboys are "cowpokes" although they prefer to be called "cowhands." The equipment for cowboys came into use because of his many practical needs. The wide-brimmed cowboy hat served as a bucket to hold water, as a sort of whip to drive cattle, and waving to other cowboys a few hills away. Cowboys began to wear tight trousers because they did not want loose pants to catch in bushes as they chased cattle. The rope is a cowboy's most important tool since they use it to catch cattle, pull wagons, tie up equipment, and even killing snakes. The famous roundup, which takes place twice a year, are important because cattle are separated, classified, and selected for market. When cowboys get together for such a roundup, they often hold a rodeo as a celebration. Rodeos give cowboys opportunities to compete in riding bareback, wrestling steer, and to rope calves. The Calgary Stampede is the modern result of these rodeos.

### EXERCISE 2 Editing Paragraphs for Errors

Correct all the punctuation and grammatical errors in the following paragraph. More than one correct answer is possible.

Once upon a time whenever I tried to make my writing interesting and imaginative with all sorts of similes and metaphors and colourful language I forgot about my grammar and spelling my essays were full of sentence fragments comma splices and run-ons moreover my syntax was always scrambled even I had trouble figuring out what I had intended to say originally although I could tell that I had started with brilliant ideas help has finally arrived however since I have done all the exercises in my grammar book I now have perfect command of English grammar whereas one time I bit my nails when I handed in an assignment I worry no more no longer do I need to worry about essays being handed back bleeding to death after being savaged by some sadistic English teacher wielding his or her red pen no longer will my sleep be curtailed by hours of tedious rewrites moreover from now on I'm expecting straight As all the way.

**EXERCISE 3**

## Editing Paragraphs for Errors

Correct all the punctuation, capitalization, and grammatical errors in the following paragraphs. More than one correct answer is possible.

Sleep is one of those things you never think about. As long as you're getting your full 40 winks at night. As soon as a bout of insomnia hits though sleep is the only thing on your mind. The ancient greeks had a god of sleep called hypnos who could appear as a bird, child, or friendly warrior those images don't suggest sleep to modern people though we prefer fields of sheep and mr. sandman.

Since the greeks scientists have made much progress in unravelling the secrets of sleep but many mysteries remain. They can't explain for example exactly how we fall asleep. Or wake up. Or what dreams are. However they know a lot about insomnia and other sleep disorder. Such as narcolepsy, sudden attacks of deep sleep, sleep apnea (the sleeper stops breathing for several seconds at a time) and, sleepwalking. Which are more amusing to hear about than to experience.

Millions of people suffer from insomnia either chronically, or from time to time. They will try anything to break the curse and science and folklore offers them a carload of choices everything from warm milk and lavender sachets to sleeping pills and sleep clinics. Not that any of these things help the true insomniac of course. And, how maddening it must be for someone who hasnt slept in weeks to come across a bus passenger fast asleep sitting up. Surrounded by strangers. These innocents are like people who stay skinny without having to diet.

## Working Together: Remembering 9/11

Work with a group of your classmates. Each student should write a paragraph remembering what 9/11 was like either for him or her or for his or her family. If you choose not to remember, pretend you are a tourist on a street in New York who sees the plane (in the picture on this page), and write a paragraph about what might be going through your mind. Double-space your paragraph, and take about ten minutes to write it.

Once your paragraph is finished, trade it with someone else's. Check the other student's paragraph for **fragments, run-ons, lack of parallel structure, misplaced and dangling modifiers, and errors with pronouns, subject-verb agreement, punctuation, capitalization, and so on.** When you are finished, hand it back and discuss the grammar (and the content if you wish to do so).

# UNIT TWO

# II

# The Writing Process


**CHAPTER 14** THE FOUR STAGES OF WRITING FOR A PARAGRAPH OR AN ESSAY

**CHAPTER 15** THE PARAGRAPH I: STRUCTURE AND TOPIC SENTENCE

**CHAPTER 16** THE PARAGRAPH II: SUPPORTING DETAILS

**CHAPTER 17** THE ESSAY

**CHAPTER 18** REVISING AND EDITING

**CHAPTER 19** SUMMARIZING AND PARAPHRASING

**CHAPTER 20** RESEARCH AND DOCUMENTATION

CHAPTER FOURTEEN

14

# The Four Stages of Writing for a Paragraph or an Essay

Few people can go to a desk and write the perfect composition from scratch without giving any of it even a second look. Most people need to go about the process in stages. This chapter introduces the writing process (for a paragraph or an essay) in terms of four stages: (1) prewriting, (2) outlining, (3) the rough draft, and finally, (4) postwriting (revising, editing, and proofreading). The chapter begins with some prewriting techniques designed to generate writing ideas and ends with the part of the postwriting stage that is proofreading. Revising and editing (parts of stage four) are covered in this chapter, but are examined in more depth in Chapter 18 of this unit.

## Stage One: Prewriting

How many times have you heard yourself say, "I don't know what else to write"? Well, what if you really do have plenty to write about and simply don't realize it? The following **prewriting techniques** are designed to retrieve your thoughts and ideas and make sense of feelings you might have so that you can start exploring them on paper. These techniques include brainstorming, freewriting, keeping a journal, and clustering. Use any, all, or none of them—whatever works for you.

### Brainstorming

One of the best ways of collecting ideas is through **brainstorming.** Brainstorming is simple—all you need is some time. It is best accomplished in groups of four or more people, but numbers aren't as important as the ideas you generate.

Here's how brainstorming works:

1. Compile a list of ideas, as many of them as you can.
2. Don't criticize any idea initially. That will come later.
3. If any ideas generate objections, work on developing alternatives to the ideas rather than simply discarding them.
4. Use ideas to stimulate discussion and to generate other ideas.

5. Make sure that everyone in the group completely understands the ideas generated.
6. Put your list of ideas aside for a while in order to think about them at your leisure. This "back burner" process often generates other ideas.

**TIP**

**When you brainstorm, allow your mind to roam freely around the topic, letting one idea lead to another, even if the ideas seem unrelated or irrelevant. Jot down every word and phrase that pops into your mind when you think about your topic.**

Here is what a brainstorming process might look like.
First identify a topic:

hockey

Then, what things come to mind when you think of this topic?

| | |
|---|---|
| coaches | referees |
| Stanley Cup | new drafts |
| Maple Leafs | Vancouver Canucks |

Now, you may want to pick out a couple of these ideas and combine them:

Maple Leafs and Stanley Cup

Expand the idea by reflecting on what you know and/or what you believe.

The Maple Leafs can't seem to win the Stanley Cup.

At this point, a question might arise:

Why can't the Leafs win the Stanley Cup?

A possible answer suggests a topic sentence for a paragraph or a thesis statement for an essay:

If they want to win the Stanley Cup, the Maple Leafs should commit to a realistic long-term plan rather than continue to cater to the demands of their short-sighted fans.

## Freewriting

In freewriting, you don't have to worry about spelling, grammar, focus, or organization. You just write. Write whatever comes to mind. Let a force beyond your control guide your pen, be it your unconscious, your heart, or the spirit world. The idea here is to generate ideas for writing a composition at a later stage. In the meantime, just have fun exploding with words on paper.

## Keeping a Journal

When handing in her journal at the end of a semester, a young female college student once said, "The journal was better than any man I'd ever known. It listened to absolutely everything I had to say!"

You may have kept some kind of diary in your childhood. Each entry may have started with "Dear Diary, I experienced my first kiss today. It was awkward, but amazing ..." Most diaries are logs of what goes on in the daily lives of their writers. As students get older, their diaries may evolve into journals in which the format is similar, but in which the content contains more depth and other engaging qualities. Rather than mention everything you did yesterday in last night's diary entry, for example, you might concentrate on something that struck you forcefully. It might have been a dream you had that preoccupied you all day. It might have been something in a conversation you'd overheard between two other students in front of you in a bus on the way to school. Perhaps what you had heard made you angry or sad or hopeful or, at the very least, contemplative, causing one of your friends in the cafeteria, or your professor in class, to try to get you to "snap out of a daze."

## Let Your Emotions Serve as a Guide

Think of a teacher from your past whom you remember well. Chances are it was someone who caused you to feel a great deal of emotion, either positive or negative. It might have been a teacher who made you feel stupid. Or on the more positive side, it might have been a teacher who encouraged you to follow a certain path because of a talent he or she detected in you that your parents never noticed or encouraged. Emotion is often associated with memory. The same can be said for people whom you've dated in the past. You may remember some girlfriends/boyfriends more than others. Those with whom you experienced strong emotions are probably the ones you tend to remember the most, no matter how long ago you were with them. Your emotions, in this way, can be your guide when it comes to choosing the topic of your journal entries, and subsequently, your essays (if your professor gives you enough choice, that is). What moves you, after all, may cause you to want to write more and will give you more about which to write. You'll experience fewer writer's blocks, fewer occasions on which you're thinking, "I don't know what else to write."

You may be asked to respond to either fiction or nonfiction. Does the story you just read remind you of a personal experience? Do you strongly disagree with how the character or writer dealt with his or her own situation because you would have reacted very differently? What should the character or writer have done, and why? You may be encouraged to respond to a movie, a movie that made you very emotional. Again, don't try to control the direction of your entry. Let your feelings take you on paper (or on your computer screen) to wherever they seem to want to take you. Regard it as an inner journey into the unknown (where no one has gone before)—a journey into your unconscious or your psyche. *Psyche,* by the way, is Greek for "soul."

## Buy a Journal That Doesn't Remind You of School

Are you a cat lover? Buy a journal with a hard cover on which there's a picture of a richly exotic Siamese cat! Or if it's cars you're into, find a journal whose cover features a picture of a sexy sports car. In any event, try to find something that you actually look forward to writing in every day or every night before you go to bed. Or take it with you in your knapsack so that you can record fresh ideas as they come to mind throughout the day. Rather than call someone on your cell phone, do some journal writing between classes. Develop a relationship with your journal the same way you would with a good novel that you find hard to put down. Just don't allow the journal to turn into a regular assignment that you feel forced to do just for the marks. Then it turns into meaningless drudgery, like too many things in life already. Don't let your journal transform into a burden when it should be, instead, a record of the journey of your mind!

If typing your entries on a computer screen is what you'd rather do, that's fine, too. Do whatever you feel most comfortable and most inspired doing. Do whatever is likely to help you cultivate that relationship, not just the one with your journal, but also the one with yourself that you'll find you are developing as you start to write on a regular basis. Writing regularly in your journal may help you not only get in touch with your feelings and solve your personal problems; it can also help you start writing more quickly and fluently whenever you're asked to complete a task that requires any writing at all. (See *Working Together* #3 on p. 173.)

## Clustering (also known as Diagramming or Mapping)

Many students are visual learners in that they learn best by seeing something get done and not necessarily by reading or even by hearing (a lecture, tapes, etc.). The same can be said for generating ideas. Clustering is a kind of brainstorming but with the aid of a diagram. Identify a topic you either have to or want to write on. Write it in the middle of a blank page and circle it (see Figure 14.1). This topic becomes the central idea of your clustering activity. Draw a line from that circle downward, and write out another idea that is in any way related to the central topic. Don't allow yourself to think for a long time. Write down whatever comes to mind first. (What you write first does not bind you in any way to a particular outcome.) Continue to fashion a diagram in this way by building on it in several directions. Eventually, certain ideas will begin to take hold. In other words, one idea will begin to seem stronger than another depending on what is familiar and important to you at the time.

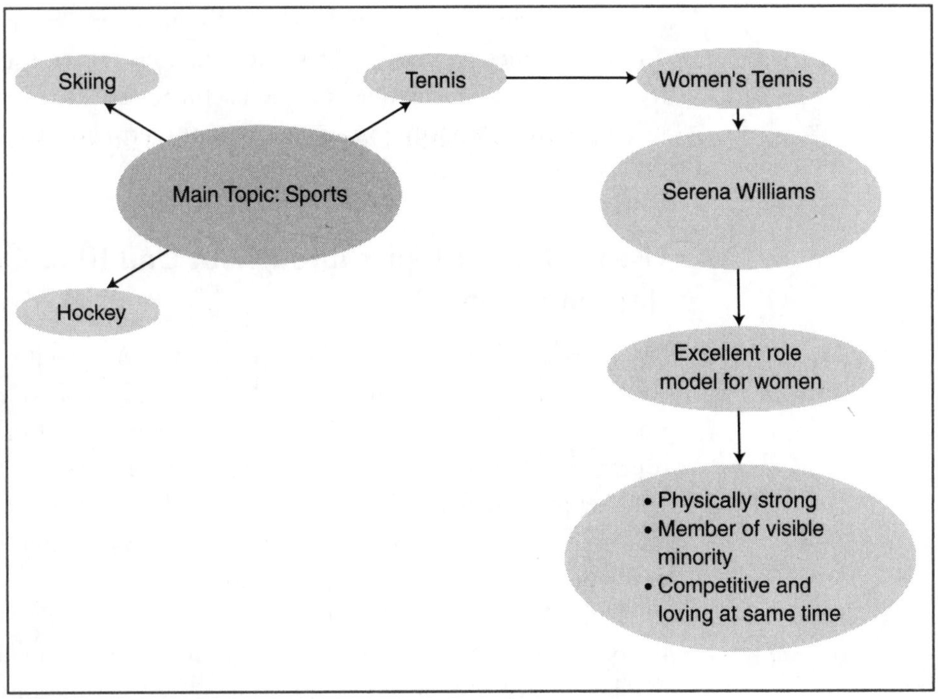


**Figure 14.1: Clustering**

Working from the cluster diagram, you could decide that you're interested in women's tennis, specifically in the top-ranked Serena Williams. If you feel strongly about the idea that Serena is an excellent role model for women, this might be a topic sentence for your paragraph.

***Topic Sentence:*** Serena Williams, in her title as the No. 1 Women's Tennis Player in the World, was an excellent role model for women everywhere.

Then you might ask yourself the following question: Why was Serena an excellent role model for women?

The answer to this question might come in three parts, all of which can be used as the supporting points for your topic sentence:

**Supporting points:**

1. She is physically strong.
2. She's a member of a visible minority, but this has not held her back in tennis.
3. She is living proof that she can be competitive and loving all at the same time, as illustrated by her relationship with her sister.

## Choosing the Topic and the Controlling Idea

Some people have no use for any of the above prewriting techniques. And that's fine. If you can come up with a topic and a controlling idea (your attitude toward the topic) right away, all the better. But remember, even if you can come up with a topic sentence (or thesis statement for an essay) without the use of prewriting techniques, these techniques can be useful for other reasons, too, such as establishing a writing routine if you have trouble getting started, dealing with personal upsets, difficulties, etc.

## Use the Lists of Topics throughout Unit III or Questions throughout Unit IV

Using the lists of topics available in each chapter in Unit III on a different writing strategy (narration, description, etc.) or using ideas of your own, jot down two or three different topics that appeal to you. From this list of possibilities, select the topic you think would give you the best opportunity for writing. Which one do you feel most strongly about? Which one do you know the most about? Which one is most likely to interest your readers? Which one is best suited to being developed into a paragraph or an essay?

Unit IV in this text contains major readings of mostly nonfiction, some fiction, and a bit of poetry by Canadian writers. Immediately following every reading, there are four sets of questions. Read a selection that interests you, and practise your paragraph or essay writing by responding to one of the questions that interests you also.

Your next step is to decide what your controlling idea should be. What is the point you want to make about the experience? What is the direction you want to take? Was the experience humiliating, absurd, or hilarious?

## Every Paragraph or Essay Must Be Persuasive

Where does the word "essay" come from? It comes from the French verb *essayer,* which means "to try." So what does the writer "try" to do in, for example, an essay? The writer tries to persuade the reader of a particular point of view. Even if the essay is considered more expository (writing that does more to point things out) than argumentative, the writer still selects certain facts that he or she hopes will "persuade" the reader to see things the way the writer does. The essay, and even the single paragraph, no matter what type it happens to be, is an exercise in persuasion. (See more on *persuasion* in Chapter 28.)

Two of the most critical elements the writer must consider in order to maximize the persuasive power of the composition are **audience** and **purpose.**

## Audience and Tone

Your primary audience is, no doubt, your professor. But whom do you have in mind when you're writing your composition? If you're writing a children's story, chances are you're not going to be discussing the topic of venereal disease, nor will you be using five-syllable words. If you're writing a formal essay, you're not going to begin by saying, "I thought I'd spill a few thoughts down on some paper." Who your intended audience is, aside from the professor who will be marking your assignment, determines not only what you write, but also how you write it.

Your intended audience, for example, determines the level of formality of your writing. If you're writing a formal research paper, use a formal tone. Don't, for example, use contractions (he's, she'd), and stay in the third person. Don't use *I* or *you*, for example.

### Purpose

The main reason for writing a composition at this stage in your life is probably to get a passing grade so that you can move on to the next level of English course in order to eventually graduate in your program. And the better your compositions are, the more likely you are to pass your English course. In the interest of pulling off a high-quality composition, be as mindful as you can of the specific reason for writing your particular composition.

This purpose should be crystal clear to you from the beginning. If it's not, it probably won't be clear to the reader either. First of all, is your purpose to inform, persuade, or entertain? Now that you've determined who your intended audience is, it's time you decided what you want that audience to think, do, or feel. Perhaps you want your audience to do all of these things. Do you want your audience to do something or simply to understand your particular point of view toward a controversial topic? Regardless, the clearer you are on the purpose of your composition, the more effective your composition will be in the end.

## Stage Two: Outlining (or Organizing)

Most texts on writing suggest elaborate outlines for paragraphs or essays, some of which seem to be as long as the paragraphs or essays themselves. Here, however, we suggest a very short outline, one that is clear and that saves you time, whether it is for a paragraph or an essay.

This outline consists of four complete sentences (sentences that appear exactly the same way within the final product).

**Outline for a paragraph:**

1. The topic sentence
2. The first major support sentence
3. The second major support sentence
4. The third major support sentence

**Outline for an essay (of five paragraphs):**

1. The thesis statement
2. The topic sentence of the second paragraph
3. The topic sentence of the third paragraph
4. The topic sentence of the fourth paragraph

Of course, by the time you've finished your composition, you may find that the wording of some or all of these sentences has changed because of improvements you've made along the way. The outline is meant to help you ensure that your composition contains persuasive power. If your outline doesn't seem logical, chances are, neither will your composition.

## Stage Three: The Rough Draft

After you have applied a prewriting technique and you have organized the material into some kind of order, the time has come to write a rough draft.

A rough draft is just what its name implies: your first attempt to write your essay. The first attempt is "rough" because it will undoubtedly undergo many changes before it is finished: parts may be missing, some paragraphs will probably lack sufficient detail, and some parts may be repetitious or inappropriate. Some sentences are likely to sound awkward, and you will need to rewrite them later. The experienced writer expects all this and does not worry. All that you should try to accomplish in the rough draft is to let your mind relax and to get down on paper all of your initial ideas, according, of course, to some kind of plan as established by your work in stages one and two. These first ideas will provide the seeds that can be better developed later on.

As you work on your rough draft, you may work alone, with a group, with a peer tutor, or directly with your instructor. (An explanation of terms that relate to the paragraph can be found in Chapters 15 and 16, to the essay in Chapter 17, and to writing strategies in Chapters 21–28.) Here are some of the basic questions you should consider at this most important stage of your work:

1. Does the rough draft satisfy the conditions for paragraph or essay form? Does it have a topic sentence or thesis statement, adequate support, and a concluding sentence or paragraph? Are there at least five sentences in every paragraph that you've written, but not more than twelve?
2. Does your paragraph or essay contain the writing strategy of your choice, such as narration, cause and effect, or description? Or does your essay combine several strategies, a different one in each paragraph? Does your composition focus on a single event rather than on a general situation? Where does the action take place? Can the reader see it? What time of day, week, or year is it?
3. Have you put the details of the paragraph or essay in an order of a certain logic?
4. Does the paragraph or essay seem complete? Do any questions come to mind upon reading what you've written that you think should be answered here as well? Is there any material that is irrelevant and should be omitted?
5. Except for what is required in openings and closings, are there sentences or paragraphs that are repetitious?

6. Are there several places where you can substitute better verbs or nouns? Can you add adjectives to give the reader better sensory images?
7. Can you think of a better way to begin or end your paragraph or essay?
8. Can you show your draft to at least two other readers, and ask for suggestions?

Armed with a first draft, you will now have something with which to work. No longer is there a blank paper staring you in the face. This accomplishment is a great relief to most writers, but remember, you are far from finished.

## Stage Four: Postwriting (Revising, Editing, and Proofreading)

If you have worked hard at revising the rough draft, you will be delighted with the improvements as you write the second draft. For a detailed examination of this part of the writing process, see Chapter 18 (Revising and Editing).

Feedback is an important aid in each of the final stages of writing a paragraph or essay. A good way to help yourself see your own work more clearly is to put the writing aside for a little while, if you can. Then read what you have written aloud to someone else, or to yourself if no one else is available. You may be surprised at the number of places in your writing where you will hear the need for a change.

### Revising and Editing the Rough Draft

If you have time, put aside your rough draft for a day or two. Then, when you reread it, you will look at it with a fresh mind. In this important revision stage, you should be concerned with how you have organized your ideas. At this point, do not yet worry about grammar, spelling, and punctuation.

Begin this important stage by asking these major questions:

1. Is the paragraph or essay unified? Do you stick to the topic you have announced? Go through the paragraph or essay and take out irrelevant material.
2. Do you repeat yourself? Look back over your paragraph or essay to determine whether you have given any information more than once. Even if you find you have used different words, you should delete the repeated material.
3. Does the paragraph or essay make sense? Can a reader follow your logic, your train of thought, and the course of events you describe? (Giving the rough draft to someone else to read will often answer this question for you.) If the paragraph or essay is confusing to the reader, you must find out where it goes wrong and why. Sometimes when you read your writing out loud, you will feel that one sentence has leaped to some point that doesn't follow from the sentence before.
4. For an essay, are the paragraphs roughly the same length? If you see a one-sentence paragraph, you know something is wrong. Aim to develop the point of each paragraph using at least five sentences. The first and last paragraphs

are usually the shortest paragraphs in the essay, but they still require approximately five sentences each. Are they long enough without being too long? Check through your essay. Do you need to change the paragraphing? You may need to develop one paragraph more fully, or a one-sentence paragraph may really belong with the paragraph that comes before or after it.

5. Do you have all the components essential to a paragraph or types of paragraphs essential to an essay? For an essay, do you have the introduction with its thesis, at least three well-developed body paragraphs with transitional devices used to connect ideas, and a concluding paragraph? For a paragraph, do you have a topic sentence that contains the topic of the paragraph and its controlling idea, strong supporting detail, and a concluding sentence?
6. Can you add more specific details? Most writing instructors agree that nearly every paper they read could be improved by adding more details, more descriptive verbs, and more sensory images to make the writing come alive. You should make sure there is sufficient detail throughout your paper, but for an essay none of the supportive detail should appear either in your introductory or concluding paragraphs.
7. Can you add dialogue or a quotation from someone?
8. Can you make the introduction, conclusion, or title more creative?

## Proofreading

An important step still remains. You must check each sentence to see that it is correct, including grammar, spelling, and punctuation. In the rush to get a paper in on time, this step is often overlooked. If you take each sentence, starting with the last and going sentence by sentence backwards to the beginning, you will more easily be able to look at the sentence structure apart from the other aspects of the essay. Taking the time to look over a paper will usually result in your spotting several sentence-level errors. (As an exercise, you might want to correct errors of grammar, spelling, and punctuation in the first draft of the student essay on pages 217–18 of Chapter 18.)

*Note:* In many cases, your professor will not accept handwritten work, and you will be expected to submit a paper produced on a computer. Do not forget to proofread your work after it has been printed out; even if you have your paper typed for you, you are still responsible for errors. If there are not too many errors, you can make corrections neatly in ink on your printed copy before handing it in.

### Proofreading

Check your second draft for
- Misspellings
- Fragments or run-ons
- Incorrect punctuation
- Consistency of voice and tense
- Verb problems
- Agreement
- Parallel structure

A checklist for the final preparation of a paragraph or essay follows.

### Checklist for the Final Copy

1. Use 21.5 cm by 28 cm (8½ by 11 inch) paper
2. Type or write (whichever is required) on one side of the paper only.
3. Double-space.
4. Leave margins approximately 2.5 cm (1 inch) wide on each side of the paper.
5. Do not hyphenate words at ends of lines without consulting a dictionary for the correct division of words into syllables.
6. Centre the title at the top of the first page.
7. Put your name, the date, and the title of your paper on a separate title page, unless your professor says otherwise.
8. If you have more than one page, number them and staple or clip them together so they will not be lost.

## Working Together: Prewriting Activities

1. Imagine yourself in the following situation: you and your classmates are guidance counsellors in a high school. You have been asked to produce a brochure that will be entitled "When a Young Person Quits School." This brochure is intended for students who are thinking of dropping out. You and the other counsellors meet to brainstorm on the topic.

   Divide into groups. Each group will brainstorm for fifteen minutes or so, and then come together again as a class. On the board make a final grouping of the ideas for this topic and discuss.
2. In groups or as a class, construct an outline for the essay to be called "When a Young Person Quits School." Use the information gathered in the brainstorming activity above. Either organize the information into main points and supporting details under those main points as it has been done above, or follow the suggestion of a brief outline under "Outlining" on page 169 in this chapter.
3. If you think the following suggestion is too personal, feel free to try #1 or #2 above, instead. Think of a movie you've seen or a dream you've had that you have found yourself thinking about over and over again. It doesn't matter

how long ago you've seen the movie or dreamt the dream because your long-term memory can be quite selective and doesn't work always on the basis of time.

Describe in writing that part of the movie or dream that you seem to be remembering over and over again. It's possible that this part you're remembering may be calling out to you to express it, to explore it, to somehow come to terms with it, and perhaps most importantly, to learn something from it, something important for you. After all, it's not the movie that's calling out to you. It's something in you that's doing the calling, perhaps something in your unconscious, the part programmed to tell the whole truth about who you are, what you should be doing, where you should be going, and perhaps whom you should be seeing!

After you write about the part of the movie or dream that you remember the most, adding as much detail as you can, start to discuss how you feel. Then try to explain where those feelings are coming from. And finally, explore what that same place in your unconscious is trying to tell you about what you're supposed to learn from your preoccupation with that part of the movie or dream. You may find yourself the wiser, and the preoccupation with that part of the movie or dream may actually stop. Discuss the results of your activity with someone else in the class. Allow your partner to ask you questions about what you've just said; now it's the other person's turn to discuss his or her results with you.

CHAPTER FIFTEEN

15

# The Paragraph I: Structure and Topic Sentence

## What Is a Paragraph?

**DEFINITION ➤** A **paragraph** is a group of sentences that develops one main idea. A paragraph may stand by itself as a complete piece of writing, or it may be a section of a longer piece of writing, such as an essay.

No single rule will tell you how long a paragraph should be, but if a paragraph is too short, the reader will feel that basic information is missing. If the paragraph is too long, the reader will be bored or confused. An effective paragraph is always long enough to develop the main idea that is being presented. This textbook suggests that, as a rule, a healthy paragraph should consist of at least five sentences and no more than twelve sentences. You have undoubtedly read paragraphs in newspapers that are only one sentence long, but in fully developed writing, this is considered unacceptable.

## What Does a Paragraph Look Like?

Margins, new-paragraph indication, and complete sentences are essential parts of paragraph form. Study the following paragraph from Elizabeth Pollet's "A Cold-Water Flat" to observe the standard form.

> I got the job. I worked in the bank's city collection department. For weeks, I was like a mouse in a maze: my feet scurried. Every seventh day, I received thirteen dollars. It wasn't much. But, standing beside the pneumatic tube, unloading the bundles of mail that pelted down and distributing them according to their texture, size, and colour to my superiors at their desks, I felt humble and useful.

A margin of adequate width is used on each side of the text (for a manuscript page, this margin should be 2.5 cm or 1 inch). If another paragraph is added, make sure there is proper indication of the new paragraph. If the first line of the first paragraph is indented (as in the example on the previous page), ensure the first line of the second paragraph is also indented. If you follow the full-block style (no indentation of the first line of a paragraph), then make sure you skip a line between paragraphs. If you're already double-spacing, skip two lines between paragraphs. If you neither indent the first line of your paragraph nor skip an extra line between paragraphs, the reader cannot be expected to know you've written two paragraphs.

You will note that the layout of this book follows a different format than that suggested for your essays. The book industry has its own standards and norms relating to page layout.

Figure 15.1 illustrates the structure of the paragraph.

***Note:*** Any space left over at the end of the last line of a paragraph, in itself, never properly indicates the end of a paragraph (if another paragraph follows). As mentioned, proper indication of a paragraph means either indenting the first line of the paragraph or skipping a line (or two, if you're already double-spacing) between paragraphs.

## What Is a Topic Sentence?

**DEFINITION ➤** A **topic sentence** states the main idea of the paragraph. It contains the topic of the paragraph and a controlling idea (the writer's attitude toward the topic). It is the most general sentence of the paragraph. All the other sentences of the paragraph serve to explain, describe, extend, or support the controlling idea in the topic sentence.

Most paragraphs you read will begin with the topic sentence. However, some topic sentences come in the middle of the paragraph; others come at the end. Some paragraphs have no stated topic sentence at all; in these cases, the main idea is implied. You are advised to use topic sentences in all your work in order to be certain that the writing has a focus and develops a single idea at a time. Whether you are taking an essay exam in a history course, doing a research paper for a sociology course, or writing an essay in a composition course, thoughtful use of the topic sentence will always bring better results. Good topic sentences help both the writer and the reader to think clearly about the main points.

The paragraph that follows makes a point, which is stated in its topic sentence. Read the paragraph and notice how the topic sentence is the most general sentence; it is the main idea of the paragraph. The other sentences explain, describe, extend, or support the topic sentence.

**Model Paragraph**

We are the great "Let's junk it" society! Mountains of disposable diapers are thrown into garbage cans every day. Tonnes of yogurt containers, pop cans,

## Two Paragraph Types

| TOPIC SENTENCE |
|---|
| REGULAR<br>(5–7 sentences including the topic sentence) |
| CONCLUDING SENTENCE |

| TOPIC SENTENCE |
|---|
| EXTENDED<br>(8–12 sentences including the topic sentence) |
| CONCLUDING SENTENCE |

## Regular or Extended Paragraphs

A **regular paragraph** has five to seven sentences. An **extended paragraph** (eight to twelve sentences) is longer because it has more supporting detail. The supporting detail of a paragraph is made up of sentences that directly support the topic sentence. These supporting sentences may be specific examples of the topic sentence, or they may be parts of an explanation. Some instructors require a concluding sentence, especially when the paragraph stands alone. See "The Concluding Sentence" on pp. 191–92.

## Sample Paragraph

One of the areas in which having choice can be extremely valuable is that of friends. Like leaving home to seek greater knowledge of yourself, picking your own friends from a greater number of people can aid in your journey to seek self-knowledge. After all, if you go out with the same group of small-town friends all the time, not because you necessarily like them all that much but because they're the only ones available, this can prove quite limiting when it comes to your growth as an individual. The big city, on the other hand, offers an endless number of opportunities to meet people of like interests. You're much more likely to cultivate relationships with people who help you to grow.

## Topic Sentence

A **topic sentence** includes two things: a *topic* and a *controlling idea.* The controlling idea is the attitude or position of the writer of the paragraph toward the topic identified in the topic sentence. The controlling idea gives direction to the paragraph. The topic sentence does not always appear first in a paragraph, but until you are well practised, place the topic sentence first.

## Transitions

**Transitional words or phrases** are used to organize the paragraph better and to make the paragraph flow more smoothly.

## Stands On Its Own

Any paragraph, even if it is part of a longer work such as an essay, should be able to stand on its own, much like a sequel to a movie.

## Paragraph Indication

There are only two ways **to indicate a new paragraph:**

1. **Indent** the first line of the paragraph (see sample paragraph above), or
2. Skip a line before starting the next paragraph. If you are already double-spacing your work, skip two lines, instead of one, before starting the next paragraph.

**Figure 15.1: Structure of the Paragraph**

The sample paragraph is from "City Life Beats the Small Town Blues"; see pp. 298–300.

and plastic items are discarded without so much as a stomp to flatten them out. If the old Chevy is not worth fixing, tow it off to sit with thousands of others on hectares of fenced-in junkyards. Radios, televisions, and toasters get the same treatment because it is easier and often less expensive to buy a new product than to fix the old one. Who wants a comfortable old sweater if a new one can be bought on sale? No thought is given to the fact that the new one will look like the old one after two or three washings. After all, what's bad for the environment is probably good for the economy!

All the examples in this paragraph support the topic sentence, that we are a "throwaway" society. Although the concluding sentence does not repeat the topic sentence in this case, it gives the paragraph a sense of closure. (See more on concluding sentences on pages 191–92 in Chapter 16.)

**PRACTICE**

### Finding the Topic Sentence of a Paragraph

Each of the following paragraphs contains a topic sentence that states the main idea of the paragraph. Find this sentence and underline it. Check your answers against those in the Answer Key on p. 465.

1. Love is a crazy, complicated affair made trickier by the tangle of superstitions that go along with it. According to the book *Cross Your Fingers, Spit in Your Hat,* you must pull a hair from the head of the one you love to make him or her love you back. Or you can offer your loved one a glass of lemonade in which you have soaked your toenail clippings, or a bowl of soup to which you have added three drops of your blood. Once your sweetheart has devoured either of these concoctions, he or she will love you always.
2. When you remember something, your brain uses more than one method to store the information. You have short-term memory, which helps you recall recent events; you have long-term memory, which brings back items that are further in the past; and you have deep retrieval, which gives you access to long-buried information that is sometimes difficult to recall. Whether these processes are chemical or electrical, we do not yet know, and much research remains to be done before we can say which with any certainty. The brain is one of the most remarkable organs, a part of the body that we have only begun to investigate. It will be years before we start to understand all its complex processes.

## How Do You Find the Topic in a Topic Sentence?

To find the topic in a topic sentence, ask yourself this question: What is the topic the writer is going to discuss? Below are two topic sentences. The first topic is underlined. Underline the topic in the second example.

Backpacking in the mountains last year was an exciting experience.
College registration can be stressful.

**PRACTICE**

### Finding the Topic in the Topic Sentence

Find the topic in each of the following topic sentences. For each example, ask yourself this question: What is the topic the writer is going to discuss? Then underline the topic. Check your answers against those in the Answer Key on p. 465.

1. Remodelling an old house can be frustrating.
2. College work demands more independence than high school work.
3. A well-made suit has three easily identified characteristics.
4. Growing up near a museum had a profound influence on my life.
5. My favourite room in the house would seem ugly to most people.
6. A student who goes to school full-time and also works part-time has to make careful use of every hour.
7. One of the disadvantages of skiing is the expense.
8. When we met for dinner that night, I was shocked at the change that had come over my friend.
9. According to the report, current tax laws greatly benefit those who own real estate.
10. Greek restaurants, to the delight of many Canadians, can be found in most of our cities.

## What Is a Controlling Idea?

Every topic sentence contains not only the topic, but also a controlling idea.

**DEFINITION ➤** The **controlling idea** tells us the position the writer has taken on the topic. It gives the paragraph direction. It is the writer's attitude toward the topic.

***Example:*** Her trip to Kenya was *exciting.*

For example, in the topic sentence "Backpacking in the mountains last year was an exciting experience," the topic is "backpacking" and the controlling idea is that this backpacking trip was "exciting." Another person on the same trip might have had another attitude toward the trip. The person might have found the trip exhausting or boring. A single topic can therefore have any number of possibilities for development since the writer can choose from a limitless number of controlling ideas, depending on his or her attitude.

### How Do You Find the Controlling Idea of a Topic Sentence?

When you look for the controlling idea in a topic sentence, ask yourself this question: What is the writer's attitude toward the topic?

In each of the following examples, the topic is underlined and the controlling idea is circled.

Sealfon's Department Store is my favourite store in town.

Sealfon's Department Store is too expensive for my budget.

**PRACTICE**

## Finding the Controlling Idea

Below are seven topic sentences. For each sentence, underline the topic and circle the controlling idea. Check your answers against those in the Answer Key on p. 465.

1. Vigorous exercise is a good way to reduce the effect of stress on the body.
2. St. John's and Corner Brook differ in four major ways.
3. Many so-called wonder foods are less than wonderful.
4. Athletic scholarships available to women are increasing.
5. Caffeine has several adverse effects on the body.
6. Madame Benoît, a famous gourmet cook, had an amusing personality.
7. Computers will make newspapers obsolete by 2020.

# Choosing Your Own Controlling Idea

Professors often assign one general topic on which all students must write. Likewise, when writing contests are announced, the topic is sometimes the same for all contestants. Since very few people have exactly the same view of or attitude toward a topic, it is likely that no two papers would have the same controlling idea. There could be as many controlling ideas as there are people to write them. The secret of writing a good topic sentence is to use a controlling idea that strongly and accurately expresses your attitude or feeling toward the topic.

**EXERCISE**

## Choosing Controlling Ideas for Topic Sentences

Below are two topics. For each topic, think of three different possible controlling ideas, and then write a different topic sentence for each of these controlling ideas. An example is done for you.

**Topic:** My mother

Three possible controlling ideas:

1. Unusual childhood
2. Silent woman
3. Definite ideas about alcohol

Three different topic sentences:

1. My mother had a most unusual childhood.
2. My mother is a very silent woman.
3. My mother has definite ideas about alcohol.

1. **Topic:** My neighbourhood

First controlling idea: Quite neighborhood.

First topic sentence: My neighbourhood is generally very quite.

Second controlling idea: Kids Playground.

Second topic sentence: My neighbourhood has a couple of kids playground that makes the area very life.

Third controlling idea: Walking distance

Third topic sentence: My neighbourhood is at walking distance from the shopping centre.

2. **Topic:** The Internet

First controlling idea: Source of information.

First topic sentence: the internet is a great source of information.

Second controlling idea: Connection with people

Second topic sentence: The internet helps people connect & interact easely

Third controlling idea: A tool to getting a job.

Third topic sentence: The internet is a tool that helps everyone in needs to find a job.

## Chapter Review Exercises

**EXERCISE**

### Further Practice Writing the Topic Sentence

Develop each of the following topics into a topic sentence. In each case, the controlling idea is missing. First, decide on an attitude you might take toward the topic. Then use that attitude to write your topic sentence. When you are finished, underline your topic and circle your controlling idea. Be sure your topic sentence is a complete sentence and not a fragment. An example is done for you.

***Topic:*** My brother's car accident

***Controlling idea:*** Tragic results

***Topic sentence:*** My brother's car accident had (tragic results) for the entire family.

1. **Topic:** Sending e-mail

Controlling idea: easy way of communicating

Topic sentence: Sending e-mail is an easy way of communicating with friends overseas.

2. **Topic:** Two years in the armed forces

   Controlling idea: traumatizing experience.

   Topic sentence: Spending two years in the armed forces would be enough to have a thraumatizing experience

3. **Topic:** Making new friends

   Controlling idea: Important.

   Topic sentence: Making new friends is important to increase the support system already created by the friends we have!

4. **Topic:** Working as a waiter or waitress

   Controlling idea: Exhausting but rewarding.

   Topic sentence: Working as a waiter or waitress is exhausting but rewarding in many ways.

5. **Topic:** Going on a diet

   Controlling idea: Important but ~~careful~~ cautelous decision.

   Topic sentence: Going on a diet is an important but cautelous desicion to make since there are diferent factors that we should consider.

## Working Together: Controlling Ideas

1. In this chapter, you have written many topic sentences in various exercises. Choose one of your best sentences to put on the board. After several students have written some of their sentences on the board, other students will underline the topics and circle the controlling ideas. If the sentences need improvements, students can write their own versions under the other sentences so the class can compare and contrast them.
2. Every topic contains numerous possibilities for controlling ideas. Take, for example, the topic of education. Each student thinks for a moment and jots down one or two controlling ideas that come to mind. Then a class member lists on the blackboard all the different controlling ideas that the members of the class have generated. Your instructor may want the class to use the remainder of the period to write a paragraph by selecting one of these controlling ideas on education.

CHAPTER SIXTEEN 16

# The Paragraph II: Supporting Details

## What Is a Supporting Detail?

**DEFINITION ➤** A **supporting detail** is a piece of evidence used by the writer to make the controlling idea of the topic sentence convincing to the reader.

Once you have constructed your topic sentence with its topic and controlling idea, you are ready to move on to supporting your idea with details. These details will convince your readers that what you are claiming in the topic sentence is believable or reasonable.

### State Facts

As you choose these supporting details, realize that readers do not necessarily have to agree with your point of view. However, your supporting details must be good enough and numerous enough to convince your readers at least to respect your position. Remember to state facts rather than opinion. You are likely not the only one who has knowledge of a particular subject, so be sure that you don't present vague assertions that leave you open to contradiction. You may have had many problems with a particular make of car that you purchased, for example, and want to write a paragraph detailing its faults. However, your reader may have had a positive experience with this same make of car, or may work for the company that built it. Respect the possible point of view of your reader.

### Be Specific

Remember, too, that specific details tend to stay in readers' minds much longer than general ideas. The statement that over 34 600 males died of cancer in Canada in 2000 is much more effective and memorable than a statement saying only that cancer killed many people. Specific details also make a piece of writing more interesting. When the reader has concrete objects, particular people, or recognizable places to hang on to, the contents of the writing become a pleasure to read.

It is important to notice that longer paragraphs with complicated topics usually contain a large number of supporting details. The following paragraph is taken from an essay about the richness of Aboriginal people's languages. It begins with a good topic sentence. Then several strong details support the topic sentence.

> Languages are remarkably adaptable, easily borrowing or coining new words as circumstances change. The horse, unknown to Aboriginals when the Spanish landed, soon took on a central role among Aboriginal peoples, and words for the horse and its many uses were introduced. One device was to borrow some form of the Spanish word *caballo*. Another was to invent a descriptive term. Native people of eastern New York State used a word meaning "one rides its back"; in the western part of the state, the word for horse means "it hauls out logs." Presumably these were the first uses of horses seen in the two areas. Among the Kwakiutl of British Columbia, a steamboat was "fire on its back moving in the water." To the Tsimshian of the same area, the word for rice was "looking like maggots."

Notice that the topic sentence gives us the topic (language) and the writer's attitude toward the topic (remarkably adaptable). Each of the sentences that follow this topic sentence is a supporting detail that convinces us that the controlling idea is a reasonable attitude. The writer provides more than one example and chooses these examples from more than one group of Aboriginal people. This wide range makes the topic sentence more convincing and interesting.

| | |
|---|---|
| *Topic sentence:* | Languages are remarkably adaptable, easily borrowing or coining new words as circumstances change. |
| *First supporting detail:* | The word for "horse" was adapted to meet certain situations among Aboriginal peoples. |
| *Second supporting detail:* | Spanish was adapted. |
| *Third supporting detail:* | Descriptive terms were used. |
| *Fourth supporting detail:* | The word "steamboat" was adapted by the First Nations peoples of British Columbia to serve a descriptive purpose. |
| *Fifth supporting detail:* | Another British Columbia Nation had a descriptive word for "rice." |

**EXERCISE**

## Finding the Topic Sentence and Supporting Details

For the following paragraph, write down the topic sentence, and then list the supporting details.

> The time when the darkness that envelops me is most disturbing is the moment when I roll over onto my back and face the ceiling, still encased in the web of drowsiness sleep has woven, and from which it is reluctant to release me. As I become more aware of the sounds around me in the darkness, the tick-

ing of my alarm clock draws my attention, and I look toward it to see what time this morning I have awakened. I am unable to comprehend why I can't locate its familiar face when I know it should be there. It is at this moment that reality crashes in and reminds me, once again, that morning never comes for me anymore. Life has indeed abandoned me to the night, which is, and always will be, my constant companion. After this moment passes, I reach out into the void toward the sound of the clock. Grasping it and tracing the face that had eluded me moments ago, I sense it forfeit the time to my touch, and thus I broach another day.

Glenn David du Moulin, blind student, "Five Hours in a Life"

Topic sentence: ~~The time within the darkness that~~ envelops me is most disturbing is the moment when I roll over onto my back....

First supporting detail: ~~I become~~ more aware of the sounds around me in the darkness.

Second supporting detail: The ticking of my alarm clock draws my attention.

Third supporting detail: morning never comes for me any more.

Fourth supporting detail: Life has indeed abandoned me to the night, wich is, and always will be, my constant companion.

Fifth supporting detail: Grasping it & tracing the face that had eluded me moments ago, I sense it forfeit the time to my touch, and thus I broach another day.

## Using Examples as Supporting Details

**DEFINITION ➤** An **example** is a very specific illustration or piece of evidence that supports a writer's point of view. Examples make general ideas more concrete and therefore easier to comprehend and remember. An example may be part of a sentence, or an entire sentence on its own, or more than one sentence long.

### Respect Other Points of View

When you use examples in your writing, you are trying to convince your reader that what you are saying is true and worthy of belief. At the same time, you must assume that some readers will be knowledgeable in your subject area, so be sure to respect that, and make your examples as clear and concise as you can.

Remember that no matter how good your examples are, they might not convince some readers, who may have education and experience you lack. So don't "preach" to the reader or consider that your point of view is the only one that is valid.

## Use Specific Examples

Examples are supporting details that support or further explain main supporting details.

See the paragraph below that starts with "Not only are weather forecasters often wrong ..." The second sentence contains the first main supporting detail. The third sentence contains an example that supports the second sentence. The more precise your examples, the more clearly your reader will be able to see what you mean, and the more memorable your writing will be.

Examples may be given in more than one way. They may appear as lists of specific items to illustrate a particular point, or they may be written as extended examples.

**DEFINITION ➤** **Extended examples** include lengthy descriptions or stories that are usually several sentences long (or even an entire paragraph long in a longer piece of writing, such as an essay).

A good piece of writing is filled with both kinds of examples—specific items and extended examples—that fit together to create a well-developed, convincing whole. Read the following paragraph on the terminology used in weather forecasting. As you read, look for different examples that show how listening to the weather forecast can be a challenge.

> Not only are weather forecasters often wrong with their forecasts, but they speak a language that only the most knowledgeable meteorologist can understand. For the average television viewer or radio listener, a dictionary is a necessity when listening to the weather forecast. "Watch out for the Alberta clipper, folks. It's coming this way!" seems to be part of the forecasters' lexicon in the winter. Or maybe it's the summer. In any case, what is an Alberta clipper? Are we supposed to hide under a table when it approaches? I've never understood the term, nor have I understood the significance of the dew point or a temperature inversion. How could I ever understand these terms when no one has ever defined them for me? Yet they roll off the tongues of weather forecasters as if *everyone* should know what is happening. The relative humidity mystifies me, as do troughs and ridges of pressure. I know one thing, however: if the forecast is for a sunny day, be sure to take an umbrella.

**EXERCISE 1**

### Finding Examples

Analyze the paragraph on weather forecasting (on the previous page). What kind(s) of examples can you find in the paragraph? (specific examples & extended).

**EXERCISE 2**

### Finding Examples

Find a newspaper or magazine article on a current topic or other subject that interests you. Examine the article for paragraphs containing lists of examples and paragraphs containing extended examples. How has the writer made the article interesting and memorable through the use of examples?

## Avoid Restating the Topic Sentence

One of your most important jobs as you write a paragraph is to recognize the difference between a genuine supporting detail and a simple restatement of the topic sentence. The following is a poor paragraph with its sentences merely restating the topic sentence, which has been underlined:

> My grandmother's photograph dates from a period when she and her family came to live in St. Petersburg. I like to look at the photograph and wonder about how life was in those days. From the clothes that my grandmother is wearing in the old photograph, it looks as if she is ready for a formal occasion. It is difficult to tell, though, because the photograph is old and faded. I don't think she enjoyed formal occasions.

The supporting sentences tell the reader very little about the period in which the photograph was taken. There is no description given of the clothing or why the writer might feel that it was a formal occasion. And even though the photograph is old and faded enough that details can't be seen, the writer is assuming that his or her grandmother isn't having a good time.

By contrast, the following paragraph, from Michael Ignatieff's *The Russian Album,* has good supporting details:

> In the family album there is a photograph of my grandmother, Natasha Ignatieff, that dates from the period when she and her family came to live in St. Petersburg in the dark and cluttered apartment two blocks from the Neva river. She is dressed for a formal winter evening, a fox fur draped over her shoulders. Brussels lace [decorates] the bodice of her velvet gown, her hair [is] swept back in a tight chignon, and a twelve-strand pearl choker [hugs] her stiffly upright neck. She is thin and pale, the cheekbones of her long angular face taking the light, the eyes deep-set and dark. Her expression is guarded, and she seems at odds with the occasion. She was a private soul: in the public glare, she shrank back. She hated Petersburg society: paying courtesy calls on the wives of Paul's superiors, making curtsies and small talk and all the while feeling she was up on a high wire one step from a fall.

Ignatieff's paragraph has vivid illustrations of life in Russia during his grandmother's time. In the first place, naming her Natasha gives a personal element to the paragraph. His descriptions of the apartment ("dark and cluttered"), her formal wear ("fox fur," "Brussels lace," "twelve-strand pearl choker"), and her appearance ("hair [is] swept back," "thin and pale," "cheekbones of her long angular face") all contribute to the overall topic, that of the photograph mentioned in the first sentence. Rather than assuming she is not enjoying herself, the author points to concrete aspects of her features to reinforce the statement that she hated St. Petersburg society: her "guarded" expression, her "private soul," and the feeling that she was "on a high wire one step from a fall" tend to give a clarity and personality to the old picture.

**PRACTICE**

## Avoid Restating the Topic Sentence

Each of the topic sentences below is followed by four additional sentences. Three of these additional sentences contain acceptable supporting details, but one of the sentences is simply a restatement of the topic sentence. In the space provided, identify each sentence as *SD* for supporting detail or *R* for restatement. Check your answers against those in the Answer Key on p. 466.

1. I am surprised at myself when I think how neat I used to be before I started school full-time.

    ____________ a. In my closet, I had my clothes arranged in matching outfits with shoes, hats, and even jewellery to go with them.

    ____________ b. I always used to take great pride in having all my things in order.

    ____________ c. If I opened my desk drawer, compartments of paper clips, erasers, staples, pens, pencils, stamps, and rulers greeted me without one lost penny or safety pin thrown in out of place.

    ____________ d. On top of my chest of drawers sat a comb and brush, two oval frames with pictures of my best friends, and that was all.

2. Iceland has a very barren landscape.

    ____________ a. One-tenth of the island is covered with ice.

    ____________ b. Not one forest with magnificent trees is to be found.

    ____________ c. Nature has not been kind to the people of Iceland.

    ____________ d. Three-fourths of the island is uninhabitable.

**EXERCISE**

### Distinguishing a Supporting Detail from a Restatement of the Topic Sentence

Each of the topic sentences below is followed by four additional sentences. Three of these additional sentences contain acceptable supporting details, but one of the sentences is simply a restatement of the topic sentence. In the space provided, identify each sentence as *SD* for supporting detail or *R* for restatement.

1. In the last thirty years, the number of people living alone in Canada has increased by 400 percent.

   ____________ a. People are living alone because the number of divorces has dramatically increased.

   ____________ b. Many young people are putting off marriage until they are financially more secure or emotionally ready.

   ____________ c. More and more Canadians are finding themselves living alone.

   ____________ d. An increasing percentage of our population is in the over-65 age group, which includes many widows and widowers.

2. Writing as Sandra Field and Jocelyn Haley, Jill MacLean makes love pay the bills.

   ____________ a. Her first book, *To Trust My Love,* was published by Harlequin.

   ____________ b. Jill received a royalty cheque of about $1800 for her first book.

   ____________ c. She is the author of thirty-six full-fledged romance novels.

   ____________ d. Jill MacLean writes love stories under two pen names.

## How Do You Make Supporting Details Specific?

Students often write paragraphs that are made up of only general statements. When you read such paragraphs, you doubt the author's knowledge and you suspect that the point being made may have no basis in fact. Here is one such paragraph that never gets off the ground.

> Doctors are terrible. They cause more problems than they solve. I don't believe most of their treatments are necessary. History is full of the mistakes doctors have made. We don't need all those operations. We should never ingest all those drugs doctors prescribe. We shouldn't allow them to give us all those unnecessary tests. I've heard plenty of stories that prove my point. Doctors' ideas can kill you.

Here is another paragraph on the same topic. This paragraph is much more interesting and convincing because the general statements throughout the essay have been changed to supporting details.

Evidence shows that "medical progress" has been the cause of tragic consequences and even death for thousands of people. X-ray therapy was thought to help patients with tonsillitis. Now many of these people are found to have developed cancer from these X-rays. Not so long ago, women were kept in bed for several weeks following childbirth. Unfortunately, this cost many women their lives, since they developed fatal blood clots from being kept in bed day after day. One recent study estimates that 30 000 people each year die from the side effects of drugs that were prescribed by doctors. Recently, the Centers for Disease Control reported that 25 percent of the tests done by clinical laboratories were done poorly. All this is not to belittle the good done by the medical profession, but to impress on readers that it would be foolish to rely totally on the medical profession to solve all our health problems.

This second paragraph is much more likely to be of real interest. Even if you would like to disprove the author's point, it would be very hard to dismiss these supporting details, which are based on facts and information that can be researched. Because the author sounds reasonable, you can respect him or her even if you have a different position on the topic.

In writing effectively, the ability to go beyond the general statement and get to accurate pieces of information is what counts. A writer who has a statistic, a quotation, an historical example, or a descriptive detail can use these items to clarify the theme, especially if the examples are well chosen and appropriate. Readers should go away wanting to share with the next person they meet the surprising information they have just learned.

Good writing is filled with supporting details that are specific, correct, and appropriate for the subject. Poor nonfictional writing is filled with generalizations, stereotypes, vagueness, untruths, and/or insults.

**EXERCISE**

## Creating Supporting Details

Below are five topic sentences. Supply three supporting details for each one. Be sure each detail is specific and not general or vague.

1. Jim's entire wardrobe should be burned.

   a. ______________________________

   b. ______________________________

   c. ______________________________

2. The Internet is more valuable than television.

   a. ______________________________

   b. ______________________________

   c. ______________________________

3. Dr. Kline is an easy instructor.

   a. ______________________________

   b. ______________________________

   c. ______________________________

4. It is difficult to stop eating junk food.

   a. ______________________________

   b. ______________________________

   c. ______________________________

5. Learning another language will make your life richer.

   a. ______________________________

   b. ______________________________

   c. ______________________________

## The Concluding Sentence

Some instructors will require that you add a concluding sentence to your paragraph, especially if you're writing a paragraph that stands on its own and not as part of a larger essay. The concluding sentence should give the paragraph a sense of closure. It should be logical and appropriate. It may or may not restate the topic sentence, but it must not introduce new evidence (supporting detail). It is more general than the supporting detail. It also should be the last sentence in the paragraph. Look at the two sample paragraphs on medicine in the previous section on making supporting details specific (pp. 189–90). Find the concluding sentence in each paragraph. Notice that in each case, the controlling idea of the concluding sentence seems either a bit stronger or weaker than that of the topic sentence. Either way, however, the concluding sentence still reinforces the original controlling idea and does not contradict it.

**Concluding Sentences**

A concluding sentence
- is not part of the supporting detail.
- is more general than any individual supporting detail.
- should be the last sentence in the paragraph.
- restates or at least reinforces the controlling idea established in the topic sentence (and, therefore, does not contradict the controlling idea of the paragraph).
- gives the paragraph closure.
- may offer a final commentary on the paragraph.

## Outline Format

Now that you have learned what all the components of a good paragraph are, it is time to piece them all together. What follows is an outline format that can be used for an **extended paragraph.** How many supporting details to include, and how many examples, and how many sentences for each example, and so on, depend on the paragraph being written and what evidence comes to mind when you are writing. So the following format is merely a suggested one to help you see how everything might fit together. Feel free to use it if it can help guide you as you're practising paragraph development.

For a reminder of the difference between supporting sentences and examples, review "Use Specific Examples" on page 186 earlier in this chapter.

**Topic sentence:** ____________________

**Supporting sentence #1:** ____________________

**Example: (2 sentences)** ____________________

____________________

**Supporting sentence #2:** ____________________

**Example: (2 sentences)** ____________________

____________________

**Supporting sentence #3:** ____________________

**Example: (1 sentence)** ____________________

**Concluding sentence:** ____________________

**Total: 10 sentences**

## Working Together: Supporting Details

1. Divide into groups. Select one of the topic sentences on pages 190–91. Together make a list of as many supporting details or examples as you can. Then each student writes a paragraph selecting details from the list prepared by his or her group.
2. Circulate everyone's answers to the assignment within the group. Be sure to give every member of the group enough time to read through all the papers. Then discuss the various paragraphs that have been written. Even though each paragraph began with the same topic sentence and supporting details, all of the paragraphs have turned out differently. Why?

CHAPTER SEVENTEEN

17

# The Essay

## Writing Is a Skill

Very few writers can "dash off" a masterpiece. We sometimes think that a person is "a born dancer" or "a born writer," but the reality is that the person has worked long hours for many years to achieve his or her level of skill. Writing is no exception. Like playing the piano, cleaning a patient's teeth, or managing a restaurant, writing is a skill. It helps to have talent, but talent must still be developed, and skills must still be mastered.

When you learned to write a well-developed paragraph in Chapters 15 and 16, you were creating something that could be a support paragraph for the essay. An essay is a longer piece of writing, usually five or more paragraphs, in which you can develop a topic in much more depth than you can in a single paragraph. The essay may also be called a composition, thesis, or paper. In most schools, such writing is an important part of many courses, not only English composition.

### Transferability

While the essay is required in any number of courses—law enforcement, business studies, office administration, technology, social sciences, journalism, broadcasting, and the like—its purpose goes beyond fulfilling the requirements of a post-secondary-level education. Writing essays also helps prepare students for careers by providing the skills necessary to write corporate reports, evaluations, summaries, research papers, letters, memos, and job applications. Although the structures of various forms of writing may vary, the essay is still the basic form of writing. Spelling, grammar, and logic, essential to the composition of an effective essay, remain paramount in all forms of writing, as does the ability to express yourself clearly. In short, the skills you develop when you learn how to write an essay are transferable in countless ways.

You learned in Chapters 15 and 16 that the paragraph, with its topic sentence and supporting details, must have an organization that is both unified and coherent. The essay must also have these characteristics. Furthermore, since the essay develops a topic at greater length and depth, making all the parts work together becomes an added challenge. Figure 17.1 illustrates the structure of the essay.

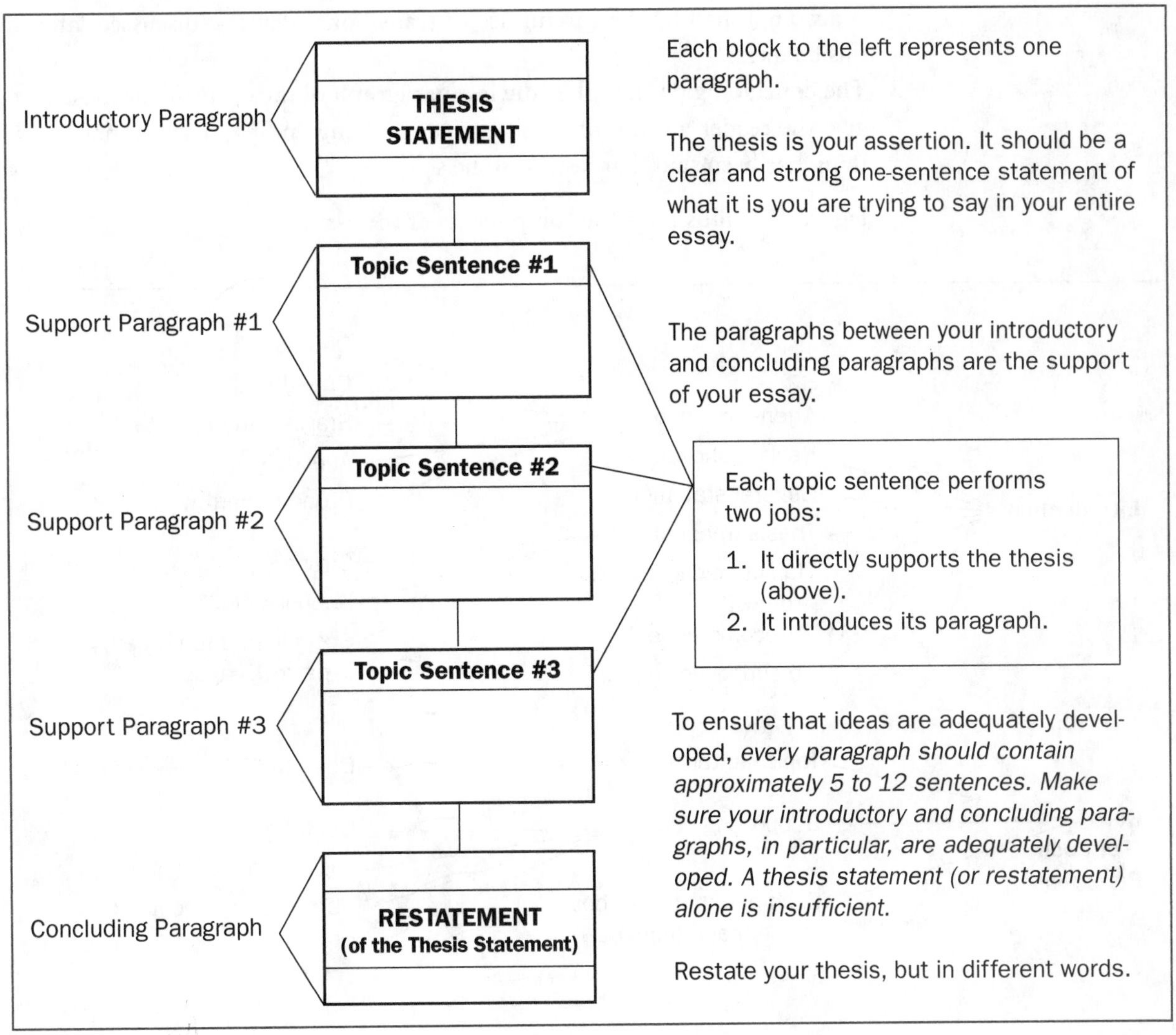


**Figure 17.1: The Structure of an Essay**

## The Components of an Essay

Three types of paragraphs must always be present in an essay: an introductory paragraph, support paragraphs, and a concluding paragraph.

1. **The introductory paragraph is the first paragraph of the essay.** Its purpose is to be so inviting that the reader will not want to stop reading. This introduction must contain a **thesis statement.**
2. **Support paragraphs (sometimes called body paragraphs) provide the evidence that shows your thesis is valid.** An essay normally has at least three well-developed support paragraphs. (You have studied these kinds of paragraphs in Chapter 16.) One paragraph must flow logically into the next. This

is accomplished by the careful use of **transitional devices** (discussed later in this chapter).

3. **The concluding paragraph is the last paragraph of the essay.** Its purpose is to give the reader a sense of coming to a satisfying ending, a sense that everything has been said that needed to be said.

Figure 17.2 illustrates the components of the essay.

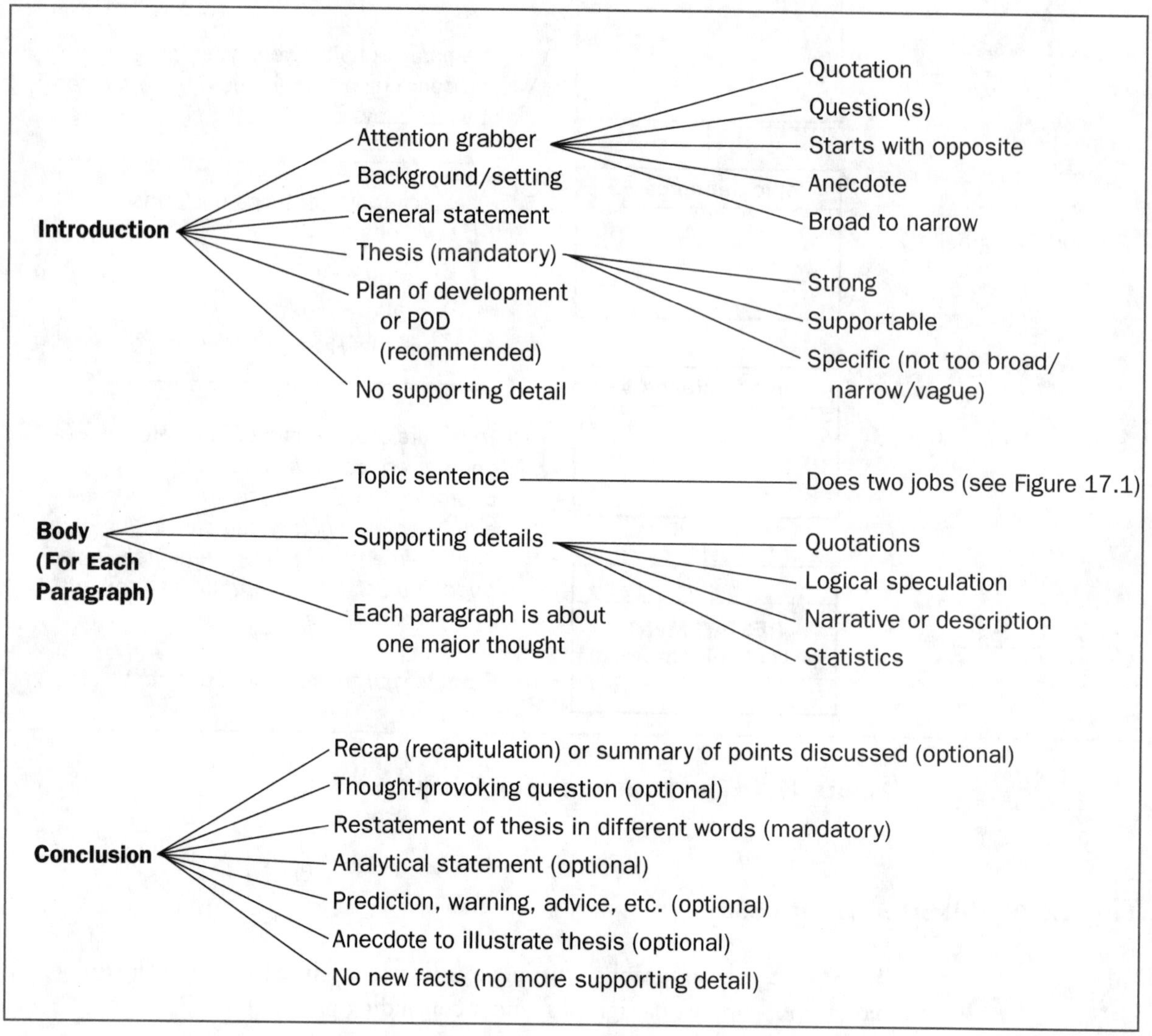


**Figure 17.2: Components of the Essay**

Before you begin the process of writing your own essays, this chapter will prepare you to understand and work with these special essay features:

Thesis statement
Introductory paragraph
Transitions between body paragraphs
Concluding paragraph

## What Is a Thesis Statement?

**DEFINITION ➤** The **thesis** of an essay is a statement of the main idea of that essay. It usually contains an element of opinion or argument. It is sometimes referred to as the claim that evidence in the rest of the essay is expected to support.

The thesis states what you are going to explain, defend, or prove about your topic. It is usually placed in the middle or at the end of the introductory paragraph.

### Plan of Development or POD

**DEFINITION ➤** A **plan of development or POD** is an introduction to the main points that are intended to support the thesis statement. The best place for this POD is immediately after the thesis in the introductory paragraph.

You might have learned before that a thesis statement itself should contain within it three points that you will discuss throughout the supporting paragraphs of your essay. For purposes of this book, this type of thesis is not necessary. It is recommended here, in fact, that if it's important to you that your main points be introduced in the first paragraph, introduce them after the thesis statement. Either a general or specific introduction to these points, according to Figure 17.2, is referred to as the plan of development (POD). Such separation of the thesis from the points that will be used to support it may enable you to formulate a more forceful and effective thesis statement. That said, if your thesis contains three points and is still clear, brief, and strong, feel free to go with it.

### How to Recognize the Thesis Statement

1. **The thesis statement is a complete sentence.** Students sometimes confuse a title with a thesis. Remember that titles are usually phrases rather than complete sentences.

   ***Title:*** The Advantages of All-Day Kindergarten

*Thesis:* Schools should offer parents the option of an all-day kindergarten program for their children, not only for the benefit of mothers who work outside the home, but also for the advantages to the children.

2. **The thesis statement presents a viewpoint about the topic that will be defended or shown in your essay. It may be based on facts, but it is not itself a fact.**

*Fact:* Nearly all kindergartens in Canada offer a half day of instruction.

*Thesis:* Parents know there is more than one reason why most children at five years of age should be in school for only half a day.

**PRACTICE 1**

### Thesis or Fact?

Read each of the following statements. If you think the statement is a fact, mark it with an *F*. If you think the statement is a thesis, mark it with a *T*. Check your answers against those in the Answer Key on p. 466.

____________ 1. In Canada, kindergarten is not compulsory.

____________ 2. Children should begin learning to read in kindergarten.

____________ 3. Putting a child into kindergarten before he or she is physically or emotionally ready can have several unfortunate effects on a child.

____________ 4. In some European countries, children do not begin formal schooling until age seven or eight.

**PRACTICE 2**

### Recognizing the Thesis Statement

In the space provided, identify each of the following as (1) a title, (2) a thesis, or (3) a fact that could be used to support a thesis. Check your answers against those in the Answer Key on p. 466.

____________ 1. The personal interview is the most important step in the employment process.

____________ 2. Looking for a job

____________ 3. Sixty percent of all jobs are obtained through newspaper advertisements.

____________ 4. The best time to begin learning a foreign language is in grade school.

____________ 5. The importance of learning a foreign language

____________ 6. By the year 2000, the number of students studying foreign languages declined dramatically.

____________ 7. Most Canadians doing business with Japan do not know a word of Japanese.

## Writing an Effective Thesis Statement

An effective thesis statement has two and sometimes three parts:

1. **It contains a topic that is not too broad.** Broad topics must be narrowed down in scope. You can do this by *limiting the topic* (changing the term to cover a smaller part of the topic) or *qualifying the topic* (adding phrases or words to the general term that will narrow down the topic).

   *Broad topic:* Swimming

   *Limited topic:* Learning to float (Floating is a kind of swimming, more specialized than the term swimming.)

   *Qualified topic:* Swimming for health two hours a week (The use of the phrase "for health two hours a week" narrows the topic down considerably. Now the topic concentrates on the fact that the time spent swimming and the reason for swimming are important parts of the topic.)

   There are a number of ways to narrow a topic in order to make it fit into a proper essay length, as well as make it fit your experience and knowledge.

2. **It contains a controlling idea that you can defend.** The controlling idea is what you want to show or prove about your topic; it is your attitude about that topic. The controlling idea is often an adjective, such as *beneficial, difficult,* or *maddening.*

   Learning to float at the age of 20 was a *terrifying* experience.

   Swimming two hours a week brought about a *dramatic* change in my health.

3. **Optional in a thesis statement is an indication of what strategy for development is to be used.** Often you can use words such as the following: *description, steps, stages, comparison, contrast, causes, effects, reasons, advantages, disadvantages, definition, analysis, persuasion.*

   Although not all writers include the strategy in the thesis statement, they must always have in mind what major strategy they plan to use to prove their thesis. Professional writers often use more than one strategy to prove the thesis. However, in this book, you are asked to develop your essays by using one major strategy at a time. By working in this way, you can concentrate on understanding and developing the skills needed for each specific strategy.

Study the following thesis statement:

Although a date with the right person is marvellous, going out with a group can have many advantages.

Now look back and check the parts of this thesis statement.

*General topic:* Going out
*Qualified topic:* Going out in a group (as opposed to a single date)
*Controlling idea:* To give the advantages
*Strategy for development:* Contrast between the single date and the group date

**EXERCISE**

## Writing the Thesis Statement

Below are three topics. For each one, develop a thesis statement by (1) limiting or qualifying the general topic, (2) choosing a controlling idea (what you want to explain or prove about the topic), and (3) selecting a strategy that you could use to develop that topic. An example is done for you.

***General topic:*** Senior citizens

a. ***Limited or qualified topic:***

Community services available to the senior citizens in my town

b. ***Controlling idea:***

To show the great variety of programs

c. ***Strategy for development*** (narration, description, process, comparison or contrast, definition, classification, cause and effect):

Classify the services into major groups.

***Thesis statement:*** The senior citizens of New Glasgow, Nova Scotia, are fortunate to have programs available to help them deal with health, housing, and leisure time.

1. Winnipeg (or another city with which you are familiar)

a. Limited or qualified topic:

Toronto

b. Controlling idea:

To Talk about the entertainment available.

c. Strategy for development (narration, description, process, comparison or contrast, definition, classification, cause and effect):

Describe the most ~~attended~~ entertainning places-

Thesis statement:

the city of toronto is full of places to go; specially the ones that ~~captivate the~~ entertain the visitors most such as the CN tower, the Air Canada Centre & the Harbour Front.

2. Shopping

   a. Limited or qualified topic:

   Variety of ~~products~~ in the city.

   b. Controlling idea:

   To list a variety of shopping centers in Toronto.

   c. Strategy for development (narration, description, process, comparison or contrast, definition, classification, cause and effect):

   Classify the stores into major groups.

   Thesis statement:

   There is a variety of stores in the city of Toronto, but they concentrate at the ~~Malls~~ big centers - like Yorkdale Mall, Dufferin Mall and Eaton Centre.

*3. Canadians

   a. Limited or qualified topic:

   ______________________________

   b. Controlling idea: (Attitude)

   ______________________________

   c. Strategy for development (narration, description, process, comparison or contrast, definition, classification, cause and effect): comparison or contra

   Thesis statement:

   ______________________________

   ______________________________

## Answering a Question in the Form of a Thesis Statement

One of the most effective ways to begin an essay is to start with a thesis statement that directly answers a question. Your thesis statement should include the important parts of the question and should also give a clear indication of the approach you intend to take in your answer.

For example, suppose you were going to write an essay in response to the following question:

> Why did the Conservatives under Stephen Harper win the federal election in 2006?

An effective way to begin would be to write the following thesis sentence:

> The Conservatives under Stephen Harper won the federal election in 2006 probably for several reasons.

The reader would then know that this was the topic you had chosen and would also know how you intended to approach this topic.

*Note:* This is not a three-point thesis statement. But the reader might expect a few reasons to be introduced immediately following the thesis in the form of a plan of development (POD).

**EXERCISE**

## Writing Thesis Statements

Answer each of the following questions in the form of a thesis statement. Read each question carefully and underline the important words or phrases in it. Then formulate a thesis that is a one-sentence direct answer to the question. An example has been done for you.

***Essay question:*** How does one learn another language?

***Thesis statement:*** The process of learning another language is complicated, but usually follows four distinct stages.

1. Essay question: Should or should not the Canadian government support young artists?

   Thesis statement:

   In my opinion, the Canadian government should support young artists for a variety of reasons.

2. Essay question: What is the value of being able to speak two languages in Canada?

   Thesis statement:

   The value of being able to speak two language in Canada is well appriced due to ~~affe~~ the diferent opportunitis it gives to a person living in a multicultural country like ~~Canada~~ this

3. Essay question: Is it harmful or beneficial to adopt a child from one culture and raise that child in another culture?

   Thesis statement:

   There ~~is~~ are advantages & disaventages ~~of~~ in adopting a child from one culture and raise that child in another culture; it all defends on how we look at that topic.

4. Essay question: In what ways can the Canadian government discourage people from smoking?

   Thesis statement:

   the Canadian government discourage people from smoking in many ways; one of them is ~~by~~ the limitation stablished as of 2005 ~~disabling~~ that doesn't allow to smoke in certain places and eateries.

5. Essay question: Are some forms of advertising harmful, and, if so, should harmful advertising be banned?

   Thesis statement:

   Some forms of advertising are harmful, and they should be banned to a certain extend, do to the diferent ~~message~~ understanding of the mesage by some, specially kids.

## The Introductory Paragraph

**DEFINITION ➤** An **introduction** has a purpose that is two-fold: to "grab" your readers' attention so that they will keep reading and to establish the thesis or your main idea. Often, in fact, without a thesis, there is no essay.

There is no one way to write an introduction. However, since many good introductions follow the same common patterns, you will find it helpful to look at a few examples of the more typical patterns to help you write your own introductions. In the following examples, most thesis statements are at the end.

1. **Begin with a general subject that can be narrowed down to the specific topic of your essay.** Here is an introductory paragraph on astronomy, from *Universe* by W.J. Kaufmann:

   > Speculation about the nature of the universe is one of the most characteristic human endeavours. The study of the stars transcends all boundaries of culture, geography, and politics. The modern science of astronomy carries an ancient tradition of observation and speculation, using the newest tools of technology and mathematics. In the most literal sense, astronomy is a universal subject—its subject is indeed the universe.

2. **Begin with specifics (a brief anecdote, a specific example or fact) that will broaden into the more general topic of your essay.** Here is the introduction to Miriam Waddington's "The Hallowe'en Party," an essay about a family of Russian Jews settling on a prairie farm just outside of Winnipeg:

   > The year that I was twelve, my father came home one day and announced that he had bought a farm. My sister Helen and I could hardly wait to see the farm which, according to my father, consisted of 26 acres in St. Vital, just beyond the outskirts of Winnipeg. There were 20 acres of bush with buildings, and six acres of meadow beside the river. My father had dreamed of such a farm all the years he was shut up in the dark greasy machine shop where he earned his living. Now as I look back, I can understand my father's deep hunger for land.

3. **Give a definition of the concept that will be discussed.** Here is the introduction to "Man, Woman and Child," an essay by Lydia Bailey about the rising trend of single motherhood:

    They are a new breed of mother—single, self-sufficient, and in their thirties. They have opted for motherhood without marriage. Some call it a return to tribal times when women raised children on their own with the help of other women. Others see it as a dangerous trend, labelling them as "the most narcissistic group of people you will ever see." Regardless of how it's perceived, statistics show that in the past few years, the number of single mothers in their thirties has increased dramatically.

4. **Include a plan of development (a brief summary of points that will support your thesis statement) after your thesis statement.**

    Are you a *Law and Order* junkie? Well, if you are, you'll know that the State of New York has the death penalty. And it seems that it gets applied every now and again if the TV show is any indication. But in Canada, the death penalty was abolished, and it's time to bring it back. One reason to do so is the money that taxpayers will save by not having to maintain the lives of hardened criminals who will never be freed anyway. Secondly, there is no redemption for criminals who are sentenced to life in prison. And lastly, the punishment should fit the crime.

5. **Start with an idea or statement that is a widely held point of view.** Then surprise the reader by stating that this idea is false or that you hold a different point of view. Here is an example from "A Planet for the Taking," by David Suzuki:

    Canadians live under the remarkable illusion that we are a technologically advanced people. Everything around us denies that assumption. We are, in many ways, a Third World country, selling our natural resources in exchange for the high technology of the industrialized world. Try going through your home and looking at the country of origin of your clothes, electrical appliances, books, car. The rare technological product that does have Canada stamped on it is usually from a branch plant of a multinational company centred in another country.

6. **Start with a familiar quotation or a quotation by a famous person,** as Frank Trippett does in this example from "Getting Dizzy by the Numbers":

    "The very hairs of your head," says Matthew 10:30, "are all numbered." There is little reason to doubt it. Increasingly, everything tends to get numbered one way or another, everything that can be counted, measured, averaged, estimated or quantified. Intelligence is gauged by a quotient, the humidity by a ratio, pollen by its count, and the trends of birth, death, marriage and divorce by rates. In this epoch of runaway demographics, society is as often described and analyzed with statistics as

> with words. Politics seems more and more a game played with percentages turned up by pollsters, and economics a learned babble of ciphers and indexes that few people can translate and apparently nobody can control. Modern civilization, in sum, has begun to resemble an interminable arithmetic class in which, as Carl Sandburg put it, "numbers fly like pigeons in and out of your head."

Where is the thesis statement in Trippett's introductory paragraph?

7. **Give a number of descriptive images that will lead to the thesis of your essay.** The descriptive images can make up the plan of development, which, in the case of this paragraph, *precedes* the thesis statement.

> The nuclear family is breaking up. Both parents are working and children are left on their own for long periods of time, or are sent to daycare centres. Youngsters are learning about life from television and from movies, although the life that they learn about is often far removed from the truth. The incidence of crime is increasing among children because they receive little guidance and even less teaching on the difference between right and wrong. Social, moral, and religious values are declining. These are among the reasons why the fabric of society is decaying.

## What Not to Say in Your Introduction

1. **Avoid telling your reader that you are beginning your essay:**

   In this essay I will discuss ...
   I will talk about ...
   I am going to prove ...

2. **Don't apologize:**

   Although I am not an expert ...
   In my humble opinion ...

3. **Do not refer to later parts of your essay:**

   By the end of this essay, you will agree ...
   In the next paragraph, you will see ...

4. **Don't use trite expressions.** Since they have been so overused, they will lack interest. Using such expressions shows that you have not taken the time to use your own words to express your ideas. Some examples of trite expressions are

   busy as a bee
   you can't tell a book by its cover
   haste makes waste

## Using Transitions to Move from One Idea to the Next

Successful essays help the reader understand the logic of the writer's thinking by using transitional expressions when needed. Transitions usually occur when the writer is moving from one point to the next. They also occur whenever the idea is complicated. The writer may need to summarize the points covered thus far; the writer may need to emphasize a point already made; or the writer may want to repeat an important point. The transition may be a word, a phrase, a sentence, or even a paragraph.

Transitions are used to form links between paragraphs and the ideas in them in the same way that transitions are used to link ideas in a sentence or within a paragraph. Paragraphs are used to show a progression of ideas within an essay, a composition, or a research paper. Here are some of the transitional expressions you might use to help the reader make the right connections. Also refer to the **chart on the inside back cover of this book** and notice what other transitions could be used in the categories indicated below.

1. **To make your points stand out clearly:**

| | | |
|---|---|---|
| the first reason | second, secondly | finally |
| first of all | another example | most important |
| in the first place | even more important | all in all |
| | also, next | in conclusion |
| | then | to summarize |

2. **To present an example of what has just been said:**

   for example
   for instance

3. **To present the consequence of what has just been said:**

   therefore
   as a result
   then

4. **To make a contrasting point clear:**

   on the other hand
   but
   contrary to current thinking
   however

5. **To admit a point:**

   of course
   granted

6. **To resume your argument after admitting a point:**

    nevertheless
    even so
    nonetheless
    still

7. **To call the reader's attention to your organization:**

    Before attempting to answer these questions, let me ...
    In our discussion so far, we have seen that ...
    At this point, it is necessary to ...
    It is beyond the scope of this paper to ...

A more subtle way to link one idea to another in an essay is to repeat a word or phrase from the preceding sentence.

> I have many memories of my childhood in the Yukon. These *memories* include the aunts, uncles, grandparents, and friends I left behind when I moved to Ontario.

Sometimes instead of the actual word, a pronoun will take the place of the word.

> Like many Northerners, I've had to learn to adapt to an urban way of life. *It* hasn't been easy, but today I almost think of myself as a Torontonian.

## The Concluding Paragraph

A concluding paragraph has one main purpose: to give the reader the sense of reaching a satisfying ending to the topic discussed. Students often feel they have nothing to say at the end. A look at how professional writers frequently end their essays can ease your anxiety about writing an effective conclusion. You have more than one possibility; here are some of the most frequently used patterns for ending an essay.

1. **Come full circle; that is, return to the material in your introduction.** Finish what you started there. Remind the reader of the thesis. Be sure to restate the main idea using different wording. Here is an example from the essay "The Fatal Question," by Vivian Rakoff.

    > We are involved in an unending process of questioning and adaptation—an adaptation that, with luck, will not fall into a simple-minded rejection of the machine as the work of the devil. It is at least equally valid to see the manufacture of machines and goods as the continuous unfolding of human endowment in a cumulative history. Man the toolmaker is man expressing an ancient and important component of his true nature.

2. **Summarize by repeating the main points.** The following example of a concluding paragraph is from the essay "City Life Beats the Small Town Blues," by Zack Goodman, which appears in its entirety in Chapter 24 (pages 298–300).

   A small town has its advantages; that's true. The cost of living is lower. The streets are probably safer at night. And it might even be easier to meet someone special. But if you're an arts lover who enjoys the company of people from all over the world, and you're interested in cultivating friends who help you to grow spiritually and not just to get drunk on a Saturday night, city life is tough to beat.

3. **Show the significance of your thesis by making predictions, giving a warning, giving advice, offering a solution, suggesting an alternative, or telling the results.** This example is from the essay by David Suzuki discussed previously on page 204.

   But Canadians do value the spiritual importance of nature and want to see it survive for future generations. We also believe in the power of science to sustain a high quality of life. And while the current understanding of science's power is, I believe, misplaced, in fact the leading edges of physics and ecology may provide the insights that can get us off the current track. We need a very profound perceptual shift and soon.

4. **End with an anecdote that illustrates your thesis.** This example is from an essay by Robert Fulford on the Métis and Native people.

   The criminal trials of the Indians and the Métis in the autumn of 1885 seem, in retrospect, outrageously illogical—the rebels were convicted of treason against an empire that had conscripted them as citizens without consulting them. But the North-West Rebellion also produced a trial that was merely bizarre. Shortly after the rebellion ended, an article in the Toronto *News* said that Montreal's Sixty-fifth Battalion had conducted itself during the hostilities in a way that was mutinous, reckless, disorderly, and drunken. Officers of the battalion sued, and eventually the editor of the *News*—a notorious enemy of French Canadians and the French language—was summoned to Montreal to stand trial for criminal libel. Convicted and fined $200, he emerged from the courtroom, barely escaped with his life from a howling mob of outraged Montrealers, and went home to be treated to a torchlight parade of 4000 cheering supporters in Toronto. Two years later, fed up with the stresses of daily newspaper work, the editor, Edmund E. Sheppard, founded a new periodical, *Saturday Night*.

### What Not to Say in Your Conclusion

1. **Do not introduce a new point.**

    Something else of importance ...
    Additional information has come to light ...
    A new idea ...

2. **Do not apologize.**

    Unfortunately, this essay cannot end on a more positive note ...
    If there were more space ...
    It is impossible to be sure of every point ...

3. **Do not end up in the air, leaving the reader feeling unsatisfied.** This sometimes happens when the very last sentence is not strong enough.

    Maybe the problem will never be solved ...
    There is no obvious solution ...
    Hopefully, things will get better ...

## Titles

Be sure to follow the standard procedure for writing your title.

1. Try to think of a short and catchy phrase (approximately three to six words). Avoid complete sentences, even if they're short. Often writers wait until they have written a draft before working on a title. There may be a phrase from the essay that will be perfect. If you still cannot think of a clever title after you have written a draft, choose some key words from your thesis statement, especially that part of the thesis that suggests the point of view you have taken.
2. Capitalize the first letter of the first word and the last word; then capitalize the first letter of the other words except articles (*the, a, an*), prepositions (such as *in, of,* and *on*), and short conjunctions (such as *and, but,* and *so*).
3. Do not put quotation marks around the title when it is in a title position.
4. Centre the title at the top of the page, and remember to leave about 2.5 cm (1 inch) of space between the title and the beginning of the first paragraph.

## Model Outline

Now that you have learned the various components of an essay, it's time to put them all together. The following is a suggested outline of the essay's format. The outline includes suggestions for length, but how long the attention grabber is, and how long each supporting detail is, and how long each example is, and so on, all depend on what your instructor's requirements are, what evidence comes to mind when you are writing the essay, and so on. Next time you write an essay for practice, try using the following outline in order to get used to a proper structure.

For a reminder of the difference between a supporting detail and an example, see "Use Specific Examples" on page 186 in Chapter 16.

**Essay title:** ______________________________
**(see above)**

**First Paragraph (introduction):**

**Attention grabber: (1 sentence)** ______________________________

**General statement: (2 sentences)** ______________________________
______________________________

**Thesis: (one sentence)** ______________________________

**Plan of development: (one sentence)** ______________________________
______________________________

**Second Paragraph (first support paragraph):**

**Topic sentence:** ______________________________

**Supporting detail #1:** ______________________________

**Example:** ______________________________

**Supporting detail #2:** ______________________________

**Example:** ______________________________

**Third Paragraph (second support paragraph):**

**Topic sentence:** ______________________________

**Supporting detail #1:** ______________________________

**Example: (2 sentences)** ______________________________
______________________________

**Supporting detail #2:** ______________________________

**Example: (1 sentence)** ______________________________

**Supporting detail #3:** ______________________________

**Supporting detail #4:** ______________________________

**Fourth Paragraph (third support paragraph):**

**Topic sentence:** ______________________________

**Supporting detail #1: (2 sentences)** ______________________________

______________________________

**Supporting detail #2:** ______________________________

**Example: (2 sentences)** ______________________________

______________________________

**Supporting detail #3:** ______________________________

**Fifth Paragraph (conclusion):**

**Recap: (3 sentences)** ______________________________

______________________________

______________________________

**Thesis restatement:** ______________________________

**Question for further research:** ______________________________

**Thought-provoking idea (prediction):** ______________________________

## Working Together: Education Endangered?

1. The cartoon on the next page uses the technique of a multiple-choice quiz to suggest reasons that education in North America is in trouble. As a class or in groups, discuss each of the four areas of concern raised by the cartoonist. Then write a five-paragraph essay (an introductory paragraph, three supporting paragraphs, and a paragraph of conclusion). Use the information you have learned in this chapter to write a good introduction and conclusion. For your supporting paragraphs, choose three of the four areas of concern shown in the cartoon and make each one the main idea for one of the support paragraphs. Be sure to make use of the ideas generated during the class discussion.

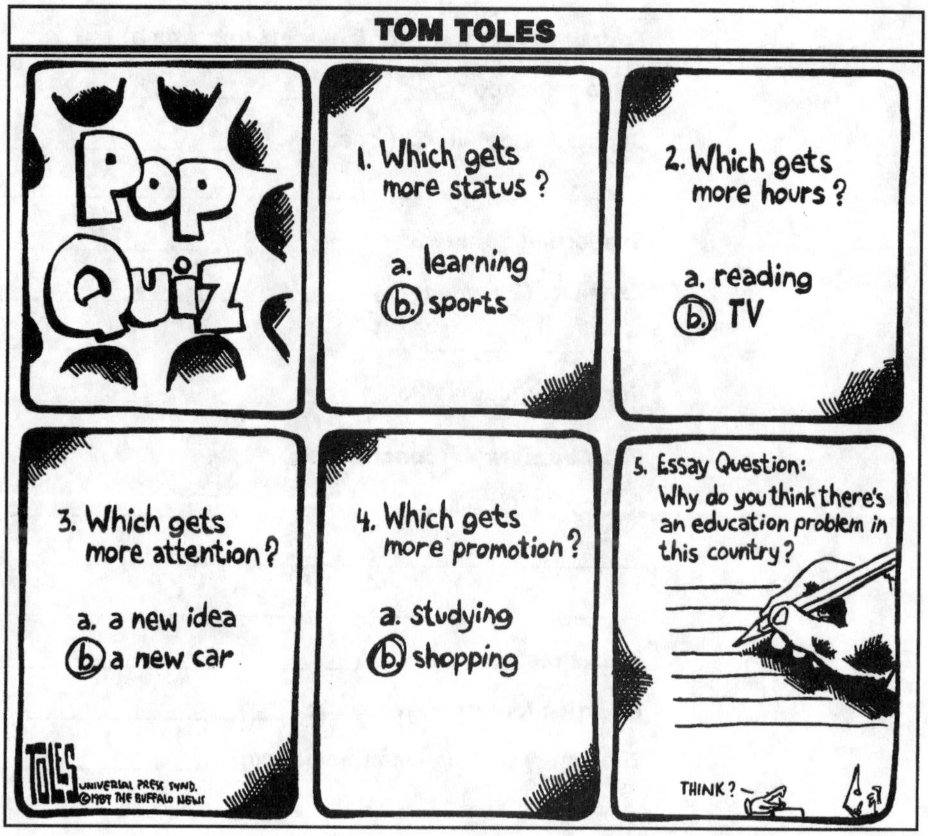




2. Divide into three groups. Each group will study the introductory and concluding paragraphs in any three of the essays in the "Readings" section of this book (Unit IV). Analyze each introduction and conclusion to decide if the author has chosen one of the patterns suggested in this chapter. Can you point to one sentence as the author's thesis statement?

CHAPTER EIGHTEEN

18

# Revising and Editing

## The Final Stage

Too many writers finish their first draft and then start rereading to catch mistakes. Their idea is to get the editing process over with as soon as possible. If the writer misses a few little mistakes, who's going to notice? But revising and editing involve much more than proofreading or rereading and hoping any mistakes jump out. This stage involves a well-planned approach to making improvements, finding mistakes, and discovering better ways of writing.

Revising and editing your writing are necessary before word processing the final copy of your work. They are essential components of the writing process. Of course, you'll need to proofread your final copy for typos and other mistakes you may have made, but revision and editing must precede proofreading. And if the essay is not being word processed, revising and editing, of course, are still required.

### What Is the Difference between Revising and Editing?

Revising and editing are often thought of as one and the same thing. They are not. Specifically, revising is rereading your first draft very carefully and making major improvements. You might replace an entire paragraph with a new one, for example. You might cut the length of a large anecdote in half and add a smaller, but completely different one. Editing, on the other hand, usually means smaller, but still important changes. Revising often refers to changing the content, whereas editing often refers to improving the organization of the composition and the style of writing. Too many people do not spend enough time on these parts of the writing process. However, it's better to make improvements at this stage than to have your professor point out the need for them later.

## Proofreading

After the revising and editing are finished, proofreading begins. Proofreading refers, mostly, to correcting mistakes that might be, for example, grammatical in nature. Minor factual errors in content might also be caught at this stage.

## The Right Conditions for the Tasks

When you've finished the first draft of your work, set it aside for a day or two if you can. Then read through the whole thing, making notes, corrections, or additions based on the checklists on pages 214–16. These checklists are adapted from *The Reluctant Writer* by Roger Mann and John Roberts. Many instructors recommend that you read your essay out loud. Some say that writers can catch up to 70 percent of their own errors this way. It is also important to make sure you've printed off a hard copy of your final draft in order to proofread your work. After all, the eyes read better with reflected light (off paper) than with emitted light (from a computer screen). There is a better chance of spotting errors on hard copy as a result.

What you need first is a quiet place and a block of time that will allow you to complete the task in one sitting. You might also ask someone to read your material and offer a second opinion on the quality of your work when you've completed your revising and editing. And finally, keep in mind that your computer's spell check and grammar check programs are not infallible. As the writer, you are ultimately responsible for your own work, and that includes the revising, the editing, and the proofreading.

### Master Checklist for Revising and Editing

1. Check the macrocomposition: the content and the overall arrangement of ideas. (See Macrocomposition Checklist below.)
2. Check the microcomposition: the flow of thought, the sentence structure, and the wording, grammar, and usage. (See Microcomposition Checklist on the next page.)
3. Check the spelling.
4. Check the punctuation.
5. Check the manuscript form.

### Macrocomposition Checklist

1. Have you provided enough background explanation at the outset for the reader to
   a. recognize the context?
   b. understand what follows?
   c. want to read further?
2. Do the ideas introduced in the beginning connect logically to a continuous line of thought that moves sensibly from introduction to discussion and ends in a conclusion? Are appropriate connecting words used?
3. Are the thoughts packaged in small chunks of information that the audience is capable of following? Will the sequence of ideas convince and enlighten the reader?
4. Is the information sufficient to do the job it is intended to do? Are there any gaps? Is all of the discussion relevant to the subject and the purpose?
5. Is the point of view toward the reader consistent throughout the text?
6. Are the time sequences logical and consistent? Check verbs for uniformity of tense and mood.

*(continued)*

*(continued)*

7. Is the wording concise, and are physical references precise and concrete? If you are dealing with ideas and concepts, are they adequately explained and illustrated? Is the wording geared to the presumed reading level of the reader?
8. Is the tone appropriate to the situation, the purpose, and the reader? Is it consistent throughout the text?
9. Does the conclusion fulfill the intended purpose? At the end, will the reader understand the message, agree with what you have said, and be motivated to act?

## Microcomposition Checklist

**Check your sentences for *grammar:***

1. Is every sentence grammatically complete, with no sentence fragments?
2. In sentences with two or more independent clauses, are the clauses grammatically parallel, and either connected by coordinating conjunctions or separated by semicolons, with no run-ons or comma splices?
3. Are subordinate clauses and verb phrases clearly related to the words they modify, with no dangling or misplaced modifiers?
4. Are the elements of each sentence consistent in grammar and in thought?
   - Do subjects agree with verbs?
   - Do pronouns agree with their antecedents and with each other in person and in number?
   - Is it clear which nouns the pronouns stand in for?
   - Are the verb tenses consistent?
   - If you have used lists, are the elements of each list grammatically parallel?
   - Is the word order appropriate and easy to follow?

**Check your sentences for *style:***

1. Are the beginnings of your sentences varied—do some start with the subject, some with introductory phrases or clauses, and a select few with reversed word order?
2. Have you varied the clause structure of your sentences—some simple, some compound, some complex, some compound–complex?
3. Have you mixed your sentence lengths effectively—long sentences to convey information and establish a rhythm, short sentences to get important points across?

**Check your *wording and usage:***

1. Have you used vocabulary suitable to the reader and the situation?
2. Are your nouns concrete, tangible, and specific?
3. Are your verbs active or passive, as is appropriate to the context?
4. Have you used adjectives and adverbs selectively and sparingly? Can you replace any adjective–noun or adverb–verb combinations with carefully selected single nouns or verbs?
5. Could you explain the reason for your choice of every word and its placement in the sentence?
6. Have you used any words that you are not entirely sure about—the spelling, the meaning, or the way the words should be used?
7. Have you used any clichés? If so, can you justify using them? If not, can you think of original expressions to replace them?
8. Have you used any idiomatic expressions? If so, are you sure you have used them correctly and appropriately?
9. Have you used jargon, such as technical terms or acronyms? Are you sure the reader will understand these terms?

*(continued)*

*(continued)*

**Check your *punctuation:***

1. Have you used periods at the ends of sentences and after abbreviations?
2. Do question marks indicate the ends of interrogative sentences?
3. Have you used exclamation marks to emphasize especially important points or statements? (Do not overuse this device!)
4. Have you used quotation marks properly—for all direct speech, direct quotations from sources, and titles of short works?
5. Have you used, but not overused, commas to pace the reader's understanding of the text, to separate internal parts of your sentences, and to clarify potentially ambiguous word combinations?
6. Have you used semicolons to separate parts of a sentence that are grammatically distinct, or to separate items in a complex list?
7. Have you used dashes and colons correctly?

**Check your *spelling, capitalization,* and *apostrophes:***

1. Have you checked the words you traditionally have trouble with?
2. Have you checked *ie* combinations, spelling changes caused by suffixes, and consonants that must be doubled or not?
3. Have you used capital letters properly—for titles, names, places, months, countries, etc.?
4. Have you used apostrophes correctly—for possessive nouns and indefinite pronouns, or for shortened forms of words?

**Check your *manuscript form:***

1. Has all your source material been suitably acknowledged and documented?
2. Have you used the proper format conventions for the form you are writing—memo, letter, report, essay?

Now that the final stage of the composition has been discussed in detail, it's time to apply this stage of the writing process to an actual sample of a student essay. Of course, just as no two chefs or carpenters or painters approach their work in the same way, no two writers work in the same way either. In spite of this individuality, each writer goes through a surprisingly similar series of steps to reach the finished product.

Again, here is a summary of the steps in the final stage of the writing process.

**Stage Four (Postwriting: Revising, Editing, and Proofreading)**

1. Revising and editing the rough draft (some writers revise their work through many, many drafts before they are satisfied).
2. Writing the second draft.
3. Proofreading (grammar, spelling, style, etc.).
4. Typing or word processing the final copy.
5. Checking for errors (especially typos).

## A Sample Student Essay in Its Fourth Stage

Some instructors prefer that their students not write essays from the first-person point of view (using the word *I*, for example). In the case that follows, however, a student named Allison Hickman has been asked specifically to write a personal-experience narrative essay (see Chapter 21) about fear or anxiety. (For model essays written in a more formal tone, see other chapters such as 20: "Research and Documentation"; 25: "Definition"; 26: "Classification"; and 28: "Argumentation.")

### Sample Student Essay: Revising and Editing the Rough Draft

What follows is a rough draft that Allison has written. In the margin are comments (plus some editing marks in the essay itself) that have been added by Allison's writing instructor to aid in revision. No corrections of punctuation, spelling, or grammar have been made yet. At this stage, the student should focus on the organization and content. As the student works with the text, she may correct some of the grammar errors when she rewrites, deletes, or adds material.

**A more creative title?**

**Performing on the Piano**

**Student has another idea for an introduction.**

**This is the end of the Introduction. Should begin a new paragraph.**

Sometimes I wonder why I play the piano. It makes me so nervous when I have to play in front of people. I want to do well. But I can never play my best when I'm so nervous. I'm going to tell you about a typical performance I gave last February. ¶ On a Saturday afternoon I walked up the long driveway to my piano teachers house. My hands were already shaking and my stomach felt upset. I was not looking forward to this at all. In fact, I had been dreading this moment for over a month. This day would not be the end of my terror. In the Spring I would be playing in a special contest where I would be judged and given a score.

**Paragraph 2 is too short.**

Today, as usual, I felt my piece was not securely memorized. I never had enough time to practise. Although I wanted to please my teacher, I felt funny being nearly the oldest student in her class. I should be the best, I thought.

**Paragraph 3 is too short. Belongs to paragraph 2.**

Now I hoped I wouldn't make a fool of myself in front of the younger kids in my teacher's class, especially that little wizard, Leonard.

**Needs to be a new paragraph.**

He was skinny with big glasses. When he looked at you it seemed to be with a laugh. He was as great at the violin, the computer, and everything else as he was at the piano. ¶ At least I could always count on Michelle to mess up her piece. She never practised but it didn't seem to bother her. She always acted as if she was pleased with herself. At least I knew I sounded better than she did.

**Be more specific.**

I was late as usual the class had begun. Mrs. Stuart was pleased to see me and she motioned to me to take a chair near the piano. The house was so nice. Filled with beautiful furniture and things on the shelves and tables.

**Be more specific.**

Mrs. Stuart was kind to everyone, always trying to make us feel like "somebody." There was something about her looks and personality that made everybody who knew her like her. She had dark eyes and brown hair, was not too tall, and never seemed to wear makeup.

**Use a quotation here.**

Before I knew it, it was my turn. Everyone was watching me. I said what piece I was going to play and sat down. Starting was always the worst. This piece had hard trills and runs and I was really scared. I counted to ten, took a deep breath, and began.

**Paragraph too short. Give more detail.**

It went better than I thought. The trills weren't so great, my runs were shaky, but at least I got through it without forgetting any part. What a relief when it was over.

**Use a quotation here.**

My teacher seemed pleased. She says a few nice words and then moves on to the next student. People were beginning to get tired of sitting. One little girl yawned. Then it was Leonard's turn. He got up and announced that he was going to play the same piece as me. My heart started to beat faster. I was really upset. This little kid was going to play my piece.

**Slang—not appropriate. Give more thought to your reactions.**

You can guess what happened. He played better than me. The teacher praised him to the sky and I ended up feeling like a jerk. Why should I even bother to play piano when there are kids like Leonard?

## Preparing the Final Copy

If you have worked hard in revising and editing the rough draft, you will be delighted with the improvements as you write the final copy.

At this stage of the writing process, it is time to proofread and to use the "Checklist for the Final Copy," which can be found on page 173 in Chapter 14.

READ

### *A Student Essay in Progress: The Final Copy*

**Sonata in C Major, Opus 35**
**by Allison Hickman**

Have you ever been to a children's piano recital? The little seven-year-olds walk eagerly up to the piano, play their 30-second piece that is 16 bars long, feel very pleased with themselves, and walk back to their seats to wait for everyone else to finish. All they are thinking about is the cookies and punch. I, on the other hand, sit pale and still, twisting my hands, dreading the moment when I must take my place at the piano. I must play well. What if I don't play well? What if I make a mess? The thought of forgetting the piece or stumbling through a difficult passage in front of an audience is unnerving. My experience last month at a class recital still makes me shudder.

It was a bleak Saturday afternoon in February. I trudged up the long driveway to my piano teacher's house. My hands were already shaking, and my stomach felt upset. I had been dreading this moment all week. I had to perform my contest piece in front of my teacher and 15 other talented students. Later in the spring, I would be performing the same piece for a judge who would give me a score.

Today, as usual, I felt my piece was not securely memorized. I never had enough time to practise. Even though I practised one hour a day, I really needed to spend at least two hours to get the Mozart sonata that I was playing in good shape. To make matters worse, I was the oldest student. This made me feel that I should be the best even though I knew that several of the others had been playing much longer than I had. Now, I could only hope I didn't make a fool of myself in front of the younger kids in my teacher's class. They never seemed to make any mistakes when they played, especially that little Leonard.

Leonard was a skinny little kid with a mat of black hair slicked smoothly back against his egg-shaped head. His thick glasses made him look like the stereotype of a brainy kid. When he looked at anyone, it was always with a look of amusement. I guess he knew his grey matter was far superior to whatever was in the rest of our heads! He was as good in computer programming, creative writing, and chemistry as he was at the piano. He had been taking lessons for only three years and was already playing pieces at an advanced level. What's more, I heard his mother complaining once that Leonard didn't spend much time at the piano. The worst part of performing in the same room with Leonard was his age. He was only nine!

Now, a student like Michelle made me feel better about myself. I could always count on her to break down in the middle of her piece. She seldom practised. Nevertheless, she was content to do what she could. At least I knew I sounded better than she sounded.

I entered the large Victorian house through the back door as the sound of a familiar Bach prelude drifted out from the heavy doors of the music room. As usual, I was late. I took off my shoes and crept noiselessly into the room, where I slipped into an armchair near the door. Oh, if only I could sit here and just listen. My eyes wandered across the large room filled with beautiful antique furniture and treasures from around the world. In the far corner stood the black ebony grand piano. How much more beautiful its tone was than the old spinet on which I practised. Children ranging in age from five to twelve sat motionless in the rows of sturdy wooden folding chairs set up across a large Oriental rug.

Mrs. Stuart looked over and smiled, seeming to know how nervous I was. She had tried for years to assure me of my talent, yet I still tended to doubt it—particularly on these occasions. Mrs. Stuart was not your typical overbearing piano instructor. She was kind and always encouraging. She was in her mid-thirties, yet appeared younger. Her face was free of makeup, yet her high cheekbones and large dark eyes seemed not to need it. She radiated a warmth that was felt by all of her students.

As soon as the music ceased, I was jolted back into the reality of my situation. I was next. I approached the piano cautiously, feeling the eyes of the younger children riveted upon me. "Uhm ... this piece is a Mozart sonata," I murmured quietly. Filled with difficult runs and countless trills, it was the kind of piece that could easily fall apart, especially when the performer is nervous. I counted to ten in an attempt to calm my nerves, and with one deep breath, I began.

To my surprise, I played the first movement smoothly, hardly missing a note. In the second movement, I made a small memory slip, but I managed to keep going. The third movement gave me some trouble. My fingers didn't seem to be able to move fast enough for the trills. I had to slow down. I missed two of the hard runs. Finally, I reached the last notes of the sonata, heaved a great sigh of relief, and stood up from the bench.

"Beautiful, Allison. I think that was the best I've heard you play this piece. By April you will sound more secure." The reassuring voice of Mrs. Stuart broke the silence, and I started to relax. The younger students were beginning to get restless. One girl yawned, and two boys in the back were poking at each other. Then it was Leonard's turn.

Leonard marched up to the piano with the posture of a West Point cadet. In a high, somewhat nasal voice, he announced, "This afternoon I will perform the Mozart Sonata in C Major, Opus 35." My heart started to beat faster. I was disgraced! Leonard was going to play my piece. How could Mrs. Stuart have given us both the same piece?

Of course all of my hopes were shattered as he began to play. The sound of the music took everyone by surprise. I stared at my teacher in disbelief. I could hardly recognize this as the same piece. The evenness of the trills, the beauty of the melody, the flawless technique on the runs—I had to admit the piece was more beautiful than I had imagined. I was thrilled and devastated. The piece was gorgeous, but my performance had been mediocre, and I felt discouraged.

So now I ask myself, "What keeps me going back to the piano? How can all this misery be worth it?" Well, the answer seems clear to me, now more than ever. It's the thrill of hearing a beautiful piece. And it's the challenge of my re-creating that beauty.

## Working Together: Revising and Editing Activity

Write two to three paragraphs in answering the following question:

> Should volunteer work be a required component of a postsecondary (college or university) education?

Take twenty minutes to write a first draft. Then exchange it with someone else in class. Based on the content of this chapter, revise and edit the draft you've been given; then discuss what you've done with the student whose draft you've worked on. What have you learned from this revision and editing process?

CHAPTER NINETEEN

19

# Summarizing and Paraphrasing

Many companies assign reading to their employees, much like instructors do to their students. At a Monday morning staff meeting, for example, each employee might be expected to summarize a booklet, manual, catalogue, or document for the benefit of everyone. If you are that employee, you might also be expected to produce a written summary for everyone who isn't at the meeting.

The ability to **summarize and paraphrase** well is perhaps one of the most useful skills you will learn. Summarizing and paraphrasing are techniques for rewriting something you have read; they require putting in your own words the main idea or ideas of the original text. They are especially useful techniques when studying for tests and exams and writing research essays because they develop and demonstrate your understanding of the material you have read. When writing a research assignment, the techniques of summarizing and paraphrasing are important in making a coherent document out of your various sources. Translating ideas and information into your own words also helps you remember them better because in order to summarize, you must have a complete understanding of what you have read. You probably will not forget something once you understand it.

## Summarizing

**DEFINITION ➤** A **summary** is written in your own words, but it is a condensed version of an original source.

We practise summarizing all the time in our day-to-day lives. When telling friends about a movie, you don't repeat the story or dialogue from beginning to end. Instead, you will probably relate the main points in the plot or things about the movie that captured your interest.

A summary states the main idea of a passage. The purpose of a summary is to shorten the original piece of writing, providing only important information and eliminating nonessential points. A summary allows the reader to understand the main facts and ideas in the original without actually having to read the entire passage. A summary should be no more than one-third the length of the original passage. The words you use should be your own. To avoid charges of plagiarism, you should not use more than three words at a time from the original. (See more on plagiarism later in this chapter.)

## Tips on Writing a Successful Summary

1. **Read the passage and identify the topic sentence and controlling idea.** Underline the sentence that you think best expresses the main point of the passage. Rewrite this sentence in your own words.
2. **Identify and eliminate minor supporting ideas.** Specific facts or examples may be important in developing a main idea, but they are not to be included in a summary.
3. **Write out the major supporting details in full sentences of your own.** Use as few words as possible, and remember not to use more than three words at a time from the original.
4. **Count the words.** Make sure the total is no more than one-third of the original.
5. **Reread your summary.** Make sure that the meaning of the passage is conveyed clearly and that your sentences work together.
6. **Edit for spelling and grammar.**

**EXERCISE 1** **Writing Summaries**

Find single words to replace the following phrases. Answers will vary.

1. perform an analysis of ______________________________
2. create a reduction in ______________________________
3. engage in the preparation of ______________________________
4. give consideration to ______________________________
5. is dependent on ______________________________

The following passage is taken from a longer piece entitled "Canadian Internet Use Survey" from *The Daily,* published by Statistics Canada on August 15, 2006. Immediately following this excerpt is a summary in the length of a third of its original.

> Two-thirds of adult Canadians surfed the Internet in 2005, and those living in larger cities were much more likely to have done so than those in rural areas and small towns, according to the Canadian Internet Use Survey.
>
> An estimated 16.8 million adult Canadians, or 68%, used the Internet for personal non-business reasons during the 12 months prior to the survey.
>
> Only 58% of residents living in small towns or rural areas accessed the World Wide Web, well below the national average. In contrast, rates in Canada's largest census metropolitan areas ranged from 68% in Montreal to 77% in both Ottawa-Gatineau and Calgary.

The survey also showed that the Internet has changed the way many Canadians do banking and access news. Roughly 6 of every 10 Internet users used it to read news or sports, or to conduct their banking online. Even so, three-quarters of Canadians expressed strong concerns about privacy and security.

The new survey, which replaces the Household Internet Use Survey, was redesigned to focus on individual Internet use. The CIUS did show that in 2005, an estimated 7.9 million Canadian households (61%) were connected to the Internet, up slightly from the nearly 60% reported in 2004 by the Survey on Household Spending.

(206 words)

### *Acceptable Summary:*

Two-thirds of adult Canadians (16.8 million) used the Internet in 2005. Usage in small towns averaged 58% compared to 68% to 77% in Canada's large cities. Also revealed was that many people who accessed the Internet to do online banking also have strong privacy concerns. And finally, the survey shows that the number of households connected to the Internet was up slightly in 2005 from 2004 (61% from 60%).

(67 words)

**EXERCISE 2**

## Summarizing a Paragraph

Summarize the following passage, reducing it to approximately one-third of its original length:

Canadian society in the twenty-first century is very different from that of early Canadians, and not just because we have televisions and VCRs. Two hundred years ago, people lived half as long as they do today, and families had twice as many children. In general, all Canadians are living longer, which means not only is our working life extended, but we can expect to retire from work and live another 15 to 20 years to enjoy the fruits of our labours. Canadians born in 1700 had an average life expectancy of 30 to 35 years due to poor diet, disease, and accidents. By 1831, four generations had passed, and there had been a slight improvement in life expectancy, with males expecting to live to age 40 and females to 42. During the next four generations, major medical breakthroughs and public health education eliminated a number of infectious diseases and reduced infant mortality, so that Canadians' life spans were almost double what they were a little more than a century previously. But while Canadians can expect a long and healthy life, with many living well into their seventies or eighties, the average life span will not increase indefinitely. While we can expect to live longer than the Canadians of the 1700s, we can't expect to live forever.

**EXERCISE 3**

## Summarizing an Article

John Cleland and Thérèse Zarb wrote this 435-word article. Write a summary of it that is one-third its length (approx. 100–150 words).

### Steer Away from Road Rage

According to a Steel Alliance-Canada Safety Council survey, drivers in B.C. are more likely than those in other regions to tailgate and change lanes without signalling. Ontario drivers are more likely to drive through a yellow light turning red, and steal parking spaces.

Road aggression is not a new phenomenon. It gained attention when the media recharged it by coining the term "road rage." According to Claudia Palucci, media and public affairs specialist for CAA Central Ontario, "what was rude and careless driving before, now has a sexy new term [road rage]. But aggressive driving hasn't suddenly appeared on our roadways; it was always there." In public opinion surveys, Canadians perceive an increase in roadway aggression despite a lack of objective data to confirm this.

***

Although systematic observational studies are lacking, traffic researchers have suggested several factors that increase the likelihood of aggressive driving.

"Driving is tailor-made to engender anger," says Dr. Lorne Korman, clinical psychologist and head of the Anger and Addictions Program at the Centre for Addiction and Mental Health in Toronto. He explains that the inherent goal of driving is to get from point A to point B, and reality dictates that there will always be obstacles along the path: other automobiles, pedestrians, road signs, and construction. The more congested our roads become, the more thwarted we feel on the way toward our goal. For many, this interference amounts to personal violation. And it is when we feel violated, says Dr. Korman, that we react with anger. Angry drivers seem to attribute the situational barriers to other drivers' deliberate interference. Furthermore, drivers are less likely to inhibit this aggression because "driving is life and death. You are moving fast, you have to make fast decisions, and your body is aroused physiologically."

Dr. Korman also believes that the deluge of car chases and smashes in the media contributes to our feeling of empowerment and recklessness behind the wheel; the automobile becomes an aggressive tool rather than a means of transportation.

***

Due to the anonymity of driving, we are more likely to express our annoyance in our car than on the sidewalk. We believe that we can get away with an anti-social act because we are not face-to-face and do not know our opponent. Escape is easy when we rely on the protection and speed of our automobile.

Finally, we can roll out the usual suspects believed to fuel dangerous driving. We transport our personal and professional stress with us in our cars. Combine that with a "me-first," rat-race mentality and we may find ourselves skidding toward a head-on collision with aggression.

*Wellness Options* (February–March 2001)

## Paraphrasing

**DEFINITION ➤** **Paraphrasing** is the process of putting another writer's work into your own words. A paraphrase can be as long as or even longer than the original.

An effective **paraphrase** follows not only the line of reasoning in the original source, but also the sequence of ideas or evidence. You paraphrase in an essay when it is important that every sentence of the original work be conveyed to your reader. But like summarizing, paraphrasing should be done in your own words. Paraphrasing is typically done for shorter passages that are about a paragraph or two in length. Don't worry, your instructor won't ask you to paraphrase a whole book!

### Writing a Successful Paraphrase

1. **Read the passage and define all unfamiliar or technical terms.** Write all unfamiliar terms and their definitions on a separate sheet of paper.
2. **Reread the passage, paying closer attention to the content and the order in which the ideas develop.** Make sure you have a clear understanding of the passage you are reading before you begin paraphrasing it.
3. **Begin converting the language of the passage into your own words, sentence by sentence.** Look for synonyms of words used in the passage. Alter sentence structure and vocabulary until you are conveying the original ideas in your own voice. If the original uses the first person (*I*), change it to the third person (*he* or *she*).
4. **Write out your paraphrase in full sentences of your own.** Remember not to use more than three words at a time from the original.
5. **Edit for spelling and grammar.**

**EXERCISE**

### Writing Paraphrases

Use your own words or phrases to express the following. Answers will vary.

1. utterly

___

2. Every cloud has a silver lining.

___

3. No pain, no gain.

_______________________________________________

4. He's like a wolf in sheep's clothing.

_______________________________________________

5. The apple doesn't fall far from the tree.

_______________________________________________

The sample paragraph below is followed by unacceptable and acceptable paraphrases.

### *Original:*

"Reality-based" TV programs, which have become very popular recently, appear to capture spontaneous events on film. However, most viewers are not aware that much of the action that transpires on these programs is staged. People who appear on these shows are often selected because producers think they will appeal to the audience, and directors often script important pieces of dialogue at critical moments during production. Therefore, relationships that develop between participants on these shows are often as contrived as those between characters on a TV sitcom or a soap opera.

### *Unacceptable:*

"Reality-based" TV shows, which have become popular recently, seem to depict spontaneous events on film. Most people, however, do not know that a lot of the action that takes place on these programs is staged. The people on shows like these are often selected because the producers believe they will appeal to viewers, and directors frequently write important pieces of dialogue at crucial moments during the filming of the show. Therefore, relationships that develop are frequently as phony as those between personalities on TV sitcoms or soap operas.

This is an unsuccessful paraphrase because the underlined structure and phrasing are almost identical to the original. In fact, much of the structure and phrasing has not changed at all from the original.

### *Acceptable:*

The popularity of "reality-based" TV shows is founded on the belief that live events are being filmed, but many viewers do not know that much of what they see is made purposely dramatic. Producers of these shows often choose participants because they believe viewers will find them attractive, and the shows' directors often have them acting from scripts to heighten the drama. Thus, participants create relationships that are no more real than those we see on other TV shows, such as sitcoms or soap operas.

This passage is an example of good paraphrasing. The writer has taken the main idea of the original paragraph and restated it using his or her own words. All of the original details and examples appear, but they have been reworded and the sentences restructured.

**Plagiarism: A Serious Offence**

Students who write unacceptable paraphrases can be accused of plagiarism. Plagiarism is a form of intellectual theft. It occurs when a student uses the ideas or words of another person *without giving credit to the original source or author.* You can avoid plagiarism by ensuring that credit for work other than your own is cited. (See Chapter 20: "Research and Documentation.") When you paraphrase a passage, be sure to inform your reader about who the original author is and where the original work appeared.

Plagiarism often results in a mark of zero on an assignment. If this is a major assignment, one case of plagiarism can result in the overall failure of a course. Plagiarism is not only contrary to school policy; it is also against the law. If you are not sure about how to avoid being accused of plagiarism, ask your professor for advice.

## Avoid Unintentional Plagiarism

With so much information at our fingertips today, there may be a tendency and, perhaps, an irresistible temptation to use what is in front of us (such as something on a website) for our papers without even realizing that we might be opening ourselves up to charges of plagiarism. Many instructors consider as few as three words together that are lifted from someone else's text to be plagiarism if these words are not in quotation marks and attributed to their original author.

So if you are summarizing or paraphrasing, and you want to avoid the plagiarism trap, here is a trick of the trade: Read something closely enough that you understand what it is you have read. Then close the book, or the window on the computer (or reduce it so that you cannot see it for now). Write what you remember or as much as you think you need for the purpose of your paper. Then go back to the original if necessary to check for accuracy. You also might want to check to make sure you haven't, by accident, ended up with phrases three words or longer that are in the original. If you have, change the wording of these phrases. If the original is relatively long, do this one paragraph at a time. Not only will you protect yourself, in this way, from accusations of intellectual thievery, but you will find yourself absorbing the reading material more efficiently. Such development of better work habits can lead to all sorts of rewards when doing assignments that involve reading and writing.

**EXERCISE**

### Paraphrasing a Paragraph

The following passage was excerpted from an article entitled "A Dead End for Humanity," by Wade Davis. Write a paraphrase of this paragraph. The passage contains 79 words, so your paraphrase should be about the same length.

> Of the 6000 languages spoken today, fully half are not being taught to children. Effectively, these languages are already dead. By the end of the twenty-first century, linguistic diversity may be reduced to as few as 500 languages. A language, of course, is not simply vocabulary and grammar; it is a flash of the human spirit, the vehicle by which the soul of a culture comes into the material realm. Each language represents a unique intellectual and spiritual achievement.
>
> *The Globe and Mail* (December 28, 2000)

## Analyzing and Critiquing

Eventually, your professor will ask you not only to repeat what someone else has already written, but to agree or disagree and explain the reasons why. If you look at Unit IV of this book, you'll notice several questions at the end of each reading, questions that are classified into four groups. This first of four groups is called "Comprehension Questions." These are questions that require some summarizing and paraphrasing. They require that you recall or look back at what you've read and that you repeat, in one way or another, what the author has written.

"Questions for Discussion" and "Questions about Form," on the other hand, require more thinking on your part. They require analysis and argumentation. You, at times, will have to support or refute what the author has written. One skill you will develop in this area is usually referred to as critical thinking. It is often a requirement in courses across the curriculum at the postsecondary level, a requirement that can only help you in any workplace. For more on critical thinking and analysis, see Chapter 28: "Argumentation."

## Working Together: Summarizing Opposing Points of View

Form groups of three or four. Look in your local newspaper for feature articles on controversial topics that are of concern to many Canadians, such as the effects of global warming or genetic engineering. Try to find one article that looks at the problem from one perspective, and another article that takes an opposing view. For instance, find an article that supports high-speed police chases and another that takes the view that high-speed police chases are too dangerous. Each person then writes a summary of one of these articles, making sure that the opposing points of view are clearly indicated. You might use this information to discuss ways in which the media attempt to influence the attitudes of Canadians.

CHAPTER TWENTY

20

# Research and Documentation

## The Research Paper

With the research paper, you are given the opportunity to showcase your work. You finally have a chance to "sink your teeth" into something you've been curious about. You can devote more time to thinking about, reading for, and writing on a subject that interests you. As the research paper generally requires a fair amount of independent reading, you should start it early—as soon as the project is assigned. You'll maximize your potential not only for a higher grade, but also for major insights. Indeed, the research paper enables you to go on a journey of intellectual discovery.

**DEFINITION ➤** A **research paper** is an essay that presents research in support of a thesis. All ideas that are not the writer's own are expected to be fully documented according to a specific academic style such as MLA or APA. A good research essay should be well researched, well documented, and, most of all, insightful.

### Responsible Research

Once you have your topic and you have some idea of the direction you want to take, it's time to start your research. Don't worry about a thesis until after you've done some serious reading. And once you've decided on a thesis and the points you want to make in support of your thesis, make sure you can find at least two pieces of evidence for every point you want to make. If you're finding this difficult to do, change your point, or even your thesis if necessary. If students report having trouble finding sources, it's often because they've set off in a certain direction (with a particular thesis in mind) far too early in their research process. As you do more reading on your subject, the direction your paper should take becomes more and more clear. Knowing too quickly what you want to say and trying to force your research to support your ideas can cause you to waste a great deal of time, not to mention frustrate you very early in the process. Allow yourself to learn. Find what exists, not what you want to see.

### Books, Periodicals, and the Internet

If your topic is current, such as the topic of the sample research essay in this chapter (cell phones and their effects on our health), you may find that most of your sources will have to come from periodicals (materials published on a regular basis such as newspapers, magazines, and academic journals) and the Internet. But if your topic is a well-established one, a good place to start would be the library's catalogue for a search of relevant books. Ask the librarian for help. Every library is different. Until you are well acquainted with its resources, the librarian can give you some excellent advice to start you on your way.

## The Literary Research Paper

### Primary vs. Secondary Sources

If your instructor has assigned a research paper on literature, you may have to research both primary and secondary sources. **Primary sources** are the works of literature themselves. For example, if you are writing about Margaret Atwood, you might look up some of the novels she has written: *Cat's Eye*, *The Handmaid's Tale*, and so on. These are primary sources. If your instructor wants you to also include works by critics about her writing, these works are considered **secondary sources.**

## The General Topic Research Paper

### Primary vs. Secondary Research

For a general topic research paper, your instructor might require that you conduct primary research as well as secondary research. The first can be more time consuming than the latter. **Secondary research** is done upon a trip to the library or by research on the Internet; **primary research,** however, might consist of an interview with an expert on the subject, an experiment that you have designed and conducted, a survey that you have circulated among certain people who qualify, and so on. You can always control the amount of time you spend in a library. But when it comes to primary research, the process tends to get more unpredictable, and the plans you make don't always work out. Just setting up an interview, for example, can take more time than expected. Because the interview involves another human being, his or her schedule might not coincide with your own. The more time you give yourself to work on all of these things, the better.

## Internet vs. Library Research

More and more students have computers at home nowadays with access to the Internet. As a result, whenever a research paper is assigned, the Internet is, for reasons of convenience, the first step in the research process. Too often, unfortunately, students do not go beyond the Internet. Your instructor, however, may require you to do so. You may, for example, be instructed to go to a library to do the kinds of research that are not possible via the Internet. If so, ask a librarian for help. In any event, whether or not the Internet is the only source of research you use, it is important to determine the legitimacy of online sources (see pages 232–33).

## Internet Research

If you already have a very specific topic in mind, start with search engines. Put in a string of keywords that are critical to your search, and see what "hits" you make. The best way to determine an appropriate search engine is to visit and use various search engines yourself. The best one for you might depend on the project you are engaged in as well as overall personal preferences. The following are some suggestions:

### Search Engines

Google (www.google.com) is the most popular search engine on the Internet. It has introduced "Google Scholar" (scholar.google.com), which is academically oriented, pointing the researcher toward technical reports, academic papers, books, and so on.

Other excellent search engines include the following:

- AlltheWeb.com (www.alltheweb.com)
- Alta Vista™ (www.altavista.com)
- Lycos® (www.lycos.com)
- Ask Jeeves (www.ask.com)

### Academic Directories

The majority of websites are commercial and therefore profit-oriented. Their domains end with *.com*, so domains that end differently are often more useful for academic purposes: *.ca, .org, .edu, .net, or .gov.*

General directories such as Yahoo! (www.dir.yahoo.com) aim to accommodate the general public. They do not meet the needs that are considered more academic in nature. Here is a list of academic directories that are designed to help you in specific areas:

- The Internet Public Library (www.ipl.org), organized by librarians, has links to thousands of articles, theses, magazines, newspapers, and books from around the world.
- The Librarians' Index to the Internet (lii.org) includes 14 000 sites assessed by librarians for their academic value.
- WWW Virtual Library (www.vlib.org), a multidisciplinary academic directory.
- www.infotrac-college.com (free four-month membership comes with this book) provides articles from the *New York Times.*
- www.freefulltext.com includes over 7000 scholarly journals, but is browsable by title only.
- etext.Virginia.edu contains 70 000 texts in 13 languages, with links to research resources.

**TIP**

**The use of quotation marks can help you reduce the number of useless hits. It is particularly useful for names. You may want to look up London, Ontario, for example. But if you want to avoid all hits for London, England, type in "London Ontario."**

**EXERCISE**

### Using a Search Engine

Pick one of the following subjects and see what you can find using more than one search engine. List three sources dealing with the subject of your choice.

1. Effects of global warming

 ______________________________

 ______________________________

 ______________________________

2. Sonny Bono's political career

 ______________________________

 ______________________________

 ______________________________

3. Canadian soldiers in Afghanistan

 ______________________________

 ______________________________

 ______________________________

4. Medicinal uses for marijuana

 ______________________________

 ______________________________

 ______________________________

## Analyzing the Legitimacy of Online Sources

A great deal of excellent material can be found on the Internet, much of it for free. But not everything online is legitimate. In fact, because the electronic medium is so difficult to regulate by governmental regulatory bodies, much illegitimate and even illegal material, such as hate literature, goes unchecked and its producers not prosecuted. However, there are guidelines you can follow to make sure you are using only proper sources. (Much of the following can also be used to assess the legitimacy of regular print sources.)

1. Look for the name of the writer. If you find one, do an independent online search of the name to see what, if anything, anyone else says about this person, and what associations this person has. Are the associations with reputable organizations? If the source is not attributed to an actual name of a person, make sure that, at the very least, a reputable organization claims responsibility for the material. Do an independent online search of the organization. See what other organizations say about it, and, ultimately, based on the information you have gathered, use your common sense.
2. Is the writer of the source biased toward a particular point of view because of a connection to an organization with a specific agenda? Be aware of the one-sided approach of such writers. Does he or she give the other side fair play in his or her writing? Is there a demonstrated respect for the other side of the argument? Try to discern between a point of view and an attack on an individual or identifiable group. (See "Common Fallacies" in Chapter 28.) There are countless organizations especially on the World Wide Web whose only purpose, it seems, is to spew hatred at a particular group or groups of people. Avoid these attacks altogether. It is without question that writers with no obvious agenda and with no particular stake in the matter tend to have the most credibility and to develop the best arguments. The pieces they write, therefore, often make the best sources for your research paper.
3. Is the writing well edited and relatively free of errors? Is the site well designed and professionally presented? Has the site been revised recently, or does it seem to have been abandoned after being established a long time ago? In other words, how well is the site being maintained?
4. Are there links on the website? If so, where do they lead? Do they lead to other academic materials? Or do they lead to commercial or entertainment sites instead?

The answers to any of these questions may not provide you with conclusive evidence of anything. But with more information at your disposal, you'll be better equipped to assess the legitimacy of the sources you have found.

**EXERCISE**

### Evaluating Online Sources

Use the three sources that you found as a result of doing the previous exercise on using search engines (on page 232). Discuss the legitimacy of these sources using the above criteria.

## Using Quotations

By the word *quotation,* this textbook means the exact words used by an author or speaker. Therefore, the most important thing when it comes to quotations is that you must be careful to use the precise word-for-word text of the author (or the person who has quoted within the source you are using). Some quoting is good because it breaks up your text and makes your essay more interesting to read in general. However, try to keep your quoting to a minimum. Quote only those things that you cannot say better yourself, and remember, whenever you include a quotation, you are expected to explain to the reader why the quotation appears in your essay and how it connects to your thesis. You might also be expected to interpret the quotation if its meaning is not straightforward enough already.

How you incorporate a quotation into your essay depends on how long the quotation is. Short quotations are embedded within your regular paragraphs. Longer quotations are indented and set apart from your regular paragraphs.

## Short (Integrated) Quotation

**RULE ➤** **For a short quotation, four lines or under (some say forty words or under), place quotation marks around the quotation and integrate the quotation within the regular paragraph. Such a short quotation might be a sentence or two, or even a spot quotation, meaning a quotation that is a partial sentence integrated within your own sentence.**

### *Example of a short quotation:*

Notice the introduction (without quotation marks) of the quotation followed by a comma.

Notice the absence of the word *that* between the word *says* and the quotation. The word *that* is reserved for paraphrases (see Chapter 19).

> The professor said *that* Campbell was a great mythologist.
> The professor said, "Campbell was an accomplished mythologist." (no *that* between the introduction of the quotation and the quotation itself)

Notice that there is no indentation of the quotation.

A common theme in the study of mythology is that of the hero and the hero's journey. In his most famous book, *The Hero with a Thousand Faces,* Joseph Campbell says, "The battlefield is symbolic of the field of life, where every creature lives on the death of another."

Notice how the final period goes inside the quotation mark. If this is a documented paper, however, there would be no period inside the quotation mark. Instead, a set of parentheses (for the internal documentation) would follow the last quotation mark, and a final period would follow the parentheses. See examples under APA and MLA for internal documentation below; pp. 237–39 (APA) and pp. 240–43 (MLA).

### Longer (Block) Quotation

**RULE ➤** **If your quotation is longer than four lines (or forty words), you must set it apart from your regular paragraph. When you do this, indent (by a few spaces) the part that is quoted. Do not use quotation marks around or within this quotation at all unless there are quotation marks already within the original quotation.**

***Example of a block quotation:***

The first two lines of the quotation are Campbell's words, so there are no quotation marks yet. But in the third line, there is a set of quotation marks around the words "after long, long years." These words are words that Campbell, himself, has taken from another source (the story by the Grimm Brothers).

In his most famous book, *The Hero with a Thousand Faces,* Joseph Campbell begins to tell the story of "Sleeping Beauty":

Indent the entire quotation.

> Little Briar-rose (Sleeping Beauty) was put to sleep by a jealous hag (an unconscious evil-mother image). And not only the child, her entire world went off to sleep; but at last, "after long, long years," there came a prince to wake her. "The king and queen (the conscious good-parent images), who had just come home and were entering the hall, began to fall asleep, and with them the whole estate...."

Note the four periods at the end of the quotation before the final quotation mark. These four periods at the end of a quoted sentence indicate that the original quotation continues, but for the purposes of the quotation by Campbell, this is all that is necessary to support whatever point he is making.

## Documentation

**DEFINITION ➤** **Documentation** is the formal acknowledgment of sources in your research paper that protects you against charges of plagiarism (theft of ideas). It involves a combination of citations (internal documentation) and a listing of sources (end documentation). The citations are inserted within the text of the research paper, while the listing of sources is always on a separate page (or pages) at the end of the research paper. A particular academic format, such as MLA or APA, must be applied to both the citations and list of sources.

For more on plagiarism, see page 227.

### Two Academic Styles of Documentation: APA and MLA

Although there are several academic styles of documentation, APA and MLA are the two most common. APA stands for American Psychological Association. MLA stands for Modern Language Association. They are universal styles in that they are known and used in research throughout the world. Which one is used depends on the subject matter. Generally speaking, APA is commonly used for the physical and social sciences: physics, medicine, psychology, sociology, and so on. MLA, on the other hand, is used for subjects in the humanities: literature, philosophy, religion, the arts, and so on. **In business, no one style is dominant.** If the program in which you are enrolled requires that you apply one of these two styles to your research, it would be wise to continue to apply the same style as long as your English professor does not object. If it does not matter to anyone which style you choose, you might want to briefly examine the differences between the two styles outlined below and choose the one that you think most suits your needs. Regardless of which one you end up choosing, you must apply it correctly and consistently to both your internal and end documentation.

## Two Mandatory Parts of Documentation: Internal and End

There are two kinds of documentation that you must incorporate into your research paper regardless of which academic style you choose:

- Internal documentation (using sets of parentheses throughout the essay)
- End documentation (list of entries of sources at the end of your paper)

### Connection between Internal and End Documentation

Often, students do not see the reason that both forms of documentation must be provided in a research paper. They do not understand the connection between the two and therefore their interdependent relationship (one needs the other to be valid). A citation in the form of parentheses with information inside them (usually author and page number for MLA) is used to show exactly where an author's idea has been used in your paper, either in the form of a direct quotation or a paraphrased or summarized idea. (For summarizing and paraphrasing, see Chapter 19.) Using the limited information between the parentheses, one can then go to the list of sources at the end of the paper and find out exactly from what publication (or website) the idea was taken. One can then locate the source if necessary for fact checking, further research, and so on.

### Citations Not Just after Direct Quotations

Many students believe that citations are required only after direct quotations. They believe that if they put someone else's idea into their own words, then documentation is no longer required. This is not true. If an idea from another author has been paraphrased or summarized and is not considered common knowledge, its source must also be acknowledged in the form of both a citation and its listing at the end of the paper. If you are not sure whether or not the idea you're thinking of paraphrasing is common knowledge, check with your professor. It's better, after all, to be safe than sorry.

## American Psychological Association (APA)

### APA Format

APA

Follow these guidelines for formatting your APA paper.

- **Title Page:** On a separate page, include the title (double-spaced if more than one line), your name, the course code, the professor's name, and the date of submission. Double-space everything on the title page, and centre everything, left to right and top to bottom. Do not italicize, underline, or place quotation marks around your title. Capitalize key words (see capitalization for titles on page 148). See the sample title page on page 245.
- **Running Head:** On every page, place a shortened version of the title and page number at the top right margin.
- **Abstract (if your instructor requires it):** On a separate page following the title page, include an abstract, which is a block-paragraph (no indentation) summary of your paper. The title (Abstract) should appear centred 2.5 cm (one inch) from the top of the page. Start your abstract one double line space after the title. The length of your abstract should be somewhere between 75 and 150 words.

### Internal Documentation: Print Sources (APA)

Internal documentation in APA is referred to as reference citations. These citations must appear throughout the body of your research paper (approx. 3–4 per page). What they include (between parentheses) depends on what is already included in your text leading up to the citation. A common reference citation immediately following a quotation would include the author's name, the year of publication, and the page number. See the following example.

#### ***When you do not name the author in your text:***

> "The battlefield is symbolic of the field of life, where every creature lives on the death of another" (Campbell, 1973, p. 238).

See how the above reference citation corresponds to the APA bibliographic entry starting with Campbell on page 239, under "Entry (from a References list)."

On the other hand, if the author is already named in your text, it is common practice to put the year in parentheses immediately after the author's name when it is mentioned. After the quotation, the only citation necessary is that of the page number. See the following example.

### *When you do name the author in your text:*

> In *The Hero with a Thousand Faces*, Joseph Campbell (1973) wrote, "The battlefield is symbolic of the field of life, where every creature lives on the death of another" (p. 238).

### *When you paraphrase or summarize:*

When developing citations for paraphrased or summarized ideas rather than quotations, there is no need for the page numbers. See the following example.

> War is like life, in which some people have to die so that others can live (Campbell, 1973).

Or

> Campbell (1973) says that war is like life, in which some people have to die so that others can live.

Or if two books or more by Campbell are being used:

> Campbell (1973) says that war is like life, in which some people have to die so that others can live (*The Hero*).

(*The Hero* is short for the full book title *The Hero with a Thousand Faces.*)

## Internal Documentation: Electronic Sources (APA)

Electronic sources include the same information as other sources, though most of the time, for an electronic source, there will be no page number. In this case, if there is a paragraph number, use this after the abbreviation "para." instead of "p." If there is no paragraph number, the author's last name and year of publication will suffice:

> (Jones, 2002)

If there is no author, use part of the title:

> ("Cell Phone Links," 2004).

**TIP**

**Remember to put article titles (or parts of article titles) in quotation marks, but italicize titles of major works such as books, journals, and newspapers.**

APA

## End Documentation: Print Sources (APA)

The list of sources in APA style at the end of your essay is referred to as References. This is the word that should appear as the title of this list. The list of entries under this title must be alphabetized according to the first word (usually the author's last name) of each entry. If two entries begin with the same name, apply the same principle by which the phonebook works: go to the year after the name and put the entry with the most recent year first, and so on.

### *Entry (from a References list):*

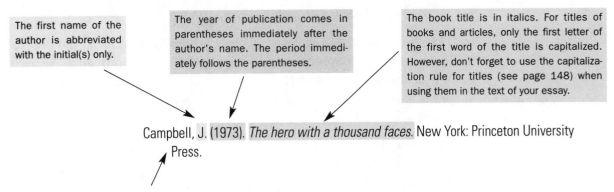

The first name of the author is abbreviated with the initial(s) only.

The year of publication comes in parentheses immediately after the author's name. The period immediately follows the parentheses.

The book title is in italics. For titles of books and articles, only the first letter of the first word of the title is capitalized. However, don't forget to use the capitalization rule for titles (see page 148) when using them in the text of your essay.

Campbell, J. (1973). *The hero with a thousand faces.* New York: Princeton University Press.

The second (and any subsequent line) of the References list for APA must be indented. If there were a third line, it would align with the second line.

## End Documentation: Electronic Sources (APA)

The general principle with electronic sources is that you should include as much information as you can so that someone else can find your source. Make sure the URL (website address) is copied with complete accuracy. The slightest incorrect detail (a hyphen, for example) can invalidate the entire URL. The URL is without hyperlink. To eliminate a hyperlink, right-click on the hyperlink, go to "remove hyperlink," and left click on this.

The following model is commonly used when in comes to electronic sources for APA.

### *Article in a periodical:*

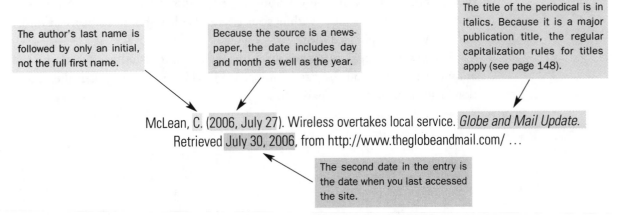

The author's last name is followed by only an initial, not the full first name.

Because the source is a newspaper, the date includes day and month as well as the year.

The title of the periodical is in italics. Because it is a major publication title, the regular capitalization rules for titles apply (see page 148).

McLean, C. (2006, July 27). Wireless overtakes local service. *Globe and Mail Update.* Retrieved July 30, 2006, from http://www.theglobeandmail.com/ ...

The second date in the entry is the date when you last accessed the site.

**EXERCISE**

### Formatting APA Entries for a References List

Use the sources you have found as a result of the search engines exercise on page 232. Formulate their entries for a References list of sources according to APA style. Remember to list them alphabetically according to the first word of the entry.

MLA

## Modern Language Association (MLA)

MLA

### MLA Format

Follow these guidelines for formatting your MLA paper.

- **Title Page:** For MLA, a separate title page is not required unless your instructor requires one. If none is required, type the following information flush left and double-spaced and start 2.5 cm (one inch) from the top of your first page: your name, your professor's name, your course code, and the date submitted.

  Johann Hilton
  Professor Einstein
  COMM 301
  23 April 2007

  If your instructor does require a separate title page, centre your title (not underlined, not in quotation marks, and not in italics). Apply capitalization rules for titles (see pp. 148–49). Centre the above information underneath the title. Double-space this information, also.

- **Headers:** Create a header with your last name and the page number (Hilton 1) for the top right corner of all pages beginning with the first page of your paper (whether this is a separate title page or not). You will find the "header" option under the "view" menu in most word-processing programs. A header is found on the separate page with the Works Cited list, also.

### Internal Documentation: Print Sources (MLA)

Internal documentation in MLA is made up of parenthetical references or parenthetical citations. As mentioned above, a parenthetical reference must appear after you refer to a source within your essay whether this reference is a direct quotation or paraphrased idea.

The parenthetical reference is information that usually consists of the author's last name and the page number from which you have taken the quotation or idea inside a set of parentheses.

### *When you do not name the author in your text:*

"The battlefield is symbolic of the field of life, where every creature lives on the death of another" (Campbell 238).

Notice that there is no period before the end quotation mark. The period that ends the sentence comes after the reference in parentheses. Secondly, notice there is no comma between the author's last name and the page number inside the parenthetical reference.

When you include the author's name in the body of your text, there is no need to include the name of the author within the parenthetical reference. The page number is enough.

### *When you include the author's name in your text leading up to the quotation or paraphrased idea:*

Campbell states, "The battlefield is symbolic of the field of life, where every creature lives on the death of another" (238).

Notice there is still no period before the second (end) quotation mark. The period still comes after the parentheses.

### *For a source with two authors:*

"Perhaps the Canadian experience can serve as a paradigm, since Canadian writers also searched for a voice through much of the twentieth century" (Sullivan and Levene 9).

### *For an author of at least two sources listed in your Works Cited list:*

"The battlefield is symbolic of the field of life, where every creature lives on the death of another" (Campbell, *The Hero* 238).

Notice that there is a need to mention the title in the parenthetical reference if the author is responsible for two different sources in your paper. But the title of the book need not be complete (*The Hero with a Thousand Faces*), as long as an important part of the title is present. Any title of a book must be italicized (or underlined); the parenthetical reference is no exception.

## Internal Documentation: Electronic Sources (MLA)

Electronic sources don't always provide page numbers. In this case, use the paragraph number preceded by the abbreviation *par.* If neither the page number nor the paragraph is provided, use the author's last name only. This is sufficient to link the citation to more information in the Works Cited list at the end of your paper.

(Statistics Canada, par. 28)
(Rogers)

## End Documentation: Print Sources (MLA)

As already discussed, documentation would not be complete without a Works Cited list in which all your sources are listed, starting on a new page. When a reader sees your parenthetical reference such as (Campbell 238), he or she may look right away at your Works Cited list to see more information on the book to which you have referred. In the Works Cited list, the first thing the reader looks for is the name Campbell since it is the first thing you see in the parenthetical reference: (Campbell 238). The reader might see a Works Cited *entry* like this:

### ***Works Cited entry:***

The last name of the author comes first. If there are two authors, the second author's name is given first name first and last name last.

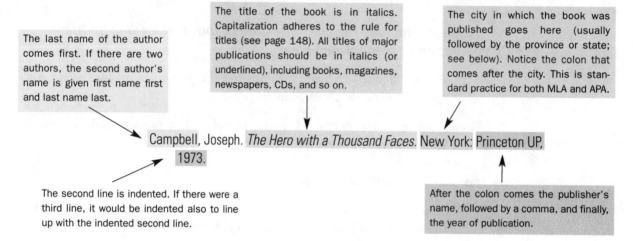

The title of the book is in italics. Capitalization adheres to the rule for titles (see page 148). All titles of major publications should be in italics (or underlined), including books, magazines, newspapers, CDs, and so on.

The city in which the book was published goes here (usually followed by the province or state; see below). Notice the colon that comes after the city. This is standard practice for both MLA and APA.

Campbell, Joseph. *The Hero with a Thousand Faces.* New York: Princeton UP,
    1973.

The second line is indented. If there were a third line, it would be indented also to line up with the indented second line.

After the colon comes the publisher's name, followed by a comma, and finally, the year of publication.

Notice that this city is not followed by the name of the state (which is also New York, of course) because New York is a famous enough city that its state or country is not necessary. But if the city were Moose Jaw, instead, it should be followed by *SK* to help people locate it in Saskatchewan.

**TIP** **MLA requires that provinces and states be abbreviated using postal abbreviations (e.g., SK, ON, CA).**

## End Documentation: Electronic Sources (MLA)

The general rule for electronic sources in the Works Cited list is to include as much information as you can find. And the URL (uniform resource locator) alone is never sufficient. You must give your readers sufficient information so that they can find on the Internet exactly what you have found.

MLA

### *Citation for a web page with an author given:*

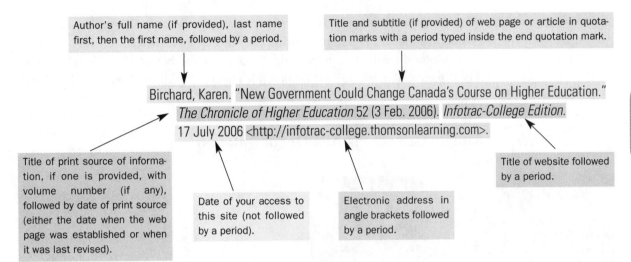

Author's full name (if provided), last name first, then the first name, followed by a period.

Title and subtitle (if provided) of web page or article in quotation marks with a period typed inside the end quotation mark.

Birchard, Karen. "New Government Could Change Canada's Course on Higher Education." *The Chronicle of Higher Education* 52 (3 Feb. 2006). *Infotrac-College Edition.* 17 July 2006 <http://infotrac-college.thomsonlearning.com>.

Title of print source of information, if one is provided, with volume number (if any), followed by date of print source (either the date when the web page was established or when it was last revised).

Date of your access to this site (not followed by a period).

Electronic address in angle brackets followed by a period.

Title of website followed by a period.

- Both the title of a print source and the title of a website are italicized or underlined.
- Page not applicable for the print source given on web page.
- City (if provided) and publisher, followed by a period.
- If editor(s) of the print source are provided, add "Ed." and then the name(s) (names not inverted, followed by a period) after the title of the journal.

### *Article in a periodical (with author's name):*

McLean, Catherine. "Wireless Overtakes Local Service." *Globe and Mail Update* 27 July 2006. 30 July 2006 <http://www.theglobeandmail.com>.

### *Article in a periodical (without author's name):*

"Cellphone Radiation." *CBC News Online* 3 June 2004. 29 July 2006 <http://www.cbc.ca>.

### *Article from a database:*

"Long Mobile Phone Use Raises Brain Tumor Risk: Study." *Information Week* 3 April 2006. *Infotrac College Edition from Gale Group and Thomson Learning.* 28 July 2006 <http://infotrac-college.thomsonlearning.com>.

**EXERCISE**

### Formatting MLA Entries for a Works Cited List

Use the sources you have found as a result of the exercise on search engines on page 232. Formulate their entries for a Works Cited page according to MLA style. Remember to list them alphabetically according to the first word of the entry.

## Sample Research Paper

READ

What follows is a formal research paper. It will first be shown using the APA style of documentation. Next, one paragraph, rather than the entire essay, and end documentation will be repeated for the purpose of showing how MLA applies. The topic is cell phones and their possible effects on the human brain. (See related reading, "How R Tngz, Dude?" in Unit IV.)

APA

### Sample Essay Using APA Documentation

It was always important for a tobacco company to portray someone who smoked as "cool."

Some scientists say cell phone usage is the modern version of smoking. It might seem "cool" to some, but like smoking, it might prove to be addictive and dangerous.

The Cell Phone: Tomorrow's Medical Menace?

By Leila Sayeed

ENG 101

Professor P. Muldoon

March 17, 2008

Cell Phone 2

Cell phones are the latest craze—a modern addiction. For young people, the cell phone not only contributes to the look of "cool" in the way smoking once did and perhaps still does for some, but also offers them a degree of independence—a way to stay in touch with friends without having to check at home for messages. Like smoking, however, not everything about the cell phone is positive. The cell phone, for example, is being blamed for an increasing number of car accidents. And some claim that the cell phone, like the computer and the television, is just another piece of technology that people use—unconsciously, perhaps—to avoid real intimacy. But what might be the worst consequence of all is the one that users seem to be ignoring the most. Startling evidence from scientists around the world has shown that the cell phone does, in fact, interfere with DNA and the human brain. The trouble is no one is absolutely sure of the long-term effects because the technology is simply not old enough. Until it is known for certain whether people will develop serious diseases such as dementia or cancer directly due to cell phone use, it would be wise for cell phone users to err on the side of caution and take steps to minimize potential damage to the brain.

The cell phone is a microwave transmitter. It uses electromagnetic energy to transmit signals from fixed base stations. The growth rate of cell phone technology has been massive and rapid. The number of cell phone users reached 2 billion around the world at the end of 2005 (Reuters, 2005). In Canada, the number of cell phone users increased by 13 percent in 2005 to 17 million (McLean, 2006). Despite the enormity of the industry's expansion, the technology (the cell phone in its present form) has only been around since the 1980s. And those researchers who believe cell phones will cause cancer also say cancer takes decades to develop. It may be years if not decades, therefore, before we start to hear about cases of direct linkage between cell phones and brain cancer, making it easy for cell phone companies to insist in the meantime that their product is safe. This is ominously reminiscent of the decades during which tobacco companies had insisted smoking could not be linked to lung cancer.

Several studies of cancer and its possible link to cell phone use have been conducted in the United States and Europe between 1993 and the present day. One such study was sparked by a lawsuit that a Florida man filed in 1993. He claimed his wife's brain tumour had been caused by her cell phone. In response to this lawsuit, the Cellular Telecommunications Industry Association (CTIA) formed Wireless Technology Research (WTR) and granted it more than $25 million to study possible health risks of cell phone use. After six years, George Carlo, public health scientist and WTR's chairman announced an alarming conclusion:

> We found evidence of genetic damage in human blood. We have suggestions of excessive mortality from brain cancers among wireless phone users, and we have very clear evidence of a statistically significant higher risk of neuroepithelial tumors. We now have more data suggesting problems with wireless phones than the FDA (U.S. Food and Drug Administration) had when it banned silicone breast implants. The CTIA, which funded the study, is, in turn, funded by huge companies that produce mobile phones and communications infrastructure. It is not surprising, therefore, that these results were not widely publicized. (Bass, 1999, p. 62)

In the book *Cell Phones: Invisible Hazards in the Wireless Age*, Dr. Carlo and syndicated columnist Martin Schram (2001) write how Carlo, after running the cell phone industry's research program for six years, quit due to a conscience he could no longer ignore. He could not say what the industry wanted him to—that all was well. "The big picture is becoming disturbingly clear: There is a definite risk that the radiation plume that emanates from a cell phone antenna can cause cancer and other health problems" (p. 248).

Links between microwave radiation and DNA damage in rat brains have been established by several scientists in the U.S. alone. U.S. neurosurgeons Henry Lai and N.P. Singh of the University of Washington in Seattle in 1997 reported damage to the brain cells of rats exposed to microwave radiation, according to U.S. magazine *Business Insurance*. The two neurosurgeons claim a "hot spot may develop in the brain, causing cell damage which could lead to neurodegenerative diseases [such as Alzheimer's] and cancer" (Aldred, 1997, p. 25). Although human brains are not rat brains, "we have similar physiology, and our brain cells work basically in similar ways to theirs," says Sheila Rogers (2003), founder and director of the international nonprofit organization Association for Comprehensive NeuroTherapy. Ross Adey is a professor of biochemistry at the University of California at Riverside. He found a link between low-intensity microwaves and DNA damage in rat brain cells. Even if cell phone microwaves do not damage human DNA, their interference alone may impede the ability of DNA to repair itself when damaged by other causes (Bass, 1999).

In Europe, one of the most alarming major research studies was conducted in Sweden in 2006. Researchers at the Swedish National Institute for Working Life looked at 2200 cancer patients and compared them with an equal number of healthy control cases. Of the cancer patients, 905 had a malignant brain tumour, and a tenth of these were heavy users of cell phones (usage of at least one hour a day for at least

10 years). There was also a high incidence of the tumour appearing on the side of the head that the phone was generally used. Researchers in this study concluded that long-term mobile phone use raises the risk of brain tumours, especially in people who start using by the age of 20 (Reuters, 2005). And if anyone thinks cordless phones are safer, they should think again. Cordless phones (marked 900 megahertz or 2.4 gigahertz) give off the same microwave radiation as cell phones do (Worthington, 1998).

Not all of the research has resulted in negative findings. The National Cancer Institute (U.S.) supported an earlier study of approximately 1600 people in the year 2000. It found that cell phone users are "no more likely than anyone else to develop benign tumors or malignant brain cancers" (Kolata, 2000). The American Health Foundation, a private, nonprofit research organization in Valhalla, New York, conducted a smaller study in the same year. It found similar results after examining 1000 people. The latter study was funded by the U.S. government and the cell phone industry (Kolata, 2000).

It is extremely unlikely that an essay like this will convince anyone to get rid of his or her cell phone. But at the very least, there are some tips gathered from CBC News Online and CTV.ca that aim to minimize the damage to one's brain:

- Use a headset whenever possible, especially in a location where the signal to the phone is weak, such as in a basement. Headsets and cell phones with speakerphone capability are highly recommended. Both allow the phone to be positioned safely away from the user's brain.
- Try to use the cell phone only for emergency purposes, not for long conversations. When and where possible, use a landline or phone booth instead. The British government currently advises cell phone users to keep their calls short.
- Using the cell in a moving car is particularly dangerous, so minimize this usage as much as possible. Not only can it cause accidents, but a cell phone works particularly hard to receive a signal when the car is moving, so the electromagnetic field is stronger, putting one's brain further at risk.
- If you are not using a headset, do not put the cell phone to your head until after the call is established. Until the signal is established, the phone is working harder to find the signal, therefore increasing the electromagnetic field.
- Try as much as possible to use the cell phone only when it is fully charged or when the signal it receives is at its strongest (check the signal bars). Again, the harder the cell phone has to work to receive a signal, the harder it is on your brain.

Cell Phone 5

- A person under the age of 16 should only use a cell phone for essential calls since his or her head and nervous system might still be developing. Children under the age of 10 should not use cell phones at all.

Someone walking down the street with a cell phone at his or her ear, for many young people, still rates high on the meter of "cool." It makes some people feel important when it looks like they are "well connected." It can appear to take the loneliness out of being alone. But today's craze might be tomorrow's tragedy. Smoking has already proven to be the medical menace of today. What seems like a new addiction (especially among the youth) may prove to be the medical menace of tomorrow. For those who cannot quit using cell phones any more easily than it is for some to quit smoking, they might want to try the tips listed in this essay. But if others are more serious about self-improvement, the best solution is obvious: they should go back to using a landline. They might be saving some money. They might also be saving their lives.

Cell Phone 6

## References


magazine article — Aldred, C. (1997, January 6). Cell phone dangers require further study. *Business Insurance, 31*(1), 25.

magazine article — Bass, G. (1999, December). Radar: Is your cell phone killing you? *PC/Computing*, 62.

book with two authors — Carlo, G., & Schram, M. (2001). *Cell phones: Invisible hazards in the wireless age*. New York: Carroll & Graf.

online newspaper article — Cell phones not linked to brain cancer: Study. (2005, August 31). *CTV News, Shows and Sports*. Retrieved July 18, 2006, from http://www.ctv.ca

online newspaper article — Cellphone radiation. (2004, June 3). *CBC News Online*. Retrieved July 29, 2006, from http://www.cbc.ca/news/background/cellphones/radiation.html

newspaper article — Kolata, G. (2000, December 20). Two studies report no links to cancer in cell phones' use. *New York Times*, p. A1.

magazine article from online database — Long mobile phone use raises brain tumor risk: Study. (2006, April 3). *Information Week*. CMP Media Inc. Retrieved July 28, 2006, from *Infotrac College Edition from Gale Group and Thomson Learning*: http://infotrac-college.thomsonlearning.com

online newspaper article — McLean, C. (2006, July 27). Wireless overtakes local service. *Globe and Mail Update*. Retrieved July 30, 2006, from http://www.theglobeandmail.com

posting to a web forum — Rogers, S. (2003, January 31). Electromagnetic radiation: New study on mobile phones and brain. Message posted to ACN Forums. Retrieved July 29, 2006, from http://www.latitudes.org/forums/index.php?act=Print&client=printer&f=10&t=90

online magazine article — Worthington, A. (1998). Cellphones shrink brain cells. *Health, Wealth & Happiness*. Retrieved July 17, 2006, from http://www.relfe.com/cellphones_brain_cancer.html

MLA

## Sample Essay Using MLA Documentation

A portion of the previous essay is being repeated here to demonstrate how MLA parenthetical references (citations) apply to the same text. A Works Cited list (in full) appears later.

Sayeed 3

Links between microwave radiation and DNA damage in rat brains have been established by several scientists in the U.S. alone. U.S. neurosurgeons Henry Lai and N.P. Singh of the University of Washington in Seattle in 1997 reported damage to the brain cells of rats exposed to microwave radiation, according to U.S. magazine *Business Insurance*. The two neurosurgeons claim a "hot spot may develop in the brain, causing cell damage which could lead to Alzheimer's disease and cancer" (Aldred 25). Although human brains are not rat brains, "we have similar physiology, and our brain cells work basically in similar ways to theirs," says Sheila Rogers, founder and director of the international nonprofit organization Association for Comprehensive NeuroTherapy. Ross Adey is a professor of biochemistry at the University of California at Riverside. He found a link between low-intensity microwaves and DNA damage in rat brain cells. Even if cell phone microwaves do not damage human DNA, their interference alone may impede the ability of DNA to repair itself when damaged by natural causes (Bass 62).

What follows is the MLA equivalent of the *References* list. Note the title *Works Cited*.

Sayeed 6

## Works Cited


magazine article

Aldred, Carolyn. "Cell Phone Dangers Require Further Study." *Business Insurance* 6 Jan. 1997: 25.

magazine article

Bass, Gordon. "Radar: Is Your Cell Phone Killing You?" *PC/Computing* Dec. 1999: 62.

book with two authors

Carlo, George, and Martin Schram. *Cell Phones: Invisible Hazards in the Wireless Age.* New York: Carroll & Graf, 2001.

online newspaper article

"Cell Phones Not Linked to Brain Cancer: Study." *CTV News, Shows and Sports* 31 Aug. 2005. 18 July 2006 <http://www.ctv.ca>.

online newspaper article

"Cellphone Radiation." *CBC News Online* 3 June 2004. 29 July 2006 <http://www.cbc.ca>.

newspaper article—late edition

Kolata, Gina. "Two Studies Report No Links to Cancer in Cell Phones' Use." *New York Times* 20 Dec. 2000, late ed.: A1.

magazine article from online database

"Long Mobile Phone Use Raises Brain Tumor Risk: Study." *Information Week* 3 April 2006. *Infotrac College Edition from Gale Group and Thomson Learning.* 28 July 2006 <http://infotrac-college.thomsonlearning.com>.

online newspaper article

McLean, Catherine. "Wireless Overtakes Local Service." *Globe and Mail Update* 27 July 2006. 30 July 2006 <http://www.theglobeandmail.com>.

posting to a web forum

Rogers, Sheila. "Electromagnetic Radiation: New Study on Mobile Phones and Brain." Online posting. 31 Jan. 2003. ACN Forums. 29 July 2006 <http://www.latitudes.org/forums/index.php?act=Print&client=printer&f=10&t=90>.

online magazine article

Worthington, Amy. "Cellphones Shrink Brain Cells." *Health, Wealth & Happiness* 1998. 17 July 2006 <http://www.relfe.com/cellphones_brain_cancer.html>.

## Questions for Analysis

1. What, in your own words, in one sentence, is the thesis of this research essay?
2. Which sentence in particular is the author's thesis?
3. What is the evidence that supports the thesis?
4. Does the author provide evidence that contradicts her thesis? If so, what is it?
5. If the answer to question 4 is yes, does this evidence help or hinder the author's argument?
6. Is the author's argument effective? Why or why not?
7. Who is the intended audience?
8. What does the author want her audience to think or do as a result of reading this essay?
9. Do the sources seem legitimate? Why or why not?
10. Consider the line at the end of paragraph 6: "Researchers in this study concluded that long-term mobile phone use raises the risk of brain tumours, especially in people who start using by the age of 20." What do the last few words, "who start using ..." suggest? Does this suggestion correspond to anything else in the essay? Discuss.

## Working Together: Finding Appropriate Sources

Find *five* sources on the Internet that seem to oppose the point of view taken in the sample research paper in this chapter. Create bibliographic entries (end documentation) for them according to MLA or APA style. Then answer the questions below, and discuss your answers with others in your group or class.

1. How do you know if the sources you have located are legitimate?
2. What were the subject headings (or search terms) you used?
3. Did you use any other tips or information from the chapter to help you find appropriate sources?
4. Answer the following based on the information in this chapter and your reading of the full text of some of the sources that you've found:
   a. What observations have you made about these sources?
   b. What observations have you made about the overall issue of the possible health effects of cell phone usage?

UNIT THREE

III

# Writing Strategies for the Paragraph and Essay


**CHAPTER 21** NARRATION

**CHAPTER 22** DESCRIPTION

**CHAPTER 23** PROCESS

**CHAPTER 24** COMPARISON AND/OR CONTRAST

**CHAPTER 25** DEFINITION

**CHAPTER 26** CLASSIFICATION

**CHAPTER 27** CAUSE AND EFFECT

**CHAPTER 28** ARGUMENTATION

CHAPTER TWENTY-ONE

21

# Narration

All of the chapters in this unit apply to both the paragraph AND the essay. The flexibility of this text enables you to move immediately to the essay portion (roughly in the middle of each chapter) if you wish to do so. Even if you do choose this option, you might want to scan the first half of the chapter to see if you can pick up anything that might be of value to your writing experience. After all, where the various writing strategies are concerned, a great deal of what applies to the paragraph applies to the essay as well. Suggested topics for paragraphs, for example, can also be used for essay topics, and vice versa.

## What Is Narration?

**DEFINITION ➤** **Narration** is the oldest and best-known form of verbal communication. It is, quite simply, the telling of a story.

Every culture in the world, past and present, has used narration to provide entertainment as well as information for the people of that culture. Since everyone likes a good story, the many forms of narration, such as novels, short stories, soap operas, and full-length movies, are always popular.

## Developing Paragraphs: Narration

The following narrative paragraph, taken from an essay by Al Purdy titled "The Iron Road," tells the story of Purdy's trip westward in 1937, the height of the Great Depression, when he was looking for work. In this passage, Purdy has been caught illegally riding a freight train by the railway police, and he is imprisoned in a caboose.

### Model Paragraph

When returned to my prison-on-wheels, I felt panic-stricken. I was only seventeen, and this was the first time I'd ventured far away from home. I examined the caboose-prison closely, thinking: two years. Why, I'd be nineteen when I got out, an old man! And of course it was hopeless to think of escape. Other prisoners had tried without success, and windows were broken where they'd tried to wrench out the bars. And the door: it was wood, locked on the outside with a padlock, opening inward. It was a very springy door, though. I could squeeze my fingertips between sill and door, one hand at the top and the other a foot below. That gave me hope, blessed hope, for the first time. My six-foot-three body was suspended in air by my hands, doubled up like a coiled spring, and I pulled. The door bent inward until I could see a couple of daylight inches between door and sill. Then Snap! and screws fell out of the steel hasp outside. I fell flat on my back.

## Working with Narration: Using Narration to Make a Point

At one time or another, you have met a person who loves to talk on and on without making any real point. This person is likely to tell you everything that happened in one day, including every cough and sideways glance. Your reaction to the seemingly needless and endless supply of details is probably one of fatigue and hope for a quick getaway. This is not narration at its best! A good story is almost always told to make a point: it can make us laugh, it can make us understand, or it can change our attitudes.

When Al Purdy tells the story of his escape from the caboose, he is careful to use only those details that are relevant to his story. For example, the way the door is constructed is important. Had it not been wooden and springy, he might never have been able to get his fingertips in and force an opening. He might have had to spend two years in prison. Then Purdy would have had a different story to tell.

What is Purdy's point in this paragraph? The excerpt is part of an essay about Purdy's experiences during the Depression, and specifically, in this part, about the dangers of travelling illegally by train during that time, which many thousands of people had to do, illegal and dangerous or not. On its surface, then, the story is merely about a trip, although an unusual one. Being imprisoned in the caboose, however, might be metaphorical: the caboose in which Purdy was imprisoned might represent the life of hopeless despair caused by unemployment that he and thousands of others were imprisoned in, and Purdy's escape was the escape from despair toward the hope that a trip to the West could bring, with its opportunities for a better life.

**EXERCISE**

### Using Narration to Make a Point

Each of the following examples is the beginning of a topic sentence for a narrative paragraph. Complete each sentence by providing a controlling idea that could be the point for the story.

1. During my trip to the East Coast, I was surprised by ______________________

______________________________________________

2. When I couldn't get a job, I realized ______________________________

______________________________________________

3. After going to the movies every Saturday for many years, I discovered ________

______________________________________________

4. When I arrived at the room where my business class was to meet, I found ____

______________________________________________

5. When my best friend got married, I began to see that ________________

______________________________________________

## Coherence in Narration: Placing Details in Order of Time Sequence

Ordering details in a paragraph of narration usually follows a time sequence. That is, you tell what happened first, then next, and next, until finally you get to the end of the story. An event could take place in a matter of minutes or over a period of many years.

In the following paragraph, the story takes place in a single day. The six events that made the day a disaster are given in the order in which they happened. Although some stories flash back to the past or forward to the future, most use the natural chronological order of the events.

**Model Paragraph**

My day was a disaster. First, it had snowed during the night, which meant I had to shovel before I could leave for work. I was mad that I hadn't gotten up earlier. Then I had trouble starting my car, and to make matters worse, my daughter wasn't feeling well and said she didn't think she should go to school. When I eventually did arrive at school, I was twenty minutes late. Soon I found out the secretary had forgotten to type the exam I was supposed to give my class that day. I quickly had to make another plan. By three o'clock, I was looking forward to getting my paycheque. Foolish woman! When I went to pick it up, the woman in the office told me that something had gone wrong with the computers. I would not be able to get my cheque until Tuesday. Disappointed, I walked down the hill to the parking lot. There I met my final defeat. In my hurry to park the car in the morning, I had left my parking lights on. Now my battery was dead. Even an optimist like me had the right to be discouraged!

**PRACTICE**

### Coherence: Placing Details in Order of Time Sequence

Each of the topics below is followed by six supporting details. These supporting details are listed in random order. Order the events according to time sequence by placing the appropriate number in the space provided. The first one is done for you. Check your answers against those in the Answer Key on p. 466.

1. The driving test

| | |
|---|---|
| 2 | She had her last lesson with Mr. Panakos on Saturday morning. |
| 5 | As she ate breakfast Monday morning, Daniela read the driver's manual one more time because she knew it was her last chance to review. |
| 1 | Daniela's driving test was scheduled for Monday morning. |
| 3 | On Sunday afternoon her father gave her some advice on what to be careful of when she took her road test. |
| 6 | As her mother drove her to the motor vehicle bureau, Daniela tried to relax and not think about the test. |
| 4 | The night before her test, Daniela had phone calls from two friends who wished her good luck. |

2. Making up my mind

| | |
|---|---|
| ________ | By the time I saw the dean for final approval of the change, I knew I had made the right decision. |
| ________ | When I registered for my new courses for the next semester, I knew that I was doing what I should have done all along. |
| ________ | I spent the summer of my second year thinking about the career I really wanted to follow. |
| ________ | I suppose the experience taught me that you should always make a change in your life after you have thought it through completely. |
| ________ | When I finally did decide to change majors, my friends acted as though I had decided to change my citizenship. |
| ________ | When I told my favourite professor about my change of mind, he was very supportive, even though I had begun my major with him. |

## Writing the Narrative Paragraph Step by Step

To learn a skill with some degree of ease, it is best to follow a step-by-step approach so that various steps can be worked on one at a time. This approach will ensure that you are not missing a crucial point or misunderstanding a part of the whole. There are other ways to go about writing an effective paragraph, but here is one logical method you can use to achieve results.

**Steps for Writing the Narrative Paragraph**

1. Study the given topic, and then plan your topic sentence with its controlling idea.
2. List the events that come to mind when you think about the topic you have chosen.
3. Choose the five or six most important events from your list.
4. Put your final list in order.
5. Write at least one complete sentence for each of the events you have chosen from your list.
6. Write a concluding statement that gives some point to the events of the story.
7. Finally, copy your sentences into standard paragraph form.

## Step-by-Step Example of Writing a Narrative Paragraph

The following example starts with a suggested topic and then uses the seven steps above to work through each stage of the writing process.

**Topic:** At one time or another, most people have to buy a car. Often it's not the type of car purchased that leads to a story, but the process of buying it. Write a narrative paragraph about buying a car (or some other expensive item, such as a stereo).

1. Topic sentence: Because my classes were at different campuses, and because I lived quite a distance from the college, I decided to buy a car.
2. Make a list of events.
   a. Tired of waiting for the bus
   b. Budget—gas, insurance, licence, repairs, financing
   c. Car loan
   d. Newspaper ads—dealerships
   e. Want ads
   f. Comparison shopping
3. Circle the five or six events you believe are the most important for the point of the story.
4. Put your final choices in order by numbering them.
5. Using your final list, write at least one sentence for each event you have chosen.
   a. I was tired of waiting for the bus on cold and rainy days, and being late for class when the bus was late didn't impress my professors.
   b. My budget didn't allow me to purchase a new car, especially when I calculated the price of gasoline, insurance, repairs, licensing, and finance charges.
   c. My bank manager was very helpful when it came to arranging a car loan, but even though the payments were spread out over a long period of time, it was still an expensive proposition.
   d. I looked in the newspaper for ads from car dealerships, trying to decide whether I'd be better off buying from a dealer, with at least a minimal warranty on the car, or from a private seller.

e. Comparison shopping was a long and tedious, but necessary, process.

6. Write a concluding statement: I finally bought a car, although it wasn't what I really wanted because of my financial situation. At least I don't have to wait for the bus any more.
7. Copy your sentences into standard paragraph form.

Because my classes were at different campuses, and because I lived quite a distance from the college, I decided to buy a car. I was tired of waiting for the bus on cold and rainy days, and being late for class when the bus was late didn't impress my professors. My budget didn't allow me to purchase a new car, especially when I calculated the price of gasoline, insurance, repairs, licensing, and finance charges. My bank manager was very helpful when it came to arranging a car loan, but even though the payments were spread out over a long period of time, it was still an expensive proposition. I looked in the newspaper for ads from car dealerships, trying to decide whether I'd be better off buying from a dealer, with at least a minimal warranty on the car, or from a private seller. Comparison shopping was a long and tedious, but necessary, process. I finally bought a car, although it wasn't really what I wanted. At least I don't have to wait for the bus anymore.

**EXERCISE**

## Writing the Narrative Paragraph Step by Step

The following exercise will guide you through the construction of a narrative paragraph. Start with the suggested topic. Use the seven steps (repeated below) and the example on pages 261–62 to help you work through each stage of the writing process. Refer to the section above for a completed sample.

**Topic:** Recount the plot of a book you have read recently or a movie you have seen within the last few weeks.

1. Write a topic sentence.
2. Make a list of events.
3. Circle the five or six events you believe are the most important for the point of the story.
4. Put your choices in order by numbering them.
5. Using your final list, write at least one sentence for each event you have chosen.
6. Write a concluding statement.
7. On a separate sheet of paper, copy your sentences into standard paragraph form.

## On Your Own: Writing Narrative Paragraphs from Model Paragraphs

### Model Paragraph

I hate to be late. So, when I began my new job, I was determined to be on time for my first day. I awoke early, had a leisurely breakfast, and gave myself lots of time to get through the traffic. I entered my new office building and sat down at my new desk a good fifteen minutes before starting time. My boss noticed me, smiled, and came over to my desk. "I'm glad you're early," she said. "In fact, you're a week early. You start *next* Monday."

**ASSIGNMENT**

### Narrative Paragraph

Write a paragraph telling the story of a day or part of a day in which you faced an important challenge of some kind. It could have been a challenge you faced in school, at home, or on the job. The preceding paragraph is an example of such an experience.

**SUGGESTED TOPICS:**

(For more suggested topics, see the list on pp. 265–66.)

1. The day I started a new job
2. Becoming a member of a sports team
3. The morning of my big job interview
4. Facing a large debt
5. Sharing the telephone
6. The day I started driving lessons
7. Losing

## Writing the Narrative Essay

Like the narrative paragraph, the narrative essay also tells a story. The essay, however, gives you the opportunity to write a longer story with more detail. Although the narrative is the most informal type of essay, you still need to organize it. You might, for example, devote each support paragraph to a single event or a different character in your story. At the very least, make sure that some sort of shift has taken place, one that warrants a new paragraph. Don't fall into the trap of starting a new paragraph simply because the old one is getting too long.

**For an in-depth look at the essay and its standard format (for all writing strategies in this unit), see Chapter 17: "The Essay." Also review Chapter 14: "The Four Stages of Writing," which can be applied to both the paragraph and the essay.**

**An extensive list of transitional words and phrases categorized by their function is found on the inside back cover of this book and in Chapter 17: "The Essay."**

The following narrative essay was a winning entry in Centennial College's Student Writing Contest (2001–2002). As you read, see how Akis keeps you in suspense, but follows a logical sequence of events all at the same time.

READ

### Model Essay: Transparent Silhouette

**by Akis Stylianou**

On many lonely nights when I am too far from home to remember where home is and too beat to care where I lay my head, I have often heard an echo or seen a reflection that reminded me of a woman I knew. A silhouette through the window reflects the image of a petite yet shapely figure with long strands of silken hair falling over her shoulders. The wind whistling through the trees calls her name, taking me to another place where I can delay my misery.

We met early in life as classmates in elementary school. She used to stand alone in the schoolyard, surrounding herself with the walls she had built. It was a few years later before I could find the strength to enter those walls and discover her world. She told me she came from a broken home with an alcoholic mother and an abusive father. Being the only child, she was often the target of their frustration and rage, though she constantly dreamt of escaping her parents. By the time we reached our teens, she was running out of ways to numb her pain, and, soon after, she left home to live on the streets. Caring as much as I did, it tore me apart knowing there was nothing I could do to help.

She met the wrong kind of people and got involved with their crowds. She did many things she would come to regret, but, if the price was fitting, she was willing to sacrifice herself. My role as her friend was never to judge the path she had chosen; thus, friendship was never compromised. Most people considered her character unethical and immoral. However, she could smile with relief because she had finally escaped from the chains that weighed her down in the past.

One night, she was working as a dancer in a sleazy downtown bar when one of her customers began boasting about his position as an adult film producer. He told her that she had the look he was interested in. Soon after, she started acting, and her status as an adult film star rocketed. Before her twenty-fifth birthday, she had a brand new sports car, a beautiful apartment in the heart of the city, and a bank account holding her six-figure salary. On one occasion, we met at a restaurant for dinner. As she entered the room, all eyes were on her, as if they were in a hypnotic state. The men wanted to be with her, and the women were jealous of her graceful presence. Behind all her jewellery, fur coat and expensive clothing, I could still see the frightened, bruised little girl I cared about. She pretended it didn't bother her, but beneath her polished exterior, I could see inside she wanted to explode.

That was the last chance I had to see her before her body was found lying lifeless in an empty apartment. The police said it was a burglary that went wrong and resulted in a homicide. She taught me to accept the good with the bad. After the rain falls, I walk the streets where she once lived, and the dried up puddles remind me of her permanent tears.

## Questions for Analysis

1. What, in your own words, do you think is the writer's thesis?
2. What is the writer's tone?
3. What is the meaning of the essay's title?
4. How do you think the writer feels about his friend?
5. Did the writer foreshadow the ending of the essay? (In other words, are there lots of clues throughout the essay that enable the reader to predict the eventual death of the writer's friend?)
6. If your answer to question 5 was yes, why did the writer foreshadow the ending? If your answer was no, why not?
7. Identify the transitions in the writer's essay.
8. Speculate on what might have caused the writer's friend's demise?

A model paragraph that answers question 5 above can be found on page 342 in Chapter 28: "Argumentation."

**ASSIGNMENT**

### Rewrite the Conclusion

Rewrite the last paragraph of the essay using your own ideas. Try to stay faithful to the rest of the narrative essay so that you don't end up contradicting anything that comes before the new last paragraph.

**ASSIGNMENT**

### Narrative Essay

Choose one of the following topics and write a narrative essay of at least five paragraphs to develop that topic.

**SUGGESTED TOPICS:**

(See more suggested topics in the list on p. 263.)

1. My worst classroom experience
2. A parent who would not listen
3. My first ____________________

4. When I tried to convince someone to hire me for a job
5. My experience with an aggressive salesperson
6. A day when nothing went right
7. A misunderstanding with a friend
8. Trouble at the workplace
9. A day that changed my life
10. A major disappointment
11. How my nervousness made matters worse
12. A perfect evening
13. The best summer of my life
14. An embarrassing experience
15. Learning something surprising about myself

**For helpful hints on the following subjects, all of which will assist you in developing your narrative essay, see Chapter 14:**

**Brainstorming**
**Choosing the Topic and the Controlling Idea**
**Outlining**
**The Rough Draft**
**Revising and Editing the Rough Draft**
**Proofreading**
**Checklist for the Final Copy**

## Working Together: Spontaneous Creativity or Combustion?

1. A parlour game that is amusing is telling a story by creating it on the spot. One person begins with a sentence that sets the scene. Then it is continued sentence by sentence as each person takes a turn. Do this for perhaps twenty minutes. Elect one student in charge of putting the sentences on the board. Then discuss the outcome. In what ways is the narrative a success? What are its weaknesses?
2. In this chapter, each student is invited to write a narrative essay. Divide into groups and share the narrative essays in your group. Attach a sheet of paper to each essay in which you critique the essay by answering two questions:
   a. In your opinion, what is one aspect of the essay that you believe is very strong? Explain.
   b. In your opinion, what is one aspect of the essay that still needs improvement? Explain.

CHAPTER TWENTY-TWO

22

# Description

## What Is Description?

**DEFINITION ➤** **Description** is the usage of words to help the reader understand how people, places, or things are perceived. How a particular food tastes, looks, and smells, for example, might be the subject of a descriptive paragraph or essay.

Description is one of the basic building blocks of good writing. When you are able to write an effective description of a person, an object, a place, or even an idea, you are in control of your writing. Good description also makes you able to control what your reader sees and does not see.

The key to writing a good description is the choice of the **specific details** you will use. Specific details make your descriptions real and help your reader remember what you have written. A careful writer always pays special attention to specific details in any piece of writing.

A second important aspect of good description is the use of **sensory images.**

**DEFINITION ➤** **Sensory images** are details that relate to your sense of sight, smell, touch, taste, or hearing.

***Example:*** The deafening screams and relentless yelling of the children on the school bus drove its driver mad.

When you appeal to at least some of the five senses in your descriptive writing, your reader will be able to relate directly to what you are saying. Sensory images also help your reader remember what you have written.

A third important aspect of good description is the **order** in which you place the details you have chosen. The combination of specific details, sensory images, and the order in which you present these details and impressions will help your reader form a **dominant impression** of what you are describing.

Some descriptive writing is more objective than subjective (such as in a police report). If your descriptive piece is more objective, give the readers enough facts to allow them to come up with their own dominant impressions. If your descriptive piece is subjective, instead, your dominant impression should be suggested from the outset, even if it's not completely obvious. The establishment of your dominant impression is the job of the topic sentence of the paragraph or the thesis statement of the essay.

## Developing Paragraphs: Description

The following example of a descriptive paragraph shows all of the elements of a good description. As you read this description of a typical neighbourhood delicatessen, note the specific details and the sensory images the writer uses. After you have read the description, ask yourself whether the writer has provided a dominant impression. If so, what, in your own words, is that dominant impression? What is your evidence for this conclusion? Is the paragraph one of subjective or objective description?

**Model Paragraph**

The delicatessen was a wide store with high ceilings that were a dark brown colour from many years of not being painted. The rough wooden shelves on both sides of the store were filled from floor to ceiling with cans of fruits and vegetables, jars of pickles and olives, and special imported canned fish. A large refrigerator case against one wall was always humming loudly from the effort of keeping milk, cream, and several cases of pop and juice cool at all times. At the end of the store was the main counter with its gleaming white metal scale on top and its cold cuts and freshly made salads inside. Stacked on top of the counter beside the scale today were baskets of fresh rolls and breads that gave off an aroma that contained a mixture of onion, caraway seed, and pumpernickel. Behind the scale was the friendly face of Mr. Rubino, who was in his store seven days a week, fourteen hours or more each day. He was always ready with a smile or a friendly comment, or even a sample piece of cheese or smoked meat as a friendly gesture for his "growing customers," as he referred to us kids in the neighbourhood.

## Working with Description: Selecting the Dominant Impression

When you use a number of specific sensory images as you write a description, you should do more than simply write a series of sentences that deal with a single topic. You should also create a dominant impression in your reader's mind. Each individual sentence that you write is part of a picture that becomes clear when the reader finishes the paragraph.

For example, when you describe a place, the dominant impression you create might be of a place that is warm, friendly, or comfortable; or it could be a place that is formal, elegant, or artistic. When you write a description of a person, your reader could receive the dominant impression of a positive, efficient person who is outgoing and creative, or of a person who appears to be cold, distant, or hostile. All the sentences should support the dominant impression you have chosen.

Here is a list of descriptive words for you to use as a guide as you work through this chapter. (Not surprisingly, all these words are adjectives since adjectives are words that *describe* persons, places, and things.) Picking a dominant impression is essential in writing the descriptive college paragraph.

### Selecting the Dominant Impression

**Possible Dominant Impressions for Descriptions of Places**

| | | | | |
|---|---|---|---|---|
| crowded | cozy | inviting | cheerful | dazzling |
| romantic | restful | dreary | drab | uncomfortable |
| cluttered | ugly | tasteless | unfriendly | gaudy |
| stuffy | eerie | depressing | spacious | sunny |

**Possible Dominant Impressions for Descriptions of People**

| | | | | |
|---|---|---|---|---|
| creative | angry | independent | proud | withdrawn |
| tense | shy | aggressive | generous | sullen |
| silent | witty | pessimistic | responsible | efficient |
| snobbish | placid | bumbling | bitter | easygoing |

**EXERCISE**

## Selecting the Dominant Impression

Each of the following places could be the topic for a descriptive paragraph. First, the writer must decide on a dominant impression. Fill in each blank to the right of the topic with an appropriate dominant impression. Use the list above if you need help. The first one is done for you.

| Topic | Dominant Impression |
|---|---|
| 1. The college pub on pub night | loud |
| 2. A park at dusk | __________ |
| 3. The room where you are now sitting | __________ |
| 4. The variety store nearest you | __________ |
| 5. The college bookstore in September | __________ |
| 6. An overcrowded waiting room | __________ |
| 7. The kitchen in the morning | __________ |

## Revising Vague Dominant Impressions

Certain words in the English language have become so overused that they no longer have any specific meaning for a reader. Careful writers avoid these words because they are almost useless in descriptive writing. Here is a list of the most common overused words:

good, bad
nice, fine, okay
normal, typical
interesting
beautiful

The following paragraph is an example of the kind of writing that results from the continued use of vague words:

**Model Paragraph I**

I had a typical day. The weather was nice and my job was interesting. The food for lunch was okay; supper was really good. After supper, I saw my girlfriend, who is really beautiful. That's when my day really became fun.

Notice that all of the details in the paragraph are vague. The writer has told us what happened, but we cannot really see any of the details that are mentioned. This is because the writer has made the mistake of using words that have lost much of their meaning. Replacing the vague words in the paragraph will create an entirely different impression:

**Model Paragraph II**

I had an event-filled day that was typical of the kind of day I've been enjoying lately. The weather on this summer day was perfect for late June, and the challenge of my job in the health-care field made me feel that this warm and sunny day was made just for me. I had a delicious lunch in a tiny Italian restaurant, and a supper to excite the taste buds at a cozy Greek restaurant that just oozed atmosphere. After supper, I met my girlfriend, who has a warm sense of humour and who is a partner in a major law firm down the street from where I work.

The following exercise will give you practice in recognizing and eliminating overused words.

**EXERCISE**

## Revising Vague Dominant Impressions

In each of the spaces provided, change the underlined word to a more specific dominant impression. An example is done for you.

***Vague:*** The tablecloth was beautiful.
***Revised:*** The tablecloth was of white linen with delicate blue embroidery.

1. The sunset was beautiful. I felt enchanted by looking at the sunset reflecting their last minutes of the day on the ocean.
2. The water felt nice.
3. Horseback riding was fun. ______
4. The traffic was bad. ______

5. The hotel lobby was typical. ______________________________

6. The main street is interesting. ______________________________

7. The dessert tasted good. ______________________________

## Working with Description: Sensory Images

One of the basic ways all good writers communicate experiences to their readers is by using sensory impressions. We respond to writing that makes us *see* an object, *hear* a sound, *touch* a surface, *smell* an odour, or *taste* a flavour. When a writer uses one or more of these sensory images in a piece of writing, we tend to pay more attention to what he or she is saying, and we tend to remember the details of what we have read.

For example, if you come across the word *door* in a sentence, you may or may not pay attention to it. However, if the writer tells you it was a *brown wooden* door that was *rough to the touch* and *creaked loudly* when it opened, you would hardly be able to forget it. The door would stay in your mind because the writer used sensory images to make you aware of it.

The following sentences are taken from the description of Mr. Rubino's delicatessen that you read on page 268. Notice how in each sentence the writer uses at least one sensory image to make the details of that sentence remain in our minds. The physical sense the writer is appealing to by the use of one or more sensory images is indicated after the sentence.

1. A large refrigerator case against one wall was always humming loudly from the effort of keeping milk, cream, and several cases of pop and juice cool at all times.

   Physical sense: hearing

2. Stacked on top of the counter ... were baskets of fresh rolls and breads that gave off an aroma that contained a mixture of onion, caraway seed, and pumpernickel.

   Physical sense: smell

3. He was always ready with ... a sample piece of cheese or smoked meat as a friendly gesture....

   Physical sense: taste

When you use sensory images in your own writing, you will stimulate your readers' interest and create images in their minds that they will remember.

## Coherence in Description: Putting Details in Spatial Order

In descriptive paragraphs, the writer often chooses to arrange supporting details according to space. With this method, you place yourself at the scene and then use a logical order such as moving from nearby to farther away, right to left, or top to bottom. Often you move in such a way that you save the most important detail until last in order to achieve the greatest effect.

In the paragraph about the delicatessen on page 268, the writer first describes the ceilings and walls of the store, then proceeds to the shelves and large refrigerator, and ends by describing the main counter of the deli with its owner, Mr. Rubino, standing behind it. The ordering of details has been from the outer limits of the room to the inner area, which is central to the point of this paragraph. A description of a clothes closet might order the details differently. Perhaps the writer would begin with the shoes standing on the floor and finish with the hats and gloves arranged on the top shelf, an arrangement that goes from the ground up.

Here is a paragraph from Thierry Mallet's *Glimpses of the Barren Lands,* a description of his travels through the Canadian Arctic:

> Our camp had been pitched at the foot of a great, bleak, ragged hill, a few feet from the swirling waters of the Kazan River. The two small green tents, pegged down tight with heavy rocks, shivered and rippled under the faint touch of the northern breeze. A thin wisp of smoke rose from the embers of the fire.

Notice that the writer begins with a description of the landscape, then gives a description of the camp, and ends with a picture of the small fire. We are able to follow the writer through the description because there is a logic or plan. No matter which method of spatial order you choose in organizing details in a descriptive paragraph, be sure the results allow your reader to see the scene in a logical order.

**PRACTICE**

### Coherence: Putting Details in Spatial Order

Each of the following topic sentences is followed by descriptive sentences that are out of order. Put these descriptive sentences in order by placing the appropriate number in the space provided. Check your answers against those in the Answer Key on p. 466.

1. The young woman was a teen of the 21st century.
   (*Order the material from top to bottom.*)

   _______ She wore hip-hugging, low-rise faded jeans.

   _______ Her nose was pierced with a subtle gold stud.

   _______ She donned a tasteful tattoo of a single red rose on her left shoulder blade above her tight-fitted tube top.

_______ Her brown hair sported an uneven cut and blonde streaks.

_______ Her wedge sandals looked cute and comfortable all at the same time.

2. The locker room was in chaos.
   (*Order the material from near to far.*)

_______ Immediately to my right, I saw Pat and Chris slapping each other with towels.

_______ Behind the pair, a row of locker doors banged open and shut.

_______ I squeezed past a noisy group crowding the doorway.

_______ At the back, the rest of the team was hugging and congratulating our hero in celebration of her winning goal.

## Writing the Descriptive Paragraph Step by Step

To learn a skill with some degree of ease, it is best to follow a step-by-step approach so that you can work on the steps one at a time. This will ensure that you are not missing a crucial point or misunderstanding a part of the whole. There are other ways to go about writing an effective paragraph, but what follows is one logical method you can use to achieve results.

**Steps for Writing the Descriptive Paragraph**

1. Study the given topic, and then plan your topic sentence, especially the dominant impression.
2. List at least ten details that come to mind when you think about the topic.
3. Choose the five or six most important details from your list. Be sure these details support the dominant impression.
4. Put your final list in order.
5. Write at least one complete sentence for each of the details you have chosen from your list.
6. Write a concluding statement that offers some reason for describing this topic.
7. Finally, copy your sentences into standard paragraph form.

**EXERCISE**

### Writing the Descriptive Paragraph Step by Step

The following exercise will guide you through the construction of a descriptive paragraph. Start with the suggested topic. Use the seven steps to help you work through each stage in the writing process. (Refer to pages 261–62 in Chapter 21 for a completed sample paragraph.)

**Topic:** A person you admire

1. Write a topic sentence.
2. Make a list of possible supporting details.
3. Circle the five or six details you believe are the most important for the description.
4. Put your choices in order by numbering them.
5. Using your final list, write at least one sentence for each detail you have chosen.
6. Write a concluding statement.
7. On a separate sheet of paper, copy your sentences into standard paragraph form.

## On Your Own: Writing Descriptive Paragraphs from Model Paragraphs

### Description of a Person

In the following model paragraph, from Alistair MacLeod's story "The Lost Salt Gift of Blood," the author describes his mother in Nova Scotia.

**Model Paragraph**

My mother ran her house as her brothers ran their boats. Everything was clean and spotless and in order. She was tall and dark and powerfully energetic. In later years, she reminded me of the women of Thomas Hardy, particularly Eustacia Vye, in a physical way. She fed and clothed a family of seven children, making all of the meals and most of the clothes. She grew miraculous gardens and magnificent flowers and raised broods of hens and ducks. She would walk miles on berry-picking expeditions and hoist her skirts to dig for clams when the tide was low. She was fourteen years younger than my father, whom she had married when she was 26, and had been a local beauty for a period of ten years. My mother was of the sea as were all of her people, and her horizons were the very literal ones she scanned with her dark and fearless eyes.

**ASSIGNMENT**

### Descriptive Paragraph

Describe a person—preferably one you have observed more than once. If you have seen this person only once, indicate the details that made him or her stay in your mind. If you choose to describe a person with whom you are familiar, select the most outstanding details that will help your reader have a single, dominant impression.

**SUGGESTED TOPICS:**

(For more suggested topics, see the list on pp. 277–78.)

1. A loyal friend
2. A local musician
3. A cab driver
4. A fashion model
5. A gossipy neighbour
6. A police officer
7. An aerobics instructor

## Writing the Descriptive Essay

Like the topic sentence of a descriptive paragraph, the thesis of a descriptive essay identifies what is being described and contains the overall impression the author has of the topic. Each support paragraph might deal with one component of that which is being described. The following is a brief outline of a descriptive essay:

| | |
|---|---|
| ***Thesis:*** | The 100-year-old house was definitely haunted. |
| ***Topic Sentence #1:*** | First of all, every time people entered any room in the house, something seemed to be out of place, contrary to the owner's insistence that she never changes a thing. |
| ***Topic Sentence #2:*** | Secondly, visitors constantly scurry out of the house in a fright claiming later they've sighted at least one ghost. |
| ***Topic Sentence #3:*** | Scariest of all are the stories about visitors to the house constantly hearing what seems like moaning coming from the walls, as if the walls are filled with sick people struggling to break free. |

**For an in-depth look at the essay and its standard format (for all writing strategies in this unit), see Chapter 17: "The Essay." Also review Chapter 14: "The Four Stages of Writing," which can be applied to both the paragraph and the essay.**

The following descriptive essay was a winning entry in Centennial College's Student Writing Contest (2001–2002). The paragraphs are journalistic in that they are shorter than the type of paragraph this book prescribes. What was Alexandra's inspiration for writing this piece? She was driving home from school one day and happened to notice a caravan in someone's back yard. What she didn't know yet was that Daphne, the subject of the piece, was not only a carpenter and artist, but she would also turn out to be an English professor at Durham College.

## Model Essay: A Profile of Daphne

### by Alexandra Savage-Ferr

The first time I saw her sitting amidst the Gypsy caravans, I knew this was a woman I had to meet. After all, we shared a love—a love of books, a love of secret, special places, and a love of the caravans we read and dreamt about in childhood. Daphne designs and builds unique living spaces based upon English Gypsy wagons at her home in the Durham Region of Ontario.

Using the frame and wheels of old farm wagons and the occasional antique CP baggage cart, she custom-builds wooden living spaces that writers and dreamers will truly appreciate. Each caravan is uniquely hand painted and decorated with themes from literature, such as Robin Hood's Sherwood Forest and Kenneth Grahame's *The Wind in the Willows.*

Today, surrounded by sun-drenched maples, this skilled craftswoman in sweater and jeans, ponytail a-flying, leads me from one work of art to the next, while a grey, shaggy dog—a rescued stray—prances about in circles of dappled sunlight. Several brightly coloured Gypsy caravans are dotted about the six-acre wooded estate located just north of Uxbridge.

Gypsies, also known as Roma or Romany Gypsies, have their origins in India over a thousand years ago. As they entered southeastern Europe at the end of the 13th century, it was thought that they were from Egypt. They were called 'Gyptians, which is how they became known as "Gypsies."

Learning woodworking as a child, using miniature tools alongside her father building boats, Daphne discovered more than just carpentry skills. Inside her rustic country home, the walls are lined floor-to-ceiling with row upon row of books, many of which belonged to her father. No fewer than six copies of *The Secret Garden,* and the entire set of Baum's *Oz* tales—first editions, of course—are friends. This literary multitude seems as much alive as the two cats that preen themselves before the fire. Fantasy abounds as I gaze over antique photographs, carousel horses, and a brimming bag of apples picked during an early morning snowfall. She serves me Russian Caravan Tea and cuts thick slabs of sugary confection.

After building various theatre props over the years for the Scugog Choral Society and others, the old adage rang true: If you want one, build one. Conjuring magic for the stage, Daphne gazed into the crystal ball of her imagination and translated her visions into a real-life living space. Now she builds caravans for others with their own visions. "I'm interested in the ones who say, 'Wouldn't it be perfect for me?' because there's imagination there," she says. "They see it as their own spot."

These caravans are not intended for travelling, however. Rather, they are meant to be a dreaming, reading, and writing spot remote from the house, sequestered from interruptions and distractions. Since building her own personal retreat, she has crafted several more—the most recent one being commissioned as a unique guestroom for a Port Perry bed and breakfast.

Her own caravan roosts at the top of a hill overlooking the pond. "In the morning, the bulrushes are full of blackbirds," she relates. Indeed, the birds are singing now as our feet crunch through the hoarfrost-covered leaves. This earthy woman with carpenter's hands beckons me inside. I climb a small set of wooden steps and enter through the narrow Dutch door.

Inside, we are cozily sheltered from a sudden hailstorm pinging on the metal roof. Personal treasures, like sprites, peek from every nook and cranny. A crazy quilt travels the length of the platform bed beneath a window overlooking tangled briar. A hanging lantern, cherished books, photographs, and blessed gifts from her children hum with joyful verse. "This is my special place," she whispers.

I knew why I had to meet her, there by the gypsy caravans. I *knew* she had the secret. She'd had it all along.

## Questions for Analysis

1. What part of speech enriches the descriptive value of this piece more than any other?
2. Give some examples from this piece of this particular part of speech.
3. What is the object of the description in this essay? Could it be argued there are two? Why or why not?
4. In paragraph 6, the writer uses double quotation marks and single quotation marks. Explain their usage.
5. The last paragraph mentions "the secret." What "secret" did the writer know Daphne had all along?

**ASSIGNMENT**

## Descriptive Essay

Choose one of the following topics and write a descriptive essay of at least five paragraphs to develop that topic.

**SUGGESTED TOPICS:**

(For more suggested topics, see the list on p. 275.)

1. The best job I ever had
2. The career of my dreams
3. My favourite aunt or uncle
4. My pet ________________
5. My first car
6. The ideal mate
7. The most embarrassing date
8. The best dance club
9. My best friend
10. The best meal I ever had
11. The worst restaurant I've ever eaten in
12. My favourite music

13. My tattoos and/or piercings
14. The worst hospital I've ever been in
15. The best float in a certain parade

**To help you work through the stages of the writing process, see the following subjects in Chapter 14. All of them can assist you in developing your descriptive essay:**

**Brainstorming**
**Choosing the Topic and the Controlling Idea**
**Outlining**
**The Rough Draft**
**Revising and Editing the Rough Draft**
**Proofreading**
**Checklist for the Final Copy**

## Working Together: The Hunt for a Roommate

The following personal advertisement appeared in a local newspaper:

> Young man seeks neat, responsible roommate to share off-campus apartment for next academic year. Person must be a nonsmoker and respect a vegetarian who cooks at home. Furniture not needed, but CD player would be welcome!

Finding the right roommate in a college or university residence, finding the right person with whom to share an apartment, or finding the right long-term companion may be difficult. People's personal habits have a way of causing friction in everyday life. Divide into groups for a brief discussion of the kinds of problems one finds in sharing the same space with another person.

1. Imagine that you must write a paragraph or two in which you provide a character description of yourself for an agency that will match you up with a roommate. As you write, be sure you include information about your hobbies, habits, attitudes, and any other personal characteristics that could make a difference in the kind of person the agency will select for you.
2. Imagine that you must write a paragraph or two in which you provide a character sketch of the person you would like the agency to find for you.

CHAPTER TWENTY-THREE 23

# Process

## What Is Process?

**DEFINITION ➤** **Process** is the method that explains how to do something or that shows how something works. There are two kinds of process writing: **directional** and **informational.**

*A process that is directional actually shows you, step by step, how to do something.* For example, if you want to show someone how to brew a perfect cup of coffee, you would take the person through each step of the process, from selecting and grinding the coffee beans to pouring the finished product. Instructions on a test, directions on how to get to a wedding reception, or a recipe for your favourite spaghetti sauce are a few examples of the kinds of process writing you see and use regularly. You can find examples of directional process writing everywhere you look: in newspapers, magazines, and books, as well as on the containers and packages of products you use every day.

On the other hand, *a process that is informational tells you how something is or was done, for the purpose of informing you about the process.* For example, in a history course, it might be important to understand how the process of Confederation joined Upper and Lower Canada. Of course, you would not use this process yourself. The purpose is for information.

## Developing Paragraphs: Process

The following paragraph, from Mary Finlay's *Communication at Work,* is an example of directional process writing and describes certain preliminary steps to follow when preparing an oral presentation.

**Model Paragraph**

Ascertain how long your presentation is expected to take. Normally, a speech is delivered at about 150 words a minute. Make sure that your material is adequate for the time allotted. Of course, this does not mean that a ten-minute oral report will be as dense as a 1500-word essay. Rehashing points you have already made in order to fill up your time is a sure-fire way to annoy and frustrate your listeners. Leave time for questions and feedback. If there is none, don't fill in the time by answering the questions nobody asked. This suggests that you are having second thoughts about the organization and planning of your report.

The following paragraph provides an example of informational process writing, giving an overview of the process leading up to Canadian Confederation:

**Model Paragraph**

Confederation, the political union of British North America, didn't happen overnight. Starting as a topic of discussion among politicians before the 1860s, it began to take shape after 1864 with a conference in Charlottetown to discuss the possibility of a union, followed by a second conference at Quebec the same year. Details were hammered out at yet another conference in London, England, in 1866, leading to the passage of the *British North America Act* in March 1867, and resulting in the formation of the Dominion of Canada on July 1, 1867.

## Working with Process: Don't Overlook Any of the Steps

The writer of the process essay is almost always more of an authority on the subject than the person reading the essay. In giving directions or information on how something is to be done or was done, it is possible to leave out a step that you think is so obvious that it is not worth mentioning. The reader, on the other hand, does not necessarily fill in the missing step, as you did. An important part of process writing, therefore, is understanding your reader's level of ability. All of us have been given directions that, at first, seemed very clear. However, when we actually tried to carry out the process, something went wrong. A step in the process was misunderstood or missing. The giver of the information either assumed we would know certain parts of the process or didn't stop to think through the process completely. The important point is that directions must be complete and accurate. Here is one further consideration: If special equipment is required in order to perform the process, the directions must include a clear description of the necessary tools.

**EXERCISE**

### Is the Process Complete?

In the following process, try to determine what important step or steps have been omitted. Try to imagine yourself going through the process using only the information provided.

**How to Prepare for an Essay Exam**

1. Read the relevant chapters as they are assigned, well in advance of the test.
2. Take notes in class.

3. If the teacher has not described the test, ask him or her what format the test will take.
4. Get a good night's sleep the night before.
5. Bring any pens or pencils that you might need.
6. Arrive at the classroom a few minutes early in order to get yourself settled and to keep yourself calm.

Missing step or steps: ______________________________

______________________________

______________________________

## Coherence in Process: Order in Logical Sequence

When you are writing about a process, it is important to make sure not only that the steps in the process are complete, but also that they are given in the right sequence. For example, if you are describing the process of cleaning a mixer, it is important to point out that you must first unplug the appliance before you remove the blades. The importance of this step is clear when you realize that neglecting it could cost someone a finger. Improperly written instructions could cause serious injuries or even death.

**PRACTICE**

### Coherence: Order in Logical Sequence

The following steps describe the process of setting up a filing system that works. Number the steps in their proper sequence in the blanks to the left. Check your answers against those in the Answer Key on p. 466.

__________ When your mind begins to blur, stop filing for that day.

__________ Now label a file folder and slip the piece of paper in.

__________ Gather together all materials to be filed so that they are all in one location.

__________ Alphabetize your file folders and put them away into your file drawer, and you are finished for that session.

__________ Add to these materials a recycling container, folders, labels, and a pen.

__________ Pick up the next piece of paper and go through the same procedure, but ask yourself whether this new piece of paper might fit into an existing file, rather than one with a new heading.

__________ Pick up an item from the top of the pile and decide whether this item has value for you. If it does not, recycle it. If it does, go on to the next step.

__________ Finally, to maintain your file once it is established, riffle through each file folder you consult, and pick out and recycle the deadwood.

__________ If the piece of paper is worth saving, ask yourself the question "What is this paper about?"

**To make a paragraph flow smoothly and coherently, refer to the chart of transitional words and phrases (for process) on the inside back cover of this book. See also Chapter 17 (pp. 206–07), and the temporal and spatial (time and space) methods of ordering paragraphs in Chapters 21 (pp. 259–60) and 22 (pp. 272–73).**

**EXERCISE**

### Using Transitions to Go from a List to a Paragraph

Refer to the process outlined in the first exercise in this chapter, on pages 280–81. Using the chart of transitional words and phrases (for process) on the inside back cover of this text, change this list into a process paragraph that is coherent and flowing.

## Writing the Process Paragraph Step by Step

To learn a skill with some degree of ease, it is best to follow a step-by-step approach so that you can work on the steps one at a time. This will ensure that you are not missing a crucial point or misunderstanding a part of the whole. There are other ways to go about writing an effective paragraph, but here is one logical method you can use to achieve results, which in itself is a process.

**Steps for Writing the Process Paragraph**

1. Write a topic sentence.
2. List as many steps or stages in the process as you can.
3. Eliminate any irrelevant points; add equipment needed or special circumstances of the process.
4. Put your final list in order.
5. Write at least one complete sentence for each of the steps you have chosen from your list.
6. Write a concluding statement that says something about the results of completing the process.
7. Finally, copy your sentences into standard paragraph form.

**EXERCISE**

### Writing the Process Paragraph Step by Step

The following exercise will guide you through the construction of a process paragraph. Start with the suggested topic. Use the seven steps to help you work through each stage of the writing process. (Refer to pages 261–62 in Chapter 21 for a completed sample paragraph.)

**Topic:** How to burglar-proof your home

The incidence of break-and-enter crimes increases yearly, and many people are concerned about their homes when they are away on vacation. Give advice to a homeowner on how to protect a house against burglary.

1. Write a topic sentence.
2. Make a list of possible steps.
3. Circle the five or six steps you believe are the most important to complete the process.
4. Put your final choices in order by numbering them.
5. Using your final list, write at least one sentence for each step you have chosen.
6. Write a concluding statement.
7. On a separate sheet of paper, copy your sentences into standard paragraph form.

## On Your Own: Writing Process Paragraphs from Model Paragraphs

### Directional: How to Care for Your Health

Concern for health and physical fitness is enjoying great popularity, bringing in big profits to health-related magazines, health clubs, health-food producers, and sports equipment manufacturers. The following paragraph tells us how to get a good night's sleep.

**Model Paragraph**

The process of getting a good night's sleep depends on several factors. First, the conditions in your bedroom must be correct. Be sure the room temperature is around 18°C and the room is as quiet as possible. Next, pay attention to your bed and how it is furnished. A firm mattress is best, and wool blankets are better than blankets made of synthetic material. Similarly, a firm pillow is best; one that is too soft can cause a stiff neck and lead to a night of poor sleep. Also, keep in mind that what and how you eat are part of the process of preparing for bed. Do not go to bed hungry, but do not overeat, either. Avoid candy bars or cookies; the sugar they contain acts as a stimulant. Finally, do not go to bed until you are sleepy; do something relaxing until you are tired.

**ASSIGNMENT 1** **Process Paragraph**

Write a paragraph in which you give the major steps in some area of caring for your physical or mental health.

**SUGGESTED TOPICS:**

1. How to plan a daily exercise program
2. How to choose a sport that is suitable for you
3. How to live to be 100
4. How to pick a doctor
5. How to make exercise and dieting fun
6. How to stop smoking
7. How to deal with depression

### Informational: How to Accomplish a Task

The following paragraph describes how an insect builds a nest.

**Model Paragraph**

The insect known as the hunter wasp goes through a regular procedure when it builds a nest. First, it digs a small tunnel into the earth. Then it goes in search of a cicada, a large insect that resembles a cricket. After stinging and paralyzing the cicada, the hunter wasp brings it to the tunnel, lays an egg on the helpless insect, and seals the tunnel. The hunter wasp then leaves. When the egg hatches, the larva uses the cicada as a source of food.

**ASSIGNMENT 2** **Process Paragraph**

Write a paragraph in which you show how an important task is accomplished. The task may be something that is frequently done by humans or that occurs in the world of nature.

**SUGGESTED TOPICS:**

(For more suggested topics, see the list on p. 287.)

1. How cheese is made
2. How to burn a CD
3. How people obtain a divorce
4. How to get a driver's licence
5. How yeast causes bread to rise
6. How a bill becomes a law
7. How planets are formed

## Writing the Process Essay

Any process paragraph easily can be turned into a process essay by simply increasing the amount of detail in all of the steps. Follow the essay structure as it is shown in Chapter 17, and devote each support paragraph to a single step in the process.

**EXERCISE**

## When Process Goes Wrong

It is your sister's birthday. You have bought her a gift that you must first put together. Carefully following the instructions, you try to assemble the item, but something is wrong. It does not work. Either you have not followed the instructions properly, or the instructions themselves are not clear. All of us have found ourselves in this situation at one time or another. It takes careful thought to write about a process. The writer must not assume the reader knows more than he or she is likely to know.

Answer the following questions in further exploration of this topic.

1. Think of a time when you had to put something together but were not given adequate directions. What did you do?
2. When people write instructions or give directions, what do they usually neglect to keep in mind?
3. Recall a time when you had to explain a process to someone. Perhaps you had to show someone how to get somewhere or had to write a detailed description of how to do a science experiment. What was the process? Was it hard to explain? Why or why not?
4. What was your worst experience with trying to follow a process? You could have been trying to work something out yourself or follow someone else's directions. How did you overcome your difficulty?

**For an in-depth look at the essay and its standard format (for all writing strategies in this unit), see Chapter 17: "The Essay." Also review Chapter 14: "The Four Stages of Writing," which can be applied to both the paragraph and the essay.**

Much of the instruction in this book is based on a process. This very chapter, for instance, outlines the process of writing a process paragraph or essay. Another process we are all familiar with is that of assembling a bookcase or other item from printed instructions. The following essay discusses the process of doing something that everyone has heard about, but not everyone has actually done. Perhaps if people knew how easy it is, more would end up doing it themselves. It is the simple process of changing a flat tire.

Cara had never changed a flat tire until she accidentally came upon a brochure on how to do it. Until she read what the steps were, she assumed it was actually a difficult process. The power of words made her realize her fears were unfounded. So the next time her tire went flat, she proudly put her new skills to work. She hopes that her essay can serve the same purpose for others.

## Model Essay: Replacing a Tire

### by Cara Watters

What happens when you get a flat tire? Do you immediately call Roadside Assistance or CAA? Or do you consider a flat tire the equivalent of your window washer fluid running out? If you wouldn't call CAA to replace the fluid, why would you call someone to help you replace a tire, right? Well, that choice is yours. But if you haven't replaced a tire yet, and would like to know how to do it if you ever experience the need, read on. Maybe the sense of accomplishment in itself is worth forgoing the call for help. To replace a flat tire, you need to follow a few easy steps.

The first thing to do is ensure safety. As soon as you know your tire has "bitten the dust," drive the car, if you can, onto the shoulder of the road (where it is as level as possible) so that both you and the car are out of harm's way. Put the transmission into park, and apply the parking brake. If you are driving a stick shift, place the shift into gear. Turn the engine off, and turn on your hazard lights. With more and more drivers on their cell phones these days, you want to make sure you're as visible as possible. For this reason, it might also be a good idea to open your hood until you're ready to drive away.

Secondly, prepare the car for the tire change. You can start to pretend you're a doctor who's prepping for surgery. If you're not perfectly level, place a wheel chock (or large rock) either behind (if on an incline) or in front of (if on a decline) the wheel that is diagonally opposed to the one that needs changing. Get out the spare tire, a lug wrench (tire iron), and the car jack.

Thirdly, the actual changing of the tire, or surgery, so to speak, begins. Remove the hubcap, if necessary. Turning the lug wrench counterclockwise, loosen the lug nuts before jacking up the car. Loosen the lugs in star formation: this means first loosen one lug, then the one opposite, then another and so on until each lug has been loosened a few times. Carefully jack up the car. And never go under your car when only a jack is holding it up. Jack up the car a little higher than it is necessary to remove the old tire so that there is room to put the spare on. Remove the lug nuts all the way and put them in a place that is safe and where you know they will not roll away. Then remove the flat tire and put it aside. Put the spare on the threaded studs, making sure the air valve is facing out.

Now it's time to finish the job. Close up your patient by first replacing the lug nuts. Tighten them the same way you loosened them, by the star formation: tighten one a little, then tighten the one opposite a little. Go to the next lug, and so on. Every lug should be tightened a few times. Slowly lower the jack, and remove it. Give all the lug nuts a final tightening until you can't tighten any more. Replace the hubcap. Make sure everything you've put down is picked up, and you're ready to go.

Of course, once you've changed a tire the first time, it will automatically get easier the second time (if there is a second time). With these steps, the surgery promises to be quite painless. Before that first time, however, it's always a good idea to remember a few tips: for example, have a strong, hollow pipe (about two feet in length) in your car that can help you with leverage when you're using the lug wrench. Have some penetrating oil on hand that you can squirt on the lug nuts if they stick. (After you squirt some, wait a moment, and then try again.) Use gloves when removing a flat tire. If the tire is bald, after all, there may be steel strands sticking out that can cut you. And check your spare tire before any of this happens to make sure it is inflated properly. Apparently, many spare tires are flat because people don't check on this. Imagine going as far as taking your flat tire off only to find out your spare is flat too! You'd have to call for help after all.

## Questions for Analysis

1. Is this process essay more directional or informational?
2. What method did the writer use for the introduction? (See pp. 203–05.)
3. What method did the writer use for the conclusion? (See pp. 207–08.)
4. How many main steps are there to the process as the writer described it?
5. Where, at each step of the process, does the writer give specific examples to make each part of the process clear?
6. Identify some of the transitions used by the writer.

**ASSIGNMENT**

## Process Essay

Choose one or more of the following topics, and write a process essay of at least five paragraphs to develop that topic.

**SUGGESTED TOPICS:**

(For more suggested topics, see the list on p. 284.)

1. How to give a speech
2. How to do well in a job interview
3. How to plan a backpacking trip
4. How to buy a used computer
5. How to study for a test
6. How to choose the right college
7. How to redecorate a room
8. How to buy clothes on a limited budget
9. How to learn to sing
10. How to make new friends

## Writing the Process Essay: How to ...

Thousands of books and articles have been written that promise to help us accomplish some goal in life: how to start a business, how to cook, how to lose weight, how to install a shower, how to assemble a bicycle. In the essay you are about to write, you have the opportunity to describe how you once went through a process to achieve a goal of some kind.

**To help you work through the stages of the writing process, see the following subjects in Chapter 14. All of them can assist you in developing your process essay:**

**Brainstorming**
**Choosing the Topic and the Controlling Idea**
**Outlining**
**The Rough Draft**
**Revising and Editing the Rough Draft**
**Proofreading**
**Checklist for the Final Copy**

## Working Together: Campus Woes

1. The class as a whole discusses and lists some of the problems on their particular campus today. Then the class divides into groups of three or four, each group choosing one of the problems identified. After discussion, each group draws up a list of steps that need to be taken in order to improve the situation.
2. Each group chooses a secretary. The group uses the list to create sentences that will go into a letter to be sent to the appropriate college or university official suggesting the process that could be followed to solve the problem. The secretary will write the finished letter. Be sure there is an introductory paragraph that presents the problem and a conclusion that thanks the official for his or her attention.

3. Imagine you're Abby. Read the letter to the right and answer the following questions:

   If you were the one to advise this person, what would you tell her to do? Explain the process she should follow in order to solve her problem.

   In order to effectively deal with this situation, the class could divide into groups to consider the following questions:

   a. Should she confront the man who is harassing her?
   b. Should she go to her supervisor? Should she have told her co-workers about the problem?
   c. Should she share her problem with the man she is dating?
   d. Should she avoid the problem and quit her job?
   e. How important is evidence for a person in this situation? How and when should she gather documentation for a possible formal action?
   f. Does she need a lawyer? Does she need to consider the consequences of a formal action?

> **DEAR ABBY**
>
> Dear Abby: I am doing my co-op at a cable television company as a computer operator. Lately, every morning when I sign in on my computer, I find suggestive messages from the man I relieve from the night shift.
>
> I am a single mother. I am also dating another man and have no interest in this co-worker. Should I report him to my supervisor? Someone in my office suggested that I file a sexual harassment charge.
>
> —Harassed

4. Sexual harassment is not the only problem workers or students might face. In a brief discussion with your classmates, list some other common complaints workers or students might have. Are there steps that need to be followed in order to successfully resolve all such problems? Following the class discussion, write your own paragraph or essay describing the steps you feel are necessary to deal with such situations.

CHAPTER TWENTY-FOUR

24

# Comparison and/or Contrast

## What Are Comparison and Contrast?

Comparison and contrast are two related methods of explaining topics.

**DEFINITION ➤** When we use **comparison,** we emphasize the similarities between two topics. When we use **contrast,** we emphasize the differences between two topics. An essay or paragraph may deal with either similarities or differences, or both.

We sometimes use the word *comparison* to refer both to similarities and differences between people or things, but it is more precise to use *comparison* for similarities and *contrast* for differences. For example, if you were to write about twin sisters you know, and how close they are in appearance and personality, the similarities you noted would make up a comparison. On the other hand, if you wanted to emphasize some important differences between the two sisters, the result would be a contrast.

We use comparison or contrast in a variety of ways every day. We talk about what a boyfriend and girlfriend have in common; we put similar products side by side in the store before we decide to buy one of them; we listen to two politicians on television and think about the differences between their positions before we vote for one of them; and we read college and university catalogues and talk to our friends before we decide which school to attend.

## Developing Paragraphs: Comparison and/or Contrast

### Working with Comparison and/or Contrast: Choosing the Two-Part Topic

The problem with writing a good comparison and/or contrast paragraph usually centres on the two-part topic, when you compare and/or contrast two items. This demands very careful attention to the topic sentence. While you must be careful to choose two subjects that have enough in common to make them comparable, you must avoid choosing two that have so much in common that you cannot possibly handle all the comparable points in one paragraph or even ten paragraphs. For example, a student trying to compare the French word *chaise* with the English word *chair* might be able to come up with only two sentences of material. With only a dictionary to consult, the student is unlikely to find enough material for several points of comparison. On the other hand, contrasting Canada with Europe would present such an endless supply of points to compare that the student would tend to give only general facts that the reader would already know. When the subject is too broad, the writing is often too general. A better two-part topic might be to compare travelling by train in Europe with travelling by train in Canada.

Once you have chosen a two-part topic that you believe is not too limiting and not too broad, you must remember that a good comparison and/or contrast paragraph should do two things: (1) contain a topic sentence that is evaluative in nature, and (2) devote an equal or nearly equal amount of space to each of the two parts. If a writer is interested in only one of the topics, the paragraph may end up being very one-sided.

## Formulating an Evaluative Topic Sentence

In establishing the controlling idea of a comparison and/or contrast paragraph, you should make sure that the topic sentence does two things: (1) it should identify the two items you've chosen to compare and/or contrast (topic), and (2) it should tell the reader essentially what your feeling is with respect to the two things being compared and/or contrasted (controlling idea). For example, it should indicate which one is better than the other (but try to use more specific language than the word *better*).

Here is an example of an evaluative topic sentence taken from the model paragraph on the next page:

> It was going to be as difficult making an income as a freelance editor as it was as an editor on staff at the magazine, but the benefits of freelancing seemed to far outweigh the disadvantages.

There are several things from this topic sentence one can assume about the rest of the paragraph:

1. There will be a contrast. There might be some comparison, but, for sure, the paragraph will not entirely be a comparison.
2. The two things being compared and/or contrasted are being a freelance editor and working as an editor on staff at the magazine.
3. In the end, after all the comparing and contrasting are finished, one should get the distinct impression that the writer prefers freelancing.

Now, with respect to the balance of content within the paragraph, here's an example of a one-sided contrast within a sentence:

> While Canadian trains go to only a few towns, are infrequent, and are often shabby and uncomfortable, the European train is much nicer.

The following example is a more balanced contrast that gives more of an equal amount of attention to both topics:

> While Canadian trains go to only a few large cities, run very infrequently, and are often shabby and uncomfortable, European trains go to virtually every small town, are always dependable, and are clean and attractive.

**PRACTICE**

### Evaluating the Two-Part Topic

Study the following topics and decide which are too broad for a paragraph and which are suitable as topics for a paragraph of comparison and/or contrast. Mark your choice in the appropriate space to the right of each topic. The first two are done for you. Check your answers against those in the Answer Key on p. 466.

| Topic | Too Broad | Suitable |
|---|---|---|
| 1. Australia and England | ✓ | |
| 2. Indian elephants and African elephants | | ✓ |
| 3. Canadian wine and French wine | | |
| 4. Wooden furniture and plastic furniture | | |
| 5. Wood and plastic | | |
| 6. Photography and oil painting | | |

## Two Methods: Point-by-Point and Block

The first method for ordering material in a paragraph or an essay of comparison and/or contrast is known as the **point-by-point method.**

**DEFINITION ➤** The **point-by-point method** is one way to order the material in a comparison and/or contrast paragraph or essay. When you use this method, you compare and/or contrast a point of one topic with the same point of the other topic before going onto the next point.

What follows is a paragraph in which the writer uses the point-by-point method to compare the difficulties of being a freelance editor with those of working as an editor on staff at a magazine.

**Model Paragraph I**

Now, of course, I knew that it was going to be as difficult making an income as a freelance editor as it was as an editor on staff at the magazine, if not more so, but the benefits of freelancing seemed to far outweigh the disadvantages. I would be at home hustling editing contracts via telephone, while everyone else spent their mornings at the office gabbing over endless cups of coffee. I sometimes resented having to work so hard to make a living, while my old colleagues on staff sat in meetings, went to conferences, and attended company luncheons. But I never envied them on their way to work on cold, dark winter mornings. And I wondered how many of them would have gladly switched places with me as I worked outside on my patio in the summer, while they looked longingly out their office windows.

Notice how, after the opening topic sentence, the writer uses half of each sentence to describe a freelance editor's experience and the other half of the same sentence to describe the experience of an editor who works for a magazine. This technique is effective in such a paragraph, and it is most often used in longer pieces of writing in which many points of comparison are made. This method helps the reader keep the comparison and/or contrast carefully in mind at each point.

Looking at the paragraph in outline form will help you see the shape of its development.

**Point-by-Point Method**

***Topic sentence:*** Now, of course, I knew that it was going to be as difficult making an income as a freelance editor as it was as an editor on staff at the magazine, if not more so.

***First point, first topic:*** I would be at home hustling editing contracts via telephone ...

***First point, second topic:*** ... while everyone else spent their mornings at the office gabbing over endless cups of coffee.

***Second point, first topic:*** I sometimes resented having to work so hard to earn a living ...

***Second point, second topic:*** ... while my old colleagues on staff sat in meetings, went to conferences, and attended company luncheons.

***Third point, first topic:*** But I never envied them on their way to work on cold, dark winter mornings.

***Third point, second topic:*** And I wondered how many of them would have gladly switched places with me as I worked outside on my patio, while they looked longingly out their office windows.

**DEFINITION ➤** The **block method** is another way (in addition to the **point-by-point method**) to order material in a paragraph of comparison and/or contrast. When you use this approach, you present all of the facts and supporting details about one topic, and then do the same for the second topic.

What follows is another version of Model Paragraph I, on pp. 292–93, written using the **block method.**

### Model Paragraph II

Now, of course, I knew that it was going to be as difficult making an income as a freelance editor as it was as an editor on staff at the magazine, if not more so, but the benefits of freelancing seemed to far outweigh the disadvantages. I spent my mornings hustling editing contracts on the telephone, and I sometimes resented having to work so hard to earn a living. On the other hand, I didn't envy my old colleagues on their way to work on cold, dark winter mornings. They could spend as much time as they wanted to gabbing over endless cups of coffee and going to meetings, conferences, and company luncheons; but I wonder how many of them would have gladly switched places with me as I worked outside on my patio in the summer.

Notice how the first half of this version presents almost all of the details about the freelance editor, while the second half presents all of the information about the editor on staff. This method is often used in shorter pieces of writing, where it is possible for the reader to keep in mind blocks of information.

Here is the paragraph in outline form.

### Block Method

*Topic sentence:* Now, of course, I knew that it was going to be as difficult making an income as a freelance editor as it was as an editor on staff at the magazine, if not more so.

*First topic, points one, two, and three:* I spent my mornings hustling editing contracts on the telephone, and I sometimes resented having to work so hard to earn a living. On the other hand, I didn't envy my old colleagues on their way to work on cold, dark, winter mornings.

*Second topic, points one, two, and three:* They could spend as much time as they wanted to gabbing over endless cups of coffee and going to meetings, conferences, and company luncheons; but I wonder how many of them would have gladly switched places with me as I worked outside on my patio in the summer.

You will want to choose one of these methods before you write a comparison and/or contrast assignment. Although the block method is most often used in shorter writing assignments, such as a paragraph, you will have the chance to practise the point-by-point method as well.

**PRACTICE**

## Recognizing the Two Methods

Each of the following passages is an example of comparison and/or contrast. Read each paragraph carefully, and decide whether the writer has used the point-by-point method or the block method. Indicate your choice in the spaces provided after each example. Also indicate whether the piece emphasizes similarities or differences. Check your answers against those in the Answer Key on p. 466.

1. Female infants speak sooner, have larger vocabularies, and rarely demonstrate speech defects. (Stuttering, for instance, occurs almost exclusively in boys.) Girls exceed boys in language abilities, and this early linguistic bias often prevails throughout life. Girls read sooner, learn foreign languages more easily, and, as a result, are more likely to enter occupations involving language mastery. Boys, in contrast, show an early visual superiority. They are also clumsier, performing poorly at tasks such as arranging a row of beads, but excel at other activities calling for total body coordination. Their attentional mechanisms are also different. A boy will react to an inanimate object as quickly as he will to a person. A male baby will often ignore the mother and babble at a blinking light, fixate on a geometric figure, and, at a later point, manipulate it and attempt to take it apart.

   _________ Point-by-Point _________ Block

   _________ Similarities _________ Differences

2. It is hard to decide who are the better inventors, Canadians or Martians. Canadians have invented wonderful devices that have made a significant contribution to their civilization, but then so have the Martians. Canadians invented the chain saw, the paint roller, the power mower, and the zipper. But Martians are no slouches, having come up with the intergalactic spaceship, the long-range power blaster, and the moon-dust mobile home. Of course, not all Canadian inventions have been stellar successes; consider, for example, the cast-iron airship, the reverse cooking stove, and the patent medicine carrot cure-all. But neither have Martians hit a winner every time: who can forget the ill-fated interplanetary bicycle, the invisible mirror, or the boomerang rocket? In the ingenuity department, you'd have to say it's a tie.

   _________ Point-by-Point _________ Block

   _________ Similarities _________ Differences

EXERCISE

## Using the Point-by-Point and Block Methods

Choose one of the paragraphs from the above Practice and rewrite it using the opposite method for comparison and/or contrast. For instance, if a paragraph uses the point-by-point method, rewrite it using the block method.

## Tips on Transitions: *Like* vs. *As*

**TIP** ***Like*** **is a preposition and is used in the prepositional phrase "like me."**

My sister is just *like* me.

**TIP** ***As*** **is a subordinate conjunction and is used in the clause below with a subject and a verb.**

My sister sews every evening, *as* does her oldest daughter.

**See the chart on the inside back cover of this book and Chapter 17: "The Essay" (pp. 206–07) for additional transitions.**

## Writing the Comparison and/or Contrast Paragraph Step by Step

To learn a skill with some degree of ease, it is best to follow a step-by-step approach so that various skills can be worked on one at a time. This approach will ensure that you are not missing a crucial point or misunderstanding a part of the whole. There are other ways to go about writing an effective paragraph, but here is one logical method you can use to achieve results.

**Steps for Writing the Comparison and/or Contrast Paragraph**

1. Study the given topic, and then plan your topic sentence, especially the dominant impression.
2. List all your ideas for points that could be compared and/or contrasted.
3. Choose the three or four most important points from your list, and put them in order.
4. Decide whether you want to use the point-by-point method or the block method of organizing your paragraph.
5. Write at least one complete sentence for each of the points you have chosen from your list.
6. Write a concluding statement that summarizes the main points, makes a judgment, or emphasizes what you believe is the most important point.
7. Finally, copy your sentences into standard paragraph form.

**EXERCISE**

### Writing the Comparison and/or Contrast Paragraph Step by Step

The following exercise will guide you through the construction of a comparison and/or contrast paragraph. Start with the suggested topic. Use the seven steps to help you work through each stage of the writing process. (Refer to pp. 261–62 in Chapter 21 for a completed sample paragraph.)

**Topic:** Compare and/or contrast going to work with going to college immediately after high school.

1. Write a topic sentence.
2. Make a list of possible comparisons and/or contrasts.
3. Circle the three or four comparisons or contrasts that you believe are most important, and put them in order.
4. Choose either the point-by-point method or the block method.
5. Using your final list, write at least one sentence for each comparison and/or contrast you have chosen.
6. Write a concluding statement.
7. On a separate sheet of paper, copy your sentences into standard paragraph form.

ASSIGNMENT

### Comparison and/or Contrast Paragraph

Write a paragraph in which you compare and/or contrast two places you know, either from personal experience or from your reading.

SUGGESTED TOPICS:

(For more suggested topics, see the list on p. 300.)

1. Two neighbourhoods
2. Two towns or cities
3. Two vacation spots
4. Two provinces
5. Two countries
6. Two streets
7. Two colleges or universities

## The Comparison and/or Contrast Essay

In a comparison and/or contrast essay, the thesis statement (like the topic sentence in a paragraph) identifies what is being compared and/or contrasted and what the author's overall feeling toward the comparison and/or contrast is (controlling idea).

The Honda Civic beats the Toyota Corolla in many respects.

If you're using the block method, the second paragraph of the essay might be used for everything you want to say about the Honda, while the third paragraph contains everything you want to say about the Toyota (as it contrasts with everything you've said in the previous paragraph about the Honda).

A four-paragraph essay would be appropriate if you are using the block method for your comparison and/or contrast essay. The last paragraph of your four-paragraph essay, of course, would contain a restatement of your thesis but in different words (see Chapter 17: "The Essay").

If, on the other hand, you're using the point-by-point method, the second paragraph of the essay would compare and/or contrast both the Honda and the Toyota based on the first of, ideally, three points. The third paragraph of the essay would deal with the second of three points, and so on. With the point-by-point method, provided you are discussing your findings on the basis of three points, it would be appropriate to go back to a standard five-paragraph essay, rather than the four-paragraph essay recommended for the essay in which you might have chosen the block method.

**For an in-depth look at the essay and its standard format (for all writing strategies in this unit), see Chapter 17: "The Essay." Also review Chapter 14: "The Four Stages of Writing," which can be applied to both the paragraph and the essay.**

The following essay explores the differences between living in a small town and living in a big city, according to its author. Although Zack's opinion is pretty clear from the outset, someone else could just as easily argue for the opposite point of view. What's important is that the thesis is clear and that there is evidence supporting it. Determine if Zack achieves these goals.

READ

### Model Essay: City Life Beats the Small Town Blues

**by Zack Goodman**

Growing up in a small town has its perks. You might have fewer friends than you have in the big city, but you tend to keep them closer. The East Coast small town author Hugh MacLennan once said that a writer who grows up in a small town has a greater knowledge of human intimacy even if that intimacy dries up at the age of 40. Well, not everybody agrees with either of those points. In fact, city life can offer just as much intimacy if not more than small town life can. Life is better in the big city, and it all comes down to one general reason: more choice.

One of the areas in which having choice can be extremely valuable is that of friends. Like leaving home to seek greater knowledge of yourself, picking your own friends from a greater number of people can aid in your journey to seek self-knowledge. After all, if you go out with the same group of small town friends all the time, not because you necessarily like them all that much, but because they're the only ones available, this can prove quite limiting when it comes to your growth as an individual. The big city, on the other hand, offers an endless number of opportunities to meet people of like interests. You're much more likely to cultivate relationships with people who help you to grow.

If you're the type of person who enjoys learning about other cultures and meeting people of many different ethnicities, you're much more likely to do both of these things in a big city. People from all over the world prefer the big city to which to emigrate because they might already have relatives there, or at least some sort of community similar to the one they've left in their country of origin. They might not have to learn English right away to get along because there are enough people with whom they can speak in their native tongue, and in general, the big city can afford more resources to make them more comfortable. In a small town, you might have to get used to a group of people of one origin, maybe even a community in which there is only one religion. If this is what you want, there's no problem. But if you consider yourself a citizen of the world, a one-ethnicity town might be pretty boring after a while.

And finally, if you're a person who enjoys the arts, the small town probably won't be able to hold a candle to the arts community of a big city. A small town might have one cinema that shows maybe three different movies at any one time. A big city can have more than 100 theatres showing at least a hundred different movies, and not all mainstream film, but independent film, B-movies, foreign film (do Canadian movies qualify as foreign films in Canada?) and second-run movies for those who missed them the first time around. But movies are only one form of entertainment in the big city on any given night. There's the Broadway musical, the independent stage theatre, ballet, modern dance, cabaret, poetry reading, cafés and night clubs with live music including jazz, house, Latin, retro, hip-hop (you ask for it; the big city's got it), street festivals in the summer, outdoor skating and indoor tennis in the winter, and so on and so on. A small town may have some of this some of the time, but a big city is more likely to have most of it most of the time.

A small town has its advantages; that's true. The cost of living is lower. The streets are probably safer at night. And it might even be easier to meet someone special. But if you're an arts lover who enjoys the company of people from all over the world, and you're interested in cultivating friends who help you to grow spiritually and not just to get drunk on a Saturday night, city life is tough to beat.

## Questions for Analysis

1. An essay of comparison points out the similarities between two subjects, while an essay of contrast examines the differences. With this in mind, is the essay you have just read an essay of comparison or an essay of contrast or both (comparison AND contrast)? What is your evidence for your answer?
2. Does the writer use the point-by-point method or the block method in writing this essay?
3. Does the writer provide an equal number of details that relate to both the small town and the big city?
4. Specifically, how does the writer demonstrate what he thinks is the superior nature of the big city?

**ASSIGNMENT** **Comparison and/or Contrast Essay**

Choose a topic from below, and write a comparison and/or contrast essay of at least five paragraphs to develop that topic.

**SUGGESTED TOPICS:**

(For more suggested topics, see the list on p. 297.)
Compare and/or contrast:

1. High school classes with college classes
2. Life in a city with life in a rural area
3. Two movies (the acting, the cinematography, the quality of the story)
4. A friend from your childhood with a present friend
5. Two similar items you have owned (e.g., cars, bicycles, radios)
6. Seeing a play with seeing a movie
7. Two vacation spots
8. Two apartments or houses where you have lived
9. Researching in a library with researching on the Internet
10. Cooking dinner at home with eating out

**For helpful hints on the following subjects, all of which will assist you in developing your comparison and/or contrast essay, see Chapter 14:**

**Brainstorming**
**Choosing the Topic and the Controlling Idea**
**Outlining**
**The Rough Draft**
**Revising and Editing the Rough Draft**
**Proofreading**
**Checklist for the Final Copy**

## Working Together: Reaching Consensus

In a group of three to five students, decide among yourselves which two movies, fashion items, concerts, or advertisements you'd like to compare and/or contrast. Make sure that everyone in your group has seen both items. Then try to reach a consensus about your overall conclusion before you begin to compare and/or contrast the items on the basis of at least three points. Discuss your results with the rest of the class. Was it easy to reach consensus on everything? What did you learn by the process? Did most groups end up comparing or contrasting, or both?

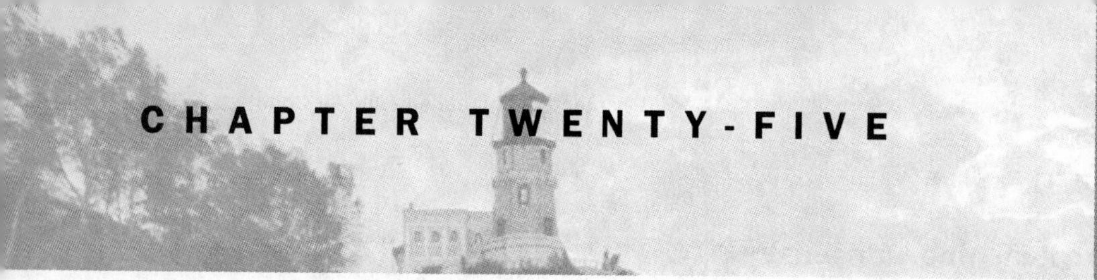

CHAPTER TWENTY-FIVE

25

# Definition

## What Is Definition?

Definition is one of the most useful forms of writing. The ability to provide accurate definitions is crucial to ensuring your audience understands your words and ideas. Most of the essays you will write in college or university will require you to define terms.

When you are asked to give a definition, you are usually asked to explain what a word means. You will often need to define terms in your writing when they are very technical or would otherwise be unfamiliar to your reader. For example, not many people would know what a contusion is, so the writer of a health-sciences report may want to explain that *contusion* is another word for a bruise. In fact, defining a term or concept is often an effective way to begin an essay. Thus, the writer of an essay on discrimination may first want to provide a definition of the term before describing examples of discrimination.

### More Personal Meaning

There may also be situations where you want to give a more personal meaning to a common term. For instance, you may think that you have a clear idea of what the word *success* means. By talking with your classmates about their definitions of success, however, you'll see that each has a different mental picture of what success looks like. For some, a successful person may have lots of money. For others, success may mean achieving a personal goal, such as competing in the Olympics. For still others, success means having a happy family life. Personal definitions are useful in writing because they cast new light on ordinary terms and make us question our conceptions about our day-to-day lives.

**DEFINITION ➤** A **definition** is an explanation of the meaning or significance of a word or term. The starting point for a good definition is to group the word into a larger category or class. (See Chapter 26 on classification.)

For example, the trout is a kind of fish, a doll is a kind of toy, and a shirt is an article of clothing. Here is a dictionary entry for the word *myth* (from the *Webster's New World Dictionary*, Second College Edition):

**myth** (mith) ***n.*** [LL. *mythos* < Gr. *mythos*, a word, speech, story, legend] **1.** a traditional story of unknown authorship, ostensibly with a historical basis, but serving usually to explain some phenomenon of nature, the origin of man, or the customs, institutions, religious rites, etc. of a people: myths usually involve the exploits of gods and heroes: cf. LEGEND **2.** such stories collectively; mythology **3.** any fictitious story, or unscientific account, theory, belief, etc. **4.** any imaginary person or thing spoken of as though existing.

To what larger category does the word *myth* belong? The myth, according to the first meaning above, is a kind of *story.*

**DEFINITION ➤** Once a word has been put into a larger class, its definition gives the **identifying characteristics** that make the word different from other members in the class.

What makes a *trout* different from a *bass,* a *doll* different from a *puppet,* a *shirt* different from a *sweater,* a *myth* different from a *parable*? With these questions, the dictionary can offer some assistance. The first dictionary definition of *myth* identifies the myth as a story that is an explanation of why individual human beings do what they do, a story about the religious practices of a people, a story about the adventures of gods and heroes.

When you write a paragraph or an essay that uses definition, the dictionary entry is only the beginning. In order for your reader to understand a difficult term or idea, you will need to expand this definition into what is called **extended definition.** It is not the function of a dictionary to go into great depth. It can provide only the basic meanings and synonyms.

**DEFINITION ➤** **Extended definition** seeks to analyze a concept in order to give the reader a more complete understanding.

For instance, you might include a historical perspective of a word or term. When or how did the concept begin? How did the term change or evolve over the years, or how do different cultures understand the term? You will become involved in the connotations of the word. Extended definition, or **analysis** as it is sometimes called, uses more than one method to arrive at an understanding of a term.

## Developing Paragraphs: Definition

Religion scholar Karen Armstrong is the author of *A Short History of Myth.* In the following passage from her book, the author's starting point resembles the first two dictionary meanings, but she sheds light on the emergence of the last two dictionary meanings as well:

### Model Paragraph

Myths are universal and timeless stories that reflect and shape our lives—they mirror our desires, our fears, our longings, and provide narratives that attempt to help us make sense of the world.... Today the word "myth" is often used to describe something that is simply not true.... When we hear of gods walking the earth, of dead men striding out of tombs, or of seas miraculously parting to let a favoured people escape from their enemies, we dismiss these stories as incredible and demonstrably untrue.... A myth is essentially a guide; it tells us what we must do in order to live more richly. If we do not apply it to our own situation and make the myth a reality in our own lives, it will remain as incomprehensible and remote as the rules of a board game, which often seem confusing and boring until we start to play.

The author, like the dictionary, puts the term into a larger class: Myths are stories. She also identifies the characteristics of these stories that are different from other stories: They are universal and timeless. They reflect and shape our lives. She also goes on to explain the relationship between one dictionary meaning and another that seems so different. A story that is about gods who walk the earth seems incredible and untrue. Therefore, a myth comes to be known as a falsehood. She explains why the term *myth* seems to have lost its real meaning as a result of science. And she explains why it is so important that humanity learn to reclaim the real meaning of myth.

**EXERCISE 1**

## Working with Definition: Class

Define each of the following terms by placing it in a larger class. Keep in mind that when you define something by class, you are placing it in a larger category so that the reader can see where it belongs. Use the dictionary if you need help. The first example is done for you.

> Chemistry is <u>one of the branches of science</u> that deals with a close study of the natural world.

1. A *motorcycle* is ______________________________
2. *Poetry* is ______________________________
3. *Democracy* is ______________________________
4. *Sugar* is ______________________________
5. A *viola* is ______________________________

**EXERCISE 2**

## Working with Definition: Distinguishing Characteristics

Using the same terms as in Exercise 1, give one or two identifying characteristics that differentiate your term from other terms in the same class. An example is done for you.

Chemistry studies the structure, properties, and reactions of matter.

1. A *motorcycle* ______________________________

______________________________

______________________________

2. *Poetry* ______________________________

______________________________

______________________________

3. *Democracy* ______________________________

______________________________

______________________________

4. *Sugar* ______________________________

______________________________

______________________________

5. A *viola* ______________________________

______________________________

______________________________

## Writing the Definition Paragraph Step by Step

To learn a skill with some degree of ease, it is best to follow a step-by-step approach so that the various aspects of the skill can be worked on one step at a time. This approach will ensure that you are not missing a crucial point or misunderstanding a part of the whole. There are other ways to go about writing an effective paragraph, but the following is one logical method you can use to achieve results.

### Steps for Writing the Definition Paragraph

1. Write a topic sentence that identifies what you are going to define.
2. List all the possible concepts for your extended definition.
3. Eliminate inappropriate concepts from your list.
4. Put your final list in order.
5. Write at least one complete sentence for each of the concepts that you have chosen from your list.
6. Write a concluding statement that summarizes the important parts of your definition.
7. Finally, copy your sentences into standard paragraph form.

EXERCISE

## Writing the Definition Paragraph Step by Step

The following exercise will guide you through the construction of a definition paragraph. Start with the suggested topic. Use the seven steps above to help you work through each stage of the writing process. (Refer to pages 261–62 in Chapter 21 for a completed sample paragraph.)

**Topic:** Intelligence

To help you get started on a topic sentence below, read the following:

> We often equate intelligence with being "smart" or with having above-average ability in some area. Yet we likely all know some rather intelligent people who don't act very smart, or who are very absent-minded. We could also have a pet that is "intelligent." What is intelligence as you understand it?

1. Write a topic sentence.
2. Make a list of possible concepts.
3. Eliminate any concepts that are not appropriate.
4. Put your final list in order.
5. Using your final list, write at least one sentence for each of the concepts you have chosen.
6. Write a concluding statement.
7. On separate sheet of paper, copy your sentences into standard paragraph form.

ASSIGNMENT

## Paragraph of Definition

Some of us are dreamers, and some of us are idealists; we all have distinguishing characteristics within the larger class of human being. Using one of the following suggested topics, write a paragraph of definition of who or what you are.

### SUGGESTED TOPICS:

(For more suggested topics, see the list on p. 309.)

1. Happy-go-lucky
2. Creative
3. A friend to all
4. A comedian
5. Reserved

## Developing an Essay of Definition

The thesis in this type of essay, of course, identifies what is being defined. It also should provide a good, but general definition. Then each support paragraph deals with an explanation of a different component or aspect of what has been defined in the first paragraph.

For example, see the essay below by Jenny Yuen on sexual addiction entitled "Love Hurts." The first support paragraph (the second paragraph of the essay) deals with the question of how common the addiction is. The third support paragraph deals with a particular example. The fifth support deals with the notion that attending twelve-step program meetings may not be enough to control this addiction, and so on.

No one support paragraph should deal with more than one component or aspect of that which is being defined. But once the support paragraph has identified the component to be discussed in its first sentence (the topic sentence of that paragraph), the author, of course, can go ahead and add various sorts of supporting details (including examples) to support the topic sentence.

**For an in-depth look at the essay and its standard format (for all writing strategies in this unit), see Chapter 17: "The Essay." Also review Chapter 14: "The Four Stages of Writing," which can be applied to both the paragraph and the essay.**

When Jenny wrote the following piece, she was a student in a journalism program. Originally, the following was a newspaper piece, which is why much of the writing seems journalistic in nature. The paragraphs are longer than typical newspaper paragraphs, however, because the story was adapted to suit a more academic style of essay for the purpose of this chapter.

READ

### Model Essay: Love Hurts

**by Jenny Yuen**

For love and sex addicts, Valentine's Day may not be simply roses and candy, but rather a traumatic reminder that love hurts. February 14 may bring back painful memories of past breakups, or trigger the need to go out and find a "special someone" who may not turn out to be all that special. Sexual and love addiction is the continuing pattern of unwanted compulsive romantic behaviour that has a negative impact on the addict's personal, social and/or economic standing.

Sex and love addiction are more common than you might imagine, says Rob Hawkings, a psychotherapist at Bellwood Health Services in North York, Ontario. These addictions are also very complex disorders in which the victims may not realize that their behaviour falls into the "addict" category. How can you tell whether you have "normal" relationship problems or that you're in love with love and sex? (See questionnaire at the end.) The answer is another question: Are you in control? But having self-control is much easier said than done. "We look for a pattern of out-of-control behaviour, whether that's with pornographic material or flirting or continually getting into romantic involvements in a serial kind of way or giving into simultaneous multiple [relationships]," says 51-year-old Hawkings, a recovering alcoholic and sex addict, himself, who has been working in the field for a decade.

Although the demographic of addicts varies, most of the people who attend the 12-step meetings are males in their late 20s to late 50s. Still, there are no definite statistics of how much of the Canadian population is affected by sexual and love addiction, although Hawkings says more patients would be checking into Bellwood for therapy if they realized it is a problem.

Judy, 37, tormented herself with obsessive sexual fantasies for four years. She had constant fantasies about extra-marital relationships, and suffered from sexual anorexia, trying to avoid her problems so she wouldn't have to deal with them. "I was in a marriage, and I started thinking about men outside my marriage so much that it was affecting my work life. I hate to use the word obsession, ... but I found myself powerless over my thoughts."

While Bellwood is new at the sex addiction game, SLAA (or Sex and Love Addicts Anonymous), also known as The Augustine Fellowship, has been working worldwide with addicts for more than 20 years. SLAA champions the Alcoholics Anonymous 12-step program as an efficient treatment program for sufferers of sex and love addiction. Currently, SLAA has more than 1200 meeting locations throughout the world, open to all who believe they may have a problem. People who believe they may suffer from love and sexual addiction may come in anonymously and tell their stories and listen to others.

Although Bellwood avidly encourages its sex addiction patients to attend these meetings, Hawkings says 12-step programs are not enough. Bellwood's program includes life-skills coaching to help addicts deal with communication and feelings. In some special cases, Bellwood prescribes medication for sex addicts. "There are situations where there are some people who need a carefully-prescribed anti-depressant," says Hawkings, who is careful not to recommend addictive medication such as Valium. "We sometimes get people coming in who have real psychiatric problems as well as addictions going on."

The question still remains: Can the love and sex addict be cured? "The classic stereotype is AA, where people are recovering for the rest of their lives, but for the rest of their lives need not forget they're alcoholics," Hawkings says. By and large, that is the case with sexual addiction. People are always going to be susceptible to using the sexual-addictive fix that they might have used in the past when they were under stress. "One thing we work very hard on in recovery is managing the stress in their lives."

Judy was fortunate enough to alter her sexual behaviours into healthier ones because of the SLAA program. "I felt freedom right away. I was really fortunate," Judy says. "You don't graduate from [a 12-step program]. They call it being 'restored to sanity,' but a better way to put it is we now have a choice over our decisions."

***

The following is a questionnaire to help determine if you are a sex and/or love addict. If you answer yes to most of these questions, you may be.

- Do you still see someone, even though you know the relationship has a destructive effect on you?
- Do you feel like you *have* to have sex?
- Do you have sex regardless of the consequences?
- Do you feel you lack dignity and wholeness?
- Is your life unmanageable because of your sexual or romantic behaviour?

Contact Information:

- SLAA Coxwell branch (416) 486-8201 or Toll-free 1-800-977-4325
- Bellwood Health Clinic: Rob Hawkings, sex psychotherapist, (416) 495-0926, ext. 107 or toll-free 1-800-387-6198
- Dr. Patrick Carnes' Website: www.sexhelp.com
- Pia Mellody's Website: www.piamellody.com

## Questions for Analysis

1. What is the central thing being defined in this essay?
2. In what ways is sexual addiction like alcoholism? In what ways is it different?
3. What surprises you the most in this piece by Jenny Yuen?
4. What do you think is the main purpose of this essay? Why?
5. Why do you think more men go to meetings for sex and love addiction than do women?
6. Do you think sex and/or love addiction can be as destructive as alcohol or substance abuse? Why or why not?

**ASSIGNMENT**

## Essay of Definition

Choose one of the topics below, or take one of your own, and write an essay of definition of at least five paragraphs to develop that topic.

### SUGGESTED TOPICS:

1. Definition of your favourite martial art
2. Definition of a particular disease or medical condition
3. Definition of love
4. Definition of a term in your particular field of study
5. Definition of "impressionism" or other kind of painting theory

**For helpful hints on the following subjects, all of which will assist you in developing your essay of definition, see Chapter 14:**

**Brainstorming**
**Choosing the Topic and the Controlling Idea**
**Outlining**
**The Rough Draft**
**Revising and Editing the Rough Draft**
**Proofreading**
**Checklist for the Final Copy**

## Working Together: What Does the Cover Mean to You?

One could argue that to interpret a picture is to define it. Look at the cover of this book, and come to a one-sentence conclusion as to what you think it means to you. This one-sentence conclusion becomes your topic sentence or thesis statement for your paragraph or essay of definition. Once you've done this, look at the various components of the picture and pick three that make the biggest impression on you. Discuss these three parts as points that support your one-sentence interpretation.

Then exchange papers with someone else in your group/class. Discuss the results with the group/class. Are there several interpretations? Are there certain universal points that everybody has made? Do any or all of the interpretations relate to the study of writing?

CHAPTER TWENTY-SIX

26

# Classification

## What Is Classification?

**DEFINITION ➤** **Classification** is the placing of items into separate categories for the purpose of helping us think about these items more clearly. This can be extremely useful and even necessary when large numbers of items are being considered.

In order to classify things properly, you must always take the items you are working with, for instance, computers, and establish a basis for classification, such as where they are made. Then put them into **distinct categories,** making sure that each item belongs in only one category. For example, if you were to classify computers into imported computers, Canadian-made computers, and used computers, this would not be an effective use of classification because a used computer does not conform to the basis for classification already established (where they are made), and an imported computer or a Canadian-made computer could also be a used computer, so the categories are not distinct.

A classification should also be **complete.** For example, if you were to classify computers into the two categories of new and used, your classification would be complete because any item can be only new or used.

## Developing Paragraphs: Classification

In the following paragraph, the writer classifies different kinds of neighbours:

**Model Paragraph**

To me, there are only two kinds of neighbours: those who are friendly and those who are not. The friendly neighbours always greet me with a smile regardless of the situation. They are the ones whose names I usually know, and they are always either asking me to come over, or they're interested in talking about what's going on in their lives or asking me about mine. The unfriendly neighbours, on the other hand, could be mistaken for complete strangers no matter how long they've lived in the neighbourhood. I don't know their names. They pass me on the street as if they've never seen me before. It's those neighbours who make me think that if I dared to try and strike up a conversation with them, they'd scowl, or, in some way, they'd make me feel sorry for ever trying. I just hope that if one day my house is on fire, my friendly neighbours are at home so that I can run up to *them* for help.

In this paragraph, the writer presents two distinct types of neighbours—friendly ones and unfriendly ones. These are the only types that have any significance for the writer. The writer's classification is complete because it covers the entire range of neighbours—there are, in the writer's opinion, no other types of neighbours. Since most of us have neighbours, we might be able to identify with the writer to some extent even if we don't think the writer's classification system is complete enough.

## EXERCISE 1 Working with Classification: Finding the Basis for a Classification

For each of the following topics, pick three different ways that topic could be classified. You may find the following example helpful.

***Topic:*** Ways to choose a vacation spot.

***Basis for classification:*** by price, by its special attraction, by the accommodations

1. **Topic:** Cellular phones

   Basis for classification: ______________________________

   ______________________________

2. **Topic:** Relatives

   Basis for classification: ______________________________

   ______________________________

3. **Topic:** Snack foods

   Basis for classification: ______________________________

   ______________________________

4. **Topic:** News sources

   Basis for classification: ______________________________

   ______________________________

5. **Topic:** Medicines

   Basis for classification: ______________________________

   ______________________________

## Making Distinct Categories

Once you have established the basis for classification, you're ready to come up with distinct categories. These are ways in which you have chosen to divide each basis for classification. In other words, they are examples of your basis for classification.

| Topic | Basis for Classification | Distinct Categories |
|---|---|---|
| Ways to choose a vacation spot | price | first class<br>medium price<br>economy |
| | special attraction | the beach<br>the mountains<br>the desert |
| | accommodation | hotel<br>motel<br>cabin |

**EXERCISE 2**

### Working with Classification: Making Distinct Categories

First pick a basis for classifying each of the following topics. Then break the basis for classification down into distinct categories. Divide the basis for classification into as many distinct categories as you think the classification requires. You don't have to stick with three.

Keep in mind that when you divide your topic, each part of your classification must belong to only one category. For example, if you were to classify cars, you would not want to make sports cars and international cars two of your categories because several kinds of sports cars are also international cars. You may find the following example helpful.

***Topic:*** Wine
***Basis for classification:*** colour
***Distinct categories:*** red, white, rosé
or
***Basis for classification:*** national origin
***Distinct categories:*** French, Australian, Italian, Canadian, Chilean, etc.

1. Clothing stores

   Basis for classification: ______________________________

   Distinct categories: ______________________________

   ______________________________

2. Television commercials

   Basis for classification: ______________________________

   Distinct categories: ______________________________

   ______________________________

3. Olympic sports

   Basis for classification: ______________________________

   Distinct categories: ______________________________

   ______________________________

4. Mail

   Basis for classification: ______________________________

   Distinct categories: ______________________________

   ______________________________

5. Art forms

   Basis for classification: ______________________________

   Distinct categories: ______________________________

   ______________________________

## Writing the Classification Paragraph Step by Step

To learn a skill with some degree of ease, it is best to follow a step-by-step approach so that various aspects of the skill can be worked on one at a time. This approach will ensure that you are not missing a crucial point or misunderstanding a part of the whole. There are other ways to go about writing an effective paragraph, but here is one logical method you can use to achieve results.

**Steps for Writing the Classification Paragraph**

1. Write a topic sentence, stating the **basis of the classification**.
2. List all the possible **distinct categories** in your classification.
3. Eliminate inappropriate **distinct categories** from your list.
4. Put your final list in order.
5. Write at least one complete sentence for each of the **distinct categories** you have chosen from your list.
6. Write a concluding sentence that emphasizes the **basis of the classification**.
7. Finally, copy your sentences into standard paragraph form.

EXERCISE

## Writing the Classification Paragraph Step by Step

This exercise will guide you through the construction of a classification paragraph. Start with the suggested topic. Use the seven steps (repeated below) to help you work through each stage of the writing process. (Refer to pp. 261–62 in Chapter 21 for a completed sample paragraph.)

**Topic**: Games

We play games as children. Some of these we continue to play as adults, and we play different types of games, as well. We are even accused of "playing games"—mind games—from time to time. There are board games, mind games, and electronic games. How many other categories of games can you think of?

1. Write a topic sentence.
2. Make a list of possible categories.
3. Eliminate any categories that are not appropriate.
4. Put your final list in order.
5. Using your final list, write at least one sentence for each category you have chosen.
6. Write a concluding statement.
7. On a separate sheet of paper, copy your sentences into standard paragraph form.

ASSIGNMENT

## Classification Paragraph

Pick a topic from the list below, and write a paragraph in which you classify relationships.

### SUGGESTED TOPICS:

(For more suggested topics, see the list on p. 320.)

1. Friends
2. Classmates or colleagues at work
3. Girlfriends/boyfriends
4. Pets
5. Teachers
6. Bosses
7. Casual acquaintances

## Developing an Essay of Classification

The thesis statement of a classification essay, like the topic sentence of the classification paragraph, identifies what is being classified. In the essay, it's important to devote each support paragraph to a distinct category of the items with which you are dealing. For example, in the first model essay below, Hussain Mohamdally classifies the types of responses to books that people read. Because three types of responses are discussed, it is a nice fit for the standard five-paragraph essay. The second essay that begins on page 318 classifies people into four groups according to what psychiatrist M. Scott Peck considers an evolution of spirituality. In this essay by Margo Fine, the first support paragraph (the second paragraph of the essay) deals only with the least spiritually evolved group (the first group). Because four groups are being classified, Margo found it appropriate to write a six-paragraph essay as opposed to the standard five, which many professors insist upon or at least strongly recommend, especially when students are required to complete the essay in a two-hour period or less. Both of the essays report on classifications made by authors in their respective books.

**For an in-depth look at the essay and its standard format (for all writing strategies in this unit), see Chapter 17: "The Essay." Also review Chapter 14: "The Four Stages of Writing," which can be applied to both the paragraph and the essay.**

In the following third-person essay of classification, Hussain looks at a book written by Royal Military College professor Stephen Bonnycastle called *In Search of Authority.* Hussain uses classification to illustrate the different types of student responses to books that English instructors choose to use for their courses.

READ

### Model Essay I: Booting Out Boredom

### by Hussain Mohamdally

English professors in college and in university face a number of challenges in the classroom. One of these challenges lies in the choice of reading material that will be of interest to their students. Professors will often choose course materials on the basis of what they consider important even if the students do not. This often becomes the source of student complaints: "The novel we're studying is boring," they often say. Stephen Bonnycastle, professor of English at the Royal Military College of Canada in Kingston, Ontario, says that every book has one of three types of reader response. In his book *In Search of Authority,* he writes that he will choose the type of book that he predicts will invoke only one particular response, and in this way, he will greatly reduce the problem of "boredom" in English classes.

The first type of reader response is one of fascination. These books, according to Bonnycastle, cause the "feeling that you want to read the book again—that it would give you pleasure to reread it." These books automatically spark interest among the students. The reader feels involved. Explanation by the teacher enhances the students' appreciation of the book, but there is no explanation required for the simple enjoyment that they experience just by reading it.

The second type of reader response is the one that can be described as a feeling of wanting to reread the book, but only upon taking a course that is related to it. Bonnycastle refers to the example of the great Russian novel *Anna Karenina*. "You might feel moderately interested by the novel, but know that for it to become really involving for you, you would need to gather some other information: a knowledge of 19th-century Russia; familiarity with other books by Tolstoy and other Russian authors of the period; and perhaps some knowledge of Tolstoy's life ..." These books need to be preserved, says the RMC professor, but they are best suited for "a university course." For without such a nurturing environment, they would not be appreciated very much.

The third and final type of reader response is quite simply, "boredom." These are the books people generally know they will never read again. And if they can help it, they will even avoid any course in which it is ever taught. Some people's responses to this type of novel may be the number two type of response, but the professor's risk in choosing this book for the curriculum is far too great for any hope of general satisfaction on the part of the class. That's not to say a teacher shouldn't take risks. But any risk should take student interest into account.

Not surprisingly, the trick is to pick as many materials that invoke a number one response from the reader. Too often, says Bonnycastle, the teacher's response to a book is a number one response, but the students' response is number three. What becomes important, therefore, is the teacher's ability to read his or her students well, and not just the books he or she assigns. A mixture of books that cause a number one and number two response is acceptable, but as many materials as possible that fascinate the students without any effort on the part of the teacher are still the best bet for an exciting English course.

## Questions for Analysis

1. What are the topic, the basis for classification, and the distinct categories in this essay of classification?
2. Is it possible for a teacher, as Bonnycastle suggests, to choose a book that he or she can assume will invoke a number one response from most students? Discuss.
3. Name a book that you have read, and classify it according to Bonnycastle's classification system. Now compare and/or contrast it (using Bonnycastle's

criteria) with another book you have read that you think belongs to another group among the three.

4. Identify at least three books that you think most people in your class would be familiar with. To which group would each of these books belong, according to Bonnycastle's system? Check with other students in your class to see if anyone else has identified any of your books. Do they agree with you or not? What are the results of this exercise?
5. Should other English professors take Bonnycastle's advice? Discuss.

Like Hussain, Margo also gets her inspiration from a book for her essay of classification that follows. Moving away from the classroom environment, she is concerned here, more generally speaking, with the spiritual state of individual human beings. This essay is a bit more complicated as it concerns more abstract concepts. But it has the potential to generate some interesting discussion.

READ

### Model Essay II: The Evolution of Spirituality

**by Margo Fine**

Psychiatrist and prolific author M. Scott Peck is probably most famous for his book *The Road Less Traveled,* which has appeared on the New York Best-Seller's List for more than 25 years. Peck entitled a sequel to this book *Further Along the Road Less Traveled*—a title that is appropriate if unoriginal. It is in this book, however, that Peck discusses a model of spiritual evolution into which, he says, every single person can be fit according to a particular classification system. Peck classifies people into four groups according to the extent to which they have spiritually evolved: the first group being the least evolved and the fourth being the most.

The first group is made up of people who are governed by their emotions. These are the quintessential charmers of the model. How nice they are, and therefore, how well they treat others, depend on whether they want something at that particular time. As soon as they get what they want, they're gone, or they're not so nice anymore: narcissism and greed are most apparent in this group. Their responses to people are generally unpredictable as these responses depend solely on these people's emotions. There is little or no self-examination or self-evaluation here.

The second group up from the bottom can quite aptly be called the "organizational clingers." These people are aware of the fact that left to their own devices, they would be completely governed by their own emotions like those in the first group. People in the second group inherently know this would prove disastrous. To avoid such a consequence, they opt to cling to an organization of some sort, one that promises to take care of them, one that offers a sense of protection and belonging, but also discipline by means of a strict code of conduct. This organization prevents them from depending on their emotions for answers to their important questions. Organized religion is often the structure to which people in this group cling. In fact, Peck would put most religious fundamentalists (of any religion) in this category.

The third group up from the bottom (and therefore, the second from the top) is the group that seems to react quite vehemently to the second group (especially to religious fundamentalists). These are the secularists. These people are often very well educated in the sciences or the arts, and they are often politically active or motivated. People in this group often pride themselves on being free thinkers, especially when they compare themselves to people in the second group. However, they, themselves, depend on a structure, however less rigid than those in the second group, for answers to their important questions. After all, the sciences, especially, are dependent upon laws and knowledge of the natural world—the world people can only perceive with any or all of their five senses, the part of existence that we can see and hear, etc. Despite their self-declaration of being the free thinkers of the world, it is often they who dismiss the idea that there is an order to the universe that is not explainable by science or that cannot be proven by anything empirical.

It is the fourth group that is most spiritually evolved, says Peck. These people, like their counterparts in the third group, are often very well educated. And although they probably call themselves secularists, they can probably be better described by the word "seekers," or perhaps "mystics." Like Albert Einstein, they may be highly regarded for their achievements in the secular world, but at the same time, they know there is more to life than that which we can see and hear or perceive with any of our five senses. People in the fourth group are very much aware of the importance of intuition, or an inner voice and the idea that something else is at work in the universe that cannot be explained by science that makes a great deal of sense whether we can understand it or not. They are not necessarily quick to call it God or Allah or a cosmic consciousness, but whatever it is, it is definitely in the realm of the supernatural. But unlike those in the second group, people in the fourth group are not satisfied with any one set of holy books or especially any one set of interpretations that a single religion can offer in its explanation of a higher power.

It's difficult to avoid value judgments (especially in the case of the first group) in this classification system of spiritual evolution, but Peck notes that the system is only a model. Most people are, most often, a combination of two or more of these groups, but he says every individual is usually more strongly associated with one group as opposed to any other. To which group does each of your friends/family belong? With which group do *you* identify? Life is constantly changing, and our spiritual evolution is no exception, says Peck. If you don't think you're in the fourth group, don't despair: self-awareness and self-examination are already indicators of upward movement.

## Questions for Analysis

1. What are the topic, basis for classification, and distinct categories in this essay of classification?
2. Do you agree with Peck's classification system? Why or why not?
3. How do you think, based on the above essay, Peck would define "spirituality"?
4. Does the author of the above essay agree with Peck's classification system? What evidence is there to suggest the author does agree? Is there evidence to the contrary?
5. Do you know people that would clearly fit into one of these categories? Discuss.
6. Do you think it is possible to go backwards on this scale of evolution? Discuss.
7. If you agree with Peck at least in principle, what do you think it usually takes for a person to progress (or regress?) from one category to another?

**ASSIGNMENT**

## Essay of Classification

Choose one of the topics below or pick one of your own, and write a classification essay of at least five paragraphs to develop that topic.

### SUGGESTED TOPICS:

(For more suggested topics, see the list on p. 315.)

1. Different kinds of beer or wine
2. Different types of music
3. Different models of Honda (or any other make of car)
4. Different types of teachers/professors
5. Different types of fashion
6. Different kinds of first dates (blind, set-up, Internet, etc.)
7. Pick a typical classification system within your field of study

**For helpful hints on the following subjects, all of which will assist you in developing your classification essay, see Chapter 14:**

- **Brainstorming**
- **Choosing the Topic and Controlling Idea**
- **Outlining**
- **The Rough Draft**
- **Revising and Editing the Rough Draft**
- **Proofreading**
- **Checklist for the Final Copy**

## Working Together: Brainstorming for Classification

Brainstorming can be wonderfully helpful when several people put their heads together. Divide into groups and brainstorm on one of the classification topics given below. After the members of each group have thought of everything they can, come together as a class, and put your classifications on the board. Compare and contrast them. What makes one more successful than another? Can you use each other's material?

**Suggested Topics for Brainstorming:**

1. Fads
   What is a fad? Classify as many different types of fads as you can.
2. Friendship
   What is friendship? Classify as many different types of friendships as you can.
3. Causes of car accidents
   What are the causes of car accidents? Classify as many different types of causes as you can.
4. Sports events
   What are the different kinds of sports events? Classify as many different types of sports events as you can.
5. Alcoholic beverages
   What are the different kinds of alcoholic beverages? Classify as many different types of alcoholic beverages as you can.

Your professor may now ask each student to write his or her own paragraph or essay using this material.

CHAPTER TWENTY-SEVEN

27

# Cause and Effect

## What Is Cause and Effect?

People have always looked at the world and asked the questions "Why did this happen?" and "What are the likely results of that event?" Ancient societies created beautiful myths and legends to explain the origin of the universe and our place in it, while modern civilization has emphasized scientific methods of observation to find the cause of a disease or to determine why the planet Mars appears to be covered by canals. When we examine the spiritual or physical mysteries of our world, we are trying to discover the connections or links between events. In this chapter, we will refer to connections between events as **causal relationships.**

**DEFINITION ➤** **Cause and effect** is an examination of either the causes of a particular effect (why something happened) or the effects of a particular cause (what is likely to happen as a result of a particular event). In either case, the establishment of causal relationships must be based on a sense of logic.

Causal relationships are part of our daily lives and provide a way of understanding the cause, result, or consequence of a particular event. The search for cause or effect is a bit like detective work. Probing an event is a way of searching for clues to discover what caused an event or what result it will have in the future.

For example, we might ask the question "Why did the car break down just after it came back from the garage?" as a way of searching for the cause of the car's new problem. Or we might ask, "What will be the side effects of a certain medicine?" in order to determine what effect a particular medicine will have on the body. This search for connections can be complex. Often the logical analysis of a problem reveals more than one possible explanation. Sometimes the best one can do is find *possible* causes or *probable* effects.

## Two Types of Cause and Effect Paragraph or Essay

There are two types of cause and effect paragraph or essay. In the **first type,** the *cause* is identified in the topic sentence (for a paragraph) or thesis statement (for an essay), and the emphasis is placed on the effects; the supporting detail, therefore, is made up of several *effects*. In the **second type,** the *effect* is identified in the topic sentence or thesis statement, but the emphasis is placed on the causes; as a result, the supporting detail, this time, is made up of several *causes*.

TIP

**DO NOT try to deal with causes *and* effects of an event in the supporting detail of a single cause and effect paragraph or essay.**

## Developing Paragraphs: Cause and Effect

### The Topic Sentence of a Cause and Effect Paragraph

The **topic sentence** of a cause and effect paragraph should reveal whether the paragraph will focus on causes or effects. For example, the following topic sentence uses the word *factors* to indicate that causes are about to follow:

> Several factors contributed to my decision to lose weight.

Losing weight is the effect, but the causes in the paragraph are about to follow.

On the other hand, this next topic sentence begins with the cause first and subsequently that a number of *effects* are about to follow:

> Losing weight had a number of positive effects on my life.

### Supporting Detail of a Cause and Effect Paragraph

Again, the supporting detail of this type of paragraph contains either causes or effects, but **not both.**

### Importance of Logic

In a good cause and effect paragraph, a cause must lead to an effect, not just precede the effect. That's why writing a cause and effect paragraph requires analysis to determine that a logical connection exists between events. For example, the fact that a person walked under a ladder just before he got hit by a car does not prove cause and effect. His walking under a ladder merely preceded the car's hitting him. To suggest that walking under a ladder caused him to get hit by a car is to use **faulty logic.** (See "Common Fallacies" on pp. 340–42 in Chapter 28.) The reader of a cause and effect paragraph is meant to understand the relationship between a cause and its effects.

**Avoid These Common Errors in Logic (Common Fallacies)**

1. Do not confuse coincidence or chronological sequence with evidence.
2. Look for underlying causes beneath the obvious ones and for far-reaching effects beyond the ones that first come to mind. Often what appears to be a single cause or a single effect is a much more complex problem.

Here is an example of a possible error in logic:

> Every time I try to write an essay in the evening, I have trouble getting to sleep. Therefore, writing must prevent me from sleeping.

In this case, writing may indeed be a stimulant that prevents the person from sleeping. However, if the person is serious about finding the cause of insomnia, he or she must observe whether any other **factors** may be to blame. For instance, if the person is drinking several cups of coffee while writing each evening, this could be a more likely cause of the person's wakefulness.

The following paragraph is an example of a good cause and effect paragraph.

**Ensure that the topic sentence reveals whether the emphasis in the paragraph will be on causes or effects.**

### Model Paragraph

A number of factors caused my car accident on Deerfoot Trail last week. First, the weather was horrible that night. It was dark, and the rain made it even harder to see where I was going. The rain also made the roads very slippery, which meant that controlling my car was more difficult than usual. There was another factor that made my car difficult to control that night. I was returning home with a very heavy concrete birdbath for our backyard. When I slammed on my brakes and turned the steering wheel to avoid getting hit, the weight in my trunk shifted and caused the back end of my small car to swing around. Perhaps the most important factor was negligence. The driver of a black sports car was speeding and driving erratically. Rather than slow down when I changed into his lane ahead of him, he sped up, swerved, and cut directly in front of me. I had to slam on my brakes and turn my steering wheel sharply to avoid hitting him. As a result, my car spun around in a complete circle in the middle of the highway. I wound up in a ditch on the side of the road, a little shaken, but realizing things could have ended much worse.

**PRACTICE 1**

## Looking for the Causal Relationship

Study each of the following situations. In each case, if the sequence of events is merely coincidental or chronological, put a *T* for time in the space provided. If the relationship is most likely causal, write *C*, instead. Be prepared to explain your answers in class. Check your answers against those in the Answer Key on p. 466.

________ 1. Every time I carry my umbrella, it doesn't rain. I am carrying my umbrella today; therefore, it won't rain.

________ 2. We put the fertilizer on the grass. A week later, the grass grew five centimetres and turned a deeper green.

________ 3. On Tuesday morning, I walked under a ladder. On Wednesday morning, I walked into my office and was told I had lost my job.

________ 4. The child was born with a serious kidney condition. Seven days later, the child died.

_________ 5. Tar and nicotine from cigarettes damage the lungs. People who smoke cigarettes increase their chances of dying from lung cancer.

_________ 6. A political scandal was exposed in the city on Friday. On Saturday night, only twenty-four hours later, a power blackout occurred in the city.

_________ 7. Very few tourists came to the island last year. The economy of the island declined last year.

**PRACTICE 2**

## Separating the Cause from the Effect

In the following practice exercise, there is an action or event above a group of related sentences. Put a *C* next to those sentences that are causes and an *E* next to those details that are effects. Check your answers against those in the Answer Key on p. 466.

1. Quitting smoking

_________ a. Smoking costs a lot of money.

_________ b. There are fewer public places that allow smoking now.

_________ c. My terrible cough is gone.

_________ d. I have gained 5 kg.

_________ e. It bothered my friends and family.

_________ f. I have found that my food tastes better.

2. Buying a new car

_________ a. I got a great deal on financing.

_________ b. My old car was unreliable.

_________ c. I have less money every month because I have to pay more for insurance and gas.

_________ d. My popularity at school has increased.

_________ e. I was tired of having to take the train whenever I wanted to visit my family.

_________ f. I was embarrassed to drive my rusted old car.

**EXERCISE**

## Separating the Cause from the Effect

In each sentence, separate the cause, problem, or reason from the effect, solution, or result. Remember, the cause is not necessarily given first.

1. More than half of the mothers with children under one year of age work outside the home, which has resulted in an unprecedented need for daycare in this country.

   Cause: ______________________________

   ______________________________

   Effect: ______________________________

   ______________________________

2. By 2000, two-thirds of all preschool children and four out of five school-age children had working mothers, facts that led to increased strain on our system of daycare.

   Cause: ______________________________

   ______________________________

   Effect: ______________________________

   ______________________________

3. In one national survey, over half the working mothers reported that they had either changed jobs or cut back on their hours in order to be more available to their children.

   Cause: ______________________________

   ______________________________

   Effect: ______________________________

   ______________________________

4. Many mothers who work do so only when their children are in school, while other mothers work only occasionally during the school year because they feel their children need the supervision of a parent.

   Cause: ______________________________

   ______________________________

   Effect: ______________________________

   ______________________________

5. Many mothers experience deep emotional crises as a result of their struggle to meet both the financial obligations of their home and their own emotional needs as parents.

   Cause: ______________________________________________

   ______________________________________________

   Effect: ______________________________________________

   ______________________________________________

**Transitional words and phrases for cause and effect paragraphs and essays can be found on pp. 206–07 in Chapter 17: "The Essay" and on the inside back cover of this book.**

## Writing the Cause or Effect Paragraph Step by Step

To learn a skill that has so many different aspects, it is best to follow a step-by-step approach, so that one aspect can be worked on at a time. This approach will ensure that you are not missing a crucial point or misunderstanding a part of the whole. There are other ways to go about writing an effective paragraph, but here is one logical method you can use to achieve results.

### Steps for Writing the Cause or Effect Paragraph

1. After you have chosen your topic, plan your topic sentence.
2. Brainstorm by jotting down all possible causes or effects. Ask others for their thoughts. Research if necessary. Consider long-range effects or underlying causes.
3. Choose the three or four best points from your list.
4. Decide on the best order for these points. (From least important to most important is one way to organize them.)
5. Write at least one complete sentence for each of the causes or effects you have chosen from your list.
6. Write a concluding statement.
7. Finally, copy your sentences into standard paragraph form.

**EXERCISE**

### Writing the Effect Paragraph Step by Step

This exercise will guide you through the effect paragraph. Start with the suggested topic. Use the seven steps (repeated below) to help you work through each stage of the writing process. (Refer to pp. 261–62 in Chapter 21 for a completed sample paragraph.)

**Topic:** What are the effects when students have part-time jobs after classes?

1. Write a topic sentence.

2. Make a list of possible effects. (Consider long-range effects.)
3. Cross out any points that may be illogical, merely coincidental, or the result of only time sequence.
4. Put your list in order.
5. Using your final list, write at least one sentence for each of the effects you have found.
6. Write a concluding statement.
7. On a separate sheet of paper, copy your sentences into standard paragraph form.

## On Your Own: Writing Cause and Effect Paragraphs from Model Paragraphs

### The Causes of Disaster

The following model paragraph looks at the causes for the loss of life in the sinking of a supposedly unsinkable ship on its maiden voyage almost a century ago.

**Model Paragraph**

One of the most tragic events of the twentieth century was the sinking of the British ship *Titanic* in the Atlantic Ocean on April 15, 1912, with the loss of over 1500 lives. The immediate cause of this terrible loss of life was a large iceberg that tore a ninety-metre gash in the side of the ship, flooding five of its watertight compartments. Some believe that the tragedy took place because the crew members did not see the iceberg in time, but others see a chain of different events that contributed to the tragedy. First was the fact that the ship was not carrying enough lifeboats for all of its passengers: it had enough boats for only about half of the people on board. Furthermore, the ship's crew showed a clear lack of concern for the third-class or "steerage" passengers, who were left in their cramped quarters below decks with little or no help as the ship went down. It has often been said that this social attitude of helping the wealthy and neglecting the poor was one of the real causes of the loss of life that night. Indeed, some of the lifeboats that were used were not filled to capacity when the rescue ships eventually found them. Finally, the tragedy of the *Titanic* was magnified by the fact that some ships nearby did not have a radio crew on duty and therefore missed the distress signals sent by the *Titanic*. Out of all this, the need to reform safety regulations on passenger ships became obvious.

**ASSIGNMENT**

### Cause and Effect Paragraph (Effects)

Select a community or area disaster that you have personally experienced or heard about. This could include a severe climatic condition or a manufactured disaster. Instead of writing a paragraph about the disaster's causes such as in the above paragraph, point out the effects it had on you or the people involved.

**SUGGESTED TOPICS:**

(For more suggested topics, see the list on p. 331.)

1. The effects of an earthquake
2. The effects of a power blackout on a major city or town
3. The effects of a flood or other extensive water damage on a home or community
4. The effects of a chemical spill on land or offshore
5. The effects of a transit strike on a community
6. The effects of a major fire on a downtown block
7. The effects of the terrorist attack on 9/11 (see photo on p. 159)

## Developing the Cause and Effect Essay

Like the cause and effect paragraph, the essay, too, should focus only on either causes or effects, but not both. And it should be self-evident from the thesis statement of your essay which one that particular essay will be discussing.

Again, the thesis appears somewhere between the middle and the end of the first paragraph. And each support paragraph deals with one cause or one effect, depending on which type of essay you've chosen to write.

Bear in mind that all the causes or all the effects should directly support your thesis, whatever it is. If not, you must make some adjustments. Whether you change your thesis or support paragraphs (perhaps only one support paragraph needs to be reworked) is up to you. At this stage, you may want to make whatever changes require the least amount of time, especially if you're writing the essay in class and you're writing under the pressure of a rigid time limit.

**For an in-depth look at the essay and its standard format (for all writing strategies in this unit), see Chapter 17: "The Essay." Also review Chapter 14: "The Four Stages of Writing," which can be applied to both the paragraph and the essay.**

Two model essays that demonstrate the strategy of cause and effect follow in the next few pages. The first, by Donald Pianissimo, is very informal and personal (notice the use of the word *I*). The second falls under "Working Together: Identifying Causes." The essay "Anything but Peaceful," by Zack Goodman, is much more formal and contains research that is used to support the author's claim.

READ

### Model Essay I: Whose Choice Is It, Anyway?

**by Donald Pianissimo**

It is so easy to think that the decisions you make are your own choices. But when you consider the events leading up to those decisions, it may not be so easy to claim the decisions as your own. My decision to go into journalism was, I thought, something I had chosen completely on my own without external influence. But when I think of three particular events in my life before leaving high school, I begin to think my say in the matter was minimal at best. I begin to think I was simply following a path that had already been laid out for me.

My mom used to be a nurse, and she confided in me long after I'd dropped chemistry in high school that she always wanted me to be a doctor. My dad, although a writer, never called himself a journalist; journalism was not the kind of writing he preferred to do. But perhaps I underestimated his influence on my choice to enter a writing career. In fact, it was he who encouraged me to publish an article in a local magazine when I was only nine years old. I still remember his editing my work. I also remember the thrill of my anticipation of seeing my name in print. It was the first taste of being published I would get, and it wouldn't be the last.

A second incident is as vivid in my memory as the first. In Grade 8, the first English teacher who would truly inspire me with his passion for teaching announced to the class one day that there were three essays he had marked that were worthy of recognition. He asked three students to read their essays out loud in front of the entire class, and I was one of them. He made me feel I had a gift, a gift worth sharing.

And finally, by the time I'd gotten to high school, a classmate and I were asked by a teacher to co-edit the school newspaper. I never thought I would have so much fun. Better still, the paper was a hit with the other students. Our high school hadn't seen so successful a student newspaper in years. I couldn't help but love the popularity that came with it, too.

I envied those students who knew they wanted to be doctors, or lawyers, or engineers since the time they could talk. I just figured I wasn't so blessed with such an ardent and focused career desire. By the time I'd graduated from high school, I chose to enter a field of study for my postsecondary education based on one of my most enjoyable pastimes: writing for an audience. Journalism seemed the logical choice. What didn't occur to me until much later was that my choice seemed the logical conclusion of a number of monumental events in my young life. Were they random events, or were they meant to lead me in a certain direction? Your guess is as good as mine.

## Questions for Analysis

1. Of the two types of cause and effect essay discussed in this chapter, which type of essay is this?
2. Does the writer support the idea of free will, or the idea of fate?
3. Is there evidence in this essay to suggest support for one or the other?
4. How much does the author attribute his choices to the influence of parents and teachers?
5. What, in your own words, is the author's thesis? Which sentence is the actual thesis? From the thesis, what do you think the support is going to be about? Why?
6. Is the thesis adequately supported?

## Exploring the Topic

1. How did you decide to enter your current field of study? Was it free will or fate? Discuss.
2. Does reading this essay make you think twice about whether or not you made the choice to enter your field of study totally independently of outside influence? Explain.

**ASSIGNMENT**

## Cause and Effect Essay

Choose one of the topics from the following list, or one of your own, and write a cause and effect essay of at least five paragraphs to develop that topic.

### SUGGESTED TOPICS:

(For more suggested topics, see the list on p. 329.)

1. The causes of war
2. The causes of failing a course
3. The causes of breaking up with a boyfriend/girlfriend
4. The causes of addiction (alcohol, drugs, sex, relationship, etc.)
5. The causes of lying
6. The effects of lying
7. The effects of parents who don't show their children affection
8. The effects of poverty in the home
9. The effects of fame
10. The effects of dating a real "hottie"

**For helpful hints on the following subjects, all of which will assist you in developing your cause and effect essay, see Chapter 14:**

**Brainstorming**
**Choosing the Topic and the Controlling Idea**
**Outlining**
**The Rough Draft**
**Revising and Editing the Rough Draft**
**Proofreading**
**Checklist for the Final Copy**

## Working Together: Identifying Causes

Listen while the following analysis of the causes for the decline of Central America's Mayan culture is read aloud to the class. The class should then divide into groups. Work with your group to list the immediate and the underlying causes for the decline of Mayan civilization. One person from each group will then read the group's complete list of immediate and underlying causes to the class. After a complete listing is agreed upon, make a judgment as to how certain scientists are about the underlying causes of this historical phenomenon.

### Model Essay II: Anything but Peaceful

**by Zack Goodman**

In the last few years, scholars have made great strides in translating the Mayas' previously indecipherable writing system. From the emerging texts and from recent excavations has emerged a new, at times bewildering, picture of the Maya civilization at its peak, from A.D. 250 to 900. Great as their cultural and economic achievements manifestly were, they had anything but a peaceful society.

Indeed, the latest feeling among scholars is that the increasing militarism of Mayan society may have undermined the ecological underpinnings of the economy. Some of them speculate that siege warfare concentrated population in urban centres, caused desperate farmers to abandon previously successful practices of diversified agriculture, and led to overexploitation of the forest.

Dr. Arthur A. Demarest, an archaeologist who directs an ambitious Maya dig in Guatemala, has said that the evidence from stone art and texts points to the surprising conclusion that "the Maya were one of the most violent state-level societies in the New World, especially after A.D. 600."

Various writings and artifacts, Dr. Demarest says, indicate continual raiding and warfare between the elites of adjacent city-states and also the practice of ritual bloodletting and human sacrifice. The prestige of ruling dynasties, and hence their power, seemed to depend on their success in battle and the sacrifice of prisoners of war. Dr. Linda Schele, a Maya scholar, wrote in an issue of *Natural History* magazine, "We don't know if the early Maya went to war mainly to acquire territory, take booty, control conquered groups for labour, take captives for sacrifice in sanctification rituals, or a combination of these."

Whatever the specific goal, archaeologists think that for centuries the wars were limited to ritualized conflicts between the elite troops of two rulers. The losing ruler was sometimes decapitated with great ceremony, as depicted in Mayan art.

CHAPTER TWENTY-EIGHT

28

# Argumentation

## What Is Argumentation?

So far, your purpose in many writing assignments in this text has been to describe, narrate, or explain by using various writing strategies for development. Still another purpose in writing is to argue.

**DEFINITION ➤** **Argumentation** is an attempt to change the reader's present viewpoint, or at least to convince her or him that your viewpoint is a valid one.

Every time you write a paper for a course, you are trying to persuade your professor that what you are presenting is a reasonable view of the subject matter. You might want to show, for example, that Canadian airlines are among the safest in the world, or that the crime novel is becoming Canada's favourite form of fiction. As you approach such types of assignments, you need to be aware of each part of the argumentative process so that you will be able to analyze other people's arguments more effectively and write better ones of your own.

## Argumentation vs. Persuasion

You could view most writing as persuasive, since one of the writer's main goals is to get the reader to see, think, and believe in a certain way. Although "persuasiveness" is a quality of *all* paragraph and essay writing strategies (narration, classification, etc.), **argumentation** is considered a separate writing strategy altogether. **Formal argumentation** follows certain guidelines. If you have ever been a member of a debating team, you have spent a good deal of time studying this special form. How to use techniques of argument in your own writing is the main subject of this chapter.

## Persuasive Appeals That Are Not Logical

Logic is always at the root of a good argument. However, persuasive techniques that can be very effective include appeal to emotion, aesthetic appeal, and appeal to practical or common points of view. These techniques are not necessarily wrong in themselves, but overuse or exclusive use of them can prove quite counterproductive.

- **Appeal to emotion:** Causing the reader to have a strong feeling can be an extremely effective persuasive technique. The writer makes the reader extremely sad, for example, by discussing the homelessness of a child. We can't help but to identify with the child in some way, perhaps because of his or her innocence.
- **Aesthetic appeal:** Everyone has a sense of what is beautiful, even if this sense changes slightly from one individual to another. Advertisements on TV (and most TV and film, it can be argued) use this type of appeal to sell products and services and boost ratings.
- **Appeal to practical or common points of view:** Writers sometimes take advantage of what they know are common beliefs, such as cultural values, to get their point across. It may be illogical, but it's a safe bet that the reader will be on their side because of the popular appeal of the belief.

## Other Argumentative Strategies

Some strategies you have already read about in this text also fall under the umbrella of argumentation. Cause and effect, for example, is argumentative most of the time, even where science is concerned. For example, the sample research essay on cell phones and their possible effects on our long-term health in Chapter 20 argues that there is a very good chance that cell phone usage and brain damage are connected. Despite the current sophistication of science, the results of this research are far from conclusive. So this paper on science is, most definitely, argumentative. All responsible scientists claim, in fact, that their findings are tentative—always subject to further analysis.

### Critical Thinking and Analysis

Students sometimes wrongly offer paraphrasing and summarizing (see Chapter 19) where argumentation is expected. Many instructors at the postsecondary level, in fact, agree that it is the original use of critical thinking and analysis that usually sets an "A" paper apart from all others. Critical thinking and analysis are vital tools in the argumentation process.

## What Is Critical Thinking?

**DEFINITION ➤** **Critical thinking** is evaluating an argument. This skill is used to determine how convincing someone else's argument is for the purpose of making a decision or to help you establish a credible argument of your own.

### Critical Thinking in Everyday Life

Critical thinking is something you should practise every day, not just when you establish arguments, but also when you listen to the arguments of others. When you listen to a TV commercial, you should be asking, "Does this make sense?" Of course, an advertisement can still be effective without a good argument. After all, it might carry with it an emotional or aesthetic appeal (making you laugh, for example, or showing you something or someone physically beautiful).

Most of the time, however, it is important that things do make sense. What you choose to eat, for instance, may not only be based on what tastes good; you might have to consider dietary needs. How you vote in the next election may not just depend on how the candidates look on TV, but also on how much sense they make in their answers to questions. You are always making decisions, and much of the time, though surely not all of the time, you are making those decisions based on some aspect of critical thinking.

## More Tools and Components of Argumentation

As mentioned earlier, the more familiar you become with the different parts of the argumentation process, the more likely you will be able to develop more effective arguments of your own.

**DEFINITION ➤** **Analysis** is the process of breaking down an argument made by someone else in order to assess its validity for the purpose of either supporting or criticizing it and, perhaps, of suggesting a better argument.

Original analysis often is what sets apart a superior student paper from all others, especially those that do not engage in analysis at all and that merely quote, paraphrase, or summarize material from research conducted.

**DEFINITION ➤** A **claim** is a position taken by the writer that must be supported in order to establish credibility in the minds of the readers. A claim may also be called the **conclusion** of an argument, or where an essay is concerned, its **thesis statement (or topic sentence** in a paragraph).

**DEFINITION ➤** **Evidence** is a collection of facts or **premises** that must be provided to support a claim made by the writer in order to establish the credibility of that claim. In a paragraph or an essay, the evidence is often referred to as **supporting detail** or just **support.**

**DEFINITION ➤** An **argument** is the combination of a claim and evidence used to support that claim. If an essay contains an argument, the essay is referred to as an **argumentative essay.**

| | |
|---|---|
| **Claim** | Capital punishment should be brought back to Canada.* |
| + **Evidence** | 1. It costs too much to keep a murderer in jail.<br>2. A serial killer is not likely to be rehabilitated.<br>3. The punishment should fit the crime. |
| **Argument** | The combination of both components (claim and evidence) above |

* Note that the words "I believe" are not used in the claim.

**Figure 28.1: Components of an Argument**

When you make a claim or write a topic sentence or thesis, there is no need to actually say, "I believe" or "I think" because these words are, in fact, implied. It is generally agreed upon that the use of the word "I," in particular, makes the argument seem less effective. The word "I" must be avoided when writing in a formal tone such as in a research paper.

## Underlying Assumptions

When an argument is made, a claim and its supporting detail are often clearly expressed. What is often not apparent is an underlying assumption, which can cause an entire argument to fail if the faulty underlying assumption is detected, identified, and discredited.

*Example:* Peter would be a great choice of a marriage partner. (claim)
Peter is rich. (evidence)
Anyone who is rich is a great choice of a marriage partner. (underlying assumption)

### Why Are Underlying Assumptions Not Expressed?

There are two basic reasons for an unexpressed underlying assumption: (1) the arguers might be unaware of their own underlying assumptions, or (2) they don't want anyone to know what their underlying assumptions are. At some level, they know their underlying assumptions (which can be beliefs attributed to upbringing, religion, community, etc.) are logically indefensible or, at the very least, unacceptable in the community at large, and they would be loathe to admit such questionable assumptions to anyone else. For example, racist sentiment or religious intolerance is often an underlying assumption for many so-called arguments. But you won't hear many people saying, "People outside of my race or religion are inferior." Arguments built on top of such underlying assumptions must be constantly questioned and critically assessed.

## Analyzing the Intention of Argument: The Importance of Virtue

Good writing should not only depend on effectiveness, but also on good intentions. A movie called *In the Company of Men* (dir. Neil Labute, 1997) includes two men who decide to target a young, deaf woman in the company at which they all work. As part of a betting game, they both try to get her to fall in love with them, and one succeeds. In the end, she is emotionally crushed when she finds out that the man she has fallen in love with has no intention of being with her. The other man, who, in the meantime, does actually fall in love with her, asks the first man why he has hurt her so. The man replies, "Because I could."

Communication, like behaviour, cannot be independent of morality. More important than the writer's ability to convince ought to be his or her intention. For example, does the writer appear to be interested only in benefiting himself or herself, or his or her own? Or is there a more honourable attempt to achieve the greater good? Richard L. Epstein and Carolyn Kernberger in their preface to their book *The Pocket Guide to Critical Thinking* wrote, "Because your reasoning can be sharpened, you can understand more and you can avoid being duped. You can reason well with those you need to convince ... But whether you will do so depends not just on method, not just on the tools of reasoning, but on your goals, your ends. And those depend on virtue."

## We Become What We Communicate

So whether you are formulating an argument of your own, or you are responding to the argument of someone else, analysis of the arguer's intention and underlying assumptions, which are often not obvious, is an essential part of critical thinking and our communication. Ultimately, the way we think and the way we communicate influence what we do and what we become. The method of arguing well is critical, but so is the reason behind the argument itself.

## Argumentative Techniques

1. **State a clear topic sentence (for a paragraph) or thesis (for an essay).** Take an obvious stand or position. You might want to use words such as *must, ought,* and *should,* although they are, of course, not necessary (see the third thesis below).

Canada's military should be better funded.
Canada must reform its prison system.
Romantic love and marriage are inevitably incompatible.
All information on the Internet should be free.

2. **Use examples.** Well-chosen examples are the heart of any paragraph or essay. Without them, the writing is flat, lifeless, and unconvincing. Providing a good example for each of your main points helps make a much stronger argument. Examples help your reader *see* what you are talking about.
3. **Use opinions from recognized authorities to support your points.** One of the oldest methods of supporting an argument is to use one or more authorities to support your particular position. People usually believe what well-known experts claim. You should use carefully chosen experts to help make your position on a topic more persuasive. However, be sure that your authority is someone who is respected in the area you are discussing. For example, if you are arguing that we must end the nuclear arms race, your argument will be stronger if you quote a respected scientist who can accurately predict the consequences of a nuclear war. A famous movie star giving the same information might be more glamorous and get more attention, but he or she would not be as great an authority as the scientist.
4. **Answer your critics in advance.** When you point out beforehand what your opposition is likely to say in answer to your argument, you are writing from a position of strength. You are letting your reader know that you are aware that there is another side to the argument you are making. By pointing out this other side and then answering its objections in advance, you are strengthening your own position.
5. **Point out the results.** Help your reader see what will happen if your argument is (or is not) believed or acted upon as you think it should be. You should be specific and rational when you point out results, making sure that you avoid exaggeration of any kind. For example, if you argue against the possession of handguns, it would be an exaggeration to say that everyone is going to be murdered if the opposition's point of view is listened to instead of yours.
6. **Define certain terms that are central to the argument.** Often there seems to be disagreement where there should not be any simply because the people who appear to be arguing have not defined their terms. For example, the term *religion* is potentially quite controversial in itself. Does it mean an organized system of beliefs that might be political as well as spiritual? Or does it refer to a narrower definition: the expression of a belief in the divine? Or perhaps its meaning refers to its Latin root: to bind back. And if it's the third definition that both parties agree upon, what does one bind back to—old ways of living and traditions, or one's spiritual instead of material values? Or perhaps religion is one's way to bring about reconciliation with the paradoxes of human life. Before arguing the benefits or harm of religion, for example, it is critical that such a term first be defined.

7. **Avoid common fallacies (errors) in your argument.** But use critical skills in analyzing the fallacies of others. The following are some types of common fallacies.

## Common Fallacies

Common fallacies help us identify bad arguments because they are based on faulty reasoning. It is impossible to present a definitive or complete list of all the fallacies, but the following are some of the most common ones. The idea is to recognize a fallacy whether you can name it or not. Recognize it so that you can criticize someone else's bad argument or prevent one of your own.

1. ***Ad hominem*:** A personal attack, or literally, an attack "on the man." Often, someone resorts to the *ad hominem* attack, in desperation, because he or she might not be able to find evidence to support a claim that makes someone else look bad.

   For example, Kim Campbell, the first and only female prime minister of Canada, ran for election against Jean Chrétien of the Liberal Party in 1993. The following was an argument made by the Liberals during the campaign, a campaign infamous for personal attacks made by both parties:

   > Kim Campbell is a divorcee. If Kim Campbell couldn't manage her marriage, how could she possibly manage the country?

   This is clearly an *ad hominem* attack on Kim Campbell. First of all, a divorce in itself is not necessarily the result of the inability to "manage a marriage." And secondly, it cannot automatically be argued that her divorce

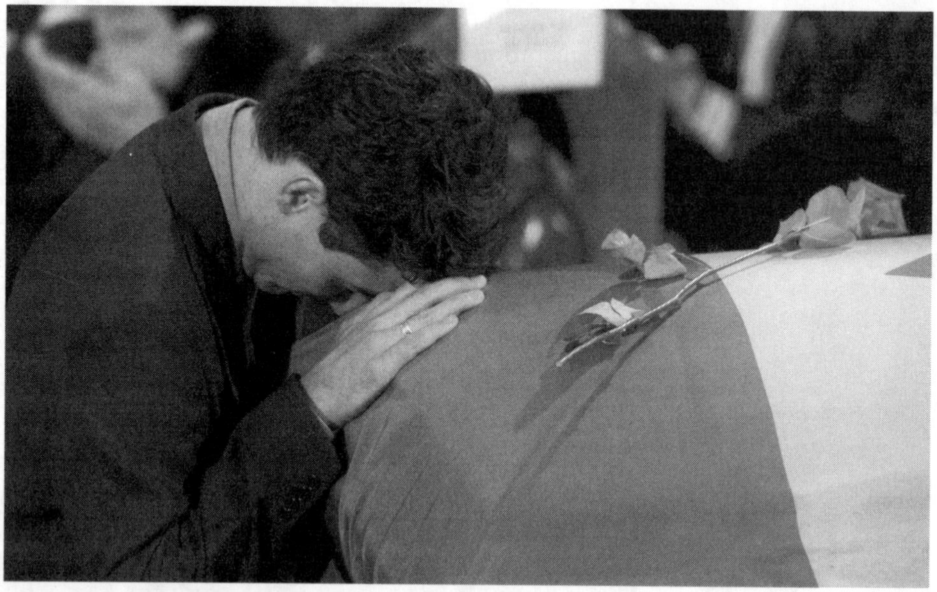

Justin Trudeau has just finished giving the eulogy at the funeral of his father, Pierre Elliott Trudeau, former prime minister of Canada.

has anything to do with whether or not she is capable of serving as prime minister.

During the same campaign, the Conservatives were also guilty of an *ad hominem* attack. A photograph in which Chrétien's partial facial paralysis was prominent was used until it was pulled amid a huge public outcry.

Justin Trudeau, son of the late Pierre Trudeau, another former prime minister of Canada, gave a eulogy at his father's funeral in 2000. He said that as a child, with the aim of gaining his father's approval, he insulted a man whom he knew was his father's political rival. His father, with a stern look on his face, told Justin that it's fine to criticize someone's point of view, but this ought to be done without attacking the individual on a personal level. Everyone, after all, deserves to live with dignity and respect. No one has the right to take those away. An *ad hominem* attack, unfortunately, enables one to do just that.

2. **Practical (common) point of view or belief (also known as the democratic fallacy):** The person making an argument takes advantage of a common point of view to persuade the reader of another point of view. The danger here is the assumption that the will of the majority determines what is right and what is wrong. Mahatma Gandhi of India, on the other hand, once said that history will judge a country not on the basis of how it treats its majority, but how it treats its minority instead. This speaks volumes.

   *Example:* The teacher asks the students, "Is it okay to lie?" One student responds, "Lying is okay because most people do it."

   First of all, there is a dangerous assumption here. The student assumes that everyone lies. He or she may have evidence that his or her parents have lied on occasion. His or her friends might lie even more often. He or she sees evidence in the news of heads of state lying. And the student's conclusion is that everyone lies. But these examples of evidence do not support the idea that everyone lies. And unless the student has evidence to this effect (which is impossible), such a broad statement should never be made. Secondly, even if it could be proven that everyone does lie, does that make it fine for the student to lie? Is it not possible that most people might be doing something that is wrong?

3. **Straw man** ("Putting words into someone's mouth"): This fallacy consists of an attack on an argument that is similar to, but not exactly the one your opponent holds. For example, former U.S. president Bill Clinton vehemently told his country that he did not have sexual relations with former White House intern Monica Lewinsky. He meant what he said very technically in that he did not have intercourse with her, when in fact he knew he was being accused of an improper relationship with her in general. He was guilty of employing a "straw man" to dispute a claim he knew to be true.
4. **False analogy:** This is an unfair comparison. Two things are so different, they cannot be compared, but someone tries anyway.

> *Example:* Guns don't kill people. People kill people. Guns are like cars. Therefore, it should be just as easy to get a gun as it is to get a car.

The fact is, guns are not like cars. A car is a vehicle. A gun is a weapon.

## Writing the Argumentative Paragraph

In all of the previous chapters in this unit, more emphasis was placed on the development of the paragraph than on the essay. With respect to the writing strategy of argumentation, the opposite will be done. The most effective arguments are those supported by several points that are treated thoroughly. For this reason, an argumentative essay would probably be a more effective piece of writing than an argumentative paragraph, so long as the points are thoughtful, well expressed, and directly supportive of your overall assertion or claim. However, that is not to say that a good argumentative paragraph cannot be written. Of course, it can. If you do attempt to write such a paragraph, just remember to establish your claim in the form of a topic sentence that is clear and strong, and make sure your supporting details are the strongest evidence in support of your claim that you can find. (See Chapters 15 and 16 on the paragraph.)

### Developing Paragraphs: Argumentation

The following argumentative paragraph was written in response to one of the questions that follows the narrative essay "Transparent Silhouette" on page 264.

> Question: Did the writer foreshadow the ending of the essay? (In other words, are there lots of clues throughout the essay that enable the reader to predict the eventual death of the writer's friend?)

**Model Paragraph**

Many clues exist in the story by Akis Stylianou that his friend will end up dead. First, there is the title of the essay itself: "Transparent Silhouette." It might conjure up the mental picture of the outline of a ghost. Second, there is the third line in the first paragraph of the story in which Stylianou mentions the words, "the woman I knew"; "knew," after all, is in the past tense, not the present. Third, the last line in the first paragraph includes the words "where I can delay my misery." If Stylianou is miserable because of his friend, whatever has happened to her cannot be good. Fourth, the second paragraph describes her sad childhood, full of abuse and the loneliness that results. A traumatic childhood is often, though not always, an omen of bad things to follow in life. And finally, the events Stylianou describes throughout the story seem to get more and more dangerous, starting with getting mixed up with the "wrong" crowd, becoming an exotic dancer, and finally becoming a porn star. All in all, the abundance of clues throughout the story strongly suggests that the writer's friend will end up in a very bad state, as she does.

### Questions for Analysis

1. With respect to the proper form of a paragraph, how do you know this is one paragraph, and not two or three?
2. Is the paragraph a proper length, according to what Chapter 15 says about paragraph structure?
3. What is the topic sentence? Does it directly answer the question?
4. Are there transitions in the paragraph? What are some examples?
5. Is there sufficient support of the topic sentence? Discuss.
6. Is the difference between the main supporting details and specific examples or explanations that support them apparent?
7. Is there a concluding sentence in this paragraph? If so, what is it?
8. Is the transition "finally" used for the last supporting detail of the paragraph or the concluding sentence?

## Developing Essays: Argumentation

The following essay by Leanne C. Southall is about the relationship between attitudes and oppression against women. As you read the essay, look for the major parts of an effective argument: strong thesis, carefully chosen examples, quotations from authorities, answers to the opposition, and predictions. Can you find any weaknesses or fallacies in the argument?

This piece was written in the form of a letter to the editor in response to an article published in the *Hamilton Spectator* on July 19, 2001. The article outlined the proposed regulations put forward by Turkey's Health Minister that female nursing students must undergo "virginity testing" to proceed with their training. These regulations were proposed "to ensure that nursing schools are not encouraging prostitution." The letter was sent on July 30, prior to the events of September 11, 2001. Because Leanne C. Southall's essay deals with a controversial topic, some people may offer counterarguments in response to the points she makes. However, the writer combines the results of several nations' experiences and those of Canada to persuade us to change our attitudes where appropriate.

READ

### Model Essay: Individuals Must Spur Change

**by Leanne C. Southall**

Once again, attitudes toward females in a fundamentalist religious realm are perpetuating women's oppression. Regulations proposed by Turkey's health minister, Osman Durmus—stating that women training to be nurses must prove their virginity—are a discriminatory offence. He has suggested that nursing students who have ever been sexually active may lead schools to become places for prostitution. His statement implies that sexually active women are immoral. Since Durmus issued the directive, Turkish newspapers have reported that he has been told by government leaders to take a vacation.

But this situation is just one of many restrictions on women around the world. Essentially, being a woman anywhere may be reason enough for targeting. In countries such as India and Jordan, daughters can be viewed as property; "honour killings" are tolerated if a woman shames her family. Recently, in Iran, where girls are forced to cover their heads and bodies from age 9, ten prostitutes were murdered. A special investigation ensued, and the deputy governor-general for law enforcement explained, "They were little and unimportant." In Pakistan, where 80 per cent of women are subjected to domestic violence, there is emerging a pattern of husbands dumping kerosene on their wives, lighting a match, and claiming their death to be a stove accident. Acid attacks are now being seen in hospitals. Reasons for getting rid of wives may include a suspicion of other sexual partners, a dowry considered too small or a woman's failure to get pregnant. (Incidentally, a woman's testimony was once only half the weight of a man's in Pakistan). Female genitalia mutilation is still a harmful custom in various countries around the world; some 4000 girls in Africa are to undergo this ritual in October.

In Afghanistan's past twenty years of war, women and girls have been beaten, raped, abducted and sold into prostitution. Since Taliban rule began in 1994, women are not permitted to work or attend school and must not make noise when they walk. They are not to leave their homes unless accompanied by a male relative, and certainly not without their restrictive burqua [a black veil that cloaks a woman's body from head to toe, leaving a small meshed window for her eyes to see through]. Their windows are painted black, ensuring that they cannot be seen from the street. In the United States, women are excluded from leading congregations because "Southern Baptists, by practice as well as conviction, believe leadership is male," as explained by Drafting Committee Chairman Reverend Adrian Rogers.

And what about Canada? Each of us should evaluate how our attitudes toward women affect lives. A mere 4 per cent of sexual assault charges result in convictions. The court process resembles a second violation, where her medical records and previous charges can be subpoenaed and her credibility is put on trial. Women still earn less than men in the same jobs. The only exception may be fashion modelling, which demonstrates the emphatic value we place on a woman's beauty, versus intelligence or contribution.

Judged far too quickly are single moms supported by social programs. Provinces have tightened eligibility for social assistance and designed policies that lead single mothers into the labour market. However, with licensed day-care costs as high as $7000 per year and limited regulated spaces available, help is far beyond the means of many single moms. Consequently, 56 per cent of single-parent families headed by women are poor.

If violence toward women reflects societal attitudes, sexism is all too alive in Canada. Some 51 per cent of Canadian women report having experienced physical or sexual violence. In 1998, more than 90 000 women and children used emergency abuse shelters across Canada. While not every woman has experienced violence, there is virtually no one who has not feared it.

Globally, we must adopt a system that embraces gender equality within political, economic and social spheres. Working toward that day, as individuals, let us each be aware of our attitudes and the part we can play to improve the status of women around the world.

## Questions for Analysis

1. In your own words, what is Southall's thesis statement? Which sentence, in particular, is *her* thesis statement?
2. What is her strongest supporting detail? Why? What is her weakest supporting detail? Why?
3. What does she want her readers to do?

Even more controversial, perhaps, is the following essay on euthanasia: the killing of dying patients. Try to keep an open mind as you read it regardless of your views. Listen to the arguments. Which ones are weak? Which ones are strong? Is there anything you need to know more about before you can make an informed decision?

The annotations in the left margin in the following essay are comments and questions provided by the author of this textbook, not the author of the article, to promote more effective analysis by the reader.

READ

### Annotated Model Essay: It's Time We Helped Patients Die

**by Dr. Howard Caplan**

Human case example

Appeal to emotion

For three years, the husband of one of my elderly patients watched helplessly as she deteriorated. She'd burst an aneurysm and later had an astrocytoma removed from her brain. Early in the ordeal, realizing that she'd never recover from a vegetative state, he'd pleaded with me to pull her nasogastric tube.

I'd refused, citing the policy of the convalescent hospital. I told him I could do it only if he got a court order. But he couldn't bring himself to start such proceedings, although the months dragged by with no signs of improvements in his wife's condition. He grieved as her skin broke down and she developed terrible bedsores. She had to have several courses of antibiotics to treat the infections in them, as well as in her bladder, which had an indwelling catheter.

Finally I got a call from a lawyer who said he'd been retained by the family to force me to comply with the husband's wishes.

"I'm on your side," I assured him. "But you'll have to get that court order just the same."

Euthanasia as best solution to problem

I went on to suggest—though none too hopefully—that we ask the court to do more than just let the patient starve to death. "If the judge will agree to let her die slowly, why won't he admit that he wants death to happen? Let's ask for permission to give her an injection and end her life in a truly humane manner."

The lawyer had no answer except to say, "Aw, come on, Doc—that's euthanasia!"

Frankly, I'd have been surprised at any other reaction. Although most states have enacted living-will laws in the past decade, none has yet taken the next logical step—legalizing euthanasia. But I believe it's time they did. Ten years of practice in geriatrics have convinced me that a proper death is a humane death, either in your sleep or being *put* to sleep.

**Evidence supporting the claim**

**Underlying assumption?**

I see appropriate patients every day in the extended-care facilities at which I practice. About 50 of the 350 people under my care have already ended their biographical lives. They've reached the stage in life at which there's no more learning, communicating, or experiencing pleasure. They're now simply existing in what is left of their biological lives.

**Concerned about people other than the patient?**

Most of these patients are the elderly demented. A typical case is that of a woman in her eighties or nineties, who speaks only in gibberish and doesn't recognize her family. She has forgotten how to eat, so she has a feeding tube coming from her nose. She is incontinent, so she has an indwelling catheter. She can no longer walk, so she is tied into a wheelchair. She's easily agitated, so she gets daily doses of a major tranquilizer. Why shouldn't I, with the concurrence of her family and an independent medical panel, be allowed to quickly and painlessly end her suffering?

**Appeal to emotion**

I think of another patient, a woman in her fifties, with end-stage multiple sclerosis, unable to move a muscle except for her eyeballs and her tongue. And younger patients: I have on my census a man in his early forties, left an aphasic triplegic by a motorcycle accident when he was nineteen. For nearly a quarter of a century, while most of us were working, raising children, travelling, reading, and otherwise going about our lives, he's been vegetating. His biographical life ended with that crash. He can't articulate—only make sounds to convey that he's hungry or wet. If he were to become acutely ill, I would prefer not to try saving him. I'd want to let pneumonia end it for him.

Of my remaining 300 patients, there are perhaps 50 to 100 borderline functional people who are nearing the end of their biographical lives and—were euthanasia legal—would probably tell me: "I'm ready to go. My bags are packed. Help me."

**Appeal to sense of compassion, pity?**

**Over-generalization?**

Anyone who's had front-line responsibility for the elderly has been asked if there wasn't "something you can give me" to end life. Such requests are made by patients who clearly see the inevitability of their deterioration and dread having to suffer through it. For these people, there is no more pleasure, let alone joy—merely misery. They want out.

***Ad hominem* fallacy?**

What is their fate? Chances are they'll be referred for psychiatric consultation on the grounds that they must be seriously depressed. The psychiatrist, usually decades younger than the patient, does indeed diagnose depression and recommends an antidepressant.

More evidence that supports claim: precedent

But if such patients lived in the Netherlands, odds are they'd get assistance in obtaining a release from the slow dying process to which our modern technology condemns them. While euthanasia is not yet legal there, it's openly practised. On a segment of the CBS show *60 Minutes* not long ago, I heard a Dutch anesthesiologist describe how doctors in his country help 5000 terminal patients slip away peacefully each year. Isn't that a promising indication of how well euthanasia would work in this country?

Acknowledgment of opposing argument

Counterargument

Pre-emption of counterargument

I realize that there are those who vigorously oppose the idea. And there are moral issues to confront—how much suffering is too much, the one-in-several-million chance that a person given no hope of improving will beat the odds. But it's time for society to seriously reconsider whether it is immoral to take the life of someone whose existence is nothing but irreversible suffering. Euthanasia ought to be treated the same way the abortion issue has been treated: people who believe it a sin to take a life even for merciful reasons would not be forced to do so. What I'm pleading for is that doctors and their patients at least have the choice.

Appeal to sense of reason, legal and medical ethics

I doubt that we'll get congressional action on such an emotionally charged issue during my lifetime. Action may have to come at the state level. Ideally, legislatures should permit each hospital and each nursing home to have a panel that would approve candidates for euthanasia. Or it might be more practical to have one panel serve several hospitals and nursing homes in a geographic area. Made up of one or two physicians and a lawyer or judge, plus the attending doctor, the panel would assess the attending's findings and recommendations, the patient's wishes, and those of the immediate family. This would ensure that getting a heart-stopping injection was truly in the patient's best interests, and that there was no ulterior motive—for example, trying to hasten an insurance payout. Needless to say, members of the board would be protected by law from liability claims.

Vague reference ("certain circumstances")

Then, if the patient had made it known while of sound mind that under certain circumstances he wanted a deadly substance administered, the process would be easy for everyone. But in most cases, it would be up to the attending to raise the question of euthanasia with the patient's relatives.

I'd start with those who've been part of the patient's recent life. If there are relatives who haven't seen the patient for years, it really shouldn't be any of their business. For instance, I'd try involving a son who's just kept in touch by phone. I'd say to him, "If you really want to stop this from happening, then you'd better come out here to see firsthand what's going on."

Is this a good point?

However, if he said, "Well, I can't really get away, Doctor, but I violently disagree," my answer would be, "Well, not violently enough. Everyone here can see what shape your mother's in. We're quite sure what she'd want if she could tell us, and we're going to help her."

Practical advice that can be applied to related issues

Before any of this can happen, though, there's going to have to be widespread public education. The media will have to do a better job of discussing the issues with living wills than it has. Among my patients who are nearing death, there aren't more than a half-dozen with living wills attached to their charts. Patients' families often haven't even heard of them, and even when large institutions encourage families to get these things taken care of while the patient is still alert, it's hardly ever done.

Not knowing about living wills, unaware of no-code options, many families plunge their loved ones—and themselves—into unwanted misery. How many rapidly deteriorating patients are rushed from a nursing home to a hospital to be intubated, simply because that's the facility's rigid policy? How many families impoverish themselves to keep alive someone who's unaware of himself and his surroundings?

**Fair reference to "souls"?**

**Good reference to irony of high technology**

Every day in my professional life, I encounter illogical, irrational, and inhumane regulations that prevent me, and those with whom I work, from doing what we know in our souls to be the right thing. Before high technology, much of this debate was irrelevant. There was little we could do, for example, when a patient arrested. And what we could do rarely worked.

**Does acceptance of the inevitable justify euthanasia?**

But times have changed. Now we have decisions to make. It helps to understand that many of the elderly infirm have accepted the inevitability—and, indeed, the desirability—of death. We who are younger must not mistake this philosophical position for depression. We need to understand the natural acceptance of death when life has lost its meaning.

**What is the main point of this paragraph?**

About 28 per cent of our huge medicare budget is spent providing care during the last year of life. Far too little of that money goes to ensure that dying patients' last months are pain-free and comfortable. Far too much is wasted on heroic, pain-inducing measures that can make no difference. It's time to turn that ratio around—and to fight for the right to provide the ultimate assistance to patients who know their own fight to prolong life is a losing one.

## Analysis

Because Dr. Caplan deals with a very sensitive subject, many people might find his position to be dangerous and even frightening. Even before we examine his essay, the title of the piece gains our attention. It's likely to shock both those for and those against euthanasia because of its bluntness.

The fact that the author is a doctor, in itself, might persuade the reader to accept whatever he says as true. But what if another doctor as familiar with dying patients as the author were to argue *against* euthanasia? Would you then have to consider the arguments more carefully? Do we, at times, trust authority too blindly?

To support his position on euthanasia, Caplan refers to the case of the Netherlands where euthanasia, although officially illegal, has become an acceptable policy of medical practice as long as certain rules are followed. Rachel Nowak, however, reported the following facts in "The Dutch Way of Death" in the book *Moral Philosophy for Modern Life* by Anthony Falikowski—facts that Caplan does not acknowledge in his essay:

At least a third of the 5000 or so Dutch patients who each year receive lethal doses of drugs from their doctors do not give their unequivocal consent. About 400 of those patients never even raise the issue of euthanasia with their doctors. Moreover, of those who willingly opt for euthanasia, only about 5 per cent do so because of unbearable pain. A much higher proportion, about a third, do so partly for fear of becoming dependent on others.

Nowak adds that each year, doctors have acknowledged that about 1300 patients are given an increased dose of painkillers, "not to alleviate their pain but to shorten their lives." Does this weaken or strengthen Caplan's point about medical policy in the Netherlands? Does this additional evidence about euthanasia affect his overall argument?

## Questions for Discussion and Further Analysis

1. Did you support euthanasia before discovering this piece in *The Canadian Writer's Workplace*? Does this section change your views at all? Explain.
2. What does Caplan mean by a "biographical life"? What part of life might Caplan not be taking into consideration in his argument? Is his understanding of life too limited?
3. Consider the point the author made about a son not having the right to contribute to the decision of his mother's fate (of living or dying) because the son says he cannot make it to a meeting. Is this a good or bad argument? Discuss.
4. Why does Caplan begin his essay with an example of a dying patient? Does this part appeal to the reader's sense of reason or emotion? Is this an effective way to start? Is it fair? Is it responsible? Discuss.
5. Are there any common fallacies in Caplan's argument? Discuss
6. Are there any underlying assumptions in Caplan's article? Discuss.
7. Is euthanasia in violation of the Hippocratic Oath? Discuss.
8. Why do you think Caplan leaves the issue of money for the last paragraph?

**ASSIGNMENT**

## Argumentative Paragraph or Essay

Choose one of the topics below, and either write an extended paragraph or an essay of at least five paragraphs. Argue for or against the topic of your choice. Use the following argumentative techniques, discussed earlier in this chapter, as a guide for your writing.

1. Write a strong thesis statement.
2. Provide examples for each of your reasons.
3. Use at least one authority to support your thesis.
4. Admit that others have a different point of view.
5. Indicate the results or your predictions in the conclusion.
6. Define certain terms that are central to your argument.

**SUGGESTED TOPICS:**

1. Capital punishment
2. Censorship of books or movies
3. Same-sex marriages
4. Gun control
5. Prayer in the public schools
6. Single-parent adoption
7. Control of pornography

Many, many more topics for both argumentative paragraphs and essays are provided under the heading of *Writing Ideas,* which can be found at the end of the section of questions immediately following each major reading in Unit IV. Questions under the heading *Questions for Discussion* (also after each major reading in Unit IV) might also be deemed suitable argumentative writing topics.

**For helpful hints on the following subjects, all of which will assist you in developing your argumentative essay, see Chapter 14:**

**Brainstorming**
**Choosing the Topic and the Controlling Idea**
**Outlining**
**The Rough Draft**
**Revising and Editing the Rough Draft**
**Proofreading**
**Checklist for the Final Copy**

**For an in-depth look at the essay and its standard format (for all writing strategies in this unit), see Chapter 17: "The Essay." Also review Chapter 14: "The Four Stages of Writing," which can be applied to both the paragraph and the essay.**

## Working Together: Identifying Good and Bad Arguments

Develop small groups of four or five. Look at several recent newspapers and choose an editorial about a subject of interest to everyone in the group. Read it and comment on the argument in terms of what you now know regarding good and bad arguments. Answer the following questions. You may want to assign a different question to each person in the group.

1. Are there any common fallacies in the writer's argument? Explain.
2. Does the writer employ the argumentative techniques listed in this chapter? Explain.
3. What is the writer's overall claim?
4. Is the evidence used to support the claim generally good or bad? Discuss.

# UNIT FOUR IV

## Readings

| | |
|---|---|
| ROSEMARY SULLIVAN | DON JUAN/DOÑA JUANA |
| DAVID SUZUKI | HIDDEN LESSONS |
| MARYA FIAMENGO | IN PRAISE OF OLD WOMEN |
| JEAN VANIER | HEART OF LONELINESS |
| GRANT ROBERTSON | THE $2-MILLION COMMA |
| TOMSON HIGHWAY | CANADA, MY CANADA |
| NAHEED MUSTAFA | MY BODY IS MY OWN BUSINESS |
| JOHN ARTIBELLO | LEAVING THE CAVE |
| RITA JOE | I LOST MY TALK |
| W. FRANK EPLING | RATS |
| HIMANI BANNERJI | THE OTHER FAMILY |
| COLIN CAMPBELL | HOW R TNGZ, DUDE? |
| NEIL BISSOONDATH | SELLING ILLUSIONS |
| GARY LIPSCHUTZ | LESSONS OF LOVE FROM STORIES OF OLD |
| SHARI GRAYDON | BAD GIRLS |
| CAMERON AINSWORTH-VINCZE | TILL FRAUD DO US PART |
| LEONARD COHEN | IN MY SECRET LIFE |

Many schools subscribe to the philosophy that reading and writing are inseparable components in the process of improving one's writing skills. The readings that follow include works of nonfiction, fiction, and poetry, all Canadian, and all written by seasoned writers. Many of these will not represent specific essay models as described earlier in this book, but as is often the case, a single essay written by a professional writer can contain a mixture of different modes and styles. These readings have been selected in the hope that they will inspire meaningful discussion and well-written student responses.

✦ ✦ ✦

## DON JUAN/DOÑA JUANA

*Rosemary Sullivan*

Professor of English at the University of Toronto, Rosemary Sullivan is also a novelist and writer of nonfiction. The following piece is taken from her book called *Labyrinth of Desire*, published in 2001, which offers a collection of perspectives on different aspects of love and sex. The term "Don Juan" (from the mythological story of a man who is a lover of thousands of women) is often considered a good thing. Sullivan, however, reveals what lies beneath the term and in the depths of the psyche of the person "honoured" with the title. She also shows that the term should by no means be restricted to men.

1 In the age-old cliché, a man will fight over a woman as if she were the prize trophy. But a woman will compete against another woman for the prize in a ruthless, predatory way.

2 Anyone who has been involved in a triangular affair knows how this works. Neither our own motives nor our man's are examined. The other woman is the enemy. She must be defeated.

3 What kind of man precipitates such **acrimony**? Traditionally, the man who indulges in multiple lovers is a Don Juan **archetype**, a narcissist. And what characterizes a **narcissist** is that the only real relationship he is capable of is one with himself.

4 The novelist Leon Whiteson once remarked that most men who play this role do so to cover their fear of intimacy. "SIN for men," he explained, "is Safety In Numbers." Having many women is a guarantee against having to deal intimately with one individual woman. It's a perfect device for protecting the bottom line: *I need no one.* As soon as such a man allows himself to acknowledge need, he opens himself to betrayal. How can he trust that he will not be abandoned?

5 The bad luck for women is that we often find men who fit the Don Juan archetype to be so attractive. They fall impulsively into erotic relationships, and we women immediately get ourselves busy searching out the heart within these transparently sensitive men. We do not recognize that their whole strategy is to

keep us unsettled: now you know him, now you don't. This kind of man can't deal with women candidly because to do so would compromise his power. And for us, the not-knowing, the continual shift in his affections, leaves us in a state of constant anxiety and self-doubt.

6 These affairs can only degenerate into very unpleasant **Tantalus** games. The dynamic is thoroughly destructive, a push/pull dance of misinterpretation. Nights of hysteria without sleep. Days plotting what to say. Then the accusatory barbs. A woman will find herself trivialized, undermined. She turns into the very thing she hates most: the **supplicating** female.

7 So much of obsessive love takes place in the head. We spend our time desperately trying to understand the other's perspective. It's as if we have failed a test we had no idea we were taking. We want to justify ourselves, to have our interpretation heard. We are left with lingering feelings of failure and guilt. We haven't the least clue what's going on.

8 I have been speaking as if there were no female equivalent to Don Juan, but of course there is a Doña Juana, though she hasn't been so named. She is variously called the *femme fatale*, the seductress, the siren, the vamp, *la Belle Dame Sans Merci*.

9 One of her most fascinating **incarnations** is as Scarlett O'Hara in the 1939 film *Gone With the Wind*. Scarlett is petulant, childish, totally limited in her feelings, and seemingly irresistible to men. She collects men as trophies for her beauty, using them for her own ends. She admits to having no real feeling for them and complains about the need to pretend she does. As a type, her power is incomprehensible to women. She is so transparent, can't men see through her?

10 But the quality of the seductress that is irresistible to men is her combination of vulnerability and willfulness. She has a passionate energy, an infectious appetite for life (Scarlett's favorite expletive is "great balls of fire"), but she trades on her helplessness. Probably men are flattered, but not fooled. They secretly admire her strength, which is, paradoxically, so unfeminine. One lover complains, with relish, that she cut her teeth on his heart.

11 Scarlett is ruthless, self-absorbed and manipulative. As the film makes clear, war brings out the best in her—her indomitable will to survive. She lies, cheats, and even steals her sister's fiancé to keep the family estate intact. At war's end, knowing there will be a building boom, she sets up her own lumber business and is as brutal as any man, replacing slave labor with that of convicts on starvation rations.

12 But while the Don Juan is often admired by other men for his swordsmanship (that old metaphor for sexual conquest), the vamp is vilified by other women for throwing herself after men, for making a spectacle of herself, and so forth. She becomes an outsider, and the only one to whom she might be vulnerable is an outsider like herself.

13 In *Gone With the Wind*, Rhett Butler is the outsider, and Scarlett's twin. He says they're made for each other—they're both selfish and ruthless, but, as he once remarks, at least they have the guts to look life in the face.

14 The vamp, like the Don Juan, is always the basis for a cautionary tale and both must get their comeuppance. By the end of the film, Scarlett discovers she really loves Rhett Butler, but it's too late. His cavalier dismissal of her final plea to stay is the stuff of legend. And he's a smart man not to give in. To do so would be foolish. He knows Scarlett's misfortune is to love only the one who resists her. After all, he's a Don Juan himself.

15 These days we are less prescriptive in our notions of sexual propriety, and so the seducers and seductresses are not nearly so coy in their behavior. And anyway, at some point most of us play at erotic games of seduction and many of us are even promiscuous. But the game of sexual conquest can still involve a cautionary tale.

16 To play at sex hardens the heart. *Why can't I meet anyone who feels anything?* we say. *Why can't I meet anyone who responds?* Yet sometimes what we are meaning is the exact opposite: *Why can't I let myself go, and love?*

## Glossary

**acrimony:** Extreme bitterness of temper; ill feeling.

**archetype:** (In Jungian psychology) an inherited primitive mental image.

**narcissist:** Anyone who has excessive interest in one's own appearance, comfort, abilities, importance, etc. (from the Greek mythological character Narcissus).

**Tantalus:** Greek mythological king doomed in the lower world to stand in water that always receded when he tried to drink it.

**supplicating:** Asking humbly and earnestly, as by prayer.

**incarnations:** Persons or things serving as the type or embodiment of a quality or concept.

## Comprehension Questions

1. How does Sullivan define "narcissist"?
2. What does the novelist Leon Whiteson say is the reason certain men have multiple lovers?
3. Why are women, according to Sullivan, so attracted to Don Juan types?

## Questions about Form

1. Take a look at the last paragraph of the piece. Is this an appropriate paragraph for the end? Why or why not?
2. *Gone with the Wind* is a particularly old movie (released in 1939, before most of the readers of this text were born). Why do you think Sullivan refers to it here?

## Questions for Discussion

1. In paragraph 8, Sullivan refers to the many labels of the female version of Don Juan. Discuss what you think is the relationship between a *Doña Juana* and what you know of a *femme fatale*.
2. Despite the indisputable similarities between the characteristics of the Don Juan and the female counterpart, do you think the male of this type is still looked upon more positively than the female as Sullivan suggests? Why or why not?
3. Consider the last paragraph of this piece. Is this problem common today? Discuss.
4. Based on the entry in the above glossary for "Tantalus," what do you think Sullivan means when she refers to "Tantalus games"?

## Writing Ideas

1. Write a paragraph or essay of cause and effect discussing either the causes or the effects (not both) of being a Don Juan or Doña Juana (pick one).
2. Much of Sullivan's piece deals with the reasons for which the Don Juan/Doña Juana type of person makes the worst kind of dating/mating partner to have. Write a paragraph or essay on the reasons such a person would make an ideal dating or mating (pick one) partner, instead. If you have to add a sarcastic tone to your composition, so be it. On the other hand, if you believe such a person would, in fact, make an ideal partner, then, of course, there's no need for the sarcasm.

✦ ✦ ✦

# HIDDEN LESSONS

*David Suzuki*

World-famous host of CBC's *The Nature of Things,* scientist David Suzuki was born in Vancouver in 1936. He's written approximately thirty books, ten of which explain nature to children. He lectures internationally and writes a syndicated newspaper column. His lifelong pursuit is literally to save the planet, and to this end, among countless other things, he has written the following piece, which first appeared in Toronto's *The Globe and Mail.*

1 In spite of the vast expanse of wilderness in this country, most Canadian children grow up in urban settings. In other words, they live in a world conceived, shaped and dominated by people. Even the farms located around cities and towns are carefully groomed and landscaped for human convenience. There's nothing

wrong with that, of course, but in such an environment, it's very easy to lose any sense of connection with nature.

2 In city apartments and dwellings, the presence of cockroaches, fleas, ants, mosquitoes or houseflies is guaranteed to elicit the spraying of insecticides. Mice and rats are poisoned or trapped, while the gardener wages a never-ending struggle with ragweed, dandelions, slugs and root-rot. We have a modern **arsenal** of chemical weapons to fight off these invaders and we use them **lavishly**.

3 We worry when kids roll in the mud or wade through a puddle because they'll get "dirty." Children learn attitudes and values very quickly and the lesson in cities is very clear—nature is an enemy, it's dirty, dangerous or a nuisance. So youngsters learn to distance themselves from nature and to try to control it. I am astonished at the number of adults who **loathe** or are terrified by snakes, spiders, butterflies, worms, birds—the list seems endless.

4 If you reflect on the history of humankind, you realize that for 99 per cent of our species' existence on the planet, we were deeply embedded in and dependent on nature. When plants and animals were plentiful, we flourished. When famine and drought struck, our numbers fell accordingly. We remain every bit as dependent upon nature today—we need plants to fix photons of energy into sugar molecules and to cleanse the air and replenish the oxygen. It is folly to forget our dependence on an intact **ecosystem.** But we do whenever we teach our offspring to fear or detest the natural world. The urban message kids get runs completely counter to what they are born with, a natural interest in other life forms. Just watch a child in a first encounter with a flower or an ant—there is instant interest and fascination. We condition them out of it.

5 The result is that when my 7-year-old daughter brings home new friends, they invariably recoil in fear or disgust when she tries to show them her favorite pets—three beautiful salamanders that her grandfather got for her in Vancouver. And when my 3-year-old comes wandering in with her treasures—millipedes, spiders, slugs and sowbugs that she catches under rocks lining the front lawn—children and adults alike usually respond by saying "yuk."

6 I can't overemphasize the tragedy of that attitude. For, inherent in this view is the assumption that human beings are special and different and that we lie outside nature. Yet it is this belief that is creating many of our environmental problems today.

7 Does it matter whether we sense our place in nature so long as we have cities and technology? Yes, for many reasons, not the least of which is that virtually all scientists were fascinated with nature as children and retained that curiosity throughout their lives. But a far more important reason is that if we retain a spiritual sense of connection with all other life forms, it can't help but profoundly affect the way we act. Whenever my daughter sees a picture of an animal dead or dying, she asks me fearfully, "Daddy, are there any more?" At 7 years, she already knows about extinction and it frightens her.

8 The yodel of a loon at sunset, the vast flocks of migrating waterfowl in the fall, the indomitable salmon returning thousands of kilometres—these images of

nature have inspired us to create music, poetry and art. And when we struggle to retain a handful of California **condors** or whooping cranes, it's clearly not from a fear of ecological collapse, it's because there is something obscene and frightening about the disappearance of another species at our hands.

9 If children grow up understanding that we are animals, they will look at other species with a sense of fellowship and community. If they understand their ecological place—the **biosphere**—then when children see the great virgin forests of the Queen Charlotte Islands being clearcut, they will feel physical pain, because they will understand that those trees are an extension of themselves.

10 When children who know their place in the ecosystem see factories spewing poison into the air, water and soil, they will feel ill because someone has violated their home. This is not mystical mumbo-jumbo. We have poisoned the life support systems that sustain all organisms because we have lost a sense of ecological place. Those of us who are parents have to realize the unspoken, negative lessons we are conveying to our children. Otherwise, they will continue to desecrate this planet as we have.

11 It's not easy to avoid giving these hidden lessons. I have struggled to cover my dismay and queasiness when Severn and Sarika come running in with a large wolf spider or when we've emerged from a ditch covered with leeches or when they have been stung accidentally by yellowjackets feeding on our leftovers. But that's nature. I believe efforts to teach children to love and respect other life forms are priceless.

## Glossary

**arsenal:** Place for storing weapons; collection.

**lavishly:** Giving or spending generously.

**loathe:** Abhor; detest.

**ecosystem:** System made up of a community of animals, plants, and bacteria and its interrelated physical and chemical environment.

**condors:** Very large vultures of the South American Andes.

**biosphere:** All the living organisms of the earth.

## Comprehension Questions

1. What are the causes, according to Suzuki, of our disdain for nature?
2. Does Suzuki think more of us should live in rural areas and not the city? Explain.
3. What is Suzuki's attitude toward the way most of us think of animals?
4. What does Suzuki mean when he mentions "a spiritual sense of connection with all other life forms" in paragraph 7?

## Questions about Form

1. How does Suzuki open the piece and therefore get your attention?
2. What writing strategy (see Unit III) does Suzuki seem to use to organize most of his article?
3. Why is paragraph 6 the shortest paragraph of the essay?
4. What is the purpose of paragraph 5, in which Suzuki refers to his daughters and their "pets"?

## Questions for Discussion

1. What do you think Suzuki is hoping to accomplish with this essay? Will he succeed? Why or why not?
2. Is paragraph 6 likely to meet with controversy among its readers? Why or why not?
3. Do movies generally help or hurt Suzuki's cause of sensitizing people to the environment? Examples of movies for discussion might include *ANTZ, Jurassic Park, The Fly, Arachnophobia, Gorillas in the Mist, Lassie, Flipper, Cujo,* etc.
4. What are your feelings toward the "less palatable" parts of the environment? In light of Suzuki's message, do you think anyone's attitude in this area can be changed? Explain.
5. It's tragic, according to Suzuki, that many human beings believe they're more special than animals. Does Suzuki undermine his argument by not mentioning how many human beings believe they're better than *other human beings*? How do we sensitize human beings to the pain of animals when we have a hard enough time sensitizing people to the pain of other people? Discuss.

## Writing Ideas

1. What could most people do, without too much effort, to reverse these "hidden lessons" that Suzuki writes about in this piece? Write a paragraph or essay of process to this effect.
2. Have you ever lived in a non-urban setting? Write a comparison or contrast paragraph or essay contrasting urban living with rural living as they relate to the environment.

✦ ✦ ✦

# In Praise of Old Women

*Marya Fiamengo*

Brought up and schooled in British Columbia, Marya Fiamengo is the child of Yugoslavian parents. She has taught literature at the University of British Columbia, and she's written several books of poetry, including *White Linen Remembered* and one named after the poem below, *In Praise of Old Women,* published in 1976. Much of her work has been included in anthologies and has been studied by students of high school, college, and university.

1 Yes, **Tadeusz Rozewicz,** I too
prefer old women.
They bend over graves
with flowers,
they wash the limbs of the dead,
they count the beads of their rosaries,
they commit no murders
they give advice
or tell fortunes,
they endure.

2 In Poland, in Russia,
in Asia, in the Balkans,
I see them shawled, kerchiefed,
bent-backed, work-wrinkled.

3 But Tadeusz,
have you been to America?

4 Where we have no old women.
No **Stara Babas,**
no haggard Madonnas.

5 Everyone, Tadeusz, is young in America.
Especially the women
with **coifed** blue hair
which gleams like the steel
of jets in the daytime sky.
Smooth-skinned at sixty,
second debuts at fifty
**renascent**
they never grow old in America.

6 And we have in America
literate, sexually liberated women
who wouldn't touch a corpse
who confuse **lechery** with love,
not out of viciousness
but boringly
out of confusion, neurosis, identity crises.

7 Tadeusz,
I go to the cemetery
with my mother
one of us stoically old,
the other aging,
and I tell you, Tadeusz,
I will grow old in America.
I will have no second debut.
I will raise my son on old battles,
Kossovo, Neretva, Thermopylae,
Stalingrad and Britain
and I will wrinkle adamantly in America.

8 I will put salt in the soup
and I will offer bread and wine
to my friends,
and I will stubbornly praise old women
until their thin taut skins
glow like Ikons ascending on escalators
like Buddhas descending in subways,
and I will liberate all women
to be old in America
because the highest manifestation of
**Hagia Sophia**
is old and a woman.

## Glossary

**Tadeusz Rozewicz:** Contemporary Polish poet.

**Stara Babas:** Old women (term common to several Slavic languages).

**coifed:** Styled.

**renascent:** Showing new strength or vigour.

**lechery:** Excessive indulgence of sexual desires.

**Hagia Sophia:** Holy Wisdom (Greek).

## Comprehension Questions

1. What is Fiamengo contrasting in her poem?
2. What does Fiamengo mean by what she says in the fourth stanza: "... we have no old women"?
3. What are some of the differences between the two items Fiamengo is contrasting?
4. What does it mean when the poet says "I will wrinkle adamantly in America" (last line, seventh stanza)? Why do you think she feels this way?

## Questions about Form

1. Why is Fiamengo speaking to someone called Tadeusz Rozewicz instead of directly to the reader? Why do you think she has chosen this particular person with whom to speak?
2. What does *Hagia* in *Hagia Sophia* (second-last line) look like in English? Contrast this answer with what *Hagia Sophia* really means. What does this discrepancy suggest? And how does it contribute to your understanding of the poem?

## Questions for Discussion

1. In one sentence, what seems to be Fiamengo's message? Do you agree with it? Why or why not?
2. Approximately how old do you think Fiamengo was when she wrote this poem? Why might she have written it at this time in her life?
3. Is this poem likely to provoke some strong emotions in anyone? Who? What emotions and why?
4. What do you think Fiamengo hopes to accomplish by writing this poem? Is she likely to achieve her goal? Why or why not?

## Writing Ideas

1. Write a paragraph or essay on the reasons there are, as the poet suggests, "no old women in America." Include toward the beginning of your composition what you believe "there are no old women in America" means.
2. In the last stanza of her poem, Fiamengo declares, "... I will liberate all women / to be old in America...." Write a paragraph or essay in which you suggest how all women in America can "liberate" themselves in this way.

✦ ✦ ✦

# Heart of Loneliness

*Jean Vanier*

Noah's Ark was a place of refuge and new beginnings. While in France, Jean Vanier founded an organization called L'Arche after the ark of the Old Testament. L'Arche is an international network of communities for people of intellectual disabilities. The son of former governor general of Canada Georges Vanier, Jean Vanier has written several books, one of which is *Becoming Human*, published in 1998, out of which the following piece has been taken. Loneliness may seem like a bad thing to most, but with the acknowledgment of certain principles, says Vanier, loneliness can be like Noah's Ark, a place that offers refuge and new beginnings.

1 A sense of loneliness can be covered up by the things we do as we seek recognition and success. This is surely what I did as a young adult. It is what we all do. We all have this drive to do things that will be seen by others as valuable, things that make us feel good about ourselves and give us a sense of being alive. We only become aware of loneliness at times when we cannot perform or when imagination seems to fail us.

2 Loneliness can appear as a faint dis-ease, an inner dissatisfaction, a restlessness in the heart.

3 Loneliness comes at any time. It comes in times of sickness or when friends are absent; it comes during sleepless nights when the heart is heavy, during times of failure at work or in relationships; it comes when we lose trust in ourselves and in others. In old age, loneliness can rise up and threaten to overwhelm us. At such times, life can lose its meaning. Loneliness can feel like death.

4 When people are physically well, performing creatively, successful in their lives, loneliness seems absent. But I believe that loneliness is something essential to human nature; it can only be covered over, it can never actually go away. Loneliness is part of being human because there is nothing in existence that can completely fulfill the needs of the human heart.

5 Loneliness in one form is, in fact, essential to our humanity. Loneliness can become a source of creative energy, the energy that drives us down new paths to create new things or to seek more truth and justice in the world. Artists, poets, mystics, prophets, those who do not seem to fit into the world or the ways of society, are frequently lonely. They feel themselves to be different, dissatisfied with the status quo and with mediocrity; dissatisfied with our competitive world where so much energy goes into **ephemeral** things. Frequently, it is the lonely man or woman who revolts against injustice and seeks new ways. It is as if a fire is burning within them, a fire fuelled by loneliness.

6 Loneliness is the fundamental force that urges mystics to a deeper union with God. For such people, loneliness has become intolerable, but, instead of slipping into **apathy** or anger, they use the energy of loneliness to seek God. It pushes them towards the absolute. An experience of God quenches this thirst for the absolute,

but at the same time, paradoxically, whets it because this is an experience that can never be total; by necessity, the knowledge of God is always practical. So loneliness opens up mystics to a desire to love each and every human being as God loves them.

7 Loneliness, then, can be a force for good. More frequently, however, loneliness shows other, less positive faces. It can be a source of apathy and depression, and even of a desire to die. It can push us into escapes and **addictions** in the need to forget our inner pain and emptiness. This apathy is how loneliness most often shows itself in the elderly and in those with disabilities. It is the loneliness we find in those who fall into depression, who have lost the sense of meaning in their lives, who are asking the question born of despair: What is left?

8 I once visited a psychiatric hospital that was a kind of warehouse of human misery. Hundreds of children with severe disabilities were lying, neglected, on their cots. There was a deadly silence. Not one of them was crying. When they realize that nobody cares, that nobody will answer them, children no longer cry. It takes too much energy. We cry out only when there is hope that someone may hear us.

9 Such loneliness is born of the most complete and utter depression, from the bottom of the deepest pit in which the human soul can find itself. The loneliness that engenders depression manifests itself as chaos. There is confusion, and coming out of this confusion there can be a desire for self-destruction, for death. So, loneliness can become agony, a scream of pain. There is no light, no consolation, no touch of peace and of the joy life brings. Such loneliness reveals the true meaning of chaos.

10 Life no longer flows in recognizable patterns. For the person engulfed in this form of loneliness there is only emptiness, anguish, and inner agitation; there are no **yearnings**, no desires to be fulfilled, no desire to live. Such a person feels completely cut off from everyone and everything. It is a life turned in upon itself. All order is gone, and those in this chaos are unable to relate or listen to others. Their lives seem to have no meaning. They live in complete confusion, closed up in themselves.

11 Thus loneliness can become such uncontrolled anguish that one can easily slip into the chaos of madness.

### Eric

12 Let me tell you some stories, from my own experience, of the damage loneliness can create. I met Eric for the first time in 1977. He was in the children's ward of the local psychiatric hospital, 40 kilometres from the l'Arche community in Trosly, France. He was blind and deaf, as well as severely intellectually disabled; he could neither walk nor eat by himself. He came to l'Arche at the age of sixteen, full of tremendous needs, anguish, and fears. He often sat on the ground, and whenever he felt someone close by, would stretch out his arms and try to clutch that person and to climb up on them. Once he had succeeded in getting someone to hold him, his actions would become wild: he would lose control, struggling to be held and, at the same time, jumping up and down. Holding Eric under these

conditions became intolerable for anyone and, inevitably, it ended in a struggle, trying to get rid of him as he fought to remain held. He was someone who seemed to be living in immense anguish.

13 Anguish is inner agitation, a chaotic, unfocused energy. Anguish breaks sleep and other patterns and brings us to a place of confusion. To be lonely is to feel unwanted and unloved, and therefore unloveable. Loneliness is a taste of death. No wonder some people who are desperately lonely lose themselves in mental illness or violence to forget the inner pain.

14 Eric was a terribly lonely young man. He needed to be loved, but his needs were so great that no one person could fulfill them. It took a long time in l'Arche before he found some inner peace. Little by little, as he learned to trust those around him, he discovered he was loved.

### Pierre

15 By way of contrast, Pierre was the seventh child in a family of thirteen, a man who had spent seven years in prison. I met him in Montreal. He had run away from home when he was twelve years old because he felt unnoticed and unwanted by his family. So, for a long time he lived with gangs on the street. In his heart, Pierre was a lonely man who felt lost. He had nowhere to go, no meaning in his life. He needed a friend, a teacher, someone who could help him find himself and a sense of purpose.

16 When he was sixteen Pierre committed a crime, which I believe was a cry for help. He went to jail for it. While he was there, he fell in love with a woman who regularly visited the prison. They got married, and his life took on new meaning; he finally had someone and something to live for. It was the beginning of his process of becoming human, and it happened because he felt loved ...

17 In Eric and Pierre, there were chaos and disorder. Yet in the midst of the chaos, there was a way out. Are not all our lives a movement from order to disorder, which in turn evolves into a new order?

### Order and Disorder

18 In human beings, there is a constant tension between order and disorder, connectedness and loneliness, evolution and revolution, security and insecurity. Our universe is constantly evolving; the old order gives way to a new order, and this in its turn crumbles when the next order appears. It is no different in our lives in the movement from birth to death.

19 Change of one sort or another is the essence of life, so there will always be the loneliness and insecurity that come with change. When we refuse to accept that loneliness and insecurity are part of life, when we refuse to accept that they are the price of change, we close the door on many possibilities for ourselves; our lives become lessened; we are less than fully human. If we try to prevent, or ignore, the movement of life, we run the risk of falling into the inevitable depression that must accompany an impossible goal. Life evolves; change is constant. When we try to prevent the forward movement of life, we may succeed for a

while but, inevitably, there is an explosion; the **groundswell** of life's constant movement, constant change, is too great to resist.

20 And so empires of ideas, as well as empires of wealth and power, come and go. To live well is to observe in today's apparent order the tiny anomalies that are the seeds of change, the harbingers of the order of tomorrow. This means living in a state of a certain insecurity, in anguish and loneliness, which, at its best, can push us towards the new. Too much security and the refusal to evolve, to embrace change, leads to a kind of death. Too much insecurity, however, can also mean death. To be human is to create sufficient order so that we can move on into insecurity and seeming disorder. In this way, we discover the new.

21 Those who have the eyes to see this new order, as it arises, will often be considered too revolutionary, too modern, too **liberal.** Dictators everywhere have clamped down on movements for liberation; those who lead are always so certain that anarchy will arise if they do not govern with a firm hand. In reality, leaders are frightened of sharing or losing power. They too are frightened of change. They want to control everything. Those who see the coming new order will frequently be alone, persecuted.

**Five Principles**

22 But how do we learn to read the signs of evolution and to see where it is going? We can only help the new to evolve if we have certain clear principles. Here are five principles that have helped me.

23 First: all humans are sacred, whatever their culture, race, or religion, whatever their capacities or incapacities, and whatever their weaknesses or strengths may be. Each of us has an instrument to bring to the vast orchestra of humanity, and each of us needs help to become all that we might be.

24 Second: our world and our individual lives are in the process of evolving. Evolution is a part of life but it is not always easy to determine the good and the bad in something that is evolving.... It is a question of loving all the essential values of the past and reflecting on how they are to be lived in the new. These values include openness, love, wholeness, unity, peace, the human potential for healing and redemption, and, most important, the necessity of forgiveness ...

25 Third: maturity comes through working with others, through dialogue, and through a sense of belonging and a searching together. In order to evolve towards greater maturity and wholeness, we humans need a certain security; only when we have attained this can we advance in insecurity with others towards the new.

26 Fourth: human beings need to be encouraged to make choices, and to become responsible for their own lives and for the lives of others. We need to be encouraged to evolve in order to become mature, and to break out of the shell of self-centredness and out of our defence mechanisms, which are as oppressive to others as they are to ourselves. In other words, we humans need to be rooted in good earth in order to produce good fruit. But for this we need to freely risk life in order to give of ourselves.

27 Fifth: in order to make such choices, we need to reflect and to seek truth and meaning. Reality is the first principle of truth. To be human means to remain

connected to our humanness and to reality. It means to abandon the loneliness of being closed up in illusions, dreams, and ideologies, frightened of reality, and to choose to move towards connectedness …

28 Each one of us needs to work at searching for truth, not be afraid of it. We need to strive to live in truth, because the truth sets us free, even if it means living in loneliness and anguish at certain moments.

29 We must not try to return to the past, but instead launch out into the future—to understand each other and what it means to be human, to understand what is happening in the world—in order to become more fully human and to work for peace and unity. It is only as we begin to integrate such a sense of reality more fully into our being, as we thirst for that which gives meaning to our lives, that we discover the fundamental meaning of loneliness: a cry, often a painful cry of anguish, for more respect and love of others, to be even more enfolded in truth, held in God. Such a cry could bring a new wholeness to humanity.

## Glossary

**ephemeral:** Lasting for only a short time.

**apathy:** Lack of concern or interest; indifference.

**addictions:** Processes of being dependent on as compulsive habits. Activities such as gambling, smoking, sex, shopping, eating, etc., become addictions when they are done *compulsively.*

**yearnings:** Strong emotional longings.

**groundswell:** Increasingly forceful presence.

**liberal:** Open-minded; generous.

## Comprehension Questions

1. Why is loneliness essential to our humanity, according to Vanier?
2. What is the relationship, according to Vanier, between loneliness and God?
3. What did Eric and Pierre have in common that led to their loneliness?
4. What is the relationship between loneliness and addictions, violence, and other forms of self-destruction, according to the author?

## Questions about Form

1. This piece begins with a discussion of what society considers a disease and ends with five principles that Vanier considers a sort of antidote. Discuss the effectiveness of this format.
2. Why does Vanier include the cases of two young men?

## Questions for Discussion

1. Compare this piece to the one entitled "Bad Girls" by Shari Graydon (also in Unit IV). Is there a cause–effect relationship between the loneliness that Vanier describes and the violence that takes place among teens that Graydon describes?
2. Do you think it's possible to be lonely if you're surrounded by people? Why or why not? What in Vanier's piece supports your answer to this question?
3. What are the possible meanings of the title of this piece?

## Writing Ideas

1. Write a paragraph or essay on how one might go about solving one's own problem of loneliness in a practical way, but by considering Vanier's five principles of evolution.
2. What are the causes predominant in North American urban culture that contribute to loneliness? Write a cause and effect paragraph or essay discussing these causes.

✦ ✦ ✦

# The $2-Million Comma

*Grant Robertson*

Since Lynne Truss published the British best-seller *Eats, Shoots and Leaves* in 2003 about the importance of punctuation, some people have become more respectful of the proper mechanics of writing. But few people would believe that a mistake involving a comma could cost more than two million dollars. Media reporter for *The Globe and Mail* Grant Robertson wrote the following piece that was published on Monday, August 7, 2006.

1 It could be the most costly piece of punctuation in Canada.

2 A grammatical blunder may force Rogers Communications Inc. to pay an extra $2.13-million to use utility poles in the Maritimes after the placement of a comma in a contract permitted the deal's cancellation.

3 The controversial comma sent lawyers and telecommunications regulators scrambling for their English textbooks in a bitter 18-month dispute that serves as an expensive reminder of the importance of punctuation.

4 Rogers thought it had a five-year deal with Aliant Inc. to string Rogers' cable lines across thousands of utility poles in the Maritimes for an annual fee of $9.60 per pole. But early last year, Rogers was informed that the contract was being

cancelled and the rates were going up. Impossible, Rogers thought, since its contract was **iron-clad** until the spring of 2007 and could potentially be renewed for another five years.

5 Armed with the rules of grammar and punctuation, Aliant disagreed. The construction of a single sentence in the 14-page contract allowed the entire deal to be scrapped with only one-year's notice, the company argued.

6 Language buffs take note—Page 7 of the contract states: The agreement "shall continue in force for a period of five years from the date it is made, and thereafter for successive five year terms, unless and until terminated by one year prior notice in writing by either party."

7 Rogers' intent in 2002 was to lock into a long-term deal of at least five years. But when regulators with the Canadian Radio-television and Telecommunications Commission (CRTC) **parsed** the wording, they reached another conclusion.

8 The validity of the contract and the millions of dollars at stake all came down to one point—the second comma in the sentence.

9 Had it not been there, the right to cancel wouldn't have applied to the first five years of the contract and Rogers would be protected from the higher rates it now faces.

10 "Based on the rules of punctuation," the comma in question "allows for the termination of the [contract] at any time, without cause, upon one-year's written notice," the regulator said.

11 Rogers was **dumbfounded.** The company said it never would have signed a contract to use roughly 91,000 utility poles that could be cancelled on such short notice. Its lawyers tried in vain to argue the intent of the deal **trumped** the significance of the comma. "This is clearly not what the parties intended," Rogers said in a letter to the CRTC.

12 But the CRTC disagreed. And the consequences are significant.

13 The contract would have shielded Rogers from rate increases that will see its costs jump as high as $28.05 per pole. Instead, the company will likely end up paying about $2.13 million more than expected, based on rough calculations.

14 Despite the victory, Aliant won't reap the bulk of the proceeds. The poles are mostly owned by Fredericton-based utility NB Power, which contracted out the administration of the business to Aliant at the time the contract was signed.

15 Neither Rogers nor Aliant could be reached for comment on the ruling. In one of several letters to the CRTC, Aliant called the matter "a basic rule of punctuation," taking a swipe at Rogers' assertion that the comma could be ignored.

16 "This is a classic case of where the placement of a comma has great importance." Aliant said.

### The Comma Conflict

17 **The disputed sentence:** "This agreement shall be effective from the date it is made and shall continue in force for a period of five (5) years from the date it is made, and thereafter for successive five (5) year terms, unless and until terminated by one year prior notice in writing by either party."

18 **How Rogers reads it:** The contract is good for five years and is automatically renewed for successive five-year terms. The deal cannot be terminated within the first five-year term.

19 **How Aliant reads it:** The contract can be cancelled at any time provided one-year notice is given.

20 **What the experts say:** The presence of the second comma means the conditions of cancelling the contract apply to both the initial five-year term and subsequent five-year terms.

## Glossary

**iron-clad:** Difficult to change or break.

**parsed:** Separated a sentence into its parts, explaining the part of speech, function, and relationship of one part to another.

**dumbfounded:** Made speechless; astonished.

**trumped:** Surpassed; outdid.

## Comprehension Questions

1. In one to two sentences and in your own words, what is the controversy in this article?
2. What is the actual sentence in which the comma in question is found?
3. Why won't Aliant Inc. reap all the benefits of the blunder?

## Questions about Form

1. Why do you think this piece was included in this textbook?
2. Why are the paragraphs in this piece generally short?
3. Do you think there is a gap in the development of the argument that prevents a full understanding of it? Discuss.

## Questions for Discussion

1. Why is it, specifically, that the second comma makes the difference that the CRTC said it does?
2. Do you think the ruling by the CRTC is fair? Why or why not?
3. What can companies learn from this situation with respect to contracts?

## Writing Ideas

1. Write a paragraph or essay on the reasons it is important to have a better-than-average knowledge of grammar and punctuation.
2. Write a paragraph or essay discussing a situation in which you or someone you know either won or lost something as a result of bad communication. Feel free to refer, in your paper, to the article by Robertson in further support of your thesis.

✦✦✦

# Canada, My Canada

*Tomson Highway*

Celebrated novelist and award-winning playwright Tomson Highway is a Cree Native from Brochet, in northern Manitoba. He holds three honorary degrees and is a member of the Order of Canada. This piece by Highway, first published in 2000, is quite flattering of our nation. How would you expect a member of an aboriginal group to view Canada today? When you finish reading the following piece by Highway, compare or contrast your answer to this question with your observation of Highway's article.

1 Three summers back, a friend and I were being hurtled by bus through the heart of Australia, the desert flashing pink and red before our disbelieving eyes. It seemed never to end, this desert, so flat, so dry. The landscape was very unlike ours—scrub growth with some exotic cacti, no lakes, no river, just sand and rock forever. Beautiful, haunting even—*what the surface of the moon must look like*, I thought as I sat in the dusk in that almost empty bus.

2 I turned to look out the front of the bus and was suddenly taken completely by surprise. Screaming out at me in great black lettering were the words CANADA NO. 1 COUNTRY IN THE WORLD. My eyes lit up, my heart gave a heave, and I felt a **pang** of homesickness so **acute** I actually almost hurt. It was all I could do to keep myself from leaping out of my seat and grabbing the newspaper from its owner.

3 As I learned within minutes (I did indeed beg to borrow the paper), this pronouncement was based on information collected by the United Nations from studies comparing standards of living for 174 nations of the world. Some people may have doubted the finding, but I didn't, not for an instant.

4 Where else in the world can you travel by bus, automobile or train (and the odd ferry) for ten, 12 or 14 days straight and see a landscape that changes so spectacularly: the Newfoundland coast with its white foam and roar; the red sand beaches of Prince Edward Island; the graceful curves and slopes of Cape Breton's Cabot Trail; the rolling dairy land of south-shore Quebec; the maple-bordered

lakes of Ontario, the haunting north shore of Lake Superior; the wheat fields of Manitoba and Saskatchewan; the ranch land of Alberta; the mountain ranges and lush rain forests of the West Coast. The list could go on for pages and still cover only the southern section of the country, a sliver of land compared with the North, the immensity of which is almost unimaginable.

5 For six years in a row now the United Nations has designated Canada the No. 1 country in which to live.

6 We are so fortunate. We are water wealthy and forest rich. Minerals, fertile land, wild animals, plant life, the rhythm of four distinct, undeniable seasons—we have it all.

7 Of course, Canada has its problems. We'd like to lower the crime rate, but ours is a relatively safe country. We struggle with our health-care system, trying to find a balance between **universality** and affordability, but no person in this country is denied medical care for lack of money. Yes, we have our concerns, but in the global scheme of things we are well off.

8 Think of our history. For the greater part, the pain and violence, tragedy, horror and evil that have scarred forever the history of too many countries are largely absent from our past. There's no denying we've had our trials, but they pale by comparison with events that have shaped many other nations.

9 Our cities are gems. Take Toronto, where I have chosen to live. My adopted city never fails to thrill me with its racial, linguistic and cultural diversity. On any ordinary day on the city's streets and subway, in stores and restaurants, I can hear the muted ebb and flow of 20 different tongues. I can feast on food from different continents, from Greek souvlaki to Thai mango salad, from Italian **prosciutto** to Jamaican jerk chicken, from Indian lamb curry to Chinese lobster.

10 And do all these people get along? Well, they all enjoy a life of relative harmony, co-operation and peace. They certainly aren't terrorizing, torturing and massacring one another. They're not igniting pubs, cars and schools with explosives that blind, cripple and maim. And they're not killing children with machetes, cleavers and axes. Dislike—**rancour**, even—may exist here and there, but not, I believe, hatred of the blistering intensity we see elsewhere.

11 Is Canada a successful experiment in racial harmony and peaceful **coexistence**? Yes, I would say so—and proudly.

12 When I, as an aboriginal citizen of this country, find myself thinking about all the people we've received into this beautiful homeland of mine, when I think of the millions to whom we've given safe haven, following agony, terror, hunger and great sadness in their own home countries, well, my little Cree heart just puffs up with pride. And I walk the streets of Canada, the streets of my home, feeling tall as a maple.

## Glossary

**pang:** Sudden and brief pain, physical or emotional.

**acute:** Severe and sharp.

**universality:** The quality of not being restricted to a privileged few.

**prosciutto:** Spicy Italian ham served in thin slices.

**rancour:** Continuing and bitter hatred.

**coexistence:** Living side by side.

## Comprehension Questions

1. What in the newspaper sparked Highway's interest? Upon what were the findings in the newspaper story based?
2. What does Highway say is the most important thing about Canada that makes it great?
3. What problems in Canada does Highway admit to, and how does he defend Canada in spite of them?

## Questions about Form

1. In paragraph 1, Highway uses italics for the words "what the surface of the moon must look like." Why do you think he uses italics here? What is his tone? What effect is he looking for? Does he achieve this effect?
2. If this is a piece about Canada, why does Highway start out by talking about Australia?

## Questions for Discussion

1. In paragraph 8, Highway refers to the history of Canada as being quite tame when compared to that of other countries. Compare or contrast this comment to the message Rita Joe is sending in her poem "I Lost My Talk," on page 383. What do you make of the fact that both of these writers are Native Canadian?
2. Do you agree with Highway when he says Canada is a "successful experiment in racial harmony and peaceful coexistence"? Why or why not?
3. At any time throughout this piece, do you expect Highway to mention the fact that Canada has not always been kind to aboriginal peoples, or that the governments of the past have even committed genocide against his people? Why do you think he doesn't? Would it help to be told this piece appeared before in a journal called *The Imperial Oil Review*? Why or why not?
4. In paragraphs 9 and 10, Highway refers to the multicultural mix of Toronto, in particular, and Canada, in general. Compare or contrast his attitude to that of Neil Bissoondath in "Selling Illusions," which begins on page 397.
5. Paragraph 10 uses some rather harsh language. What countries do you think Highway might be referring to by the examples he uses?

6. Look up poems by the American poet Walt Whitman. Is there a poem whose title is similar to Highway's title of this piece? Account for the similarity.

## Writing Ideas

1. In a paragraph or essay, compare or contrast Canada with any other one country in the world with which you are very familiar.
2. Is Canada one of the best places in the world to live? In a paragraph or essay, explain why or why not.

✦ ✦ ✦

# My Body Is My Own Business

*Naheed Mustafa*

Wearing the hijab, says Naheed Mustafa, is a requirement of her Muslim faith. But in this piece, first published in *The Globe and Mail* in 1993, her faith in this respect seems far from blind. She argues that wearing the hijab, contrary to popular belief, liberates her. Mustafa works as an editor in Toronto.

1 I often wonder whether people see me as a radical, fundamentalist Muslim terrorist packing an AK-47 assault rifle inside my jean jacket. Or maybe they see me as the poster girl for oppressed womanhood everywhere. I'm not sure which it is.

2 I get the whole gamut of strange looks, stares and covert glances. You see, I wear the *hijab*, a scarf that covers my head, neck and throat. I do this because I am a Muslim woman who believes her body is her own private concern.

3 Young Muslim women are reclaiming the *hijab*, reinterpreting it in light of its original purpose—to give back to women ultimate control of their own bodies.

4 The **Koran** teaches us that men and women are equal, that individuals should not be judged according to gender, beauty, wealth or privilege. The only thing that makes one person better than another is her or his character.

5 Nonetheless, people have a difficult time relating to me. After all, I'm young, Canadian born and raised, university-educated—why would I do this to myself, they ask.

6 Strangers speak to me in loud, slow English and often appear to be playing **charades.** They politely inquire how I like living in Canada and whether or not the cold bothers me. If I'm in the right mood, it can be very amusing.

7 But why would I, a woman with all the advantages of a North American upbringing, suddenly, at 21, want to cover myself so that with the *hijab* and the other clothes I choose to wear, only my face and hands show?

8 Because it gives me freedom.

9 Women are taught from early childhood that their worth is proportional to their attractiveness. We feel compelled to pursue **abstract** notions of beauty, half realizing that such a pursuit is futile.

10 When women reject this form of oppression, they face ridicule and contempt. Whether it's women who refuse to wear makeup or to shave their legs or to expose their bodies, society, both men and women, have trouble dealing with them.

11 In the Western world, the *hijab* has come to symbolize either forced silence or radical, **unconscionable** militancy. Actually, it's neither. It is simply a woman's assertion that judgment of her physical person is to play no role whatsoever in social interaction.

12 Wearing the *hijab* has given me freedom from constant attention to my physical self. Because my appearance is not subjected to public scrutiny, my beauty, or perhaps lack of it, has been removed from the realm of what can legitimately be discussed.

13 No one knows whether my hair looks as if I just stepped out of a salon, whether or not I can pinch an inch, or even if I have unsightly stretch marks. And because no one knows, no one cares.

14 Feeling that one has to meet the impossible male standards of beauty is tiring and often humiliating. I should know, I spent my entire teenage years trying to do it. I was a borderline bulimic and spent a lot of money I didn't have on potions and lotions in hopes of becoming the next Cindy Crawford.

15 The definition of beauty is ever-changing; **waifish** is good, waifish is bad, athletic is good—sorry, athletic is bad. Narrow hips? Great. Narrow hips? Too bad.

16 Women are not going to achieve equality with the right to bare their breasts in public, as some people would like to have you believe. That would only make us party to our own **objectification.** True equality will be had only when women don't need to display themselves to get attention and won't need to defend their decision to keep their bodies to themselves.

## Glossary

**Koran:** Holy book of Muslims.

**charades:** Games in which somebody acts out a word or phrase and players guess its meaning.

**abstract:** Not concrete; conceptual; hard to put into words.

**unconscionable:** Extremely unethical; morally wrong.

**waifish:** Skinny.

**objectification:** Act of treating like an object or "piece of meat."

## Comprehension Questions

1. According to Mustafa, what does the Koran teach about equality?
2. How does the issue of attractiveness make it difficult to achieve equality between the sexes?
3. According to the author, what in the Western world has the hijab come to represent? What does it represent in reality, instead, according to Mustafa?

## Questions about Form

1. Why does Mustafa begin her piece by referring to herself?
2. Most of Mustafa's paragraphs in this piece are extremely short, unlike those of a proper academic essay. Does the fact that this piece was written for *The Globe and Mail* (1993) offer a clue as to why it was written this way? Explain.

## Questions for Discussion

1. If a woman is not a practising Muslim, but sympathizes with Mustafa's reasons for wearing a hijab, what could she do besides wear a hijab?
2. In the last paragraph, Mustafa says baring their breasts will only make women "party to our own objectification." What does this mean? Do you agree? Why or why not?
3. Many people would argue that sexual attraction is an intrinsic part of falling in love with someone. If this is true, how does one fall in love if another doesn't reveal his/her (especially her) sexuality by wearing revealing clothes?
4. Mustafa refers to the "tiring" and "humiliating" male standards of beauty in paragraph 14. What are women's standards of attractiveness in men? Are they just as tiring and humiliating? Discuss.
5. Look at the very last line of the article. Mustafa ponders a time when true equality between the sexes will be had. Has that time arrived? Cite evidence from life in Canada that supports your answer.

## Writing Ideas

1. Write a paragraph or essay of cause and effect focusing on the causes of inequality between the sexes in North American culture. When you have finished your rough draft, decide whether you've assigned more blame to women or to men or equally to both.
2. Is attention the same as respect? If a woman gets attention because of the way she is dressed, does that mean she's going to win respect, too? Write a

paragraph or essay answering the above question and supporting your answer. Feel free to refer to Mustafa's piece for further support of your topic sentence/thesis statement regardless of your point of view.

✦ ✦ ✦

## Leaving the Cave

*John Artibello*

Plato's classic work, *The Republic,* is an account of a conversation in which the philosopher Socrates and a few of his friends are trying to lay out a plan for a perfect society. It seems we cannot understand what makes society work well without understanding what it means to be human and, especially, what makes people happy. According to Socrates, who is the main speaker in the book, human happiness depends on becoming enlightened, illustrated by the famous myth called "The Allegory of the Cave." John Artibello, a philosophy professor and self-declared seeker, who has been influenced by such thinkers as Jean Vanier (see page 362) and Marshall McLuhan, interprets this myth in his article, written in 2003, that follows.

1 So, what's the secret? What makes us happy? Is it money, success, self-confidence, relationships, God? As long as we are human, we face the questions: How can I get it all together? How can I find what I need?

2 As we all know, the answers to these questions do not come easily. In fact, some people claim that if you are really taking these questions seriously, you are probably thinking too much. As the words of the song say, "We're here for a good time, not a long time ..."

3 None of us can be blamed for suspecting that the really big questions are probably unanswerable. So, if that is the case why not take the road of least resistance? Relax, chill. If anybody asks the tough questions (say on a first date, or in an English class), just smile and say, "Ignorance is **bliss**!"

4 The philosopher Socrates would never have agreed with the idea that ignorance is bliss. In fact, he would have insisted that ignorance or what he called "unenlightenment" is actually the cause of personal unhappiness, depression, social breakdown and even war. As Socrates puts it, *"The unexamined life is not worth living."* That is, if you are not thinking about your life, it might be impossible to *really live.*

5 Fancy that! A person who claims *you are what you think*! But "thinking" for Socrates is not like going into the library to do your homework. It is more like a process of waking up, and it begins when you start to question all of the conventional, generally accepted ideas and values of the society in which we live.

6 People often say that human growth is a painful process. According to Socrates, the source of the pain is our tendency to prefer "comfortable **illusions**" to the hard realities and challenges that we all must face to become fully human. The central theme of the "**Allegory** of the Cave" is disillusion, and there is a great reward for the pain of moving away from the half-truths of common sense. As you move closer and closer to the real world, you draw closer and closer to your real Self.

7 In Socrates' story of the Cave, we are introduced to a series of powerful, but troubling images. According to the philosopher, people who are unenlightened have very little self-knowledge and they are like people who live their whole lives in a darkened cave without ever discovering what is outside the cave. In fact, they don't even know that there is an "outside." Their dark cave and the shadows on the wall of the cave are their "reality." Their lives are, therefore, lives of complete illusion. This is the beginning of Socrates' ancient parable:

8 Here is a myth to illustrate the extent to which our nature may be enlightened or unenlightened. Imagine the condition of people living in a sort of cavernous chamber, with an entrance open to the light and a long passage all down the cave. Here they have been since childhood, chained by the leg and also by the neck, so that they cannot move and can only see what is in front of them because the chains will not let them turn their heads. At some distance higher up is the light of a fire burning behind them; between the prisoners and the fire is a track with a parapet built along it, like the screen at a puppet show, which hides the performers while they show their puppets over the top.

9 Now, behind this parapet, imagine people carrying artificial objects, including figures of men and animals in wood or stone or other materials, which project above the parapet. Naturally, some of these persons will be talking, others silent.

10 ... Of course, if the prisoners were talking, their words would refer only to those passing shadows which they saw and not to the real objects which are the causes of the shadows.

11 Although this imagery is over two thousand years old, it resonates when we think, for example, of people "chained" to their televisions, watching an endless parade of chaotic, but amusing images. Of course, the deeper question is, what does it all mean?

12 At this stage of the story, Socrates is describing the lives of people who try to find happiness in material things. If you are a "material girl" or a "material boy," chances are you live pretty much on the surface of life ("the shadows"). Happiness consists of looking good, having a nice car, nice clothes, and a life based on the images and truths of popular magazines and television "reality" shows. This kind of life is for Socrates equivalent to a kind of slavery. Life is at bottom unsatisfying because it is based on a lie: the message of the advertisers, which is "Don't accept yourself as you are; there is something wrong with you. You need more stuff to be happy. You need more illusion to be real."

13 Of course, the person who begins to see through the superficial messages of materialism is beginning a process of enlightenment, of coming out of the cave. This is what happens in the next part of the story.

14 Now consider what would happen if their release from the chains and the healing of their ignorance should come about in this way. Suppose one of the prisoners was set free and forced suddenly to stand up, turn his head, and walk toward the light and the objects before the fire.

15 ... What do you think he would say if someone told him that what he had formerly seen was meaningless illusion, but now being somewhat closer to reality and turned towards more real objects, he was getting a truer view? ... Would he not be perplexed and believe that the objects now shown him to be not so real as what he formerly saw?

16 ... And if he were to look at the fire itself, would not his eyes ache, so that he would try to escape and turn back to the more comfortable shadows? ...

17 ... And suppose someone were to drag him forcibly up the steep and rugged ascent and not let him go until he hauled him up into the sunlight, would he not suffer pain and vexation at such treatment, and, when he had come into the light find his eyes so full of radiance that he could not see a single one of the things that he was now told were real?

18 ... Now imagine what would happen if he went down again to take his former seat in the cave. Coming suddenly out of the sunlight, his eyes would be filled with darkness. He might be required once more to deliver his opinion on those shadows, in competition with the prisoners who had never been

released, while his eyesight was still dim and unsteady; and it might take some time to get used to the darkness. They would laugh at him and say that he had gone up only to come back with his sight ruined.

19 The story shows the transition from looking at the "shadows" on the wall to looking at the "fire" to being hauled up into the "sunlight." These are very important symbols. The shadows represent the material world, the fire represents knowledge, and the sunlight represents goodness or morality. The ascent to the things in the "upper world," where the sunlight dwells, represents the upward journey of the mind to the world of spiritual meaning behind the physical things we see everyday. This is a metaphor for the learning process. Socrates further notes that, in the world of knowledge, the last thing to be perceived and only with great difficulty is the essential nature of Goodness (the sun). This means that our knowledge of reality is ultimately moral: when we look past the outward and obvious aspect of things, we will learn to distinguish the good from what "appears" to be good. All of our material things are thought to be essential to the good life, but after studying things more closely, we may need to change our minds.

20 So getting out of the cave involves a kind of learning that transforms us. Once we develop a deep knowledge of the world, we develop a deeper connection to it, and this is ultimately what makes us fully alive. The contrast between watching "shadows on the wall" and seeing the sun and the objects of nature (outside the cave) is meant to awaken our interest in connecting to the *real world* and to saying no to the crass commercialized world of our everyday experience. When our knowledge has called into question how we live, we are living what Socrates calls the "examined life," a life really worth living. An examined life and a passionate engagement with ideas are much more interesting than a life of working like a slave to pay for a superficial materialism and the accompanying depression that seems to be **epidemic** these days in North America.

21 Perhaps "living in the cave" is **symbolic** of a modern situation like this: think of a person riding a subway on the way to school. She does not usually read on the subway because books are pretty boring. She is attracted by an ad for a new pair of jeans. She sees herself in the shapely model wearing the clothes. The come-on is "if you don't have these jeans, you won't be happy." If you buy into the message of the ad, you are buying into a whole philosophy of life, which is that "life is about *having*, rather than *being*." And, "if you want to be beautiful, *buy, buy, buy.*"

22 Of course, at this stage of your life, you don't know much about what is behind the images and the material objects you enjoy so much. You don't care, for example, that the people who make your jeans and sweaters are working for three or four dollars a day somewhere in the Third World. Your ideas of morality are pretty basic as well. Really bad people are terrorists and suicide bombers, but they live mostly in other countries. Living in the shadows is a metaphor for our tendency to immerse ourselves in superficial things as a way to avoid deeper and potentially threatening ideas and issues.

23 Some people, however, can't help asking tough questions. Why, for example, as our society becomes technologically more powerful, do individuals feel more and more powerless? Are all of the goods and gadgets that we work so hard to get making our lives more meaningful? To answer these questions, we need to get past "the shadows"; we need to break the chains and turn towards the light. This process of enlightenment, of moving into the light, is impossible apart from the search for truth, which in terms of the story, results in our understanding not just *how* things work (technology), but *why* things and people behave as they do (philosophy).

24 Consider a modern example of what the cave might represent: someone who is "in the cave" is like a person who owns a car without knowing what effect it has on the environment. If asked what makes the car work, this person says, "Just turn on the ignition, put her in gear, and off you go." If the car breaks down, the owner has no idea how to fix it. But someone who decides to take a course in auto mechanics or engineering is "breaking the chains" of **ignorance** and attempting to look at the "real objects" involved in the working of the car: things like the engine, the transmission, the spark plugs, alternator, and the burning of the fossil fuel without which there would be no cars, no highways, no

drive-in movies and probably no wars in the Middle East! When your study has taken you "outside the cave," or to "the real world," you see the political, environmental and moral aspects of cars. A person who "sees the sun" (outside the cave) can put it all together. The person sees the bigger picture. The car that you love to drive is connected to a larger, more complex reality involving the politics of oil and the destruction of the environment, and as we all know, that can't be good!

25 In the story of the Cave, Socrates is saying that humans are confronted with a fundamental option: reality or illusion. He suggests that the journey to your true self begins by going deeper and deeper into the world to find its true beauty and meaning. The philosophers will tell you that learning is the key, especially when you *explore* what really interests you. When you love to learn, it is because you are finding yourself in your study. The journey is endless, as are the rewards. As T.S. Eliot says,

26 We shall not cease from exploration
And the end of all our exploring
Will be to arrive where we started
And know the place for the first time.

## Glossary

**bliss:** Great joy or happiness.

**illusions:** Mistaken perceptions.

**allegory:** Story in which people, things, and happenings have a hidden or symbolic meaning.

**epidemic:** Prevalent and spreading among many individuals in a community at the same time (said especially of a human contagious disease).

**symbolic:** Of something that stands for or represents another thing.

**ignorance:** Lack of knowledge or education; unawareness (of).

## Comprehension Questions

1. What do most people, according to Artibello, think happiness consists of?
2. What takes place in the cave (in Plato's myth) that relates to the material world?
3. What does Artibello cite as a modern example of what the cave symbolizes?
4. What is the difference, according to Artibello, between an ignorant person who owns a car, and an enlightened person who has a deeper knowledge of cars? How does morality relate to this contrast?

## Questions about Form

1. What effect or effects do the illustrations that accompany this article have on you?
2. Some of the "Allegory of the Cave" is taken directly from a translation of Plato's *Republic.* Would it have made any difference if Artibello had simply paraphrased these parts?
3. The "Socratic Approach" is one of asking deep, thought-provoking questions. In paragraph 23, for example, Artibello asks two questions that he does not proceed to answer directly. Do you think there is a reason for this? If so, what?

## Questions for Discussion

1. Artibello is interpreting Plato to mean that, to be fully alive, we need to prefer the world of ideas to the world of "material things" such as cars, clothes, etc. Is it possible that the "material girl or boy" cannot be whole or happy? Discuss the role of ideas in the good life.
2. In the conclusion of the article, the concept of a "fundamental" or life option is introduced. Discuss the role of fundamental options and turning points in life. In what sense do these options involve a movement from illusion to reality?
3. Plato is known as an idealist philosopher. That is, he was critical of the physical world because it passes away while the deeper things such as the ideals of truth, virtue, and beauty are eternal. What images in the story of the cave reinforce this position? Do you agree with this idea? Explain.
4. If you were to lead an examined life, what would you need to do? Would you have to make changes to your lifestyle or in what you are studying? Discuss.

## Writing Ideas

1. Write a paragraph or essay on what you think it means for people in general to lead examined lives. How would their lives have to change?
2. Now that you've read and perhaps discussed the article, write a paragraph or essay of definition explaining what "leaving the cave" means to you. What are some of your own examples of what "leaving the cave" represents?

## Further Reading and Research

1. In a book entitled *Plato not Prozac!* Lou Marinoff explores the relationship between what we think and how we feel. He is exploring an ancient idea that being passionate about thinking, especially about deep and interesting issues (such as the meaning of life), is what keeps us sane.

2. Great philosophical ideas are often conveyed in stories, poems, and myths. Read T. S. Eliot's "The Waste Land," and compare the imagery of the poem to the imagery of the cave.
3. Iris Murdoch is one of the world's great interpreters of Plato. Her novel *The Philosopher's Pupil* is a fictional account of a philosopher's journey to "the dark side."
4. One source of beautiful poems about the journey to the light is Mary Oliver's *New and Selected Poems* (Beacon Press, 1992). See especially "The Journey" and "Wild Geese."

✦ ✦ ✦

# I Lost My Talk

*Rita Joe*

The writings of Rita Joe, a Micmac Native, are about aboriginal people. She was born on a reservation in Wycocomagh on Cape Breton Island in Nova Scotia. At the age of 12, after both her parents had died, she placed herself in an Indian residential school in Shubenacadie, Nova Scotia. An acclaimed poet, Rita Joe published several collections, including *Lnu and Indians We're Called* (1991). She became a member of the Order of Canada in 1990, and was active in Native issues before her death in 2007.

1 I lost my talk
The talk you took away.
When I was a little girl
At **Shubenacadie** school.

2 You snatched it away:
I speak like you
I think like you
I create like you
The scrambled **ballad,** about my word.

3 Two ways I talk
Both ways I say,
Your way is more powerful.

4 So gently I offer my hand and ask,
Let me find my talk
So I can teach you about me.

## Glossary

**Shubenacadie:** A town in Nova Scotia.

**ballad:** A popular song, generally of a personal or political nature.

## Comprehension Questions

1. What do you think Rita Joe is saying in the first stanza of her poem?
2. What does "scrambled ballad" mean? Might it have more than one meaning?
3. What does the author mean by the word *word* in the ninth line?

## Questions about Form

1. What is the difference in tone between the first line of the poem and the very last line? How might this contribute to an interpretation of the poem's theme?
2. What do you think might be the reason for the repetition in the second stanza?
3. How would you describe the type of language being used here? Does it contribute to an overall deliberate effect? Why or why not?

## Questions for Discussion

1. What do you know of Canadian history that relates to this poem? What might have been the reasons the school authorities did what they did?
2. Does the knowledge that Rita Joe placed herself in the school at Shubenacadie affect your interpretation of her poem? Why or why not?

## Writing Ideas

1. Do some research on what Canadian school authorities did to assimilate Native Canadians, and take a position either for or against this action in a paragraph or essay.
2. In a cause and effect paragraph or essay, discuss the repercussions of one's voice being denied. You may want to talk more specifically of a child whose voice is not taken seriously, or of women whose voice is silenced in certain cultures, or of North American Blacks who have been marginalized and/or discriminated against ever since the days of slavery, and so on.
3. Besides the obvious difference between this work by Rita Joe and the piece by Tomson Highway, which begins on page 370 (they are two different genres), are there any other differences? In a paragraph or essay, compare or contrast the two works.

✦ ✦ ✦

# Rats

*W. Frank Epling*

Once named Outstanding Teacher of the Year in Psychology at the University of Alberta, Frank Epling taught behaviour analysis before he died in 1998 at the age of fifty-four. He was known as a creative researcher whose ideas continue to permeate the scientific community. In this piece, first published in 1989, Epling takes a novel approach to the controversial subject of animal rights. Some essays do not include a clear thesis statement in the first paragraph, and this essay is an example of that very type. Try to figure out Epling's thesis as you read.

1 I am an animal researcher, and I work with rats. Now, for most people, the rat is an animal that does not **elicit** great sympathy. In fact, most people would hit a rat with a shovel if it dared to run across their basement floor. Of course, in Alberta, rats do not run across basement floors because the province is "rat free" and proud of it. This is not, however, exactly correct because some rats manage to sneak in from British Columbia and Saskatchewan, and I have some in my laboratory. Nonetheless, the Alberta Rat Patrol does an excellent job, and only very sneaky rats survive the border crossing. Since most of these are new arrivals and don't have a home, the Alberta winter usually gets what the Rat Patrol misses.

2 There are good rats and there are bad rats. I know this sounds absurd but stick with me and I will explain. Some time ago I was preparing a twelve-page written document that was an **ethics** justification for some proposed research with rats. I had to make certain that my rats got the very best food, shelter, and medical care. I also had to convince the local committees that I had the overall welfare of my rats foremost in my mind. This proposal took several days to write. The reason for all this is that I have good rats. Good rats live in laboratory cages.

3 Following the second day of work on my ethics proposal, I went home, opened a beer, put up my feet and flipped on the tube. *Fifth Estate* or *W5* was on, I don't remember which. Also, I can't recall the first news item, but I certainly can the second—it was about the Alberta Rat Patrol. On this show, the dedicated people of the Rat Patrol were keeping the cities, fields, and houses of Alberta rat free. This was not a fun time for those creatures who tried to invade the province. The documentary focused on the Alberta/Saskatchewan border. There are lots of rats in Saskatchewan. Well, let me tell you, the members of the Rat Patrol were shooting, hitting, and poisoning rats; these were bad rats. Bad rats do not live in laboratory cages.

4 There are other ways to be a bad rat. Rats that escape from their cages are not protected by ethics proposals. As soon as their feet hit the laboratory floor they become pests and are subject to traps, poison, and so on. Shotguns are not used because of damage to walls, noise, and the possibility of shooting a student or researcher. Believe me though, these rats are not held in high esteem. This is

particularly true in Alberta because they could get out of the building and infest our rat-free province.

5 Another way that rats lose their good status is to be food. There are animals, like some very large snakes, that will not eat unless their prey items are alive. In order to keep these animals, they must be fed. Food is not protected by ethics committees.

6 All of this makes me wonder why I am spending a significant amount of time writing ethics proposals for rats, rather than doing research with them. Don't misunderstand me. I happen to like rats and I do not advocate mistreating them. I am against the use of these animals for testing cosmetics and for repeating research where the findings are well established and rats are made to suffer. I am, however, convinced that research with rats (and other animals) can lead to findings that promote human welfare, and I am in favour of doing that research. In order to understand why I am spending a fair amount of time writing ethics proposals for my rat research, it is necessary to consider the animal rights movement.

7 Over the past fifteen years, this movement has steadily grown in number of members, and it has received increasing attention from the press. So called "animal activists" belong to a variety of organizations and they range from moderate to extreme in their views. I think it is fair to say, though, that all animal activists think that cute furry animals are nice animals—even when they are pests or food. Rats have two strikes against them, bad press and a long hairless tail. Also, the black plague did not help their cause. This prejudice for some animals and against others is curious. Not very many people are concerned about the live lobsters found at supermarkets. I think this is because the lobster is very tasty and looks vaguely like a large underwater insect. On the other hand, baby seals look cute, warm, cuddly, and helpless. Thus, the seal, but not the lobster gets sympathy. Returning to my point, the animal rights movement has created a public concern for the welfare of animals, and some of this has reached hysterical and absurd proportions.

8 A few of the more extreme views include stopping all medical research with animals, replacing animal subjects with humans, including animals in the United States Bill of Rights, recognizing **specism** as a prejudice similar to racism and so on. I don't know about you, but I can't imagine a rat, a lobster, or even a seal with the rights of free speech, assembly, and the pursuit of happiness. How would they know they had these rights? Also what happens when one animal, say a lion, **infringes** on a deer's right to life? All in all, these views seem a bit "whacky" to me, but they are taken seriously by some people.

9 One tactic of the more extreme animal activists has been overt violence and intimidation. Some individuals have joined paramilitary animal rights movements. This is an odd development since it is the only revolutionary movement I know of where none of the members are the creatures whose rights are being fought for. Nonetheless, these people are serious, and they have bombed the houses of animal researchers, released laboratory animals, vandalized labs, threatened to inject meat products with poison, organized and promoted letter

writing campaigns to stop legitimate research, and harassed reputable scientists with threatening letters and phone calls.

10 I don't know how many of my fellow citizens are members of, or in sympathy with, the animal rights movement, but I suspect not very many. This speculation is based on the number of steaks on display at my local grocery and the notable lack of concern for pit bull dogs in Edmonton. So, why all the fuss?

11 A few years ago, the *Edmonton Sun* called and wanted to interview me and several other animal researchers. We were encouraged to participate in this interview in order to "promote the benefits of animal research." Anyway, we had one of the best run and closely supervised facilities in Canada. The reporter and a photographer showed up and asked questions about my projects, photographed my rats, thanked me for giving them time, and left. I looked forward to local fame.

12 A week or so later, the *Sunday Sun* carried the article. I was not famous. They had so garbled my name that you could not tell whose research they were talking about. This was very fortunate (or perhaps intentional to prevent a civil suit). The first page of the Sunday supplement had a full-page picture of a monkey sitting in a restraining chair looking like it had just had a tooth pulled by a student dentist. None of the people interviewed by the *Sun* worked with monkeys and I recognized the picture. The photograph was a famous one that has appeared in antivivisectionist magazines and advertising campaigns for "save the animals." I don't know why the same picture is used over and over, but it is.

13 Articles like this portray animal researchers as modern day versions of **Dr. Mengele.** It would seem that we can't wait to torture animals in order to arrive at conclusions everybody knows already. We have not received "good press." I could present a case for doing animal research, but I would digress from the point I am trying to make. Writing ethics proposals that defend research with animals that are **arbitrarily** defined as good is bizarre.

14 As I have said, there are good and bad rats. At least in Alberta, it appears there are going to be bad rats for some time to come. Being a bad rat seems to depend on "the luck of the draw." Since bad rats are not considered worthy of ethics protection, I could use them in my research. There is, however, a problem. I could ask for bad rats, but they would automatically become good when they were placed in cages in my laboratory. To appreciate this, it is necessary to understand a few things about universities and public relations.

15 The people who run universities tend to place great value on "positive press": "negative press" is very much discouraged. This makes sense; the public supports universities, and if they don't like what is going on they may withdraw their support. Animal activists would like to stop all animal experiments, and they search for an opportunity to provide unfavorable press. Forcing scientists to justify the ethics of their animal research helps protect the university from this publicity. There are, however, unfortunate side effects. Large sums of money are spent on animal care staff who police laboratories. Time is wasted on writing ethics proposals, sitting on ethics committees, and waiting for ethics approval. This and more for an animal most citizens would stomp on if given the chance.

16 I am probably more concerned about the welfare of rats than most people. I have known many rats over the years and I have liked more than a few. I am in favor of kind treatment for rats and other animals that are used in scientific research. I do think, however, that a consideration of good and bad rats and lobsters and seals points to a confusion of ethics. So what can I do? Not much, write a commentary like this and then put in another two days writing another ethics proposal. Rats!

## Glossary

**elicit:** Draw out; evoke (an admission, response, etc.).

**ethics:** Science of morals in human conduct.

**specism:** Assumption of human superiority over animals.

**infringes:** Trespasses; affects something so as to limit or restrict it.

**Dr. Mengele:** A ruthless Nazi doctor who performed experiments mostly on Jewish inmates of death camps during the Holocaust in World War II. Many of these experiments resulted in the victims' sterility or death.

**arbitrarily:** Based on the unrestricted will of a person.

## Comprehension Questions

1. What does Epling mean when he says, "Good rats live in laboratory cages" at the end of paragraph 2?
2. How does Epling feel the press handled the story for which he was interviewed, and why?

## Questions about Form

1. Why does Epling begin his article by identifying what he does for a living?
2. Although an "Alberta rat control program" does exist, there is no group of people in Alberta known officially as the "Rat Patrol." Why do you think Epling places such emphasis on this made-up label?
3. Why do you think Epling does not articulate a clear thesis in the first paragraph? Does the lack of a clear thesis weaken his essay? Discuss.

## Questions for Discussion

1. In paragraph 12, Epling says he doesn't know why the picture of the monkey keeps getting used over and over. Based on the rest of his article, what reasons might he give on further speculation?

2. What do you think, in your own words, is Epling's thesis? What is the sentence in the piece that comes closest to your answer? Do you agree with this thesis? Why or why not?

3. Why does Epling call his article "Rats"? Are there at least two meanings here?

### Writing Ideas

1. Do you favour the testing of rats for medical research purposes? Write a paragraph or essay supporting your stand. Refer to Epling's article in further support of your argument.

2. Does your attitude toward specism determine whether you favour animal research or not? Where does this attitude come from? Discuss your answers in a paragraph or essay.

✦ ✦ ✦

## THE OTHER FAMILY

*Himani Bannerji*

Himani Bannerji is an associate professor of sociology at York University in Toronto. She has an active teaching connection with India, especially West Bengal, through the School of Women's Studies, Jadavpur University, Kolkata. She has taught and published extensively in the areas of Marxist theory, antiracist feminism, and nationalism. In the following story about a little girl and her mother, Bannerji gives us a glimpse into the home of an immigrant family caught between the desire to fit into a new community and the fear of losing its identity.

1 When the little girl came home it was already getting dark. The winter twilight had transformed the sheer blue sky of the day into the colour of steel, on which were etched a few stars, the bare winter trees and the dark wedges of the housetops. A few lit windows cast a faint glow on the snow outside. The mother stood at her window and watched the little hooded figure walking toward the house. The child looked like a shadow, her blue coat blended into the shadows of the evening. This child, her own, how small and **insubstantial** she seemed, and how alone, walking home through a pavement covered with ice and snow! It felt unreal. So different was this childhood from her own, so far away from the sun, the trees and the peopled streets of her own country! What did I do, she thought, I took her away from her own people and her own language, and now here she comes walking alone, through an alien street in a country named Canada.

2 As she **contemplated** the solitary, moving figure, her own solitude rushed over her like a tide. She had drifted away from a world that she had lived in and understood, and now she stood here at the same distance from her home as from the homes which she glimpsed while walking past the sparkling clean windows of the sandblasted houses. And now the doorbell rang, and here was her daughter scraping the snow off her boots on the doormat.

3 Dinner time was a good time. A time of warmth, of putting hot, steaming food onto the table. A time to chat about the important things of the day, a time to show each other what they had acquired. Sometimes, however, her mother would be absentminded, worried perhaps about work, unsettled perhaps by letters that had arrived from home, scraping her feelings into a state of rawness. This was such an evening. She had served herself and her child, started a conversation about their two cats and fallen into a silence after a few minutes.

4 "You aren't listening to me, Mother."

5 The complaining voice got through to her, and she looked at the indignant face demanding attention from the other side of the table. She gathered herself together.

6 "So what did he do, when you gave him dried food?"

7 "Oh, I don't quite remember, I think he scratched the ground near his bowl and left."

8 The child laughed.

9 "That was smart of him! So why don't we buy tinned food for them?"

10 "Maybe we should," she said, and tried to change the topic.

11 "So what did you do in your school today?"

12 "Oh, we drew pictures like we do every day. We never study anything—not like you said you did in your school. We drew a family—our family. Want to see it?"

13 "Sure, and let's go to the living room, OK? This is messy." Scraping of chairs and the lighting of the lamps in the other room. They both made a rush for the most comfortable chair, both reached it at the same time and made a compromise.

14 "How about you sit in my lap? No? OK, sit next to me then and we will squeeze in somehow."

15 There was a remarkable resemblance between the two faces, except that the face of the child had a greater intensity, given by the wide open eyes. She was fine boned, and had black hair framing her face. Right now she was struggling with the contents of her satchel, apparently trying to feel her way to the paintings.

16 "Here it is," she said, producing a piece of paper. "Here's the family!"

17 The mother looked at the picture for a long time. She was very still. Her face had set into an expression of anger and sadness. She was trying very hard not to cry. She didn't want to frighten the child, and yet what she saw made her feel distant from her daughter, as though she was looking at her through the reverse end of a telescope. She couldn't speak at all. The little girl too sat very still, a little recoiled from the body of her mother, as though expecting a blow. Her hands were clenched into fists, but finally it was she who broke the silence.

18 "What happened?" she said. "Don't you like it?"

19 "Listen," said the mother, "this is not your family. I, you and your father are dark-skinned, dark-haired. I don't have a blond wig hidden in my closet, my eyes are black, not blue, and your father's beard is black, not red, and you, do you have a white skin, a button nose with freckles, blue eyes and blond hair tied into a ponytail? You said you drew our family. This is not it, is it?"

20 The child was now feeling distinctly cornered. At first she was startled and frightened by her mother's response, but now she was prepared to be defiant. She had the greatest authority behind her, and she now summoned it to her help.

21 "I drew it from a book," she said, "all our books have this same picture of the family. You can go and see it for yourself. And everyone else drew it too. You can ask our teacher tomorrow. She liked it, so there!"

22 The little girl was clutching at her last straw.

23 "But you? Where are you in this picture?" demanded her mother, by now thoroughly aroused. "Where are we? Is this the family you would like to have? Don't you want us anymore? You want to be a *mem-sahib*, a white girl?"

24 But even as she lashed out these questions, the mother regretted them. She could see that she made no sense to the child. She could feel the unfairness of it all. She was sorry that she was putting such a heavy burden on such young shoulders.

25 "First I bring her here," she thought, "and then I try to make her feel guilty for wanting to be the same as the others." But something had taken hold of her this evening. Panic at the thought of losing her child, despair and guilt galvanized her into speech she regretted, and she looked with anger at her only child, who it seemed wanted to be white, who had rejected her dark mother. Someday this child would be ashamed of her, she thought, someday would move out into the world of those others. Someday they would be enemies. Confusing thoughts ran through her head like images on an uncontrollable television screen, in the chaos of which she heard her **ultimate** justification flung at her by her daughter—they wanted me to draw the family, didn't they? "They" wanted "her" to draw "the family." The way her daughter pronounced the words "they" or "the family" indicated that she knew what she was talking about. The simple pronoun "they" definitely stood for authority, for that uncontrollable yet organized world immediately outside, of which the school was the ultimate expression. It surrounded their own private space. "They" had power, "they" could crush little people like her anytime "they" wanted to, and in "their" world that was the picture of the family. Whether her mother liked it or not, whether she looked like the little girl in it or not, made not one jot of difference. That was, yes, that was the right picture. As these thoughts passed through her mind, her anger ebbed away. Abandoning her fury and distance, the mother bowed her head at the image of this family and burst into sobs.

26 "What will happen to you?" she said. "What did I do to you?"

27 She cried a great deal and said many **incoherent** things. The little girl was patient, quietly absorbing her mother's change of mood. She had a thoughtful look on her face, and bit her nails from time to time. She did not protest any

more, but nor did she cry. After a while her mother took her to bed and tucked her in, and sat in the kitchen with the fearful vision of her daughter always outside of the window of the blond family, never the centre of her own life, always rejecting herself, and her life transformed into a gigantic peep show. She wept very bitterly because she had caused this destruction, and because she had hated her child in her own fear of rejection, and because she had sowed guilt into her mind.

28 When her mother went to bed and closed the door, the child, who had been waiting for long, left the bed. She crossed the corridor on her tiptoes, past the row of shoes, the silent gathering of the overcoats and the mirror with the wavy surface, and went into the washroom. Behind the door was another mirror, of full length, and clear. Deliberately and slowly the child took off the top of her pajamas and surveyed herself with grave scrutiny. She saw the brownness of her skin, the wide, staring, dark eyes, the black hair now tousled from the pillows, the scar on her nose and the brownish pink of her mouth. She stood a while lost in this act of contemplation, until the sound of soft padded feet neared the door, and a whiskered face peeped in. She stooped and picked up the cat and walked back to her own room.

[. . .]

29 It was snowing again, and little elves with bright coloured coats and snow in their boots had reappeared in the classroom. When finally the coats were hung under pegs with names and boots neatly stowed away, the little girl approached her teacher. She had her painting from the day before in her hand.

30 "I have brought it back," she said.

31 "Why?" asked her teacher, "don't you like it any more?"

32 The little girl was looking around very intently.

33 "It's not finished yet," she said. "The books I looked at didn't have something. Can I finish it now?"

34 "Go ahead," said the teacher, moving on to get the colours from the cupboard.

35 The little girl was looking at the classroom. It was full of children of all colours, of all kinds of shapes of noses and of different colours of hair. She sat on the floor, placed the incomplete picture on a big piece of newspaper and started to paint. She worked long at it—and with great concentration. Finally it was finished. She went back to her teacher.

36 "It's finished now," she said, "I drew the rest."

37 The teacher reached out for the picture and spread it neatly on a desk. There they were, the blond family arranged in a semicircle with a dip in the middle, but next to them, arranged alike, stood another group—a man, a woman, and a child, but they were dark-skinned, dark-haired, the woman wore clothes from her own country, and the little girl in the middle had a scar on her nose.

38 "Do you like it?"

39 "Who are they?" asked the teacher, though she should have known. But the little girl didn't mind answering this question one bit.

40 "It's the other family," she said.

## Glossary

**insubstantial:** Not large in size or amount; weak.

**contemplated:** Looked at or considered in a calm, reflective manner.

**ultimate:** Last, final.

**incoherent:** Unable to speak intelligibly.

## Comprehension Questions

1. Is there mutual respect between mother and daughter? Cite the evidence.
2. What was the immediate thing that upset the little girl's mother when she saw the first picture her daughter had drawn?
3. Of what does the author say the mother was afraid? Where is the evidence in the story of this?
4. How did the little girl resolve the issue?

## Questions about Form

1. Is this an essay or a story? Explain.
2. Although this piece is told in third-person narration, is the narrator more knowledgeable about a particular character? Explain.
3. Does the author make effective use of transitions in this story? Give three examples of transitions.
4. How does the extensive usage of quotations affect the story?

## Questions for Discussion

1. Because this piece is fictional, the thesis of the author is far from explicit. What do you think, in your own words, is the author's thesis? What evidence would you cite from the story in support of your answer?
2. How does the fear that the mother experiences in this story relate to the idea of young people dating people of other races and religions? How do problems in this area tend to get resolved?

### Writing Ideas

1. How important are pictures and words when it comes to helping people develop strong self-esteem? Write a paragraph or essay supporting your answer.
2. As this story is about the conflict between the desire to fit in and the fear of losing one's identity, write a paragraph or essay in which you discuss a personal experience that relates to this story, and explain how your own situation was resolved.

✦ ✦ ✦

## How R Tngz, Dude?

*Colin Campbell*

The popularity of the cell phone is growing every day, especially among young people. Besides possible long-term effects on health (see the sample research paper beginning on page 244), what are its psychological and sociological effects? In the following article published in *Maclean's* magazine on December 21, 2005, Colin Campbell takes a look at the research of a Japanese primate expert whose findings are less than flattering and less than optimistic.

1 Teenagers are acting a lot like monkeys these days, says Nobuo Masataka, a professor at Kyoto University in Japan. This may not exactly qualify as news for many parents struggling to rear teenage children, but Masataka isn't talking in metaphors. The noted **primate** expert is being quite literal when he says, "The behaviour of the young generation is very similar to monkeys'." The reason, he adds, is the cellphone—and Masataka, who calls himself a fan of **Marshall McLuhan,** has struck a chord in Japan with his theory. A book he wrote on the subject, called *Monkeys with Mobiles,* has sold 200,000 copies since it came out two years ago. And it all comes down to that **ubiquitous** piece of technology, which has been blamed for making us worse drivers and less considerate people (who speak loudly in restaurants, buses and movie theatres).

2 Cellphones, explains Masataka, have given teenagers a freedom from their parents and family life like never before. As a result, teens in Japan are spending their days hanging out in the same old places, with no particular destination in mind and no need to show up at an appointed time to eat or rest—just like the monkeys he studies. Teens have, in effect, extended their living rooms to the streets, he says. "They behave in public spaces as if they're living in private rooms," Masataka notes in a phone interview from his lab at Kyoto's Primate Research Institute. "They are not conscious of the audience." And Japanese parents, he adds, aren't concerned, since they assume their children are always just a phone call away.

3 North Americans might say this is merely part of the teenage ritual of hanging out at the mall or loitering, and has been part of teenage life long before cellphones. But the cellphone has made this type of behaviour easier—and more prevalent, Masataka contends. "Monkeys frequently communicate with one another with 'coo' calls. The function is to maintain group **cohesion.** This is very similar to the use of mobile phones among teenagers. They send messages with mobile phones. They don't communicate any meaningful content—it's about group cohesion."

4 Masataka's book is based largely on his casual observations, often while riding on the train and from interviews with teenagers. But there may be some valid science backing his argument. "The role of adolescence is an **emancipation** process," says Richard Ling, a visiting scholar at the University of Michigan who has written a book on the impact of cellphones on society. Teens need to break away from their parents, and one of the ways they do this is by spending time in peer groups, which allows them to develop their own identity. "The mobile telephone has made access to that sphere much easier," says Ling, who is also a researcher at Telenor Research and Development in Norway, where he has done extensive surveys on teens and cellphone use. "The mobile telephone gives teens direct access to each other wherever they want, however they want." And, he adds, the cellphone's ability to **colonize** public space and make it private is also "clearly one of the things that we're having to get used to"—although whether that makes us more like monkeys is beyond his expertise, he jokes.

5 Masataka is not optimistic about the future of youth in his country given the growth of mobile technologies, something that may not bode well for Canada, where cellphones are now in the hands of over half the population, and where their use has doubled in the past five years. Masataka argues that teens who have grown up with television, video games and now cellphones aren't forced to develop complex social skills. In difficult situations they tend to lash out aggressively, another similarity to his monkey subjects. "They don't have the opportunity to acquire socialization. They behave always as if they live at home, like couch potatoes."

## Glossary

**primate:** Of the highest group of mammals, including humans, apes, and monkeys.

**Marshall McLuhan:** University of Toronto English literature professor and communications theorist who pointed out that in spite of the benefits of modern media technology, the world would also be forced to deal with its unintended consequences.

**ubiquitous:** Omnipresent; being or seeming to be everywhere at the same time.

**cohesion:** The act of forming a united and consistent whole.

**emancipation:** The state of being freed from any bond or restraint.

**colonize:** To migrate to and settle in; to occupy as a colony (a group of people of the same nationality in a foreign town).

## Comprehension Questions

1. In what ways, according to the article, do teenagers resemble monkeys because of cell phones?
2. What is the Japanese researcher's evidence for his conclusions?
3. What is a positive role that the cell phone plays in the teenager's growing process, according to Richard Ling, a visiting scholar at the University of Michigan?

## Questions about Form

1. Why do you think this article was given such an ungrammatical title?
2. Is the ungrammatical title effective? Why or why not?
3. How does the author tie the issue in the article to Canada? What could he have written to make the connection seem tighter?

## Questions for Discussion

1. Compare and contrast this article with the sample research paper in Chapter 20: "Cell Phones: Tomorrow's Medical Menace?" (beginning on p. 244).
2. Does your experience with people on cell phones support or refute the conclusions proposed by the primate expert in this article? Discuss.

## Writing Ideas

1. Write a paragraph or essay supporting or criticizing the use of cell phones today.
2. Interview someone who "survived" his or her teen years and early adulthood without a cell phone. Does your interviewee think he or she would have been happier with a cell phone during those years? Why or why not? Discuss your findings in a paragraph or essay.

✦ ✦ ✦

# SELLING ILLUSIONS

*Neil Bissoondath*

Novelist, short story writer, and essayist Neil Bissoondath was born in Arima, Trinidad, in 1955, and now lives in Canada. The following piece is an excerpt from his book entitled *Selling Illusions: The Cult of Multiculturalism in Canada,* published in 1994. As this piece indicates, Bissoondath exhibits some strong feelings about multiculturalism in Canada and how perhaps it's not what it is purported to be. In the following piece, he relates his experience as an eighteen-year-old who has just come to Canada to attend York University.

1 If the York University campus was a safe haven from which to discover the pleasures of Canada, ... it was also the place where I first encountered reasons for unease.

2 York operates on a college system. New students choose, or are assigned to, one of the various colleges on the campus. Unfamiliar with the system, ignorant of the purposes behind the individual colleges, I allowed myself to be assigned to Bethune College.

3 Familiarity with the college brought a certain dismay. Bethune College, named in honour of **Dr. Norman Bethune,** is an institution devoted to Third World studies; it had a certain reputation for left-wing radicalism. The reason for my dismay was simple: my major was to be French language and literature. The bilingual Glendon College, my logical "home," was never mentioned. I can only assume that I was enrolled at Bethune in part because I had come from a Third World country and in part because my adviser assumed that I would be most comfortable in an environment where a high percentage of students were, like me, non-white. It was an assuredly benign assumption, one made with the best of intentions, but also with no regard to my personal beliefs or intellectual interests. My adviser, then, had looked at me through the lens of her own stereotype and guided me according to the presumed comforts of "sticking with your own."

4 Although I was not at first aware of it, the concept of "sticking with your own" was just then in vogue at York. This became clear the moment you entered the main cafeteria at Central Square in the massive concrete bunker of the Ross Building. It was large and brashly lit, institutional in character, a place for feeding oneself rather than enjoying a meal. I remember it as a loud and busy place, brash with the sounds of trays and cutlery roughly handled, of a multitude of voices blended into a steady roar.

5 And yet, it seemed a benign atmosphere, friendly in an impersonal way. The controlled chaos offered an anonymity that would ease the task of inserting oneself, of fitting in. Or so it seemed at first.

6 Chaos is always subtly ordered, and it did not require a very discerning eye to decode the chaos of the Central Square cafeteria. Indeed, a map could be drawn, various sections coloured in to denote defined areas. To highlight, for instance, the table at which Chinese students congregated behind a wall of Cantonese; or

the tables over in the corner protected by the raucous enthusiasm of West Indian accents; or the table more subtly framed by **yarmulkes** and Star of David pendants.

7 To approach any of these tables was to intrude on a clannish exclusivity. It was to challenge the unofficially designated territory of tables parcelled out so that each group, whether racially, culturally or religiously defined, could enjoy its little enclave, its own little "homeland," so to speak, protected by unspoken **prerogatives.**

8 The idea of "sticking with your own" was reinforced by various student organizations, many of which were financially assisted by the university. Controversy arose at one point when an application for membership in the Black Students' Federation was received from a student—a writer for the campus newspaper, as it turned out—whose skin colour seemed to disqualify him. Questions arose: Was being black a prerequisite for belonging to the Black Students' Federation? Or was a commitment to the issues raised by the association sufficient justification for belonging? Just how relevant was skin colour, how relevant cultural background, how relevant political belief?

9 A hint of the complexity of the question may be discerned in a story once told to me by a friend. One afternoon, he stopped in at his favourite coffee house in Toronto's Kensington Market, a small place brightly decorated in the tropical style. It featured reggae music and the rich Blue Mountain coffee from Jamaica. As he sipped his coffee, he eavesdropped on a conversation at the table behind him, three young men, evidently musicians, discussing their next gig. My friend understood little of what was said—their thick Jamaican accents made their words **undecipherable**—but he enjoyed listening to their speech in the same way that he enjoyed the sounds of reggae. Cup empty, he rose to leave. On his way out he glanced at the men and with delight saw, as he put it, "one black guy with dreadlocks and two white guys with blond hair and blue eyes." An encounter, then, with the wickedness of history. He left the coffee house thrilled at abandoning the wreckage of a stereotype.

10 The issue at York was eventually settled by the decision to admit the white student to the Federation—not on the grounds that race was irrelevant but that, as an organization financially assisted by the university, it had to respect the university's regulations prohibiting discrimination on the grounds of race and colour. I did not belong to the Federation, but the resolution was pleasing anyway, even though there was a tincture of discomfort at the way in which it had come about: through technicality, and not through the application of principle. None of the real questions had been grappled with, none answered.

11 Questions of segregation and **exclusivity** kept raising their heads. One day a Jewish friend invited me to join him for coffee in the Jewish Students' Federation lounge. I was reluctant—the lounge seemed to me governed by even stronger proscriptions than the table in the cafeteria—but he insisted. As he fixed us each a coffee, he said in a voice clearly intended for others in the room that I should feel free to help myself from the coffee-machine at any time. And then he added

in strained tones that the lounge, provided by the university, was open to all: I was to ignore anyone who tried to stop me. It was in this way that he sought to make me part of unsuspected **internecine** tensions, while publicly declaring his own position.

12 The issues made me wary: I neither joined the Black Students' Federation nor revisited the Jewish Students' Federation lounge. I learned instead to keep my distance from the tables that would have welcomed me not as an individual but as an individual of a certain skin colour, with a certain accent, with a certain assumed cultural outlook—the tables that would have welcomed me not for *who* I was and for what I could do but for *what* I was and for what they presumed I represented. I had not come here, I decided, in order to join a ghetto.

13 Alone in a new land, I faced inevitable questions. Questions about my past and my present, about the land left behind and the land newly found, about the nature of this society and my place in it. At eighteen, about to embark on a new life, I felt these to be weighty issues.

14 For many people at those cafeteria tables, though, these were questions of no great importance. They were almost aggressive in dismissing any discomfort they might have experienced by flaunting the only government policy that seemed to arouse no resentment: Canada as a multicultural land. Officially. Legally. Here, they insisted, you did not have to change. Here you could—indeed, it was your duty to—remain what you were. None of this American melting-pot nonsense, none of this remaking yourself to fit your new circumstances: you did not have to adjust to the society, the society was obligated to accommodate itself to you.

15 An attractive proposal, then, a policy that excused much and required little effort. And yet I found myself not easily seduced.

16 The problem was that I had come in search of a new life and a new way of looking at the world, "to expand my horizons" (to use a cliché) from the narrow perspectives of my youth in Trinidad. I had no desire to transport here life as I had known it: this seemed to me particularly onerous baggage with which to burden one's shoulders. Beyond this, though, the very act of emigration had already changed me. I was no longer the same person who had boarded the aircraft in Trinidad bound for Toronto: I had brought with me not the attitudes of the tourist but those of someone embarking on an adventure that would forever change his life. This alone was a kind of psychological revolution.

17 Multiculturalism, as perceived by those at whom it was most explicitly aimed, left me with a certain measure of discomfort.

18 At the end of my first university year, I returned to Trinidad to visit my parents. It wasn't long before I was impatient to get back to Toronto. This had to do in part with the realization that, even after so short a time, old friends had become new strangers, and that old places had remained simply old places. More importantly, though, the desire to return had to do with me and with the life I had begun constructing in my adopted city. I relished the freedom this life offered, the liberation of the anonymity of the big city. I had made new friends—some of them from among "my own kind," some not—and had found all the

books, magazines and films denied me in Trinidad. I had, for the first time in my life, found a place other than my parents' house that I wished to call home: a place where I could be myself.

19 Sharing this with those who wished me to bolster their ethnic bastion in Toronto made me distinctly unpopular. I was seen as a kind of traitor, unwilling to play the game by indulging in a life best described as "Caribbean North." If there was any **alienation**, it came not from the society at large but from those who saw themselves as the front-line practitioners of multiculturalism. By establishing cultural and racial exclusivity, they were doing their bit to preserve the multicultural character of the country, while I, seeking to go beyond the confines of my cultural heritage, was seen as acting counter to those interests.

20 To put it succinctly, they coveted the segregated tables of the cafeteria, while I sought a place at tables that would accommodate a greater variety.

## Glossary

**Dr. Norman Bethune:** A Canadian surgeon and international humanitarian revered in China for his heroic and selfless treatment of the wounded in that country's struggle for a republic. He died of blood poisoning in 1939.

**yarmulkes:** Skullcaps often worn by male Jews, especially during prayer and religious functions.

**prerogatives:** Exclusive rights or privileges.

**undecipherable:** Unable to be understood.

**exclusivity:** The act of shutting out.

**internecine:** Of or relating to a struggle within a nation, an organization, or a group.

**alienation:** Feeling estranged from one's social environment.

## Comprehension Questions

1. What does Bissoondath mean by what he refers to as the "homeland" in paragraph 7? Why does he not want to join the "homelands"?
2. Why does Bissoondath think he was assigned to Bethune College?
3. What was really happening, according to Bissoondath, when his Jewish friend served him a coffee in the Jewish Students' Federation lounge?
4. What is the story told to Bissoondath by his friend who visited Toronto's Kensington Market? What is the meaning of it? How does it support Bissoondath's overall thesis?

## Questions about Form

1. What does Bissoondath include in this piece that helps you to identify with his concerns?
2. What is the setting of Bissoondath's essay? Does this help to make the piece more effective? Why or why not?
3. What is the author doing in the last paragraph of this piece? Is it effective? Why or why not?

## Questions for Discussion

1. Do "homelands," as Bissoondath would define them, exist at your school? What do you think are the reasons they exist there? Do they do more harm than good as Bissoondath suggests?
2. Do you generally "stick" with people "of your own kind"? From your own experience, what are the advantages and disadvantages of this behaviour of yours?
3. Are there clubs at your school that seem exclusive to people of a certain skin colour, religion, or nationality? Would they refuse to accept a student who wanted to join if this student didn't seem to "belong"? Is this a violation of human rights law?
4. Judging only by this essay, what would you say is the author's attitude toward multiculturalism in this country? Do you agree with it? Why or why not?
5. Do you think Canadians in general are less racist than Americans? Why or why not? What in this article by Bissoondath supports your answer?

## Writing Ideas

1. In a paragraph or essay, argue whether you think multiculturalism, the way it is promoted at your school, contributes to or combats racism.
2. In a paragraph or essay, argue whether or not a club should be able to offer exclusivity to people of only one skin colour, or one nationality or religion, etc.
3. Imagine you are creating your own college/university cultural club. In view of Bissoondath's concerns, what would the basic guidelines regarding membership of your new club be? Support them in a paragraph or essay.
4. Identify a club or society that seems to be exclusive to your race, religion, or nationality. Write a paragraph or essay supporting or criticizing this perception of exclusivity.

✦ ✦ ✦

# LESSONS OF LOVE FROM STORIES OF OLD

*Gary Lipschutz*

Ideas we have about love are often harmful. According to the author of this argumentative essay, we get some of these ideas from the popular misinterpretations of stories—stories we've known and embraced since childhood. The stories themselves might have a great deal of wisdom to offer, but, unfortunately, these stories often are misinterpreted by a society that is generally lazy and materialistic. And the result is damage in our lives around the whole issue of love. In this essay written in 2003, Lipschutz, who teaches mythology and English at Toronto's Centennial College, not only blames "external sources" (religious organizations, businesses, the media, etc.) for this damage, but also those among us who would listen to them. Most tragic, he says, is that these misinterpretations too often defy what is in our own hearts.

1 Why is it that the very thing so many people want so badly is the one thing they never seem to find? Why is it that people, young and old, spend so much time on chat lines, so much money on dating services and so much energy obsessing over the "perfect" love and/or marriage? Why is it that the success rate of getting these things is pretty low?

2 Well, did it ever occur to you that our ideas about love are often unrealistic? We may get some of them from movies, from TV sitcoms, and worse, I dare say, from so-called reality TV shows such as *The Bachelor* or *Joe Millionaire* (a title that, in itself, suggests less-than-virtuous values). How often do we ask why the media seem to sell the idea that fashion, sex appeal and money are the most important parts of any relationship?

3 One reason for these false and damaging ideas is **commercialism.** Large businesses spend inordinate amounts of money on research into the human psyche. They know that "sex sells." They know that in their appeal to the sexual urges of a person, especially the person within a certain age range, they are more likely to exert influence over the consumer's buying choices. But is there an adverse if **inadvertent** effect as well? Do these ads in any way cause us to go after certain things in relationships that are inaccessible, things that have absolutely nothing to do with love and therefore things that do not contribute to the staying power of a relationship?

4 Advertisements and "reality" TV shows are not the only things brainwashing us. We've all grown up with certain stories: stories from religious scripture, fairy tales such as "Sleeping Beauty" and "Cinderella" and Shakespearean plays such as *Romeo and Juliet.* Most of us are familiar with the latest cinematic rendition of *Titanic,* especially the love story in it that took place between Jack and Rose.

5 Why are such stories so predominant in our lives? They help to maintain our hopes and dreams when it comes to the very thing we want the most: love, no, the perfect love. But the problem is they probably cause more harm than good, even if the intentions of those who make them up are honourable. The problem is not

the stories themselves. The problem lies in the interpretation of these stories. Let's look at a classic example of misinterpretation of the story "Sleeping Beauty."

6 Everyone knows more or less what happens in "Sleeping Beauty," regardless of the version to which one was exposed. *A king and queen give birth to a daughter after many years of trying. Upon the girl's birth, the king is so overjoyed, he decides to hold a great feast to which he invites many people. There are 13 wise women in his kingdom, but the king only invites 12 because he had only 12 golden plates from which they could eat. To get revenge for not being invited, the thirteenth "wise" (and scornful) woman arrives at the feast and cries out, "In her fifteenth year, the princess shall prick herself with a spindle and fall down dead!"*

7 *By the time this thirteenth wise woman had cursed the princess, 11 wise women who were invited had given gifts to the princess, but the twelfth had not yet spoken. Although she could not undo the evil spell, she could, however, soften it with a wish: "The princess shall not die," she said. "Instead, she shall fall into a deep sleep for one hundred years."*

8 Of course, it's the following part, more than any other, for which the whole story is known and loved:

9 *After the princess's 100-year slumber was over, a prince approaches the sleeping beauty and kisses her lips. She awakens, smiles at him fondly, and they, of course, marry each other and live happily ever after.*

10 Before discussing the interpretation of "Sleeping Beauty," it's first necessary to note the difference between an interpretation that is literal and one that is symbolic. Understanding the difference may result in a very different way of understanding not only "Sleeping Beauty," but also most other stories regardless of their source.

11 People who take things **literally** take what is spoken or written at face value. Even when it comes to religious scripture, Joseph Campbell, world-renowned mythologist, says that most of us belong to two schools of thought: in one school, there are those who believe the stories of religious scripture are true because they're believers of the miraculous; yes, Moses parted the Red Sea with his hands, or yes, Jesus raised Lazarus from the dead simply because the scriptural texts say so. And in the second school of thought, there are those who do not believe in these types of miracles simply because they are unrealistic. In other words, the difference as to whether people "believe" in scripture or not seems to depend on what they believe has literally happened two or three thousand years ago. Whether they believe in miracles or not, most people take these stories literally.

12 What if a third situation were possible? Those who study mythology may realize that myth (including religious stories) is not meant to be interpreted literally, but symbolically. In other words, things that are spoken or written might be meant to represent ideas, usually relating to some aspect of our humanity, that are otherwise difficult to understand. In fact, originally, the word myth did not mean "falsehood" the way it does today. The word myth referred to (and still does for those who are educated in the area) a story about the divine mysteries of life, thus the letters "MY..." suggesting MYstery or **MYstical.** In this context, the body of mythology is not just about Greek gods and Celtic wizards, but also heroes such as Moses of the Old Testament and Jesus of the New and, by extension, ALL of the characters of stories in every religion of the world, bar none. All such stories shed light on the mystery of humanity. They all include characters of the divine. Symbolically speaking, it could be argued that Moses represents every person in the world who eventually gets called by a higher power to do something heroic and can succeed against insurmountable odds if the holy deed is faced with a great deal of courage and conviction. Did Moses actually part the Red Sea? Only those who are literalists care, not to mention those who are bent on insisting their religion is superior to all others. The difference between "our" truth and "their" truth is what unfortunately causes **acrimony** among the religions of the world. Many present-day wars are testimony to this unfortunate side of our human nature.

13 What if the messages of these divine stories, regardless of whether we relegate them to myth, religion or fairy tales, are the same? Undeniably, regardless of interpretation, they all seem to have certain messages in common: Arrogance and selfishness are bad. Humility and sacrifice are good. Treat your neighbour as

yourself. (And don't forget, your neighbour might be of a different skin colour or religious background or social class—a detail that too often gets lost in people's interpretations, sometimes for evil reasons.) Be fair and kind to people. Don't kill people (unless you are 100 per cent sure your killing them is in self-defence). Don't lie because, as psychiatrist and prolific author M. Scott Peck (famous for his book called *The Road Less Traveled*) says in his book *People of the Lie*, the lie is the very root of human evil. Judge a person by her or his character and not on the basis of how much money he makes or how intelligent he is or how beautiful she is on the outside. And one's character, to quote the wizard in *Harry Potter and the Chamber of Secrets*, is determined not by a person's abilities but by her or his choices. Wouldn't the world be a better place if we all recognized that all these stories are telling us not only the same things, but that the important things in life are things universal to human consciousness? Doesn't it make more sense to concentrate on our similarities rather than our differences? Is religion meant to unite or divide us? Is the answer not obvious?

14 And what about Sleeping Beauty's never-ending naptime? Bruno Bettelheim, famous child psychologist and psychological interpreter of children's literature, said that what's important among other things is what Sleeping Beauty's 100-year slumber symbolizes or represents. Why, for that matter, is the 100-year sleep important at all? Literally speaking, nobody sleeps for 100 years. Then this part of the story has no meaning, right? Wrong! It has a world of meaning if it's interpreted symbolically. A cigar, symbolically speaking, is never a cigar. The 100-year sleep, it could be argued, should be the focal point of the story. The title, after all, is "*Sleeping* Beauty."

15 A more prevalent reason for ignoring the significance of the centennial snooze is that it seems to have nothing to do with the message of this story that most people desperately want to cling to: that a woman must be rescued by a man. (The first time I shot down the "rescuing" message of "Sleeping Beauty" in a class I was teaching, a young female student stormed out of the room in angry protest and promptly proceeded to drop my course.) Too many of us think, or at least hope, the rescuing part is realistic because we're basically selfish (or chauvinistic if we're male) and lazy. Too many women want to be "rescued," and too many men think they have to do the "rescuing." And that, to too many men, means making lots of money and perhaps getting a hair transplant or wearing thousand-dollar suits because if you don't look like a prince and you don't own a white horse (in modern-day terms, an expensive car and/or a condo), Sleeping Beauty won't even look at you, much less ride off with you into the sunset.

16 If the wedding of Prince Charles and Princess Diana seemed like a "fairy tale," their lives together certainly did not. Why did Sleeping Beauty and her prince get to ride off into the sunset, while Princess Diana and her lover (a lover other than her dashing prince) died a violent death? Why did a life for the world's favourite royal start out as a fairy tale and end up in a fiery and fatal car crash? Wasn't Diana meant to be "rescued" by her charming (not to mention, rich) prince?

17 If Sleeping Beauty doesn't look at you because you don't dress fashionably or you don't have a full head of hair or you don't have a nice car and condo, she's

not worth your time because these things have absolutely nothing to do with love. She may be attracted to you for your sense of style, your hair, or your money, and she may feel like she's being "saved" from poverty, or her parents, or both, but she will only stay with you until she finds a richer or better looking prince or until you lose your money or, better yet, until you leave her first when you finally realize what your "princess's values" really are.

18 The 100-year slumber, according to Bettelheim, represents a stage in a person's life (not just a female's) during which she must develop her own mind away from her parents and away from her friends. Call it mental and emotional downtime or a physical or inner journey to "find oneself," an accounting of the soul, whatever you wish. The point is, too often young people make the biggest mistakes in their lives because they don't listen to an inner voice. It's much easier to "take the path of least resistance" and do what your parents tell you in order to make them happy. It's easier to follow your friends' advice; after all, they have your best interests in mind, right? Actually they probably don't, even if they don't realize it themselves. Thomas Hobbes, a 17th-century social theorist, said that people are basically selfish. And chances are we haven't gotten less selfish in the last 400 years. If anything, with more affluence in our lives, with the Internet and other types of "instantly gratifying technology" at our fingertips, we're more selfish than ever. So when we tell our friends what they should do, we're actually telling them what WE want them to do. If we were real friends, we'd try to find out what they want and then support them unconditionally.

19 When Sleeping Beauty wakes up from her 100-year slumber, she's grown. She hasn't grown old physically, of course. If she had, Prince Charming would not be kissing her, right? But how else has she grown? Having spent the time BY herself, she's learned ABOUT herself. She's "slept," which might symbolize she's spent time understanding her **unconscious,** the voice inside, the voice we tend to hear when we turn off the cell phone, the TV and the computer—the noise and chatter we hear every day. Technology makes it even more difficult than ever before to shut out the noise. For this reason, the message of the 100-year sleep in "Sleeping Beauty" becomes more relevant today than ever. We all desperately need this downtime, this distance from the noise, if we're ever going to know what our own hearts are saying. There are two problems, as I see it. First, we don't take the time or make the effort to challenge our assumptions of the interpretations of most stories, especially ones with which we've grown up. Second, even if we did, and even if people did understand what Bettelheim was trying to say, shutting out the noise of our cell phones, the TV and our computers would still be too difficult, the usual excuse made by spiritually lazy and unawakened people.

20 "Sleeping Beauty," simply put, is not about a princess being "rescued" by a prince; it's about the importance of a **spiritual awakening.** After all, the story is called "Sleeping Beauty" (becoming beautiful from self-knowledge), not "The Poor Girl Who Turns into a Princess Because She Gets Rescued by a Rich Man." Don't forget Diana wasn't even poor to begin with. And secondly, if she were "rescued," one would think she'd live to see forty.

21 When Sleeping Beauty awoke, having learned who she was and what she really wants, she was then, and only then, able to *recognize* the right man for her. The prince doesn't rescue her; she saves her own soul by choosing the man she is meant to be with because she now knows who that man is, and she has the courage to go after him regardless of what her friends or family might say or do. To her, this right man *becomes* her prince. This prince will look handsome and rich not because he's got model-good looks and drives a Jaguar or BMW but because to her, the princess who now knows what's right for herself, the man whom she has recognized as the right one LOOKS handsome, and he SEEMS rich, but in non-material ways. That, after all, is the story of *Titanic.* Rose saved her own soul when she dumped the rich, handsome fiancé (the one her mother wanted her to marry) and made the commitment to love a penniless man whom she had just met. She *knew* he was her soulmate. Nobody else could tell her this, certainly not her mother. Those who take the time to learn about themselves and follow their own hearts once they realize what their hearts are saying—it is they who have grown up. It is they who have lived their own authentic lives. It is they who are rich.

## Glossary

**commercialism:** Emphasis on financial profit as a measure of worth.

**inadvertent:** Unintentional.

**literally:** Taking what is spoken or written at face value, without symbolic interpretation.

**mystical:** Of spiritual truth beyond human understanding.

**acrimony:** Bitter disagreement, hostility.

**unconscious:** Part of the mind of which we are unaware, but which is largely responsible for our emotions, behaviour, etc.

**spiritual awakening:** New awareness of the importance of soul as opposed to physical things.

## Comprehension Questions

1. What ideas, according to the author, do most people have about love?
2. What causes people to have these ideas?
3. How do most people interpret "Sleeping Beauty"?
4. What is different about Bruno Bettelheim's interpretation of "Sleeping Beauty"?
5. Why did the author's student walk out of his class in anger?
6. What does the author mean by the last sentence in the essay: "It is they who are rich"?

## Questions about Form

1. What does the author do to make this essay effective?
2. What are the intended audience and purpose of this essay?
3. Why do you think the author mentions the movie *Titanic*?
4. Why are paragraphs 6, 7, and 9 largely in italics?

## Questions for Discussion

1. What is the more believable fairy tale in our society, "Sleeping Beauty" or "Beauty and the Beast"? Why?
2. What is your definition of the perfect love?
3. Where do you think your idea (in your answer to question 2) of this definition comes from?
4. Do you think the perfect love according to your definition exists?
5. Compare this essay to "Don Juan/Doña Juana" by Rosemary Sullivan. What do they have in common? How do they differ?
6. Woody Allen, a very controversial film director/actor on the celebrity love scene (because of his marriage to the adopted daughter of his former partner, Mia Farrow), once interviewed a seemingly happy couple on the street in one of his movies. He asked to what they attributed their happiness as a couple. The male of the couple responded that they were both superficial: they both loved talking about fashion and other materialistic interests that they had in common. Do you think Woody Allen is saying these two people are likely to stay happy as a couple? Do you agree with him? Why or why not?

## Writing Ideas

1. In a paragraph or essay, explain where people get their ideas of love.
2. In a paragraph or essay, identify the story that you believe best illustrates your ideas about love, and explain why.
3. What are the most important things in a relationship? What often attracts us first to the one we want to date? Why do the answers to these questions often cause trouble later on? Based on your answers to the above questions, write a paragraph or essay in which you discuss the reasons behind the breakdown of many relationships.

✦ ✦ ✦

# Bad Girls

*Shari Graydon*

Shari Graydon is a writer, educator, and media analyst living in Vancouver. She's been the press secretary for former B.C. premier Ujjal Dosanjh, and she's been the president of MediaWatch, a nonprofit women's group that monitors the media for sexist content. For the *Vancouver Sun,* she's been a columnist, and for WTN, she's produced a 13-part TV series about women and media. In this piece from *Homemaker's* magazine (1999), Graydon interviews one of the murderers of Reena Virk, a B.C. teen violently murdered by a group of her classmates.

1 Dressed in a baggy T-shirt, cotton pants and runners, her long, wavy hair gelled and falling around her shoulders, she looks like an ordinary teenager. The stories she tells me about being spoiled as a child, rebelling as a young teen against her mom and hanging out at the mall with her friends sound like pretty common teenage experiences. Yet she spent her "Sweet 16" birthday behind bars, locked up in one of British Columbia's closed custody units for youth. "Janice" (the Young Offenders Act prohibits publication of her real name) is in jail for her part in the brutal murder of 14-year-old Reena Virk in November, 1997, an event that stunned the nation and prompted "Bad Girl" headlines coast to coast. About life in the detention centre, she says, "It's not so bad; I already knew lots of the kids."

2 The vicious attack leading to Virk's murder by a group of teenagers in a middle-class suburb of Victoria wasn't the first such incident to make headlines. In recent years stories of teen violence—usually involving testosterone-pumped boys carried away by their own misplaced **machismo**—have disturbed us all.

3 What made Reena Virk's case so shocking was that seven out of eight of the kids who participated in butting out a cigarette on her forehead, and punching and kicking her until she was dazed and bleeding, were girls. And one of them is alleged to have returned to the scene of the initial attack with a male friend, battered Virk unconscious and thrown her in the river, where she drowned, her body discovered a week later.

4 In the wake of **burgeoning** news reports about girl-to-girl violence, the case **galvanized** growing concerns across the country about just what young women are up to these days. The answer appears to be "No good." Statistics Canada reported in July that while the overall crime rate fell for the sixth consecutive year, it escalated among teenage girls by five per cent. The big picture seems to be even more alarming: from 1987 to 1997 the number of young women charged with violent crime grew from about 900 to 4,800, a staggering five-fold increase and twice that of same-aged boys.

5 Despite these figures and sensational Bad Girl headlines, the jury's still out on how widespread the problem is. For one thing, the actual numbers are relatively small: 1997's five per cent increase brought the rate to 472 offences per 100,000 population. That compares with 1,328 per 100,000 among male offenders,

which represents a four per cent drop from the previous year. For another, two-thirds of those charges were for minor assault, involving hitting or shoving that didn't result in bodily harm. The aggravated assault charges laid against the girls who attacked Reena Virk represented less than one per cent of the violent offence charges in that year.

6 Experts also point out that the numbers have risen because more charges are being laid. Alan Markwart, director of the Youth Justice team with the B.C. Ministry for Children and Families, attributes this in part to the "zero tolerance" policies now popular in schools struggling to deal with student violence. "Cases formerly dealt with by school principals are now more likely to result in legal charges," he says. He also speculates that police may be less inclined today to dismiss physical aggression between two girls as merely a "cat fight." Instead, they've begun to apply to girls the same standards used to determine the seriousness of crimes committed by boys.

7 **Mitigating** factors notwithstanding, criminologists and youth workers say that teenage girls are much more likely these days to express their anger over trivial things—and in increasingly physical ways. Once-persistent "sugar and spice" cultural stereotypes are dying hard as researchers point to evidence showing that girls have always felt just as much anger as boys; they've just been encouraged to channel their aggression into more socially acceptable "feminine" behaviors—like gossiping, name-calling and excluding the kids they want to punish. That girls are now expressing their anger physically is largely a sign of the times, attributable to the growing acceptance of violence in the teenage subculture. Studies have shown that exposure to violence can lead to increased violent behavior on the part of girls, desensitizing them to the point where they no longer feel emotional distress.

8 But the attack on Reena Virk was so frenzied—the girl's skull was fractured, her back broken—the issue takes on confounding proportions. How can young girls be capable of such shocking cruelty? What's going on in their heads?

9 Prying answers out of Janice isn't easy. Throughout our conversation, she is distracted by the comings and goings of people on the other side of the Plexiglas wall. At one point she interrupts herself to declare with pride, "That was my boyfriend who just walked by."

10 When I ask her about the night that Reena Virk died, I can tell that she doesn't really want to think—let alone talk—about what happened. But she does tell me that the source of the conflict was her belief that Virk had spread rumors about her and messed around with her boyfriend.

11 She says that the testimony and news stories describing her and a friend as "luring" Reena Virk to the site of a planned attack were false. "Fights happen every day," she says. "It just got out of hand."

12 Judging by the experiences of Stacey and Camille (pseudonyms), two Vancouver-area girls who have been on both the delivery and receiving ends of teen violence, the circumstances leading to Reena Virk's death were chillingly common. Rumors, jealousy, competition over boyfriends, they say, are the issues

most likely to ignite a fight among teenage girls. As to why more and more of those fights seem to be escalating into physical aggression, Stacey says: "You want to look big in front of your friends, to have a 'Don't mess with me' attitude. And if someone goes after you, you can't just sit there and take it."

13 Dr. Sibylle Artz, director of the School of Child and Youth Care at the University of Victoria, has authored one of the few studies of violence among teenage girls. Her book, *Sex, Power and the Violent School Girl* (Trifolium Books, 1998), provides insights into the profile of the "typical" violent teenage girl.

14 Violent girls often emerge from home lives in which they've been physically, sexually and/or emotionally abused, experienced significant alienation from at least one parent and observed chronic drug or alcohol misuse.

15 Not surprisingly, staying focused in school and fitting in generally are often a challenge for these kids, who quickly gravitate towards other teenagers with similar backgrounds. The subculture that develops reflects the same kinds of conflict and substance abuse that they see at home. And belonging to the rebel group becomes a desperate survival issue.

16 As Camille sees it, "If you're not getting attention at home, your friends—and belonging—are really important. You basically do whatever's necessary to get talked about"—including violence—"because attention, even if it's negative, is better than nothing."

17 This sounds perverse to most adults—and indeed, to most teenagers. But for the kids involved, says Shawn McNabb, a Youth Services worker in Burnaby, B.C., "Social interaction built around a constant battle for dominance is often consistent with what they experience at home."

18 The rites of passage required for acceptance into the tough crowd still include the traditional sources of peer pressure: smoking, drinking, taking drugs. Stacey explains that these are now accompanied by the expectation that girls, like boys, will demonstrate their worth in the gang by "beating up someone who has called you down." The ethic of revenge is often accompanied by the assumption that the victims "deserve" their treatment. Camille describes the **coveted** male attention won by "defending your rep" with fists and feet: "You get talked about and you get respect."

19 Some experts have suggested that girls are becoming more violent because they want to be more like boys, leading to speculation that feminism factors into the issue. By encouraging young women to seize power and go after what they want, the theory goes, we've created a monster—transforming girls into aggressive, insensitive takers.

20 Reality tells a different story. Youth workers say that girls who use violence as a means of resolving conflict typically have much more emotional investment in the traditional female goals of getting married and having a family than pursuing independence and a career. They are also more prone to seek validation through men than compete with them. The **icons** of popular culture—from the bikini-clad "warrior babes" to the ubiquitous Spice Girls—reinforce this notion.

Although lip service is paid to female power, the images of women predominating in the media send overwhelmingly sexist and **misogynist** messages, says Dr. Artz, teaching that "females are inferior to males and, in the last analysis, sexual objects."

21 Dr. Artz believes that understanding this dynamic is crucial to resolving violence among teenage girls. "The extent to which girls from troubled homes buy into messages about women's inferiority and see status as something to be gained through male attention supports their inclination to judge each other harshly."

22 Most experts agree that solutions do not include tightening up the Young Offenders Act. "The research is pretty clear," says Alan Markwart: "Get-tough approaches won't solve youth crime." Instead, training and education are paramount. Markwart stresses the importance of identifying kids in troubled homes at a young age. Then, he says, "there are two components: strong support for and training of parents, and enhanced early education to encourage kids' success in school."

23 Violence-prevention programs in the schools are useful too, says Dr. Artz, as long as they're geared to those they're intended to help. An antiviolence initiative she and project partner Dr. Ted Riecken, acting associate dean of education at the University of Victoria, introduced into B.C.'s Sooke school district underscores the need for gender-specific training programs.

24 This particular program, whose initiatives range from installing playground equipment to "bully-proofing" courses involving role-playing, was prompted by a University of Victoria 1993 survey of 1,500 grade 8 to 10 students, which revealed that 51 per cent of boys and 21 per cent of girls had admitted to beating up another person in the previous year. A sampling of the same age group taken last spring, five years into the project, showed a decrease in physical aggression of over 20 per cent among males and of 50 per cent among females. "Girls are clearly more ready to respond to this type of program," says Dr. Artz. Adds Dr. Riecken, "Girls respond to programs that focus on social skills training and desire to build positive relationships."

25 Angst among teenage girls is often provoked by the difficulty in forming trusting relationships with peers. When this is compounded by parental neglect and feelings of worthlessness—especially in the context of society's profoundly contradictory messages about female power, the importance of male attention and acceptable sexual behavior for women—the situation is ripe for violent behavior.

26 Violence begets violence. It also creates victims, who could be our daughters. If the price Reena Virk paid with her life has any meaning at all, it has at least sounded a wake-up call to the pressing need for more research into the real lives of teenage girls today.

## Glossary

**machismo:** Exaggerated expression of masculinity.

**burgeoning:** Quickly growing or multiplying.

**galvanized:** Stimulated.

**mitigating:** Making less severe or more moderate.

**coveted:** Desired, sought-after.

**icons:** Representative images or figures.

**misogynist:** Anti-women.

## Comprehension Questions

1. Describe the murderer being interviewed.
2. How does the crime rate for teenage girls compare to the general crime rate?
3. Why are the numbers of crimes by young women in Canada on the rise, according to the article?
4. What does "Janice" say was the reason she murdered Reena Virk?
5. What does Dr. Sibylle Artz say is the typical background profile of a young woman who becomes violent?

## Questions about Form

1. What does Graydon do to lend credibility to her article?
2. What kind of effect are quotations by "Janice" likely to have on the reader?
3. Graydon's article seems to be divided into two parts: the first on effects and the second on causes. Where does the change take place? What do you think the author is trying to achieve by doing this? Does she succeed?
4. Why is Reena Virk referred to in the first and, again, in the last paragraph? Do you think the author achieves her goal?

## Questions for Discussion

1. Based on what you have read in Graydon's article, do young males and young females fight for the same reasons?
2. What is your perception of teenage violence in this country? Do you agree with the article as to its causes?
3. Why do you think the crime rate among teenage girls is increasing? Does it have anything to do with feminism? Explain.

## Writing Ideas

1. Write a paragraph or essay explaining why you think teens often resort to violence. Refer to Graydon's article for at least one supportive detail (but not all) in your composition. Draw from your personal experience, also.
2. Write a paragraph or essay on what you think the solutions to the problem of teenage violence are. Do not discuss the causes or the effects; these should be somewhat evident from the solutions.

✦ ✦ ✦

# Till Fraud Do Us Part

*Cameron Ainsworth-Vincze*

For some, it is just a matter of time before they enter into the institution of marriage. For others, as wonderful as the prospect seems in some respects, marriage is utterly feared. Fuelling this fear in Canada today is the growing incidence of fraudulent marriage. *Maclean's* writer Cameron Ainsworth-Vincze gives us a glimpse into this type of desecration of what is still, for many, a holy institution.

1 Navdeep Dhillon left her Abbotsford, B.C., home in April 2004 along with her family and travelled to India for a moment she had long waited for. After selecting a traditional red dress with her mother and cousins in her native province of Punjab, Dhillon exchanged wedding vows in an arranged marriage with a man she had never met but with whom she expected to share the rest of her life in Canada. Three weeks later she returned to Abbotsford, where the 29-year-old works as a computer technician, and submitted a sponsorship application form along with a $1,525 immigration fee to enable her new husband to gain entry into Canada.

2 Five months later, Dhillon's husband, who had been recommended by relatives, arrived. But Dhillon's dream of a happy marriage quickly turned into a nightmare when, she says, he told her he had only wed her to immigrate to Canada, and then disappeared without a trace. "I can't really explain what's happening with me. It's really hard to tolerate," she says. "I never had any suspicion he was going to do that to me." But Dhillon's story is not a unique one. Increasing numbers of Canadians are becoming victims of **sham** marriages, sometimes being financially drained by the devious acts of foreigners who used them to enter the country. To make matters worse, Ottawa requires Canadians to support their spouses for a period of up to three years, and if a sponsored spouse receives any government assistance during that time, their provincial government is permitted to pursue repayment.

3 Dhillon believes her husband, luckily, has a job and has received no government assistance. But her family put forward a $20,000 **dowry,** not a penny of which has been returned. Dhillon doesn't even know where the man is currently living. Her family has tried contacting his family in India, but they keep disconnecting the phone. He has applied for a divorce, but Dhillon wants the marriage **annulled** and the government to deport him back to India. "If it doesn't do that, it means they are promoting fraud marriage," she says. "And people will do it over and over again."

4 To combat escalating incidents of sham marriages, the Vancouver-based Canadian Marriage Fraud Victim Society is petitioning Ottawa to change the Immigration Act to deter foreign spouses from using Canadians to obtain residency with the objective of leaving them once they reach Canadian soil. "We are suggesting they must live together or the divorce shouldn't be **sanctioned** earlier than three years," says society spokesman Krishan Bector. "They won't get married simply to come to Canada, but for life-long companionship. This is what marriage is all about."

5 New Democrat MLA Raj Chouhan, however, believes such a change would do more harm than good. "There is no quick fix," he says. "It's an issue that requires all of us to discuss, debate and then come up with some kind of suggestion." There will likely be people willing to live through three years of a sham marriage to stay in Canada; Chouhan fears that could force a woman to suffer a possibly abusive relationship for that time. "She will be just like a slave," he says.

6 To find a viable solution, Chouhan is spearheading a campaign to inform communities about fraud marriages, and he is raising the issue in the provincial legislature. He also believes it is essential to construct a support network for victims. "We need to let them know they are not alone," he says. "Public awareness is so essential for people to understand." But Dhillon hopes some type of legislation is passed soon so that others are protected from the pain she lives with. "I am really afraid now. I can't even trust in men."

## Glossary

**sham:** False; pretended.

**dowry:** Property that a woman brings to her husband in marriage.

**annulled:** Made no longer binding under the law.

**sanctioned:** Ratified by authority; authorized.

## Comprehension Questions

1. What, in your own words, is the thesis of this article?
2. What did Dhillon lose as a result of her experience?
3. What are the suggested solutions in the article for preventing the type of fraud described in this piece?

### Questions about Form

1. Why do you think the author starts his article by referring to a particular person's experience?
2. Is the title powerful? Why or why not? Discuss.

### Questions for Discussion

1. What can parents do to prevent this type of thing from happening to their daughter?
2. According to New Democrat MLA Raj Chouhan, the policy change the Vancouver-based Canadian Marriage Fraud Victim Society is suggesting is a bad one. What policy do you think the government should adopt?
3. Read "Lessons of Love from Stories of Old" (beginning on page 402). What is similar between that article and this one? Why does materialism often get in the way of a good marriage?

### Writing Ideas

1. Write a paragraph or essay on how an arranged marriage should be managed given the situation described in the article.
2. In a paragraph or essay, argue for or against the traditional notion of the "dowry." Remember, you might want to argue that another culture has its own version of the "dowry." Explain this briefly before you state your thesis. Remember to give logical reasons in support of the stand you take.

✦ ✦ ✦

## In My Secret Life

*Leonard Cohen*

Most famous for his song "Suzanne," this Montreal-born poet has put much of his internationally acclaimed poetry to music. Singers such as Jennifer Warnes and bands such as REM and the Neville Brothers have performed Cohen's work, but most of Cohen's fans prefer to hear the poet himself perform his own music. Cohen's collections of poetry, novels, and recordings have earned him the reputation as one of the most influential artists in Canada, the U.S., and Europe. The poem/song here is taken from his CD *Ten New Songs,* released in 2001.

1 I saw you this morning.
You were moving so fast.
Can't seem to loosen my grip
On the past.
And I miss you so much.
There's no one in sight.
And we're still making love
In My Secret Life.

2 I smile when I'm angry.
I cheat and I lie.
I do what I have to do
To get by.
But I know what is wrong,
And I know what is right.
And I'd die for the truth
In My Secret Life.

3 Hold on, hold on, my brother.
My sister, hold on tight.
I finally got my orders.
I'll be marching through the morning,
Marching through the night,
Moving cross the borders
Of My Secret Life.

4 Looked through the paper.
Makes you want to cry.
Nobody cares if the people
Live or die.
And the dealer wants you thinking
That it's either black or white.
Thank G-d it's not that simple
In My Secret Life.

5 I bite my lip.
I buy what I'm told:
From the latest hit,
To the wisdom of old.
But I'm always alone.
And my heart is like ice.
And it's crowded and cold
In My Secret Life.

## Glossary

**G-d:** In Judaism, a way of referring to the deity without taking His name in vain.

## Comprehension Questions

1. In stanza 4, Cohen refers to "the dealer" and how he "wants you thinking / That it's either black or white." What do you think Cohen means by this?
2. What do you think the last stanza means? In particular, focus on "It's crowded and cold / In My Secret Life."

## Questions about Form

1. What writing strategy or rhetorical mode does Cohen seem to be using, in part, within his poem/song?
2. Notice how each stanza ends with either "In" or "Of My Secret Life." Is this effective? Why?
3. What are the similarities or differences between the first and last stanzas? How does your answer contribute to the theme of the poem/song?
4. Are the words Cohen uses simple or complicated? Are they short or long? Notice how short the glossary is compared to that of other readings. What does this suggest? Do the answers to these questions contribute to the effectiveness of the work?

## Questions for Discussion

1. What do you think Cohen is trying to say in this poem/song?
2. What is Cohen's "secret life"?
3. With regard to the two parts in conflict, which stanza seems to most clearly make a value judgment about each part? Explain.
4. Does Cohen resolve his conflict? What evidence from the poem/song supports your answer?

## Writing Ideas

1. Identify two parts of you that always seem to be in conflict with each other. Write a paragraph or essay contrasting both.
2. Write a paragraph or essay interpreting the above poem/song by Leonard Cohen.

# UNIT FIVE V

# Appendices

APPENDIX A DISTINGUISHING BETWEEN WORDS OFTEN CONFUSED

APPENDIX B SOLVING SPELLING PROBLEMS

APPENDIX C IRREGULAR VERBS

APPENDIX D ANSWER KEY TO PRACTICES

APPENDIX A

# Distinguishing between Words Often Confused

## Words That Sound Alike

**allowed** (*verb*) permitted
**aloud** (*adv.*) out loud

*Example:*
The boy was finally allowed to stay up late.
Her question was stated aloud for all to hear.

**altar** (*noun*) an elevated place or table for religious rites
**alter** (*verb*) to change or adjust

*Example:*
The altar was decorated for the church service.
If you alter the plans, they won't work out.

**aural** (*adj.*) having to do with the ear or hearing
**oral** (*adj.*) having to do with the mouth or speech

*Example:*
I have poor aural skills because I won't listen.
The history of the First Nations is kept alive through their oral traditions.

**brake** (*verb*) to stop
(*noun*) a device used for slowing or stopping
**break** (*verb*) to smash, crack, or come apart
(*noun*) a crack, severing; an interruption, change

*Example:*
Apply the brake when you want to stop.
You'll have to break the lock to get in.
Give me a break!

**capital** (*adj.*) chief; major; fatal
(*noun*) leading city; money

**capitol** (*noun*) a building in which a U.S. state legislature assembles

*Example:*
Ottawa is the capital of Canada.
The capitol building for the legislature is in Albany.

**chord** (*noun*) three or more musical tones sounded together; harmony
**cord** (*noun*) a small rope of twisted strands; any ropelike structure; a unit of cut fuel wood

*Example:*
Many guitar chords are easy to play.
A strong cord is needed to tie the bundle together.

**close** (*verb*) to shut
**clothes** (*noun*) garments
**cloth** (*noun*) fabric; a piece of material

*Example:*
Close the door and keep the cold out.
T-shirts are our favourite type of summer clothes.
His coat was made of cloth, not leather.

**coarse** (*adj.*) rough; not fine; common or of inferior quality
**course** (*noun*) direction or path of something moving; part of a meal; a school subject

*Example:*
Coarse sandpaper is used to make a rough finish.
One course I'm taking this year is English grammar.

**complement** (*noun*) something that completes or makes up a whole
(*verb*) to complete; to supplement, enhance
**compliment** (*noun*) an expression of praise
(*verb*) to give praise

*Example:*
A blue blazer complements grey slacks.
Good work deserves a compliment.

**complementary** (*adj.*) complementing, often completing a pair or group of things that go together
**complimentary** (*adj.*) expressing a compliment; given free as a favour

*Example:*
With the textbook, he assigned the complementary study guide.
I have complimentary tickets to the game.

**fair** (*adj.*) unbiased; light colour; free of clouds; promising; lovely
(*noun*) an exhibition; regional event; market

**fare** (*noun*) a charge for transportation; food
(*verb*) get along; do

*Example:*
A pink sunset means a fair day will follow.
The train fare is increasing yearly.

**flour** (*noun*) the powder produced by grinding a grain
**flower** (*noun*) a blossom of a plant
(*verb*) to blossom

*Example:*
Wheat flour is used to make bread.
Tulips flower in early spring.

**for** (*prep.*) directed to; in the amount of; on behalf of; to the extent of
(*conj.*) because
**four** (*noun, adj.*) number
**forty:** Notice that this number is spelled differently from *four, fourteen,* or *twenty-four.*
**fore** (*noun, adj.*) situated near the front

*Example:*
This gift is for you.
There are four people in attendance.
His ideas came to the fore at work.

**forth** (*adv.*) onward in time, place, or order
**fourth** (*noun, adj.*) number

*Example:*
Go forth from this place.
She is fourth in line for tickets.

**forward** (*verb*) to send on to another address
(*adj.*) bold; progressive
(*adv.*) moving toward the front
**foreword** (*noun*) introduction to a book; preface

*Example:*
Move forward so you can hear the speaker.
The foreword to a book is sometimes called the preface.

**grate** (*verb*) to shred; to annoy or irritate
(*noun*) a metal grill
**grateful** (*adj.*) appreciative
**great** (*adj.*) large; significant; excellent; powerful; skillful; first-rate

*Example:*
Her negative attitude grates on my nerves.
Winning the prize was a great achievement.

**it's** contraction of *it is*
**its** possessive

*Example:*
It's a nice day today.
The bush has all of its new buds.

**knew** (*verb*) past tense of *know*
**new** (adj.) not old

*Example:*
The student knew the correct answer.
His new car is this year's model.

**know** (*verb*) to understand
**no** (*adv.*) a negative response
(*adj.*) not any; not one

*Example:*
You would know the work if you'd study.
Having no money means that you are poor.

**pain** (*noun*) suffering
**pane** (*noun*) a panel of glass

*Example:*
A cut finger can cause a lot of pain.
Windows contain panes of glass.

**passed** (*verb*) the past tense of *to pass*—to move ahead
**past** (*noun*) time before the present
(*prep.*) beyond
(*adj.*) no longer current

*Example:*
I passed the exam and moved to the next grade.
I was past the exit before I noticed that I had missed it.

**patience** (*noun*) calm endurance; tolerant understanding
**patients** (*noun*) persons under medical treatment

*Example:*
Waiting for someone usually takes patience.
Patients in hospitals often are very ill.

**peace** (*noun*) absence of war, calm
**piece** (*noun*) a portion, a part

*Example:*
Peace came when the war was over.
His piece of cake was huge.

| | |
|---|---|
| **plain** (*adj.*) | simple; ordinary; unattractive; clear |
| (*noun*) | a flat, treeless land region |
| **plane** (*noun*) | an aircraft; a flat, level surface; a carpenter's tool for levelling wood; a level of development |

*Example:*
The flat plain stretched for miles without a tree.
I used a plane to make the wood smooth.

| | |
|---|---|
| **presence** (*noun*) | the state of being present; a person's manner |
| **presents** (*noun*) | gifts |
| (*verb*) | (third person singular) to introduce; to give a gift |

*Example:*
The presence of the teacher kept the students quiet.
Presents are given on birthdays.

| | |
|---|---|
| **principal** (*adj.*) | most important; chief; main |
| (*noun*) | the head of a school; a sum of money |
| **principle** (*noun*) | rule or standard |

*Example:*
The principal rule is the most important guideline.
There are principles of conduct to be followed at school.

| | |
|---|---|
| **rain** (*noun, verb*) | water falling to earth in drops |
| **reign** (*noun, verb*) | a period of rule for a king or queen |
| **rein** (*noun*) | a strap attached to a bridle, used to control a horse |

*Example:*
A good rain will soak the crops.
The monarch's reign extended for many years.
To control a horse, learn how to use the reins.

| | |
|---|---|
| **raise** (*verb*) | to move upward; to awaken; to increase; to collect |
| (*noun*) | an increase in salary |
| **rays** (*noun*) | thin lines or beams of radiation |
| **raze** (*verb*) | to tear down or demolish |

*Example:*
A raise in pay often rewards good work.
The sun's rays contain harmful radiation.
The old building was razed to the ground.

| | |
|---|---|
| **sight** (*noun*) | the ability to see; a view |
| **site** (*noun*) | the plot of land where something is located; the place of an event |
| **cite** (*verb*) | to quote as an authority or example |

*Example:*
Some people with perfect sight don't see clearly.

The opera house's site is between two theatres.
I can cite my grammar text as my authority.

| | |
|---|---|
| **stair** (*noun*) | one of a flight of steps |
| **stare** (*noun, verb*) | a fixed gaze; to look at insistently |

*Example:*
Each stair climbed brings you farther up the steps.
A steady gaze can be considered a stare.

| | |
|---|---|
| **stake** (*noun*) | a post sharpened at one end to drive into the ground; a financial share |
| (*verb*) | to attach or support; to set limits with a stake |
| **steak** (*noun*) | a slice of meat, usually beef |

*Example:*
My stake in the profits amounted to a quarter share.
I like my steak well done and thick.

| | |
|---|---|
| **stationary** (*adj.*) | standing still |
| **stationery** (*noun*) | writing paper and envelopes |

*Example:*
Anything that is stationary does not move.
Stationery can be written upon.

| | |
|---|---|
| **they're** | contraction of *they are* |
| **their** | possessive |
| **there** | at that place |

*Example:*
They're a happy couple.
This antique is their prized possession.
I'll meet you over there, behind the store.

| | |
|---|---|
| **to** (*prep.*) | in a direction toward |
| **to** (+ *verb*) | the infinitive form of a verb |
| **too** (*adv.*) | also; excessively; very |
| **two** (*noun*) | number |

*Example:*
Go to school.
To see is to believe.
I, too, am going to the party.
Two is one more than one.

| | |
|---|---|
| **vain** (*adj.*) | conceited; unsuccessful |
| **vane** (*noun*) | a plate of wood or metal, often in the shape of a rooster, that pivots to indicate the direction of the wind; the weblike part of a feather |

**vein** (*noun*) a blood vessel; the branching framework of a leaf; an occurrence of an ore; a strip of colour; a streak; a transient attitude

*Example:*
A vain person spends a lot of time in front of a mirror.
The vane on the roof tells the wind direction.
Veins in your body contain blood.

**waist** (*noun*) the middle portion of a body, garment, or object
**waste** (*verb*) to use thoughtlessly or carelessly
(*noun*) objects discarded as useless

*Example:*
A belt around your waist holds your pants up.
Excess packaging contains much waste.

**wait** (*verb*) to remain inactive
**weight** (*noun*) the measure of the heaviness of an object

*Example:*
Remain here and wait for my arrival.
My weight goes up every time I eat.

**ware** (*noun*) an article of commerce
**wear** (*verb*) to have on
(*noun*) deterioration as a result of use
**where** (*adv.*) at or in what place

*Example:*
You can sell your wares at the flea market.
What clothes will you wear?
He asked where the museum could be found.

**weather** (*noun*) atmospheric conditions
**whether** (*conj.*) if it is the case that

*Example:*
The weather report calls for rain.
She will go whether I go or not.

**whole** (*adj.*) complete
**hole** (*noun*) an opening

*Example:*
A pie is whole before it is sliced and served.
Holes in the road need to be filled in.

**who's** contraction of *who is*
**whose** possessive

*Example:*
Who's going for pizza?
Whose garbage can is blocking the driveway?

| | |
|---|---|
| **wood** (*noun*) | the tough tissue from trees |
| **would** (*verb*) | past tense of *will* |

*Example:*
Most paper is made from wood fibre.
He would go, he said, if he could find a ride.

| | |
|---|---|
| **write** (*verb*) | to form letters and words; to compose |
| **right** (*adj.*) | conforming to justice, law, or morality; correct; toward a conservative political point of view |
| (*noun*) | that which is just, morally good, legal, or proper; a direction; a political group whose policies are conservative |
| (*adv.*) | directly; well; completely; immediately |
| **rite** (*noun*) | a traditional, solemn, and often religious ceremony |

*Example:*
Write a letter to your aunt.
You should legally do what is right.
Last rites were said over the dying person.

| | |
|---|---|
| **yoke** (*noun*) | a harness fastening two or more animals together; a form of bondage |
| **yolk** (*noun*) | the yellow of an egg |

*Example:*
Animals in a team are joined by a yoke.
Some diners like their eggs cooked without the yolks broken.

| | |
|---|---|
| **you're** | contraction of *you are* |
| **your** | possessive |

*Example:*
You're my best friend.
Take your gift to the party.

## Words That Sound or Look Almost Alike

Some words are often confused with other words that sound or look almost the same. Learning to spell these words correctly involves a careful study of pronunciations along with meanings.

| | **Pronunciation** | **Meaning** |
|---|---|---|
| **accept** | *a* as in *pat* | *verb:* to receive; to admit; to regard as true or right |
| **except** | the first *e* as in *pet* | *prep.:* other than; but; only |

*Example:*
I accepted the parcel from the courier.
Everyone was there except the two of us.

| | | |
|---|---|---|
| **access** | *a* as in *pat* | *noun:* a means of approaching; the right to enter or make use of |
| **excess** | the first *e* as in *pet* | *noun:* a quantity or amount beyond what is required |

*Example:*
Access to the files will provide you with information.
Overeating is an unnecessary excess.

| | | |
|---|---|---|
| **advice** | Pronounce *-ice* like the word *ice.* | *noun:* opinion as to what should be done about a problem |
| **advise** | Pronounce *-ise* like the word *eyes.* | *verb:* to suggest; to counsel |

*Example:*
My best advice is to accept the offer.
I advise you to do what is right.

| | | |
|---|---|---|
| **affect** | *a* as in *about* | *verb:* to influence |
| **effect** | the first *e* as the *e* in *pet* or *i* in *pit* | *noun:* result<br>*verb:* to bring about a result |

*Example:*
I can affect his decision with my advice.
The effect of the rain was to cancel the game.

| | | |
|---|---|---|
| **allusion** | *a* as in *about* | *noun:* an indirect reference |
| **illusion** | the first *i* as in *pit* | *noun:* a mistaken concept or belief |

*Example:*
An allusion was made to my great intelligence.
It is an illusion to think you will get rich without working.

| | | |
|---|---|---|
| **breath** | *ea* as the *e* in *pet* | *noun:* the air that is inhaled or exhaled in breathing |
| **breathe** | the *ea* as the *e* in *be* | *verb:* to inhale and exhale air |

*Example:*
You can see your breath on the window on a cold day.
Breathe deeply and inhale the clean country air.

| | | |
|---|---|---|
| **clothes** | *o* as the *oe* in *toe* | *noun:* garments; wearing apparel |
| **cloths** | *o* as the *aw* in *paw* | *noun:* pieces of fabric |

*Example:*
The clothes you are wearing are fashionable.
Pieces of cloth can be torn from the fabric to make rags.

| | | |
|---|---|---|
| **conscience** | kŏn′ shəns (two syllables) | *noun:* recognition of right and wrong |
| **conscientious** | kŏn shē en′ shəs (four syllables) | *adj.:* careful; thorough |
| **conscious** | kŏn′ shəs (two syllables) | *adj.:* awake; aware of one's own existence |

*Example:*
My conscience told me to do the right thing.
I conscientiously performed my duty to the best of my ability.
She was conscious of the fact that he was behind her.

| | | |
|---|---|---|
| **costume** | *o* as in *pot*, *u* as the *u* in you | *noun:* a special style of dress for a particular occasion |
| **custom** | *u* as in *cut*, *o* as in *gallop* | *noun:* a common tradition |

*Example:*
The costume he wore reflected his Ukrainian heritage.
It is our custom to wash our hands before eating.

| | | |
|---|---|---|
| **council** } | *ou* as in *out* | *noun:* a group that governs |
| **counsel** } | | *verb:* to give advice<br>*noun:* a lawyer; advice |
| **consul** | *o* as in *pot* | *noun:* a governmental official in the foreign service |

*Example:*
The town council passed a by-law.
Good counsel is advice well received.
Canada has a consul in many foreign countries.

| | | |
|---|---|---|
| **desert** | di zurt′<br>*i* as in *pit* | *verb:* to abandon<br>*noun:* something deserved (often plural) |
| | dez′ ert<br>the first *e* as in *pet* | *noun:* barren land |
| **dessert** | di zurt'<br>*i* as in pit | *noun:* last part of a meal, often a sweet |

*Example:*
The desert is usually a hot, arid place.
Our family usually eats dessert following dinner.
He got his just deserts.

| | | |
|---|---|---|
| **diner** | *i* as the *ie* in *pie* | *noun:* a person eating dinner; a restaurant with a long counter and booths |
| **dinner** | *i* as in *pit* | *noun:* chief meal of the day |

*Example:*
A diner is a place where meals are served.
Dinner is usually eaten in the early evening.

| | | |
|---|---|---|
| **emigrate** }<br>**emigrant** | *e* as in *pet* | *verb:* to go out of a country<br>*noun:* someone who leaves a country to settle in another country |
| **immigrate** }<br>**immigrant** | the first *i* as in *pit* | *verb:* to come into a country<br>*noun:* someone who enters a country to settle there |

*Example:*
Many people decided to emigrate from Ireland during the famine.
Immigrants to our country bring valuable skills.

| | | |
|---|---|---|
| **farther** | *a* as in *father* | *adj., adv.:* greater physical or measurable distance |
| **further** | *u* as in *urge* | *adj., adv.:* greater mental distance; more distant in time or degree; additional |

*Example:*
Montreal is farther than Toronto from Windsor.
We drew further apart in our approach to the problem.

| | | |
|---|---|---|
| **local** | lo′ kəl<br>*a* as in *about* | *adj.:* relating or peculiar to a place |
| **locale** | lo kal′<br>*a* as in *pat* | *noun:* a place, scene, or setting, as of a novel |

*Example:*
Everyone here goes to the local school on the next block.
Our town was the locale for a movie.

| | | |
|---|---|---|
| **moral** | mor′ al<br>*a* as in *about* | *adj.:* a sense of right and wrong<br>*noun:* the lesson of a story, fable, or event |
| **morale** | mo ral′<br>*a* as in *pat* | *noun:* the attitude or spirit of a person or group of people |

*Example:*
The moral of the story taught us never to cheat.
Their morale was shown by their enthusiasm for their jobs.

| | | |
|---|---|---|
| **personal** | per′ son al | *adj.:* pertaining to a particular person |
| **personnel** | per son nel′ | *noun:* the people employed by an organization; an administrative division of an organization concerned with the employees |

*Example:*
The matter is a personal one between him and me.
Most of the plant's personnel were laid off.

| | | |
|---|---|---|
| **precede** | the first *e* as the *i* in *pit* | *verb:* to come before |
| **proceed** | the *o* as the *oe* in *toe* | *verb:* to continue |

*Example:*
You go first and precede me down the hall.
Proceed with the story you started yesterday.

| | | |
|---|---|---|
| **quiet** | qui′ et<br>*i* as the *ie* in *pie,*<br>*e* as in *pet* | *adj.:* silent<br>*noun:* silence |
| **quit** | *i* as in *pit* | *verb:* to give up; to stop |
| **quite** | *i* as the *ie* in *pie*;<br>the *e* is silent | *adv.:* somewhat; completely; truly |

*Example:*
It was a quiet night when no sound could be heard.
Quit what you are doing and start something else.
It is quite true that I am guilty.

| | | |
|---|---|---|
| **receipt** | the first *e* as the *i* in *pit*, *ei* as in the *e* in *be*; the *p* is silent | *noun:* a bill marked as paid; the act of receiving something<br>*verb:* to mark as paid |
| **recipe** | the first *e* as in *pet*, the *i* like the *a* in *about*, the final *e* as in *be* | *noun:* a formula for preparing a mixture, especially in cooking |

*Example:*
The receipt for the dinner was marked "paid."
The recipe calls for more chocolate in the cookies.

| | | |
|---|---|---|
| **special** | spĕsh′ əl | *adj.:* exceptional; distinctive |
| **especially** | Notice the extra syllable at the beginning. | *adv.:* particularly |

*Example:*
She was a special person, one of a kind.
It is especially important to file an income tax return.

| | | |
|---|---|---|
| **than** | *a* as in *pat* | *conj.:* used to make a comparison |
| **then** | *e* as in *pet* | *adv.:* at that time; in that case |

*Example:*
She is smarter than I am.
It was then that I made up my mind.

| | | |
|---|---|---|
| **thorough** | the first *o* as the *u* in *urge, ou* as the *oe* in *toe* | *adj.:* all that is needed; fully done |
| **though** | *ou* as the *oe* in *toe* | *conj.:* despite the fact |
| **thought** | *ou* as the *aw* in *paw* | *verb:* past tense of *to think* |
| **through** | *ou* as the *oo* in *boot* | *prep.* used to indicate entrance at one side and exit from the other; finished |
| **threw** | sounds like *through* | *verb:* past tense of *to throw* |

- *Thru* is only an informal spelling for the word *through*.

*Example:*
The thorough investigation found a hidden clue.
It's not true, though, that I told a lie.
He thought of the answer before he spoke.
Go through that exit to get outside.
He threw the ball as far as he could.

## Words That Sound or Look Almost Alike: *sit/set; rise/raise; lie/lay*

These six verbs are among the most troublesome in English because each is similar in sound, spelling, and meaning to another verb. Since they are all irregular verbs, students must be careful to learn to spell the principal parts correctly. The key to learning how to use the verbs *sit, rise*, and *lie* is to remember that these are actions the subject can do without any help; no other person or thing has to be included in the sentence. When you use the verbs *set, raise*, and *lay* in a sentence, the actions of these verbs are done to other persons or objects; these persons or things have to be included directly in the sentence. For example, when you use the verb *to sit*, all you need is a subject and a form of the verb:

I sit.

However, when you use the verb *to set*, you need a subject, a form of the verb, and an object. For example:

I set the glass on the table.

The subject *I* and the verb *set* are followed by the object *glass*, which is what the subject set on the table.

| | | |
|---|---|---|
| ***sit:*** to take a sitting position<br>*never* takes an object | | ***set:*** to place something into position<br>*always* takes an object |
| ***Present:*** | I *sit.* | I *set the glass* down. |
| ***Present participle:*** | I *am sitting.* | I *am setting the glass* down. |
| ***Past:*** | I *sat.* | I *set the glass* down. |
| ***Past participle:*** | I *have sat.* | I *have set the glass* down. |

| | | |
|---|---|---|
| ***rise:*** to stand up; to move upward<br>*never* takes an object | | ***raise:*** to make something move up or grow; *always* takes an object |
| ***Present:*** | I *rise.* | I *raise the flag.* |
| ***Present participle:*** | The sun *is rising.* | I *am raising the flag.* |
| ***Past:*** | He *rose* at eight o'clock. | I *raised the flag.* |
| ***Past participle:*** | I *have risen* early today. | I *have raised the flag.* |

The verbs *lie* and *lay* are easily confused because two of their principal parts have the same spelling. It takes concentration to learn to use these two verbs correctly.

| | | |
|---|---|---|
| ***lie:*** to recline<br>*never* takes an object | | ***lay:*** to put<br>*always* takes an object |
| ***Present:*** | I *lie* down. | I *lay the pen* down. |
| ***Present participle:*** | I *am lying* down. | I *am laying the pen* down. |
| ***Past:*** | Yesterday I *lay* down. | I *laid the pen* down. |
| ***Past participle:*** | I *have lain* down. | I *have laid the pen* down. |

- The verb *lie* can also be a regular verb meaning "to tell an untruth." The principal parts of this verb are *lie, lying, lied, has lied.*

## Words That Sound or Look Almost Alike: *choose/chose; lose/loose; lead/led; die/dye*

These verbs are often misspelled because there is confusion about how to spell the vowel sounds of the verbs. Study the spelling of the principal parts below.

| **Present** | **Present Participle** | **Past** | **Past Participle** |
|---|---|---|---|
| choose | choosing | chose | has chosen |
| lose | losing | lost | has lost |
| lead | leading | led | has led |
| die | dying | died | has died |

- *Loose* is an adjective meaning "not tightly fitted." Remember, it rhymes with *goose.*
- *Lead* can also be a noun meaning a bluish-grey metal. Remember, it rhymes with *head.*

- *Dye* is another verb meaning "to colour." Its principal parts are *dye, dyeing, dyed, has dyed.*

## Words That Sound or Look Almost Alike: *use/used; suppose/supposed*

*To use* means *to bring or put into service; to make use of.*

***Present:*** I *use* my brother's bike to get to school.
***Past:*** Yesterday I *used* my father's car.

*Use to* means *to have as a custom* or *regular practice* in the past. It usually occurs in its past form, *used to*:

I *used to* take the bus downtown, but now I get a ride with my neighbour.

Note, however, that in expressions with the auxiliary *did,* you use the present form:

Did you use to take the bus?

A form of *to be* + *used to* means *to be familiar with or accustomed to.*

I *am used to* walking to school.

*To suppose* means *to guess.*

***Present:*** I *suppose* he is trying.
***Past:*** I *supposed* he was trying.

A form of *to be* + *supposed to* means *ought to* or *should.*

Waiters *are supposed to* be courteous.

Many people have difficulty knowing when to choose *used* and *supposed* in their writing because in speaking, the final *d* is often not clearly heard.

***Incorrect:*** I am *suppose to* be in school today.
***Correct:*** I am *supposed to* be in school today.

APPENDIX B

B

# Solving Spelling Problems

## Learning to Spell Commonly Mispronounced Words

Several common English words are often mispronounced or pronounced in such a way that the result is incorrect spelling. Below are sixty common words that are often misspelled. As you study them, be careful to spell each of the underlined syllables correctly.

I. Common Omission of Vowels

1. Do not omit the underlined syllable with the *a*:

| | |
|---|---|
| accidentally | literature |
| basically | miniature |
| boundary | separate |
| extraordinary | temperament |
| incidentally | temperature |

2. Do not omit the underlined syllable with the *e*:

| | |
|---|---|
| considerable | mathematics |
| difference | numerous |
| funeral | scenery |
| interesting | |

However, notice the following words in which the *e* is omitted:

| | | |
|---|---|---|
| disaster | *becomes* | disastrous |
| enter | *becomes* | entrance |
| hinder | *becomes* | hindrance |
| hunger | *becomes* | hungry |
| launder | *becomes* | laundry |
| monster | *becomes* | monstrous |
| remember | *becomes* | remembrance |

3. Do not omit the underlined syllable with the *i*:

| | | |
|---|---|---|
| aspirin | family | similar |

4. Do not omit the underlined syllable with the *o*:

   chocolate
   environment
   favourite
   humorous
   laboratory
   sophomore

5. Do not omit the underlined syllable with the *u*:

   luxury
   accuracy

6. Do not omit the underlined syllable with the *y*:

   studying

II. Common Omission of Consonants

1. *b*
   probably
2. *c*
   arctic
3. *d*
   candidate
   handkerchief
   handsome
   supposed to
   used to
4. *g*
   recognize
5. *n*
   government
6. *r*
   February
   library
   surprise
7. *t*
   authentic
   identical
   identity
   partner
   promptly
   quantity

III. Common Addition of a Syllable

Do not add unnecessary syllables (e.g., athelete):

athlete
athletic

IV. Common Transposition of Letters

Do not transpose the underlined letters:

perform
persuade
prefer
tragedy

PRACTICE

### Identifying the Correct Spelling

Circle the correct spelling for each of the following words. Check your answers against those in the Answer Key on p. 466.

| | | |
|---|---|---|
| 1. separate | seprate | seperate |
| 2. probably | probaly | probly |
| 3. ardic | arctic | artic |
| 4. suprise | saprize | surprise |
| 5. tragedy | tradgedy | trajedy |
| 6. quantity | quantidy | quanity |
| 7. litrature | literature | literture |
| 8. hungery | hungary | hungry |
| 9. handsome | hansome | handsom |
| 10. favourite | faverite | favrite |
| 11. nucular | nuclear | nuclar |

## Learning to Spell *ie* and *ei* Words

Use this rhyme to help you remember how to spell most *ie* and *ei* words:

*i* before *e*
except after *c*
or when sounded like *a*
as in *neighbour* or *weigh*.

*i* before *e*

The majority of all the *ie* and *ei* words use *ie*.

believe
chief
friend
shriek
yield

except after *c*

ceiling
conceit
conceive
receipt
receive

or when sounded like *a*

beige
eight
reins
sleigh
vein

Once you have learned the rhyme, concentrate on learning the following groups of words that are the exceptions to this rhyme.

| | | |
|---|---|---|
| caffeine | leisure | ancient |
| codeine | seize | conscience |
| protein | seizure | efficient |
| | | sufficient |
| neither | counterfeit | |
| either | Fahrenheit | |
| | foreign | |
| sheik | height | |
| stein | | |
| their | | |
| weird | | |

PRACTICE

## Choosing *ie* or *ei*

Choose the correct combination of *ie* or *ei* for the following words. Check your answers against those in the Answer Key on p. 466.

| | |
|---|---|
| 1. sl______gh | 6. dec______t |
| 2. bel______ve | 7. n______ce |
| 3. s______ge | 8. w______ght |
| 4. v______l | 9. prot______n |
| 5. l______sure | 10. anc______nt |

Almost all nouns are made plural simply by adding *-s* to the singular form:

| | | |
|---|---|---|
| girl | *becomes* | girl*s* |
| dinner | *becomes* | dinner*s* |

However, each of the following groups of words has its own special rule for forming the plural.

1. **Words ending in *-y*:**

   In words ending in *-y* preceded by a *consonant*, change the *y* to *i* and add *es*.

| | | |
|---|---|---|
| lad*y* | *becomes* | lad*ies* |
| ceremon*y* | *becomes* | ceremon*ies* |

   Words ending in *-y* preceded by a *vowel* form their plurals in the regular way, by just adding *-s*.

| | | |
|---|---|---|
| d*ay* | *becomes* | day*s* |
| monk*ey* | *becomes* | monkey*s* |
| vall*ey* | *becomes* | valley*s* |

2. **Words ending in *-o*:**

   Most words ending in *-o* preceded by a consonant add *-es* to form the plural.

| | | |
|---|---|---|
| ec*h*o | *becomes* | echo*es* |
| he*r*o | *becomes* | hero*es* |
| pota*t*o | *becomes* | potato*es* |

   However, musical terms or names of musical instruments (which derive from Italian) add only *-s*.

| | | |
|---|---|---|
| piano | *becomes* | piano*s* |
| solo | *becomes* | solo*s* |
| soprano | *becomes* | soprano*s* |

   Words ending in *-o* preceded by a *vowel* add *-s*.

| | | |
|---|---|---|
| pat*i*o | *becomes* | patio*s* |
| rad*i*o | *becomes* | radio*s* |
| rod*e*o | *becomes* | rodeo*s* |

   Some words ending in *-o* may form their plural with *-s* or *-es*.

| | | | | |
|---|---|---|---|---|
| memento | *becomes* | memento*s* | *or* | memento*es* |
| pinto | *becomes* | pinto*s* | *or* | pinto*es* |
| zero | *becomes* | zero*s* | *or* | zero*es* |

   If you are uncertain about the plural ending of a word ending in *-o*, it is best to use the dictionary. The dictionary gives all the endings of irregular plurals. If no plural form is given, you know the word will form its plural in the regular way, by adding only *-s*.

3. **Words ending in *-ch*, *-sh*, *-s*, *-x*, and *-z*:**

   For words ending in *-ch*, *-sh*, *-s*, *-x*, and *-z*, add *-es*.

   witch*es*
   dish*es*
   dress*es*
   tax*es*
   buzz*es*

4. **Words ending in *-fe* or *-f*:**

   Some words ending in *-fe* or *-f* change the *f* to *v* and add *-es*. You can hear the change from the *f* sound to the *v* sound in the plural.

| | | |
|---|---|---|
| wi*fe* | *becomes* | wi*ves* |
| lea*f* | *becomes* | lea*ves* |

Other words ending in *-f* or *-ef* keep the *f* and just add *-s*.

| | | |
|---|---|---|
| sheri*ff* | *becomes* | sheriff*s* |
| belie*f* | *becomes* | belief*s* |

Again, you can hear that the *f* sound is kept in the plural. Some words can form their plural either way. If so, the dictionary will give the preferred way first.

5. **Foreign words:**

Some words borrowed from other languages keep the plurals from those languages to form the plural in English.

| | | |
|---|---|---|
| alg*a* | *becomes* | alg*ae* |
| alumn*a* | *becomes* | alumn*ae* |
| alumn*us* | *becomes* | alumn*i* |
| cris*is* | *becomes* | cris*es* |
| phenomen*on* | *becomes* | phenomen*a* |

6. **Compound nouns:**

Compound nouns make their plurals by putting the *-s* on the end of the main word.

| | | |
|---|---|---|
| brother-in-law | *becomes* | brother*s*-in-law |
| passer-by | *becomes* | passer*s*-by |

7. **Irregular plurals:**

Some nouns in English have irregular plurals.

| **Singular** | **Plural** |
|---|---|
| child | children |
| deer | deer |
| foot | feet |
| goose | geese |
| man, woman | men, women |
| moose | moose |
| mouse | mice |
| ox | oxen |
| sheep | sheep |
| tooth | teeth |

**PRACTICE**

### Forming the Plurals of Nouns

Using the rules you have learned, make the following words plural. Check your answers against those in the Answer Key on p. 466.

1. puppy ______________________
2. mother-in-law ______________________
3. tooth ______________________
4. cameo ______________________
5. phenomenon ______________________
6. loaf ______________________
7. match ______________________
8. mix ______________________
9. enemy ______________________
10. bag ______________________

## Prefixes and Suffixes

Like everything else in this world, words had to begin somewhere. Many English words come from (had their *roots* in) other languages; others were created to describe something new. For example, modern English has many roots in Old English, ancient Greek, and Latin. For example:

***Roots and Derivatives***

| **Old English** | | **Latin** | |
|---|---|---|---|
| *akr* | a field, acre | *audio* | to hear, audience |
| *foda* | food, fodder | *dignus* | dignity, worth |
| *haelan* | to heal, health | *clarus* | clear, clarify |
| *war* | defence, war | *nomen* | name |

| **Greek** | |
|---|---|
| *angelos* | angel |
| *gramma* | a letter |
| *kosmos* | the world |
| *logos* | word |

Prefixes and suffixes can be added to the roots of words to alter the meaning of the words or to create new words with new meanings. A *prefix* is a word or part of a word placed before the root of a word, and a *suffix* is placed after the root. As is the case with root words, the English language derives many of its prefixes and suffixes from Latin and Greek. For example:

**Some Latin Prefixes**

| | |
|---|---|
| *ante-* | before |
| *contra-* | against |
| *extra-* | beyond |
| *in-* | in, into |
| *non-* | not |
| *post-* | after |
| *pro-* | before |
| *super-* | above |

**Some Greek Prefixes**

| | |
|---|---|
| *ampli-* | on both sides |
| *anti-* | opposite |
| *auto-* | self |
| *hemi-* | half |
| *hyper-* | over, above |
| *mono-* | alone, single |
| *para-* | beside |
| *pro-* | before |

**Some Latin Suffixes**

| | |
|---|---|
| *-ary* | belonging to |
| *-ess* | feminine of |
| *-et, ette* | denoting diminution |
| *-ty* | quality, state, condition |

**Some Greek Suffixes**

| | |
|---|---|
| *-ic* | pertaining to |
| *-ism* | act, state, condition |
| *-ist* | a doer |

Some examples of English words with prefixes and suffixes added include

| | | | | |
|---|---|---|---|---|
| anti | + | biotic | = | antibiotic |
| benefit | + | ary | = | beneficiary |
| communist | + | ism | = | communism |
| hemi | + | sphere | = | hemisphere |
| host | + | ess | = | hostess |
| in | + | dispensable | = | indispensable |
| pro | + | claim | = | proclaim |

Adding prefixes and suffixes may change the spelling of the former roots. This occurs most frequently when suffixes are added to words. Consult the basic spelling rules on the following pages when prefixes and suffixes are parts of words.

## Should the Final Consonant Be Doubled?

The answer to the question of whether a final consonant should be doubled involves the most complicated spelling rule. However, the rule is well worth learning because once you know it, you will suddenly be able to spell thousands of words correctly.

In order to understand the rule, remember first the difference between vowels (*a, e, i, o, u,* and sometimes *y*) and consonants (all the other letters in the alphabet). The problem in spelling occurs when you want to add an ending that begins with a vowel, such as *-ed, -er, -est, or -ing*. Sometimes a word will double the last letter before adding an ending:

trap + ing = trapping    The fur traders spent their time tra*pp*ing animals.

Sometimes the word will *not* double the last letter before adding the ending:

turn + er = turner    He dropped the pancake tur*n*er.

How do you know when to double the final consonant?

**Rule for Doubling One-Syllable Words**

Double the final consonant of a one-syllable word when adding an ending that begins with a vowel only if the last three letters of the word are a consonant-vowel-consonant combination.

Since *rap* in the word *trap* is a consonant-vowel-consonant combination, this one-syllable word will double the final consonant when adding an ending beginning with a vowel. Since the last three letters *urn* in the word *turn* are a vowel-consonant-consonant combination, this one-syllable word does not double the final consonant when adding an ending beginning with a vowel.

Note that in words with *qu* like *quit* or *quiz*, you should think of the *qu* as a consonant. (The *u* does have a consonant *w* sound.) *quit* + *ing* = quit*t*ing.

**Rule for Doubling the Consonant in Words of More Than One Syllable**

For words of more than one syllable, the rule adds more condition: if the first syllable is accented in the newly formed word, you do not double the final consonant.

pre fer′ + ed = pre ferred′

but

pre fer′ + ence = pref′ er ence
(The accent has changed to the first syllable.)

PRACTICE

## Doubling the Consonant?

For each of the following one-syllable words, determine whether or not the word will double the final consonant when adding an ending beginning with a vowel. The first two are done for you. Check your answers against those in the Answer Key on p. 467.

| One-Syllable Word | Consonant-Vowel-Consonant Combination? | Double? | Add *-ing* Ending |
|---|---|---|---|
| drag | yes | yes | dragging |
| drain | no | no | draining |
| slip | | | |
| crack | | | |
| broil | | | |
| win | | | |

Try these two-syllable words:

con *trol′* + ing = ______________________

fe′ *ver* + ish = ______________________

For each of the following words of more than one syllable, determine whether or not the word will double the final consonant when adding an ending beginning with a vowel.

com *pel′* + ed = ______________________

dif′ *fer* + ence = ______________________

be *gin′* + ing = ______________________

PRACTICE

## Doubling the Final Consonant When Adding Endings That Begin with Vowels?

Decide whether or not to double the final consonant when adding the endings to the following words. Check your answers against those in the Answer Key on p. 467.

| Word | Ending | | New Word |
|---|---|---|---|
| 1. bit | + en | = | ______________________ |
| 2. oc cur′ | + ence | = | ______________________ |
| 3. wa′ ver | + ing | = | ______________________ |
| 4. pre fer′ | + ed | = | ______________________ |
| 5. pre′ fer | + ence | = | ______________________ |
| 6. thin | + er | = | ______________________ |
| 7. trans fer′ | + ed | = | ______________________ |
| 8. sail | + ing | = | ______________________ |
| 9. pro pel′ | + ent | = | ______________________ |
| 10. o mit′ | + ed | = | ______________________ |

## Words Ending in *-y*

1. When a *y* at the end of a word is preceded by a consonant, change *y* to *i* and add the ending.

| | | | | |
|---|---|---|---|---|
| car*ry* | + | er | = | carr*ier* |
| mer*ry* | + | ment | = | merr*iment* |
| fun*ny* | + | er | = | ____________________ |
| pret*ty* | + | ness | = | ____________________ |
| va*ry* | + | es | = | ____________________ |

Exceptions: Do not change the *y* to *i* if the ending starts with an *i*. Few English words have two *i*'s together.

| | | | | |
|---|---|---|---|---|
| stu*dy* | + | ing | = | stud*ying* (not studiing) |
| rea*dy* | + | ing | = | ____________________ |

Some long words drop the *y* when adding the ending. You can hear that the *y* syllable is missing when you pronounce the word correctly.

| | | | | |
|---|---|---|---|---|
| milita*ry* | + | ism | = | milita*rism* |
| accompany | + | ist | = | ____________________ |

2. When *y* at the end of a word is preceded by a vowel, do *not* change the *y* when adding the ending. Simply add the ending.

| | | | | |
|---|---|---|---|---|
| sur*vey* | + | s | = | sur*veys* |
| enj*oy* | + | ment | = | ____________________ |

**PRACTICE**

### Adding Endings to Words That End in *-y*

Add endings to the following words, being sure to change the *y* to *i* whenever necessary. Check your answers against those in the Answer Key on p. 467.

| Word | | Ending | | New Word |
|---|---|---|---|---|
| 1. key | + | s | = | ____________________ |
| 2. lonely | + | ness | = | ____________________ |
| 3. cry | + | ing | = | ____________________ |
| 4. cry | + | s | = | ____________________ |
| 5. pray | + | er | = | ____________________ |
| 6. employ | + | ment | = | ____________________ |

| | | | | |
|---|---|---|---|---|
| 7. monkey | + | ing | = | ______________ |
| 8. beauty | + | ful | = | ______________ |
| 9. theory | + | es | = | ______________ |
| 10. ceremony | + | al | = | ______________ |

## Is It One Word or Two?

There is often confusion about whether certain word combinations should be joined together to form compound words. Study the following groups of words to avoid this common confusion.

These words are always written as one word:

| | | |
|---|---|---|
| another | everything | playroom |
| bathroom | grandmother | schoolteacher |
| bedroom | nearby | southeast, northwest, etc. |
| bookkeeper | nevertheless | workplace |
| cannot | newspaper | yourself |
| downstairs | | |

These words are always written as two words:

| | |
|---|---|
| a lot | high school |
| all right | living room |
| dining room | no one |
| good night | |

These words are written as one or two words depending on their use:

| | |
|---|---|
| **all ready** (*pronoun and adj.*) | completely prepared |
| **already** (*adv.*) | previously; before |
| **all together** (*pronoun and adj.*) | in a group |
| **altogether** (*adv.*) | completely |
| **all ways** (*adj. and noun*) | every road or path |
| **always** (*adverb*) | on every occasion |
| **any one** (*adj. and pronoun*) | one person or thing in a specific group |
| **anyone** (*indef. pronoun*) | any person at all |
| **every one** (*adj. and pronoun*) | every person or thing in a specific group |
| **everyone** (*indef. pronoun*) | all of the people |
| **may be** (*verb*) | might be |
| **maybe** (*adv.*) | perhaps |

**PRACTICE**

### One Word or Two?

Fill in the blank in each of the following sentences by choosing the correct word or words to complete that sentence. Check your answers against those in the Answer Key on p. 467.

1. The blue rug looks beautiful in the white ______________.
   (bed room, bedroom)
2. The room is usually occupied by our ______________ but she is not here right now.
   (grandmother, grand mother)
3. She has ______________ left for a winter vacation.
   (all ready, already)
4. Last night we all called her and ______________ we sang "Happy Birthday" over the phone.
   (all together, altogether)
5. We ______________ remember her birthday, no matter where we are.
   (all ways, always)
6. ______________ likes to be remembered on special days, particularly a birthday.
   (Every one, Everyone)
7. Next year, ______________ all the members of the family will be able to
   (may be, maybe)
   celebrate her birthday with us.
8. If she ______________ come to us, we will drive up and surprise her.
   (cannot, can not)
9. Most families have members who do not live ______________.
   (near by, nearby)
10. ______________, we can keep in touch by letter, phone, or visits.
    (Never the less, Nevertheless)

## Spelling 200 Tough Words

### Word List 1: Silent Letters

**b**
clim*b*
crum*b*
de*b*t
dou*b*t
su*b*tle

**c**
indi*c*t

**d**
knowle*d*ge
We*d*nesday

**h**
ex*h*ibit
r*h*etoric
r*h*ythm
sc*h*ool

**l**
co*l*onel

**n**
autum*n*
colum*n*
condem*n*

**p**
*p*neumonia
*p*sychology

**s**
ai*s*le
debri*s*
i*s*land

**t**
depo*t*
lis*t*en
mor*t*gage

**w**
ans*w*er

## Word List 2: Double Letters

| | | |
|---|---|---|
| a*cc*identa*ll*y | exa*gg*erate | questio*nn*aire |
| a*cc*o*mm*odate | fina*ll*y | reco*mm*end |
| acro*ss* | guarant*ee* | sheri*ff* |
| a*dd*re*ss* | hara*ss* | su*ccee*d |
| a*nn*ual | nece*ss*ary | su*cc*e*ss* |
| a*pp*arently | o*cc*asiona*ll*y | su*gg*est |
| a*rr*angement | omi*ss*ion | su*mm*arize |
| co*mmittee* | po*ss*e*ss*ion | tomo*rr*ow |
| emba*rr*ass | prefe*rr*ed | wri*tt*en *but* wri*t*ing |

## Word List 3: *-able* or *-ible*

**-able**

Usually, when you begin with a complete word, the ending is *-able*.

acceptable
agreeable

- These words keep the *e* when adding the ending:

| | |
|---|---|
| peaceable | manageable |
| noticeable | knowledgeable |

- These words drop the *e* when adding the ending:

| | |
|---|---|
| conceivable | dispensable |
| desirable | imaginable |

**-ible**

Usually, if you start with a root that is not a word, the ending is *-ible*.

| | | |
|---|---|---|
| audible | illegible | possible |
| compatible | incredible | sensible |
| eligible | permissible | susceptible |
| feasible | plausible | tangible |

## Word List 4: *de-* or *di-*

| de- | di- |
|---|---|
| decide | dilemma |
| decision | dilute |
| delinquent | discipline |
| descend | discuss |
| describe | disease |
| despair | disguise |
| despicable | dispense |

| | |
|---|---|
| despise | dispute |
| despite | dissent |
| despondent | divide |
| destructive | divine |
| develop | division |
| device | |

## Word List 5: The *-er* Sound

Most words ending with the *-er* sound are spelled with *-er*, as in the words *prisoner*, *customer*, and *hunger*. Words that are exceptions to this should be learned carefully.

**-ar**

| | | |
|---|---|---|
| beggar | dollar | polar |
| burglar | grammar | similar |
| calendar | pillar | vulgar |
| collar | | |

**-or**

| | | |
|---|---|---|
| actor | emperor | professor |
| author | governor | sailor |
| bachelor | motor | scissors |
| doctor | | |

| **-our** | **-re** | **-ur** | -yr |
|---|---|---|---|
| humour | centre | murmur | martyr |
| labour | litre | | |
| neighbour | theatre | | |

## Word List 6: *-ance* or *-ence*

Most words with the *-ence* sound at the end are spelled *-ence*. Here are a few examples:

| | |
|---|---|
| audience | insistence |
| correspondence | intelligence |
| excellence | licence (noun) |
| existence | presence |
| independence | reference |

Learn these exceptions:

**-ance**

allowance
ambulance
appearance
assistance
attendance
balance
deliverance
dominance
guidance
ignorance
nuisance
observance
resistance
significance
tolerance

**-ense**

license (verb)

**-eance**

vengeance

## Word List 7: Problems with *s, c, z, x,* and *k*

absence
alcohol
analyze/analyse
auxiliary
awkward
biscuit
complexion
concede
consensus
criticize
ecstasy
emphasize
especially
exceed
exercise
fascinate
magazine
medicine
muscle
prejudice
recede
sincerely
supersede
vacillate
vicious

## Word List 8: Twenty-four Demons

acquire
argument
benefit
cafeteria
category
cemetery
conquer
corroborate
courageous
extremely
frightening
grateful
inoculate
lightning
ninety
ninth
occurred
occurrence
privilege
ridiculous
secretary
truly
until
village

APPENDIX C

C

# Irregular Verbs

## Principal Parts of Irregular Verbs

| Simple Form | Past Form | Past Participle |
|---|---|---|
| 1. Principal parts are the same. | | |
| beat | beat | beat or beaten |
| bet | bet | bet |
| burst | burst | burst |
| cast | cast | cast |
| cost | cost | cost |
| cut | cut | cut |
| fit | fit | fit |
| hit | hit | hit |
| hurt | hurt | hurt |
| let | let | let |
| put | put | put |
| quit | quit | quit |
| read | *read | *read |
| rid | rid | rid |
| set | set | set |
| shut | shut | shut |
| split | split | split |
| spread | spread | spread |
| wet | wet | wet |
| 2. The past form and past participle are the same. | | |
| bend | bent | bent |
| lend | lent | lent |
| send | sent | sent |
| spend | spent | spent |
| build | built | built |

*Pronunciation changes.

| Simple Form | Past Form | Past Participle |
|---|---|---|
| creep | crept | crept |
| feel | felt | felt |
| keep | kept | kept |
| sleep | slept | slept |
| sweep | swept | swept |
| deal | dealt | dealt |
| mean | meant | meant |
| leave | left | left |
| bleed | bled | bled |
| feed | fed | fed |
| flee | fled | fled |
| lead | led | led |
| speed | sped | sped |
| cling | clung | clung |
| dig | dug | dug |
| spin | spun | spun |
| stick | stuck | stuck |
| sting | stung | stung |
| strike | struck | struck |
| swing | swung | swung |
| wring | wrung | wrung |
| win | won | won |
| lay (to put) | laid | laid |
| pay | paid | paid |
| say | said | said |
| sell | sold | sold |
| tell | told | told |
| bind | bound | bound |
| find | found | found |
| grind | ground | ground |
| wind | wound | wound |
| bring | brought | brought |
| buy | bought | bought |
| fight | fought | fought |
| find | found | found |
| think | thought | thought |
| seek | sought | sought |
| catch | caught | caught |
| teach | taught | taught |

| Simple Form | Past Form | Past Participle |
|---|---|---|
| have | had | had |
| sit | sat | sat |
| hear | heard | heard |
| hold | held | held |
| shoot | shot | shot |
| stand | stood | stood |

3. All forms are different

| | | |
|---|---|---|
| draw | drew | drawn |
| fall | fell | fallen |
| shake | shook | shaken |
| take | took | taken |
| bear | bore | borne |
| swear | swore | sworn |
| tear | tore | torn |
| wear | wore | worn |
| blow | blew | blown |
| fly | flew | flown |
| grow | grew | grown |
| know | knew | known |
| throw | threw | thrown |
| begin | began | begun |
| drink | drank | drunk |
| ring | rang | rung |
| shrink | shrank | shrunk |
| sing | sang | sung |
| sink | sank | sunk |
| spring | sprang | sprung |
| swim | swam | swum |
| bite | bit | bitten (or bit) |
| hide | hid | hidden (or hid) |
| drive | drove | driven |
| ride | rode | ridden |
| stride | strode | stridden |
| rise | rose | risen |
| write | wrote | written |
| dive | dove | dived |
| break | broke | broken |
| freeze | froze | frozen |
| speak | spoke | spoken |

| Simple Form | Past Form | Past Participle |
|---|---|---|
| steal | stole | stolen |
| weave | wove | woven |
| get | got | gotten |
| forget | forgot | forgotten |
| choose | chose | chosen |
| give | gave | given |
| forgive | forgave | forgiven |
| forbid | forbade | forbidden |
| do | did | done |
| eat | ate | eaten |
| go | went | gone |
| lie (to recline) | lay | lain |
| see | saw | seen |

**PRACTICE**

## Irregular Verbs

Supply the past form or the past participle for each verb in parentheses. Check your answers against those in the Answer Key on p. 467.

1. We ________________ four trout in the stream.
   (to catch)
2. I shouldn't have ________________ my gloves on the counter.
   (to lay)
3. The audience ________________ when the singer attempted the high notes.
   (to flee)
4. The pipe ________________ yesterday; we are waiting for a plumber.
   (to burst)
5. He has ________________ aimlessly around the city for several hours.
   (to ride)
6. The firefighters ________________ down the ladder.
   (to slide)
7. The elevator ________________ quickly to the tenth floor.
   (to rise)
8. She had ________________ her job because of her medical condition.
   (to quit)
9. It was clear he had ________________ about our agreement.
   (to forget)
10. He had washed and ________________ out all his clothes in the bathtub.
    (to wring)

APPENDIX D

D

# Answer Key to Practices

## UNIT I: GRAMMAR

### Chapter 2: Recognizing Subjects and Verbs

#### Finding the Subject of a Sentence

**PRACTICE (P. 17)**

1. The plane landed.
2. Michelle Bates gathered her bags.
3. She was so excited.
4. Strange sounds filled her ears.
5. A mother and her three children shared a lunch.
6. The battered red taxi idled outside.
7. A light rain had fallen recently.

#### Finding Hidden Subjects

**PRACTICE (P. 22)**

1. (You) look ~~at a map of South America.~~
2. Where is the ancient city ~~of Chan Chan~~?
3. Here ~~on the coastal desert of northern Peru~~ stand the remains ~~of this city of the kings~~.
4. Chan Chan, ~~once the fabulously wealthy centre of the Chimor~~, is situated ~~in one of the driest, bleakest regions in the world~~.
5. It was the largest pre-Columbian city ~~in South America.~~
6. ~~In the ruins of this city~~, scientists have found fragments to piece together the mystery ~~of the past~~.
7. How could this civilization have survived this hostile environment and become so advanced?

#### Finding Action Verbs

**PRACTICE (P. 24)**

1. Some people collect very strange objects. (present)
2. One man saved the fortunes ~~from fortune cookies~~. (past)
3. A group of people ~~in Alberta~~ often met to discuss their spark plug collections. (past)
4. People ~~in Brandon~~ will gather many types ~~of barbed wire~~. (future)
5. Collectors take pride ~~in the possession of unusual items~~. (present)
6. A collection, ~~like odd rocks or unique automobiles,~~ will let a person express his or her individuality. (future)
7. Collections keep us entertained ~~from childhood to old age~~. (present)

#### Chapter Review Exercises

#### Finding Subjects and Verbs in Simple Sentences

**PRACTICE (P. 27)**

1. Mother and Dad always blame me ~~for any trouble with my sister~~.
2. My sister, ~~the most popular girl in her class~~, is two years older than I.
3. Yesterday, ~~for instance~~, she was trying on her new graduation dress.
4. Helpfully, I took out her new shoes and purse ~~for her~~.
5. Margaret instantly became furious ~~with me~~.
6. I was only sharing Margaret's excitement ~~about her new clothes~~.

### Chapter 3: More Work with Verbs

#### Correcting Unnecessary Shifts in Verb Tense

**PRACTICE 1 (P. 35)**

Answers will vary. These are sample answers.

1. After I complete that writing course, I will take the required history course.
2. In the beginning of the movie, the action was slow; by the end, I was sitting on the edge of my seat.

3. The textbook gives the rules for writing a works cited page, but it doesn't explain how to do parenthetical references.
4. I was walking in the park when all of a sudden I saw her running toward me.
5. The encyclopedia gave several pages of information about astronomy, but it didn't give anything about black holes.
6. The invitation requested that Juan be at the ceremony and that he attend the banquet as well.
7. That website gives you excellent information, but it is too cluttered.

**PRACTICE 2 (P. 36)**

Doctor Norman Bethune grew up in Gravenhurst, Ontario. He was educated in Toronto and served as a stretcher bearer in World War I. He contracted tuberculosis and thereafter devoted himself to helping other victims of the disease when he practised surgery in Montreal. He also invented or redesigned twelve medical and surgical instruments. Bethune travelled to Russia in 1935, joined the Communist Party, and went to Spain in 1936, where he organized the first mobile blood transfusion service during the Spanish Civil War. After returning to Canada, he shortly left for overseas again, this time to China, where he helped the Chinese Communists in their fight against Japan. "Spain and China," he wrote, "are part of the same battle." While there, he contracted an infection and died. Mao's essay "In Memory of Norman Bethune," prescribed reading during China's Cultural Revolution, urges all Communists to follow Bethune's example of selfless dedication to others. Bethune is the best-known Canadian to the Chinese, and many Chinese visit his Canadian birthplace.

## Using the Correct Tense

**PRACTICE (P. 38)**

1. have stopped
2. would have
3. will buy
4. had never been
5. liked
6. will soon be
7. is

## Choosing the Right Voice

**PRACTICE (P. 43)**

1. The Canadian health minister made no policy or funding announcements at the International AIDS Conference in Toronto.
   The active is more appropriate. Others did make policy announcements. Knowing who didn't is important.
2. Microsoft founder Bill Gates gave $650 million (U.S.) to the war against HIV/AIDS.
   The passive is probably just as appropriate as the active here. Bill Gates is famous throughout the world, but the amount that he gave is extraordinary, also.
3. Zimbabwe's foreign minister was allowed into Canada for the international conference despite a ban on visits by senior officials from that country.
   The passive is more appropriate. The doer of the action would be Canadian authorities—too insignificant to even mention. The subject in this sentence, Zimbabwe's foreign minister, is the centre of the controversy here.
4. Former U.S. president Bill Clinton told the audience that a lot of mistakes were made during his presidency, but underfunding AIDS research was not one of them.
   The active is more appropriate. Former U.S. President Bill Clinton is more well known than anyone at this conference, even Bill Gates.
5. Twenty-two thousand delegates and 8000 journalists, exhibitors, volunteers, and staff attended the International AIDS Conference in 2006.
   Both active and passive are equally appropriate. The number of attendees is massive, but the event itself is worthy of attention.
6. Many at the conference discussed in great detail the impact that poverty has on HIV and AIDS in developing countries.
   The passive is more appropriate. The topic of discussion is more important than the general population that discussed it. Also, the sentence using active voice above is awkward sounding.
7. The importance of the role of media in spreading the word about HIV/AIDS was stressed by actor and activist Richard Gere.
   The active voice is more appropriate. Richard Gere is a celebrity activist. It doesn't really matter what he says so much as the fact that he is at the conference in the first place.

### Chapter Review Exercises

### Solving Problems with Verbs

**PRACTICE (P. 45)**

1. He ought not to drive so fast *or* He shouldn't drive so fast.
2. It is essential that Lynn take her dog to the vet.
3. I wish I were a chef.
4. She sang for a huge crowd Saturday night.
5. I was shaken up by the accident *or* The accident shook me up.
6. The skiers climbed the hill.
7. My father asked me last night to help him build a deck.

## Chapter 4: Subject-Verb Agreement

### Making the Subject and Verb Agree

**PRACTICE 1 (P. 48)**

1. cycles
2. amazes
3. vary
4. cheer
5. hope

**PRACTICE 2 (P. 48)**

1. are
2. move
3. move
4. are
5. are

**PRACTICE 3 (P. 50)**

1. is
2. has
3. is
4. specifies
5. is
6. are
7. is

**PRACTICE 4 (P. 50)**

1. is
2. was
3. seem
4. takes
5. has

**PRACTICE 5 (P. 51)**

1. are
2. is
3. are
4. are
5. is

**PRACTICE 6 (P. 52)**

1. are
2. are
3. has
4. have
5. claps

**PRACTICE 7 (P. 52)**

1. do
2. were
3. does
4. do
5. were

### Chapter Review Exercises

**PRACTICE 1 (P. 53)**

1. doesn't
2. were
3. doesn't
4. Were
5. doesn't

**PRACTICE 2 (P. 53)**

1. price, has
2. decision, requires
3. She, doesn't
4. guide or security guard, sees
5. committee, agrees
6. Potato chips and cola, are
7. One, is

## Chapter 5: Coordination and Subordination

### Recognizing the Comma and Coordinating Conjunction

**PRACTICE (P. 58)**

1. The audience was packed into the room (, for) this was a man with an international reputation.
2. He could have told about all his successes (, but) instead he spoke about his disappointments.
3. His words were electric (, so) the crowd was attentive.
4. I should have brought a tape recorder (, or) at least I should have taken notes.

### Recognizing the Semicolon, Adverbial Conjunction, and Comma

**PRACTICE 1 (P. 61)**

1. The restaurant is always too crowded on Saturdays (; nevertheless,) it serves the best food in town.
2. The land was not for sale (; however,) the house could be rented.
3. The lawsuit cost the company several million dollars (; consequently,) the company went out of business a short time later.
4. The doctor told him to lose weight (; furthermore,) she insisted he also stop smoking.

### Combining Sentences Using Adverbial Conjuctions

**PRACTICE 2 (P. 62)**

Answers will vary. These are sample answers.

1. People once preferred to write with a pen or pencil; however, the computer has now become a favourite writing tool.

2. Computers provide a powerful way to create and store pieces of writing; furthermore, they make the editing process fast and efficient.
3. Computers have revolutionized today's offices; consequently, no modern business is without them.
4. Computers have become relatively inexpensive; accordingly, most people own a computer.
5. Many children know more about computers than many adults; moreover, many children are teaching adults how to operate computers.
6. Professional writers have become enthusiastic about the use of computers; nonetheless, there are still some writers who will use only a ballpoint pen.
7. We have many technological aids for writing; nevertheless, let us not forget that the source of all our ideas is the human brain.

### Recognizing Dependent and Independent Clauses

**PRACTICE 1 (P. 68)**

| | | | |
|---|---|---|---|
| 1. DC | 3. IC | 5. IC | 7. DC |
| 2. DC | 4. DC | 6. DC | |

### Combining Sentences Using Subordination

**PRACTICE 2 (P. 68)**

Answers will vary. These are sample answers.

1. While he was eating breakfast, the results of the election came over the radio.
2. Simon gave up his plan to launch a dot-com company because he felt it was too risky.
3. I will see my teacher tonight, as she is speaking at the university this evening.
4. The designer hoped for a promotion, although not one person in the department was promoted last year.
5. Since the designer hoped for a promotion, she made sure all her work was done accurately and on time.

### Combining Sentences Using a Relative Pronoun

**PRACTICE (P. 71)**

Answers will vary. These are sample answers.

1. The chemistry lab that I attend is two hours long.
2. The student assistant who is standing by the door is very knowledgeable.
3. The equipment that was purchased last year will make possible some important new research.

### Recognizing Restrictive and Nonrestrictive Clauses

**PRACTICE (P. 72)**

1. Canada's first census, which was taken in 1667, showed 3215 non-Native inhabitants in 668 families.
2. Most of the families who lived near the St. Lawrence River were French Canadians.
3. By the time of Confederation, the population of the country had risen to 3 463 000, which was an increase of 1077 percent over 200 years.
4. If the population, which is about 30 000 000 persons in Canada now, increases by a similar percentage, we'll have a population of 280 200 000 by the year 2167.
5. Where, do you think, will we put everyone who will live in Canada then?

### Chapter Review Exercises

### Combining Sentences Using Coordination and Subordination

**PRACTICE (P. 74)**

Answers will vary. This is a sample paragraph.

The wind is strong; the waves are choppy and growing larger. I paddle my kayak harder, but my arms are getting tired. As the energy drains from them, they grow limp and heavy. The other side of the harbour seems distant. The glow of the setting sun is behind me, spreading orange and purple fingers across the sky. The wall of rocks that lies offshore picks up the last light of the setting sun, becoming a silver beacon. I focus on that wall and paddle harder. The sea smashes against my bow, pushing me away from shore. As flecks of spray hit my face, I taste the salt on my lips. With that taste of the sea, the beauty of the sea and shore strikes me. I am distracted from my labour and absorbed by the world around me. As my kayak finally glides past the rocks to the sheltered beach beyond, I am exhilarated and exhausted.

## Chapter 6: Correcting Fragments

### Understanding Fragments

**PRACTICE 1 (P. 80)**

1. a. subject
2. b. verb
3. c. both subject and verb

4. b. verb
5. b. verb
6. a. subject
7. d. contains subject and verb, but lacks complete thought

### Turning Fragments into Sentences

**PRACTICE 2 (P. 81)**

Answers will vary. These are sample answers.

1. The otter returned to the river.
2. A bird on the oak branch sang.
3. The river flowed between the island and the mainland.
4. The hawk in a soaring motion flew into the sky.
5. The fishing boats on the lake glided over the water.
6. The loon dropped like a stone into the water.
7. Because the fisherman put the net away, the fish were safe at last.

**PRACTICE 3 (P. 82)**

1. As long as it's a windy day, we'll be able to fly the kite.
2. Into the forest, armed with a machine gun, the fugitive dashed.
3. Complete
4. The college student jogged along a deserted and dusty road.
5. The meadow below is where the deer and the antelope play.
6. The groundhog was run over by three different cars.
7. Complete

### Identifying Phrases

**PRACTICE 1 (P. 84)**

1. infinitive
2. infinitive
3. prepositional
4. prepositional
5. noun
6. noun
7. prepositional

**PRACTICE 2 (P. 85)**

1. prepositional
2. infinitive
3. prepositional
4. noun
5. verb
6. prepositional
7. infinitive
8. verb
9. infinitive
10. prepositional

### Correcting the Fragment That Contains a Participle

**PRACTICE 1 (P. 86)**

Answers will vary. These are sample answers.

1. a. He is climbing in the Rockies.
   b. He climbs in the Rockies.
   c. Climbing in the Rockies, he left his stereo behind.
   d. Climbing in the Rockies is the thing to do.
2. a. He is playing video games.
   b. He plays video games.
   c. Playing video games, he didn't hear the robbers.
   d. Playing video games is time-consuming.
3. a. She is going clubbing on Tuesdays.
   b. She goes clubbing on Tuesdays.
   c. Going clubbing on Tuesdays, she met her best friend.
   d. Going clubbing on Tuesdays is tiring.

### Recognizing the Fragment

**PRACTICE 2 (P. 87)**

1. complete
2. fragment
3. fragment
4. fragment
5. complete
6. fragment
7. complete
8. fragment
9. fragment
10. fragment

### Editing for Fragments

**PRACTICE 3 (P. 88)**

Fragments:

Which took the game to 5–3 for Italy.
But 10 minutes before the end of extra time.
For head-butting Marco Materazzi.
And had insulted both his mother and his sister.
Partying with abandon.
Because he didn't take the moral high road.
While millions of fans watched his every move.

Corrected paragraph (answers will vary):

Soccer's World Cup in 2006 was won by Italy for the first time in 24 years, but it is public disgrace for which the game will be remembered by the world. By half time, the final game between Italy and France was tied 1–1. After 120 minutes, the game was still tied. The final victory depended on the penalty shootout, which took the game to 5–3 for Italy. But 10 minutes before the end of extra time, France's illustrious captain, Zinedine

Zidane, was expelled for head-butting Marco Materazzi. Apparently, Marco had called him a terrorist and had insulted both his mother and his sister. Was this a deliberate, desperate, and cheap attempt to achieve final victory in what had become a gruelling final game? Celebrations by Italians around the world were unstoppable. They partied with abandon. But soccer scandal continues to loom over the Italian team. And Zinedine Zidane exited from his last World Cup under an umbrella of shame because he didn't take the moral high road while millions of fans watched his every move.

## Chapter 7: Correcting Run-ons

### Correcting Run-ons

**PRACTICE 1 (P. 94)**

Answers will vary. These are sample answers.

1. Simple: Five-year-old Davie asked Grandpa for an iPod for his birthday. He started crying because Grandpa didn't know what that was.
   Compound: Five-year-old Davie asked Grandpa for an iPod for his birthday, but he started crying because Grandpa didn't know what that was.
   Five-year-old Davie asked Grandpa for an iPod for his birthday; however, he started crying because Grandpa didn't know what that was.
   Complex: When five-year-old Davie asked Grandpa for an iPod for his birthday, he started crying because Grandpa didn't know what that was.
2. Simple: Many people are opposed to gambling in all its forms. They will not even buy a lottery ticket.
   Compound: Many people are opposed to gambling in all its forms, so they will not even buy a lottery ticket.
   Many people are opposed to gambling in all its forms; indeed, they will not even buy a lottery ticket.
   Complex: Since many people are opposed to gambling in all its forms, they will not even buy a lottery ticket.
3. Simple: Hockey may be Canada's national sport. The game can be quite brutal.
   Compound: Hockey may be Canada's national sport, but the game can be quite brutal.
   Hockey may be Canada's national sport; however, the game can be quite brutal.
   Complex: Although the game can be quite brutal, hockey may be Canada's national sport.
4. Simple: Many young people manage to travel. They find ways to do it cheaply.
   Compound: Many young people manage to travel, for they find ways to do it cheaply.
   Many young people manage to travel; they find ways to do it cheaply.
   Complex: Many young people manage to travel because they find ways to do it cheaply.
5. Simple: The need for a proper diet is important in any health program. All the junk food on the grocery shelves makes it hard to be consistent.
   Compound: The need for a proper diet is important in any health program, yet all the junk food on the grocery shelves makes it hard to be consistent.
   The need for a proper diet is important in any health program; however, all the junk food on the grocery shelves makes it hard to be consistent.
   Complex: Even though the need for a proper diet is important in any health program, all the junk food on the grocery shelves makes it hard to be consistent.

**PRACTICE 2 (P. 96)**

Answers will vary. These are sample answers.

1. Simple: The airline has begun its new route to the islands. Everyone is looking forward to flying there.
   Compound: The airline has begun its new route to the islands, so everyone is looking forward to flying there.
   The airline has begun its new route to the islands; consequently, everyone is looking forward to flying there.
   Complex: Ever since the airline began its new route to the islands, everyone has been looking forward to flying there.
2. Simple: The movie begins at nine o'clock. Let's have dinner before the show.
   Compound: The movie begins at nine o'clock, so let's have dinner before the show.
   The movie begins at nine o'clock; therefore, let's have dinner before the show.
   Complex: Since the movie begins at nine o'clock, let's have dinner before the show.
3. Simple: The studio audience screamed at the contestant. They wanted her to try for the big prize.
   Compound: The studio audience screamed at the contestant, for they wanted her to try for the big prize.

The studio audience screamed at the contestant; they wanted her to try for the big prize.

Complex: The studio audience screamed at the contestant because they wanted her to try for the big prize.

4. Simple: Maya needs new shoes. She is running in the marathon.

   Compound: Maya needs new shoes, for she is running in the marathon.

   Maya needs new shoes; she is running in the marathon.

   Complex: Since she is running in the marathon, Maya needs new shoes.

5. Simple: My actor friend grabbed my arm. She wanted to tell me about her new part in the movie.

   Compound: My actor friend grabbed my arm; she wanted to tell me about her new part in the movie.

   My actor friend grabbed my arm, for she wanted to tell me about her new part in the movie.

   Complex: My actor friend grabbed my arm because she wanted to tell me about her new part in the movie.

### Editing for Run-ons

**PRACTICE 3 (P. 99)**

Every sentence in the paragraph is a run-on sentence.
Corrected paragraph (answers may vary):

Mythology is the study of myths, and myths are known as the oldest form of literature. The oldest myths are creation myths. Cultures from around the world have their own creation myths. All of them are amazingly similar despite the vast geographical distances between these cultures and the fact that there are no known ways in which communication could have taken place between certain ones. Details of these myths change from one culture to the next; however, various themes of the myths remain the same. For example, although characters (most of the time, but not all of the time) take on new names from one culture to another, every culture refers to the existence of a creator. Also, the number of gods often differs from one mythology to another; nevertheless, every mythology has at least one god or one heroic figure in it. All in all, myths are incredible stories that, in many cases, have lasted thousands of years. No matter where they come from and what they are about, they bear striking similarities from one culture to another, and they all share a wisdom about something that never changes: our human nature.

**PRACTICE 4 (P. 99)**

Every sentence in the paragraph is a run-on sentence.
Corrected paragraph (answers may vary):

Sigmund Freud and Carl G. Jung were both psychiatrists who have had a great deal of influence on the study of psychology to this day. For example, each psychiatrist is famous for his own model of the human psyche. In Freud's model, there are three main parts. They are the ego, the id, and the superego. In Jung's model, there are also three main parts: the conscious, the personal unconscious, and the collective unconscious. Freud (Jung's teacher and subsequent collaborator until they parted due to a major disagreement in 1912) and Jung both believed that dreams come from the unconscious part of our psyche (for Freud, this meant the id and superego); nevertheless, they disagreed a great deal in the area of dream interpretation.

## Chapter 8: Parallel Structure

### Making Sentences Parallel

**PRACTICE 1 (P. 104)**

1. dirty
2. sewing her own clothes
3. willingly explain material more than once

**PRACTICE 2 (P. 104)**

Answers will vary. These are sample answers.

1. Winter in Edmonton is very windy and bitterly cold.
2. I would prefer fixing an old car to watching television.
3. Alex is a talented athlete, a top student, and even a generous friend.
4. The apartment is crowded and dark.
5. The dancer is slender and graceful.
6. The trees were tall and leafy.
7. My friend loves to play chess, to read science fiction, and to work out at the gym.

**PRACTICE 3 (P. 105)**

Answers will vary. These are sample answers.

1. The dog had to choose between jumping over the fence or digging a hole underneath it.
2. She was great at swimming, canoeing, and rock climbing.
3. As I looked down the city street, I could see the soft lights from restaurant windows, I could hear the

mellow sounds of a nightclub band, and I could sense the carefree moods of people walking by.

4. The singers have been on several road tours, have recorded for two record companies, and have expressed a desire to make a movie someday.
5. They would rather order a pizza than eat home cooking.
6. I explained to the teacher that my car had broken down, my books had been stolen, and my assignment pad had been left at home.
7. That night the prisoner was sick, discouraged, and lonely.

## Chapter 9: Pronouns

### Chapter Review Exercises

### Making Pronouns and Antecedents Agree

**PRACTICE (P. 117)**

Answers will vary. These are sample answers.

1. The father mailed his son's high school yearbook to him.
2. No one wants his or her income reduced.
3. When a company fails to update its equipment, it often pays a price in the long run.
4. Graduates today have many more options open to them than ever before.
5. Everybody knows his or her own strengths best.
6. All the soccer players put effort into their game.
7. If the campers want to eat quickly, they should help themselves.

## Chapter 10: Modifiers: Misplaced and Dangling

### Chapter Review Exercises

### Revising Misplaced or Dangling Modifiers

**PRACTICE (P. 123)**

Answers will vary. These are sample answers.

1. Wearing his tuxedo, Victor fed the dog.
2. While we were visiting Vancouver Aquarium, the otters entertained us.
3. Wanting to make a good impression, I wore a conservative, well-cut suit.
4. A band that we had heard earlier was playing in the park.
5. After running over the hill, I noticed that the farm was visible in the valley below.
6. The truck, which was broken down on the highway, caused a traffic jam for kilometres.
7. I saw three spiders hanging from the ceiling in my bedroom.

## Chapter 11: Punctuation

### Insert Necessary Commas

**PRACTICE 1 (P. 127)**

1. Problems with the water supply of Canada, the United States, Europe, and other parts of the world are growing.
2. Water is colourless, tasteless, odourless, and free of calories.
3. You will use on an average day 90 L of water for flushing, 120 L for bathing and washing clothes, and 95 L for other uses.
4. It took 450 L of water to create the eggs you ate for breakfast, 13 250 L for the steak you might eat for dinner, and over 200 000 L to produce the steel used to make your car.
5. The English–Wabigoon river system runs through Grassy Narrows, Ontario, and had become polluted with mercury.

**PRACTICE 2 (P. 128)**

1. The most overused bodies of water are our rivers, but they continue to serve us daily.
2. Canadian cities often developed next to rivers, and industries followed soon after in the same locations.
3. The people of the industrial age can try to clean the water they use, or they can watch pollution take over.
4. The Great Lakes are showing signs of renewal, yet the struggle against pollution there must continue.
5. Most people have not been educated about the dangerous state of our water supply, nor are all our members of Parliament fully aware of the problem.

**PRACTICE 3 (P. 129)**

1. A total solar eclipse, when the moon's shadow blots out the sun completely, is an outstanding cosmic event.
2. Once you see your first solar eclipse, you start looking forward to the next one.
3. However, witnessing this spectacle takes planning and the ability to travel to the best viewing spots.

4. In eastern Turkey, on August 11, 1999, a crowd of astronomers and "eclipse chasers" watched the last total eclipse of the millennium.
5. At the moment of totality, people cheer, clap, and often cry.

**PRACTICE 4 (P. 131)**

1. Natural disasters, I believe, have not been historically significant.
2. They have, however, significantly affected the lives of many Canadians.
3. Canada's worst coal-mine disaster, at Hillcrest, Alberta, occurred on June 19, 1914.
4. In Springhill, Nova Scotia, furthermore, 424 persons were killed in the mines between 1881 and 1969.
5. Avalanches, storms, and floods, which are natural disasters, have also made their marks on the face of our country.

**PRACTICE 5 (P. 131)**

1. Honey, I hope you're not planning to wear that hat.
2. I wonder, Samir, if the game has been cancelled.
3. Dad, could I borrow five dollars?
4. Can you help me, Doctor?
5. Ayesha, is that you?

**PRACTICE 6 (P. 132)**

1. "I'm innocent," he cried, "of all charges against me."
2. He mumbled, "I won't incriminate myself."
3. "I was told," the defendant explained, "to answer every question."
4. "This court," the judge announced, "will be adjourned."
5. "The jury," said Al Tarvin of *The Star,* "was handpicked."

**PRACTICE 7 (P. 132)**

1. Kicking, the child was carried off to bed.
2. To Maria, Suzuki was the boss from hell.
3. When you can, come and visit us.
4. Whoever that is, is going to be surprised.
5. Skin cancer seldom kills, doctors say.

## Using the Apostrophe

**PRACTICE 1 (P. 136)**

1. boys'
2. their
3. Moses's or Moses'
4. Antony and Maria's
5. nobody's
6. his
7. 1700's or 1700s
8. It's
9. Vancouver's
10. Wendy's

**PRACTICE 2 (P. 137)**

1. Cherry's
2. geese's
3. Carol's and Tess's
4. somebody's
5. hers
6. two's
7. can't

## Insert Necessary Quotation Marks

**PRACTICE 1 (P. 139)**

1. "The Hot House" is one of the stories contained in Rosemary Sullivan's *More Stories by Canadian Women.*
2. Nellie McClung said, "I'll never believe I'm dead until I see it in the papers."
3. no quotation marks needed
4. To "diss" is a slang term meaning to show disrespect.
5. She read the article "Whiz Kids" in *The Review.*

## Using Semicolons

**PRACTICE 2 (P. 140)**

1. One of the best ways to remember a vacation is to take numerous photos; one of the best ways to recall the contents of a book is to take notes.
2. The problem of street crime must be solved; otherwise, the number of vigilantes will increase.
3. The meal was composed of bruschetta, an appetizer; roast duck, the house specialty; and lemon mousse, a tart dessert.
4. The bank president was very cordial; however, he would not approve the loan.
5. New methods of production are being used in the factories of Japan; eventually they will be common in this country as well.

## Using Colons

**PRACTICE 3 (P. 141)**

1. Two Canadian-born comedians have achieved great success in the United States: Jim Carrey and Mike Myers.

2. The official has one major flaw in his personality: greed.
3. No colons needed
4. The college offers four courses in English literature: Romantic Poetry, Shakespeare's Plays, The British Short Story, and The Modern Novel.
5. Arriving at 6:15 in the morning, Marlene brought me a sausage-and-cheese pizza, ginger ale, and a litre of ice cream.

### Using Dashes or Parentheses

**PRACTICE (P. 144)**

1. Herbert Simon is—and I don't think this is an exaggeration—a genius.
2. George Eliot (her real name was Mary Ann Evans) wrote *Silas Marner.*
3. You should—in fact I insist—see a doctor.
4. Health Canada's website has suggestions to help smokers quit (visit www.infotobacco.com).
5. Mass media (television, radio, movies, magazines, and newspapers) are able to transmit information over a wide range and to a large number of people.

### Chapter Review Exercises

### Punctuation Overview

**PRACTICE 1 (P. 144)**

1. To measure crime, sociologists have used three different techniques: official statistics, victimization surveys, and self-report studies.
2. "David" is one of the best-loved poems of Earle Birney.
3. That show uses one thing I hate: a laugh track.
4. Farley Mowat has written numerous books for adults; however, he also writes very popular books for children.
5. Tuberculosis (also known as consumption) has been nearly eliminated by medical science.
6. The Victorian Period (1837–1901) saw a rapid expansion in industry.
7. He told me—I remember the day—that he would never give up.

**PRACTICE 2 (P. 145)**

1. Many young people have two feelings about science and technology: awe and fear.
2. Mr. Doyle, the realtor; Mrs. Tong, the bank officer; and Ivan Petroff, the lawyer, are the three people to help work out the real-estate transaction.
3. The book was entitled *English Literature: The Victorian Age.*
4. "My computer," she said, "has been crashing all day."
5. She brought a bathing suit, towel, sunglasses, and several books to the beach. (no colon after brought)
6. The meeting to discuss a pay increase—I'll believe it when I see it—has been rescheduled for Friday.
7. The complex lab experiment has these two major problems: too many difficult calculations and too many variables.

## Chapter 12: Capitalization

### Capitalization

**PRACTICE (P. 150)**

1. Italian
2. Canadian Rockies
3. Bible
4. University of Alberta
5. Hallowe'en
6. Bell Canada, Friday, Winnipeg, Manitoba
7. Cobalt-60, Canadian, Dr. Donald Green
8. Why
9. Canadian Auto Workers
10. *Women of the Klondike*, North

## Chapter 13: Unit I Review: Using All You Have Learned

### Identifying Parts of Speech

**PRACTICE 1 (P. 153)**

2. constant: adjective modifying the noun *source*
3. of: preposition, which starts the prepositional phrase *of creativity and inspiration*
4. and: coordinating conjunction (one of the FANBOYS) joining two items
5. him: pronoun in the objective case
6. inspired: action verb in the past tense
7. throughout: preposition, which starts the prepositional phrase *throughout his life*
8. his: possessive adjective modifying the noun *ideas*
9. was: helping verb *to be* in the past tense
10. when: subordinate conjunction that begins a dependent clause
11. often: adverb modifying the past tense verb *led*

12. the: definite article
13. right: adjective modifying the noun *direction*
14. had: past tense of the irregular action verb *to have*
15. impending: adjective modifying the noun *death*
16. become: past participle of the irregular action verb *to become*
17. a: indefinite article
18. symbol: common noun
19. properly: adverb modifying the verb *understood*
20. only: adverb modifying *from his inner experiences*
21. outer: adjective modifying the noun *world*
22. for: preposition, which begins the prepositional phrase *for him*
23. he: pronoun in the subjective case
24. could: modal auxiliary (helping verb)
25. happenings: common abstract noun

There is more than one way to correct the fragments and run-ons in the following practices in this chapter. The following answers are possible.

### Editing Sentences for Errors

**PRACTICE 2 (P. 153)**

1. Roma (also known as Gypsies or Romany Gypsies) now are living in many countries of the world.
2. The international community of scientists agrees that these Roma originally came from India thousands of years ago.
3. After the original Roma people left India, they went to Persia; there they divided into groups.
4. One branch of Roma went west to Europe, while the other group decided to go east.
5. In the Middle Ages ... Little Egypt.
6. C
7. Today, Roma families may be found from Canada to Chile, living much as their ancestors did thousands of years ago.

**PRACTICE 3 (P. 154)**

1. The laser beam, a miracle of modern science, already has many practical uses in today's world.
2. Laser beams are narrow, highly concentrated beams of light that burn brighter than the light of the sun.
3. Scientists have found many possible military uses for the laser, but they are hoping these can be converted into constructive uses.
4. C
5. The possibility of making a laser was first described in 1958, and two years later, in California, the first laser beam was created.
6. Since they are so precise, laser beams are used in medicine to help make a specific diagnosis and to perform operations such as repairing delicate retinas and removing cancerous tumours.
7. The future uses of the laser seem endless, and it is up to us to decide whether we want to use this invention for war or for peaceful purposes.

# UNIT II: THE WRITING PROCESS

## Chapter 15: The Paragraph I: Structure and Topic Sentence

### Finding the Topic Sentence of a Paragraph

**PRACTICE (P. 178)**

1. Love is a crazy, complicated affair, made trickier by the tangle of superstitions that go along with it.
2. The brain is one of the most remarkable organs, a part of the body that we have only begun to investigate.

### Finding the Topic in the Topic Sentence

**PRACTICE (P. 179)**

1. Remodelling an old house
2. College work and high school work
3. A well-made suit
4. Growing up near a museum
5. My favourite room in the house
6. A student who goes to school full-time and also works part-time
7. The expense of skiing
8. The change that had come over my friend
9. Current tax laws
10. Greek restaurants

### Finding the Controlling Idea

**PRACTICE (P. 180)**

1. T: vigorous exercise CI: reduces stress
2. T: St. John's and Corner Brook CI: differ
3. T: wonder foods CI: less than wonderful
4. T: athletic scholarships available to women CI: increasing
5. T: caffeine CI: adverse effects
6. T: Madame Benoît CI: amusing personality
7. T: computers CI: will make newspapers obsolete

## Chapter 16: The Paragraph II: Supporting Details

### Avoid Restating the Topic Sentence

**PRACTICE (P. 188)**

| | | | | |
|---|---|---|---|---|
| 1. | a. SD | b. R | c. SD | d. SD |
| 2. | a. SD | b. SD | c. R | d. SD |

## Chapter 17: The Essay

### Thesis or Fact?

**PRACTICE 1 (P. 198)**

1. F
2. T
3. T
4. F

### Recognizing the Thesis Statement

**PRACTICE 2 (P. 198)**

1. thesis
2. title
3. fact
4. thesis
5. title
6. fact
7. fact

# UNIT III: WRITING STRATEGIES

## Chapter 21: Narration

### Coherence: Placing Details in Order of Time Sequence

**PRACTICE (P. 259)**

2. 4, 5, 1, 6, 2, 3

## Chapter 22: Description

### Coherence: Putting Details in Spatial Order

**PRACTICE (P. 272)**

1. 4, 2, 3, 1, 5
2. 2, 3, 1, 4

## Chapter 23: Process

### Coherence: Order in Logical Sequence

**PRACTICE (P. 281)**

7, 5, 1, 8, 2, 6, 3, 9, 4

## Chapter 24: Comparison and/or Contrast

### Evaluating the Two-Part Topic

**PRACTICE (P. 292)**

Answers could vary depending on the purpose of the paragraph.

3. too broad
4. suitable
5. too broad
6. too broad

### Recognizing the Two Methods

**PRACTICE (P. 294)**

1. block; differences
2. point-by-point; similarities

## Chapter 27: Cause and Effect

### Looking for the Causal Relationship

**PRACTICE 1 (P. 324)**

1. T
2. C
3. T
4. C
5. C
6. T
7. C

### Separating the Cause from the Effect

**PRACTICE 2 (P. 325)**

| | | | | | | |
|---|---|---|---|---|---|---|
| 1. | a. C | b. C | c. E | d. E | e. C | f. E |
| 2. | a. C | b. C | c. E | d. E | e. C | f. C |

# UNIT V: APPENDICES

## Appendix B: Solving Spelling Problems

### Identifying the Correct Spelling

**PRACTICE (P. 437)**

1. separate
2. probably
3. arctic
4. surprise
5. tragedy
6. quantity
7. literature
8. hungry
9. handsome
10. favourite
11. nuclear

### Choosing *ie* or *ei*

**PRACTICE (P. 438)**

1. sleigh
2. believe
3. siege
4. veil
5. leisure
6. deceit
7. niece
8. weight
9. protein
10. ancient

### Forming the Plurals of Nouns

**PRACTICE (P. 441)**

1. puppies
2. mothers-in-law
3. teeth
4. cameos
5. phenomena
6. loaves
7. matches
8. mixes
9. enemies
10. bags

### Doubling the Consonant?

**PRACTICE (P. 443)**

slip: yes, yes, slipping
crack: no, no, cracking
broil: no, no, broiling
win: yes, yes, winning
control: controlling
fever: feverish
compel: compelled
differ: difference
begin: beginning

### Doubling the Final Consonant When Adding Endings That Begin with Vowels?

**PRACTICE (P. 444)**

1. bitten
2. occurrence
3. wavering
4. preferred
5. preference
6. thinner
7. transferred
8. sailing
9. propellent
10. omitted

### Adding Endings to Words That End in *-y*

**PRACTICE (P. 445)**

1. keys
2. loneliness
3. crying
4. cries
5. prayer
6. employment
7. monkeying
8. beautiful
9. theories
10. ceremonial

### One Word or Two?

**PRACTICE (P. 447)**

1. bedroom
2. grandmother
3. already
4. all together
5. always
6. Everyone
7. maybe
8. cannot
9. nearby
10. Nevertheless

## APPENDIX C: IRREGULAR VERBS

### Irregular Verbs

**PRACTICE (P. 454)**

1. caught
2. laid
3. fled
4. burst
5. ridden
6. slid
7. rose
8. quit
9. forgotten
10. wrung

# Credits



**Page 91:** Audi Quattro. Reprinted by kind permission of Volkswagen Canada Inc.

**Page 159:** AP Photo/Carmen Taylor.

**Page 212:** TOLES © 1989 The Washington Post. Reprinted with permission of UNIVERSAL PRESS SYNDICATE. All rights reserved.

**Page 222:** Excerpt from article entitled "Canadian Internet Use Survey, 2005," published in the Statistics Canada publication "The Daily," Catalogue 11-001, Tuesday, August 15, 2006, URL: http://www.statcan.ca/Daily/English/060815/d060815b.htm.

**Page 244:** © Shutterstock, Inc./absolut.

**Page 244:** © iStock.com/Eva Serrabassa.

**Page 264:** Akis Stylianou, "Transparent Silhouette." Reprinted by permission of the author.

**Page 276:** Alexandra Savage-Ferr, "A Profile of Daphne." Reprinted by permission of the author.

**Page 307:** "Love Hurts." Reprinted by permission of Jenny Yuen.

**Page 340:** CP/Paul Chiasson.

**Page 343:** Leanne C. Southall, "Individuals Must Spur Change." Reprinted by permission of the author.

**Page 345:** Caplan, H. "It's Time We Helped Patients Die." *RN Magazine*, 50 (11), Nov. 1987.

**Page 352:** LABYRINTH OF DESIRE: WOMEN, PASSION, AND ROMANTIC OBSESSION by Rosemary Sullivan. Published by HarperCollins Publishers Ltd. Copyright © 2001 by Rosemary Sullivan. All rights reserved.

**Page 355:** David Suzuki, "Hidden Lessons." Reprinted by permission of the author.

**Page 359:** Marya Fiamengo, "In Praise of Old Women." © Copyright 1976 Mosaic Press, Oakville. Reprinted with permission.

**Page 362:** Excerpt from BECOMING HUMAN copyright © 1998 by Jean Vanier and the Canadian Broadcasting Corporation. Reprinted by permission of House of Anansi Press.

**Page 367:** "The $2-Million Comma" by Grant Robertson. Reprinted with permission from The Globe and Mail.

**Page 370:** "Canada, My Canada" by Tomson Highway. Copyright © 2000 by Tomson Highway. First published by *Imperial Oil Review,* Spring 2000, Volume 84, No. 436. Reprinted by permission of Tomson Highway and Susan Schulman, A Literary Agency, New York.

**Page 373:** Naheed Mustafa, "My Body Is My Own Business." Reprinted by permission of the author.

**Page 376:** John Artibello, "Leaving the Cave." Reprinted by permission of the author.

**Pages 377 and 379:** Courtesy of Jock MacRae.

**Page 383:** "I Lost My Talk" by Rita Joe. From SONG OF ESKASONI. Reprinted by permission of Canadian Scholar's Press Inc. and Women's Press.

**Page 385:** W. Frank Epling, "Rats." Reprinted with permission of the author's estate.

**Page 389:** Himani Bannerji, "The Other Family." Reprinted by permission of the author.

**Page 394:** Colin Campbell, "How R tngz, dude?" *Maclean's* Magazine, 21 December 2005.

**Page 397:** From SELLING ILLUSIONS by Neil Bissoondath. Copyright © Neil Bissoondath, 1994. Reprinted by permission of Penguin Group (Canada), a Division of Pearson Canada Inc.

**Page 403:** Courtesy of Jock MacRae.

**Page 409:** Shari Graydon, "Bad Girls." Reprinted by permission of the author.

**Page 414:** Cameron Ainsworth-Vincze, "Till fraud do us part." *Maclean's* Magazine, 24 July 2006.

**Page 416:** "In My Secret Life." Written by Leonard Cohen & Sharon Robinson. Published by Sony/ATV Music Publishing Canada & Robinhill Music. Administered by Sony/ATV Music Publishing Canada (1670 Bayview Avenue, Ste. 408, Toronto, ON, M4G 3C2) and Wixen Music Publishing Inc. All rights reserved. Used by Permission.

# Index


*a, an,* 11
Abstract noun, 5
Academic directories, 231
*accept, except,* 427
*access, excess,* 428
Action verbs, 7, 23–24
Active voice, 41–44
Adjective, 6. *See also* Possessive adjective
*Ad hominem* attack, 340
Adverb, 8, 27
Adverbial conjunctions, 10, 60, 61
Adverbs of degree, 8
Adverbs of frequency, 8
*advise, advice,* 428
Aesthetic appeal, 335
*affect, effect,* 428
Agreement
  pronoun–antecedent, 112–115
  subject–verb, 47–55
Ainsworth-Vincze, Cameron, "Till Fraud Do Us Part," 414–416
*allowed, aloud,* 420
*allusion, illusion,* 428
*altar, alter,* 420
Analysis, 303, 336
Analyzing, 228
"and" run-on, 93
Answer key to practices, 455–467
Antecedent, 112
APA documentation style, 237–240, 244–250
Apostrophe, 134–138
Appeal to emotion, 335
Appositive phrase, 21–22
Argument, 337
Argumentation, 334–350
  analysis, 336
  argument, 337
  argumentative techniques, 338–340
  claim, 336
  critical thinking, 335–336
  defined, 334
  essay development, 343–348
  evidence, 336
  fallacies, 340–342
  paragraph development, 342
  persuasive appeal, 334–335
  underlying assumptions, 337–338
  virtue, 338
Argumentative essay, 337
Argumentative techniques, 338–340
Artibello, John, "Leaving the Cave," 376–383
Article, 11
Audience, 168–169
*aural, oral,* 420
Auxiliary verbs, 7, 26–27

"Bad Girls" (Graydon), 409–414
Bannerji, Himani, "The Other Family," 389–394
*be,* 52
Bissoondath, Neil, "Selling Illusions," 397–401
Block method, 293–294
Body paragraphs, 195
Brainstorming, 163–164
*brake, break,* 420
*breath, breathe,* 428

Campbell, Colin, "How R Tngz, Dude?", 394–396
"Canada, My Canada" (Highway), 370–373
*capital, capitol,* 420–421
Capitalization, 147–151
  practice quiz, 147
  rules, explained, 147–150
  rules, listed, 150
Causal relationship, 322, 324
Cause and effect, 322–333
  causal relationship, 322, 324
  defined, 322
  essay development, 329–333
  logic, 323–324
  paragraph development, 323–324, 327–328
  step-by-step writing process, 327
  supporting detail, 323
  topic sentence, 323
  types of paragraphs, 322–323
*choose, chose,* 433
*chord, cord,* 421
Citations. *See* Documentation
*cite, sight, site,* 424
Claim, 336
Classification, 311–321
  defined, 311

distinct categories, 313
essay development, 316–319
paragraph development, 311–312, 313
step-by-step writing process, 313
*close, clothes, cloth,* 421
*clothes, cloths,* 428
Clustering, 166–167
*coarse, course,* 421
Cohen, Leonard, "In My Secret Life," 416–418
Colon, 140–141
Comma, 126–134
before coordinating conjunction, 128
dialogue, 132
interruptions, 130
introductory material, 129
lists, 127
misunderstandings, 132
noun being directly addressed, 131
numbers, 132
rules, listed, 133
Comma splice, 93
Common noun, 4, 15
Comparison and contrast, 290–301
block method, 293–294
definitions, 290
essay development, 297–300
paragraph development, 296–297
point-by-point method, 292–293
step-by-step writing process, 296
topic sentence, 291–292
two-part topic, 290–292
*complement, compliment,* 421
*complementary, complimentary,* 421
Complete sentence, 13–14, 79
Complex sentence, 65–74
Compound subject, 16
Concluding paragraph, 207–209
Concluding sentence, 191, 192
Concrete noun, 4–5
Conjunction, 9–10, 57
Conjunctive adverbs, 10
*conscience, conscientious, conscious,* 429
Contrast. *See* Comparison and contrast
Controlling idea, 179–181
Coordinating conjunctions, 10, 58
Coordination
comma plus coordinating conjunction, 57–60
coordinating conjunctions, but not two independent clauses, 60
defined, 57
semicolon, adverbial conjunction, comma, 60–63
semicolon by itself, 64–65
Correlative conjunctions, 10
*costume, custom,* 429
*council, counsel, consul,* 429
Countable noun, 5
Critical thinking, 335–336
Critiquing, 228

Dangling modifier, 122–123
Dash, 143–144
Definite article, 11
Definition, 302–310
defined, 302
essay development, 307–309
extended, 303
identifying characteristics, 303
paragraph development, 303–305
step-by-step writing process, 305
Democratic fallacy, 341
Demonstrative pronoun, 6
Dependent clause, 37, 66
Description, 267–278
coherence, 272
defined, 267
dominant impression, 268–270
essay development, 275–277
key points, 267
paragraph development, 268, 273–274
sensory images, 267, 271
spatial order, 272
step-by-step writing process, 273
*desert, dessert,* 429
Diagramming, 166–167
Dialogue, 132
*die, dye,* 433
*diner, dinner,* 429
Directional process, 279, 283
*do,* 52
Documentation, 235–252
APA format, 237–240, 244–250
basic rules, 236–237
defined, 235
MLA format, 240–243, 251–252
sample essays, 244–252
Dominant impression, 268–270
"Don Juan/Doña Juana" (Sullivan), 352–355

Editing, 171–172, 213, 214
*effect, affect,* 428
*emigrate, emigrant,* 430
Emotions, 165
Epling, W. Frank, "Rats," 385–389
*especially, special,* 431
Essay, 194–212
argumentation, 343–348
cause and effect, 329–333
classification, 316–319
comparison and contrast, 297–300
components, 195–196

concluding paragraph, 207–209
contrast, 297–300
definition, 307–309
description, 275–277
introductory paragraph, 203–205
narration, 263–265
outline, 209–211
plan of development (POD), 197
process, 284–287
structure, 195
support paragraphs, 195–196
thesis statement, 197–203
title, 209
transferability, 194
transitions, 206–207
Evidence, 336
*except, accept,* 427
*excess, access,* 428
Extended definition, 303
Extended examples, 186
Extended paragraph, 177

*fair, fare,* 421–422
Fallacies, 340–342
False analogy, 341–342
FANBOYS, 10, 58
*farther, further,* 430
Fiamengo, Marya, "In Praise of Old Women," 359–361
Final copy, 173, 217–220
Finding the subject
command, 21
gerund, 22
guide/tips, 17
*here, there,* 21
in sentence with appositive phrase, 21–22
in sentence with prepositional phrase, 17–20
questions, 21
*flour, flower,* 422
*for, four, forty, fore,* 422
*forth, fourth,* 422
*forward, foreword,* 422
Fragments
defined, 79–80
participle, 86–87, 88
phrases, 83–85
recognizing, 87
turning fragments into sentences, 81–83
verbal, 85
Freewriting, 164
Frequently confused words, 420–434
Fused run-on, 93

General topic research paper, 230
Gerund, 22, 85
Gerund phrase, 84, 85
*grate, grateful, great,* 422
Graydon, Shari, "Bad Girls," 409–414
Group noun, 51

"Heart of Loneliness" (Vanier), 362–367
Helping verbs, 7, 26–27
*here,* 21
"Hidden Lessons" (Suzuki), 355–358
Highway, Tomson, "Canada, My Canada," 370–373
*hole, whole,* 426
"How R Tngz, Dude?" (Campbell), 394–396
Hyphen, 142–143

Identifying characteristics, 303
*illusion, allusion,* 428
"I Lost My Talk" (Joe), 383–384
*immigrate, immigrant,* 430
Indefinite article, 11
Indefinite pronoun, 6, 49–50, 113
Independent clause, 37, 57, 65
Infinitive, 85
Infinitive phrase, 84, 85
Informational process, 279, 284
"In My Secret Life" (Cohen), 416–418
"In Praise of Old Women" (Fiamengo), 359–361
Interjection, 11
Internet research, 230–233
*In the Company of Men,* 338
Introduction, 203
Introductory paragraph, 203–205
Irregular verbs, 30–35, 451–454
*it's, its,* 423

Joe, Rita, "I Lost My Talk," 383–384
Journal, 165, 166

*knew, new,* 423
*know, no,* 423

*lead, led,* 433
"Leaving the Cave" (Artibello), 376–383
"Lessons of Love from Stories of Old" (Lipschutz), 402–408
Library research, 230–231
*lie, lay,* 433
Linking verbs, 7, 25–26
Lipschutz, Gary, "Lessons of Love from Stories of Old," 402–408
Lists
comma, 127
parallel structure, 102–108 (*see also* Parallel structure)
Literary research paper, 230

*local, locale,* 430
Logic, 323–324
Logic errors, 323–324
Look-a-likes, 427–434
*lose, loose,* 433

Macrocomposition checklist, 214–215
Making a point, 258
Mapping, 166–167
Microcomposition checklist, 215–216
Misplaced modifier, 121–122
MLA documentation style, 240–243, 251–252
Modal auxiliary verb, 7–8, 26, 45
Modifier, 120–125
  dangling, 122–123
  defined, 120
  misplaced, 121–122
*moral, morale,* 430
Mustafa, Naheed, "My Body Is My Own Business," 373–376
"My Body Is My Own Business" (Mustafa), 373–376

Narration, 257–266
  coherence, 259–260
  defined, 257
  essay development, 263–265
  making a point, 258
  paragraph development, 260–263
  step-by-step writing process, 260–262
  time sequence order, 259–260
*new, knew,* 423
*no, know,* 423
Non-countable noun, 5
Nonrestrictive clause, 72
Noun
  concrete/abstract, 4–5
  countable/non-countable, 5
  defined, 4
  group, 51
  proper/common, 4, 15
  subject, as, 15
Noun phrase, 84
Numbers, 132

Online sources, legitimacy of, 232–233
*oral, aural,* 420
"Other Family, The" (Bannerji), 389–394
Outline, 169–170, 192, 209–211

*pain, pane,* 423
Paragraph, 175–193
  argumentation, 342
  cause and effect, 323–324, 327–328
  classification, 311–312, 313
  comparison and contrast, 296–297
  concluding sentence, 191, 192
  contrast, 296–297
  controlling idea, 179–181
  defined, 175
  definition, 303–305
  description, 268, 273–274
  narration, 260–263
  outline, 192
  process, 279–280, 282–284
  sample, 175, 177
  structure, 177
  supporting details, 183–193 (*see also* Supporting details)
  topic sentence, 176–179
Parallel structure, 102–108
  clauses in list, 103
  defined, 102
  phrases in list, 103
  words in list, 103
Paraphrasing, 225–227
Parentheses, 143–144
Participial phrase, 85
Participle, 85
Parts of speech
  adjective, 6
  adverb, 8, 27
  article, 11
  conjunction, 9–10
  interjection, 11
  noun (*see* Noun)
  preposition, 9, 19
  pronoun (*see* Pronoun)
  verb (*see* Verb)
*passed, past,* 423
Passive voice, 41–44
Past participle, 31–33
Past perfect tense, 40
Past tense, 31–35
*patience, patients,* 423
*peace, piece,* 423
Perfect tenses, 39–40
*personal, personnel,* 430
Personal pronoun, 6
Persuasive appeal, 334–335
Phrase, 83
Plagiarism, 227
*plain, plane,* 424
Plan of development (POD), 197
*Pocket Guide to Critical Thinking, The,* 338
POD (plan of development), 197
Point-by-point method, 292–293
Possessive adjective, 6, 110, 111
Postwriting, 171–173, 213–220
Practical point of view, 341
Practice questions, answer key, 455–467
*precede, proceed,* 431

Preposition, 9, 19
Prepositional combinations, 19
Prepositional phrase, 9, 18, 84
*presence, presents,* 424
Present perfect tense, 39
Present tense, 31–35
Prewriting, 163–169
  audience, 168–169
  brainstorming, 163–164
  clustering, 166–167
  emotions, 165
  freewriting, 164
  journal, 165, 166
  persuasiveness, 168
  purpose, 169
  tone, 169
  topic selection, 167–168
Primary research, 230
Primary sources, 230
*principal, principle,* 424
Process, 279–289
  coherence, 281
  complete/accurate instructions required, 280
  defined, 279
  directional, 279, 283
  essay development, 284–287
  informational, 279, 284
  logical sequence order, 281
  paragraph development, 279–280, 282–284
  step-by-step writing process, 282
  transitions, 282
Pronoun, 109–119
  ambiguous antecedent, 116
  antecedent, and, 112–115
  case, 6, 110–111
  defined, 5
  demonstrative, 6
  indefinite, 6, 49, 113
  missing antecedent, 115–116
  personal, 6
  relative, 6, 70
  repetitious antecedent, 116
  subject, as, 16
  *who, whom,* 111
Pronoun–antecedent agreement, 112–115
Pronoun case, 6, 110–111
Proofreading, 172, 173, 213
Proper noun, 4, 15
Punctuation, 126–146
  apostrophe, 134–138
  colon, 140–141
  comma, 126–134 (*see also* Comma)
  dash, 143–144
  hyphen, 142–143
  importance, 126
  parentheses, 143–144
  quotation mark, 138–139
  semicolon, 139–140
Purpose, 169

*quiet, quit, quite,* 431
Quotation, 233–235
Quotation mark, 138–139

*rain, reign, rein,* 424
*raise, rays, raze,* 424
"Rats" (Epling), 385–389
Readings, 352–418
*receipt, recipe,* 431
References (documentation), 237–240, 244–250
Regular paragraph, 177
Relative pronoun, 6, 70
Research paper, 229–253
  APA format, 237–240
  defined, 229
  documentation, 235–243
  Internet research, 230–233
  library research, 230–231
  MLA format, 240–243
  online sources, legitimacy of, 232–233
  primary *vs.* secondary research, 230
  primary *vs.* secondary sources, 230
  quotation, 233–235
  responsible research, 229–230
  sample essay (APA style), 244–250
  sample essay (MLA style), 251–252
Restatement of topic sentence, 187–189
Restrictive clause, 72
Revising, 171–172, 213, 214
*right, rite, write,* 427
*rise, raise,* 433
Robertson, Grant, "The $2 Million Comma," 367–370
Rough draft, 170–171
Run-on, 92–101
  "and," 93
  comma splice, 93
  defined, 92
  fused, 93
  rules for correcting, 93
  types of, 93

Search engine, 231
Secondary research, 230
Secondary sources, 230
"Selling Illusions" (Bissoondath), 397–401
Semicolon, 139–140
Sensory images, 267, 271
Sentence
  complete, 13–14, 79
  complex, 37, 65–74

fragments (*see* Fragments)
joining (*see* Coordination; Subordination)
parallel structure (*see* Parallel structure)
prepositional phrase, 19
run-on (*see* Run-on)
Sentence fragments, 78–91. *See also* Fragments
Sequence of tenses, 37–38
Shifted tense, 35–37
*should of, would of,* 45
*sight, site, cite,* 424
*sit, set,* 433
Sound-a-likes, 420–434
Spatial order, 272
*special, especially,* 431
Specific details, 183–184, 189–190
Spelling, 435–450
doubling the final consonant, 442–444
*ie* and *ei* words, 437–438
list of tough words, 447–450
mispronounced words, 435–436
one word or two?, 446–447
plurals, 438–441
prefixes, 441–442
suffixes, 441–442
tough words, list of, 447–450
words ending in *-y,* 445–446
*stair, stare,* 425
*stake, steak,* 425
*stationary, stationery,* 425
Storytelling. *See* Narration
Straw man fallacy, 341
Student exercises, answer key, 455–467
Subject
compound, 16
defined, 14
finding (*see* Finding the subject)
nouns, 15
pronouns, 16
verb, and (*see* Subject–verb agreement)
Subject–verb agreement, 47–55
*be,* 52
*do,* 52
finding the subject, 48, 51 (*see also* Finding the subject)
group noun, 51
indefinite pronoun, 49–50
pair of conjunctions, 50
Subjunctive, 44–45
Subordinating conjunction, 10, 66–70
Subordination
defined, 65
relative pronoun, 70–74
subordinating conjunction, 66–70
Sullivan, Rosemary, "Don Juan/Doña Juana," 352–355
Summarizing, 221–225, 227
Summary, 221
Supporting details, 183–193
examples, 185–187
restatement of topic sentence, 187–189
specific details, 183–184, 189–190
state facts, 183
Support paragraphs, 195–196
*suppose, supposed,* 434
Suzuki, David, "Hidden Lessons," 355–358

Term paper. *See* Research paper
*than, then,* 431
*there,* 21
Thesis, 197
Thesis statement, 197–203
*they're, their, there,* 425
*thorough, though, thought, through, threw,* 432
"Till Fraud Do Us Part" (Ainsworth-Vincze), 414–416
Time sequence order, 259–260
Title, 209
*to, too, two,* 425
Tone, 169
Topic sentence, 176–179
Transitional words/phrases, 177
Transitions, 206–207, 282
"$2 Million Comma, The" (Robertson), 367–370
Two-part topic, 290–292

*use, used,* 434

*vain, vane, vein,* 425–426
Vanier, Jean, "Heart of Loneliness," 362–367
Verb
action, 7, 23–24
auxiliary, 7, 26–27
defined, 6
finding, 23–27
helping, 7, 26–27
irregular, 30–35, 451–454
linking, 7, 25–26
modal auxiliary, 26, 45
subjunctive, 44–45
tense (*see* Verb tense)
voice (active/passive), 41–44
Verbal, 85
Verb phrase, 84
Verb tense
past tense, 31–35
perfect tenses, 39–40
present tense, 31–35
sequence of tenses, 37–38
shift in tense, 35–37

Virtue, 338
Voice (active/passive), 41–44

*waist, waste,* 426
*wait, weight,* 426
*ware, wear, where,* 426
*weather, whether,* 426
*who, whom,* 111
*whole, hole,* 426
*who's, whose,* 426
*wood, would,* 427
Works cited, 240–243, 251–252
*write, right, rite,* 427
Writing process
  final copy, 173, 217–220
  macrocomposition checklist, 214–215
  microcomposition checklist, 215–216
  outline, 169–170
  postwriting, 171–173, 213–220
  prewriting (*see* Prewriting)
  proofreading, 172, 173, 213
  revising and editing, 171–172, 213, 214
  rough draft, 170–171

*yoke, yolk,* 427
*you're, your,* 427